John Hunt is to liberal theology what Rich- awkins is to evolutionary biology... a read-' challenging work.
Christian Marketplace

Knowledgeable in theo   science and history. Time and again it is re.   how he brings the important issues into relation with one another... thought provoking in almost every sentence, difficult to put down.
Faith and Freedom

Very accessible for every man and woman who cares about their faith, I would like to see it made compulsory reading for every budding theologian before he is allowed to put pen to paper.
The Presbyterian

A breath-taking project. But don't be put off by the scope of the book. The writer has such an easy-going style that we dance our way through aeons of time. And, of course, any book about God and religion is going to cover life, death and everything in between. A courageous book. It makes compulsive reading. We feel we are in the author's company, carried along by his fervor. But like all great spiritual books, the fervor is undermined by a radical acceptance of life.
Sea of Faith Network

An absorbing and highly readable book, profound and wide ranging.
The Unitarian

This is a well-informed and daring book in its call for a radically new approach to religious understanding. Expertly summarizing vast conceptual and historical stretches... even readers who find his conclusions objectionable should be thankful for his effort. It

is a hopeful and exciting book. With challenges and epiphanies on every page it is a rewarding encounter with the art of believing in God and living accordingly.
Nimble Spirit

I salute him. He is exactly the kind of Christian the church must produce if it is to live another 100 years!
John S. Spong, Former Bishop of Newark and author of *A New Christianity for a New World* and other titles

I found much to enjoy and even sympathize with.
Rowan Williams, former Archbishop of Canterbury, author of *Being Christian* and many other titles

Highly readable and well informed, this book is a refreshing personal view of the evolution of Christianity and the spiritual condition of our time.
Network Review

A most enjoyable and exhilarating book.
Interreligious Insight

The best modern religious book I have read. A masterwork.
Robert Van de Weyer, author of *A World Religions Bible, Celtic Fire*, and many other titles

Answers all the questions you ever wanted to ask about God and some you never even thought of.
Richard Holloway, former President of the Scottish Episcopal Church, author of *Doubts and Loves* and many other titles

Bringing God Up to Date

and why Christians need to catch up

Bringing God Up to Date

and why Christians need to catch up

John Hunt

CHRISTIAN ALTERNATIVE
BOOKS

Winchester, UK
Washington, USA

JOHN HUNT PUBLISHING

First published by Christian Alternative Books, 2021
Christian Alternative Books is an imprint of John Hunt Publishing Ltd.,
No. 3 East St., Alresford, Hampshire SO24 9EE, UK
office@jhpbooks.com
www.johnhuntpublishing.com

For distributor details and how to order please visit the 'Ordering' section on our website.

ISBN: 978 1 78904 703 5
978 1 78904 811 7 (ebook)
Library of Congress Control Number: 2021931161

A CIP catalogue record for this book is available from the British Library.

Design: Stuart Davies

UK: Printed and bound by CPI Group (UK) Ltd, Croydon, CR0 4YY
Printed in North America by CPI GPS partners

We operate a distinctive and ethical publishing philosophy in all areas of our business, from our global network of authors to production and worldwide distribution.

Contents

First published in 2004 as *Bringing God Back to Earth*.
Reissued in 2021.
John Hunt is also the author of *The Alaskan Chronicles*.

Acknowledgements

With love to Ros, and thanks for everything over the last 40 years. Thanks to our sons Matt and Sie, and to all family and friends. To everyone in the business, who made this possible, particularly Dominic. And to Robert, for supporting the business when we needed it.

Note to Reader

Being a conservative, traditional kind of a guy, who still thinks in Fahrenheit rather than Celsius, in feet and inches rather than meters, I've stuck to a number of old fashioned routines.

Quotations from the Bible are from the Authorized (King James) Version except where mentioned. I've used BC and AD rather than BCE or CE. It's not as if we're changing the date, making it less Christo-centric. If we dated from the time of recorded history, or from the beginning of Homo sapiens, we might gain a different perspective. I still refer to the "Old Testament," though most theologians today would probably call it the "Jewish Scriptures," or *Tanakh*.

God is usually thought of as "He," though for most of our history (like, probably, 99%) it's been more "She" (or "Them" or "It" etc...), and following Genesis 1:27 (and other verses and traditions) God is androgynous. But I've stuck with the male, just to make it easier to read.

I've followed American spelling rather than English.

Preface to the second edition

This is basically a rehash of a couple of books I wrote a couple of decades and more ago, now out of print for a while: *Daddy, Do You Believe in God?* and *Bringing God Back to Earth*.

Since then, North America and Europe have seen a steady decline in church attendance, though worldwide numbers of Christians are still rising. Indeed, increasingly, it doesn't seem possible to understand the way the world works today without taking religion into account – particularly Christianity. In all the political, economic and social commentary, it's usually the elephant in the room, rarely discussed. It tends to be categorized as a private matter, as if personal faith has no public relevance. But whether you have any kind of faith or not, to whatever degree of conviction, or whether you're simply indifferent to it (which covers most people I know – they see it as a distraction or even a hindrance to living a "good" life, in the best sense of the word), it's still important to understand how and why religion works. Because what people believe influences, even determines, how they behave and who they vote for. And over the next few decades, what people around the world believe will determine our future. Religion is not going to go away in a hurry, so we need to come to terms with it.

There's nothing wacky or controversial here; nothing that runs counter to the summary academic consensus in places like Wikipedia, which is why I haven't bothered with footnotes. It's basically just mashing up what historians, anthropologists, biologists, physicists, theologians and so on (of the serious academic kind, rather than those promoting a party line), are saying, and seeing what comes out of it. It's not for hardline atheists on the one hand or evangelicals and fundamentalists on the other. It's for people who have some sympathy with the religious outlook on life, and want to get a handle on it, but couldn't quote any of the creeds from memory, and might keep their fingers crossed if they had to recite one. For people who want to understand why, and how, we believe in something, and why we always will. It's about how beliefs are never neutral, but can be good or bad, often in extreme forms.

I'll have a go at arguing that you don't have to put your brain on hold to be religious, even to believe in God (in some form, not necessarily the one that Christians describe), and even if you take Him out of the equation, Jesus still gave us a good model for relating to the world. So it's about which bits of religion are functioning well, and which we should try and leave behind; what direction religious belief as a whole should take to make the world a better place, and how to get there.

As for the "details," I don't really know, for instance, whether the universe is 10 or 15 billion years old, whether Jesus thought of himself as a son of man or the Son of God, whether the Qur'an or the Bible is the more inspired book, whether dowsing works or not. I'm not a specialist in any of the many areas covered here. What I am sure of is that the age of the universe is measured in billions rather than thousands of years, or the stars wouldn't have got around to forming yet, let alone the earth, or life on it. It's difficult to know exactly what Jesus meant by certain phrases, or whether he even said them, which is why there are so many Christian denominations. Several billion people believe with equal conviction that either the Qur'an or the Bible is uniquely inspired, and there's no way of getting an answer from the God they both believe in that both sides will accept. Dowsing may work, but drilling is more reliable. That's good enough for me. I want to know what the probabilities are, how they tie together, if they do.

How we believe, around the world – it's so basic as to how we act, that we could pick virtually any topic to illustrate its importance. But let me give you just one example – climate change; an issue which was less prominent when I first wrote the books twenty plus years ago. Being "global" rather than "personal," it may not immediately seem a "religious" issue. But you can't find a more "religious" topic than this. Because for 95% of our time on earth we've been hunter-gatherers, leaving little trace. Nature, life itself, was seen as sacred. Then things changed. If it were possible to look back over the human library in a thousand years' time, this might be seen as the key sentence ever written, in Genesis 1:26, around 2,500 years ago (though it represents an oral tradition going back to the Middle Bronze Age – a myth which half the people in the world – Jews, Christians and Muslims – believe in):

> *And God said, Let us make man in our image, after our likeness: and let them have dominion over the fish of the sea, and over the fowl of the air, and over the cattle, and over all the earth, and over every creeping thing that creepeth upon the earth.*

Genesis represents a new understanding that had been emerging around the world for millennia; that we're not in a reciprocal relationship with Nature, part of it – we're in charge of it, above it. It's there for our use. And as far as monotheistic religions go, this verse is written into their DNA (many theistic religions take a different, even opposite approach). So, for instance, we take food for granted now. We no longer, like we used to, thank the animal who provided the food – if we say grace, we thank God (and I'm a bit ashamed to say that I no longer do either). And so we've spent the last few thousand years increasingly dominating nature, reshaping the landscape, genetically manipulating animals and crops, pushing the wild to extinction.

Then, around 300 years ago, we moved up a gear. A relatively small Christian nation (in global terms) on the northwestern fringe of Europe, the UK, developed a technological edge through burning fossil fuels, to kick-start the Industrial Revolution. Since then, the amount of carbon – the cycle of which is crucial to life –

in the atmosphere has increased by a third. Over half of that has happened in the last three decades.

The overwhelming consensus among climate scientists (or the 99% of them who agree that global warming is influenced by human activity, rather than the 1% who are funded by oil companies), the conclusion of all the models, is that as a result of this, without radical action – of the kind we're not remotely close to putting into effect – we're heading for a rise of three to four degrees C by the end of this century. That's a global average – temperatures over land as opposed to over the oceans would be several times higher – and it's probably conservative. The last time the planet was this warm was 15 million years ago in the Miocene period, around the time when our ancestors diverged from the common ones we had with the orangutans and other apes. Sea levels were over a hundred feet higher. There were forests at the Poles. In that scenario, we get into a vicious spiral of economic depression, political upheaval, social breakdown, war and civilizational collapse. The band around the Equator, between the Tropics of Cancer and Capricorn, where half the global population live, would be uninhabitable, because of heat stress. All of the USA and most of Europe would be desert. You could live in Canada, or Scandinavia, or Siberia, or the tip of South America, if you could fight off the billions of other people desperate to get there, but there would be little food – it takes thousands of years for weathering to produce topsoil deep enough for agriculture. You can't turn permafrost into farmland overnight. Sure, life has weathered temperature increases before, and will do again. But civilization hasn't, and this speed of change is unprecedented.

In a couple of decades it will be too late to stop this happening. Even now, the cost of doing so is rising exponentially. It's not difficult to imagine a scenario in the next century where our great-great-grandchildren, far less than a thousandth of the current population, could only wish for the comparative ease of the hunter-gatherer life, let alone the life we currently enjoy, as they huddle in the ruined shells of our cities, scavenging for food in the desolate land we have made of our Eden; fighting over rats and cats, scrawling curses on the walls against the generation that allowed it to happen (ours), and pleading to indifferent gods.

That final, brilliant, scorching – and some would say mentally unhinged – book in the collection of texts that were chosen by some churches in the fourth and fifth centuries AD to make up the Bible, the Book of Revelation, with its fantastic beasts and dragons (there's never been unanimity on which books should be in the Bible, and Revelation was variously in and out for many centuries, more on that in chapter 35) may actually be the one that got it right, with its Four Horsemen of the Apocalypse: war, famine, pandemic and death.

Of course, we need to stop this happening. We know this. If the political will were there, if we collectively put our minds to it, if we were prepared to cooperate globally, and sacrifice some consumer-driven growth (the vast bulk of which is on non-essentials), this could be avoided. Whether we do or not is in large part down to Christians, particularly in the USA, which produces twice the carbon emissions of China, and a good proportion of China's comes from making consumer goods for sale in the USA and other countries. Christian nations and their allies control the bulk of the word's capital, cash and weaponry. Our governments have the power to act on climate change, but need a democratic mandate to do so.

And that needs a change of heart, a change of viewpoint, in the Christian community. 90% or so of Americans say they believe in a Higher Power, 70% identify as Christian, and over 40% go to church (a proportion only found elsewhere in similarly violent societies – the USA has around 5% of the world population but 25% of its prisoners, with 80,000 in solitary confinement at any one time – where faith and fundamentalism are strong; the most compelling argument against taking Christianity or any kind of highly organized, credal religion seriously is not an intellectual one, it's simply looking closely enough at the societies that do). Evangelical Protestants are the largest single religious group in the USA. But the trouble is, most of them deny that climate change is the result of human activity, or even that it is happening at all. And polls consistently suggest that around half of all Americans believe Jesus Christ will return by 2050 (about the same number who don't accept evolution – maybe there's some link between these two fantasies). So why would they cooperate with unbelievers to try and prevent this imminent disaster? The Second Coming will happen first. For many Christians, it doesn't really matter how much we trash the planet, because they'll be leaving it. We live on a "disposable planet," according to one of the most influential American pastors, John MacArthur, author of the bestselling *The MacArthur Study Bible*, promoted as "Unleashing God's Truth One Verse at a Time".

Indeed most Christians, if you count them worldwide, believe in a strange idea called the "Rapture," as an article of faith, which would be over a billion people. When Christ comes again all the "saved" will be physically transported up to heaven in an instant, their shoes and clothes (and any unsaved family and friends) left behind, trains and cars crashing if the drivers happened to be amongst the lucky ones, leaving the rest of humanity to face the terrible End Times (there are various interpretations of this, called millennial, premillennial, dispensational, etc., which aren't worth getting into here). It's doubly strange because as a teaching it was only really developed in 1830 by a preacher called John Nelson Darby. He belonged to a sect called the Plymouth Brethren, but that Church wasn't pure enough for him, so he founded the Exclusive Brethren (which later split into Open and Closed, and is still splitting into different subgroups). There's no mention of the word "Rapture" in the Bible, itself, though it's brimful of events, ideas and teachings both bizarre and wonderful. The closest is a reference in 1 Thessalonians 4:16-17:

The dead in Christ shall rise first: Then we which are alive and
remain shall be caught up together with them in the clouds, to meet
the Lord in the air: and so shall we ever be with the Lord.

There's one more ambiguous reference in the gospel of Matthew, but that's it, out of 33,173 verses.

There are only three million or so Brethren today, but the idea has spread like a pathogen through evangelical churches. It seems a small hook to hold the future of humanity on (and it doesn't sound at all comfortable; it's freezing cold up there in the air, with little oxygen and lots of planes to dodge). But it's easier believing in fairy tales than investing in the future for your grandchildren.

That's an example of bad religion. Equally, there's plenty of good religion, across many traditions, and there are common threads. In all of them, there are strong cultural and social reasons for believing as a community. They all have their myths that can give shape and direction to our individual lives. Above all, there's the moral teaching. Across the board, the overarching themes are about living for others rather than yourself; treating them as you would like to be treated, even loving your enemy. Living in the here and now. Seeing God in everyone, and in all things, rather than creeds and doctrine. Working for reconciliation, and rejecting violence. Favoring the poor, disabled and ill – how we treat them is a measure of our humanity. Being oblivious to race, gender and sexuality. Refusing to accumulate personal wealth – and if you happen to get it, then giving it away. Respecting Nature. Simply "doing good." "Being good." Even just "being kind." It's perhaps nowhere summed up better than in the teaching of Jesus on the Kingdom of God. That's how it started, with the first Christians; it's a teaching that virtually disappeared early on, as churches became organized, and powerful, and

Christianity became the religion of a series of empires, down to the present day, turning the teaching of Jesus back to front. How all that occurred is one of the most intriguing stories in history, shaping the world we know today. To understand how it happened might help us recover and live by at least a little of the original teaching.

Part I

Why We Believe

1. Starting Out

Truth is open to everyone, and the claims aren't all staked yet.
Seneca (first century AD)

Perhaps you may think all talk of God is so much gibberish. Or maybe you reckon you know Him. You may have a clear idea of who He is. Maybe you believe it's the only right one. The Christian Church does. God may be Almighty, Omniscient, the Ground of All Being, and so on, but he also has a Son, a Church that interprets Him through a cartload of Capital Letter Doctrines, and His very own book, called the Bible, where He shares his thoughts about who He is and how we should approach Him and why we should do what He commands (though He used an indeterminate number of "ghost" writers, in publishing parlance, to put His words down on the page). This book covers the history of His involvement with His favorite tribe, in what we now call the Middle East, mainly from about 1500 BC to AD 50, and other related issues.

Over the years I've held both these positions. I still don't know which is right. I'm generally somewhere in the middle. And even if God doesn't exist, in any shape or form, that makes the best of religious teaching (which is essentially psychological, social and practical – and of course many religions don't postulate a God at all) even more relevant – because we have to do the work of healing ourselves and the planet on our own. He is not going to save us.

Indulge me for a page to explain where I'm coming from. I was naïve and pretty clueless when I started work in a publishing house in my early twenties (this is back in the 1970s). The one thing a degree in English literature had given me was the feeling that words were kind of sacred. In writing things down, you can figure out what you think. And if you get into poetry, or drama,

11

or fiction, you can go way beyond that. You can expand your understanding of who and where you are by teasing these things out. Pluck on a thought in your brain, and you can make art out of it. You can even create alternative worlds, which feed back into your understanding and appreciation of this one.

So I thought authors in the publishing world, who live in this domain of words, using it like potters use clay, would be living on some kind of higher plane, especially if they were the kind who went to church (the company published a lot of Christian books – I'd lost the kind of religious conviction I'd had as a teenager, but was still sympathetic). Obviously, the pursuit of money was gross, and here I'd never have to do math in my head or worry about which way round creditors and debtors were (I've never quite understood the reason why in ordinary life debts are money you owe someone else, whereas in business it's money others owe you). People in publishing were bound to be nice to each other and have long, intelligent conversations about the meaning of life over a bottle or two of wine after work in the evenings.

And, boy, was I committed. Sometimes I'd sleep in the office. It seemed like the ideal job; learning about business, and life, within a framework that seemed basically altruistic – to do with service as much as sales; working for a higher good as well as paying the rent.

Within a few years I was running a division of a company with its headquarters in Grand Rapids, Michigan, itself soon to become a division of a company which was a division of a media company, in itself a division of something whose remote boss was so distant as to make God seem like a friendly neighbor. I was spending most of my time on spreadsheets, crossing the Atlantic several times a year (I think of myself as part-American, went to school as a teenager in Minneapolis, and have seen more of the country than most Americans), making people redundant in the week before Christmas, and publishing books I'm too embarrassed to mention. It was all a far cry from a year or two spent bumming around Europe and the Middle East with hair down to my shoulders, living on a dollar a day, back in the time when Vietnam was a war zone and Kabul in Afghanistan was the friendly Mecca for hitchhikers (we really should learn to stop invading other countries and messing them up; we have Departments and Ministries of "Defense," not "Offense").

One of many low points I remember: we used to sell lorry loads of books every month to the Protestant community in Northern Ireland. I remember the excitement of receiving a big cardboard box of tapes of the Revd. Ian Paisley's sermons (he was the leader of the dominant Democratic Unionist Party in Northern Ireland) with a view to making them into a book. Gold dust! Maybe he was a few centuries out of his time, but a guaranteed market! I was ready to do it. Young and enthusiastic, I was ready to pass over his organization of private armies (well, you could argue it was self-defense against the IRA), denunciation of homosexuals (put it down as a cultural issue – this was before LGBT rights rose so high in public profile), ecumenism (didn't really understand what that was about anyway – tough enough to understand your own church, why bother with others, let alone other religions?). I put the tape on the old analog recorder, and his voice thundered out, repeatedly rising to crescendos, organ music swelling in the background, denouncing the whore of Babylon, the Antichrist in the Vatican (he accused the Queen Mother – by all accounts, a devout Christian, like her daughter, the current Queen – of "spiritual adultery and fornication" for simply *meeting* Pope John XXIII). It sounded more like a Nazi Nuremberg rally than a Christian sermon. No wonder Protestants and Catholics in Northern Ireland couldn't manage to live in peace together. Surely, people in the twenty-first century, knowing what we do about the history of Christian religious wars, let alone the First World War and the Second with the Holocaust, couldn't still think in this kind of way. This vitriol didn't have anything to do with the teaching of Jesus. And it didn't represent the kind of God I wanted to have anything to do with. If there really was such a thing as good and evil in the world, this kind of language was evil, and I was on the wrong side.

There were a number of issues for me that episodes like this brought into focus. Given the overwhelming thrust of the Gospels on treating others as you would like to be treated; loving your neighbor as yourself; everyone being equal in the eyes of God; the emphasis on children, the poor and sick; the irrelevance of race, gender and creed – why don't Christians appear to be more concerned and loving than other people (on average, I realize many are extraordinary)? Why is the historical record so mixed? How far can you take the details of scriptures from two to three thousand years ago and apply them today, in the light of different understandings of the world we've gained through the sciences? How sure can you be of what you believe, and is certainty such a good thing if it leads to such division? Why are there so many different beliefs? Might not God be bigger than the various limited ways we describe Him? Or are we better off without God? Was this a good way to spend a working life? And so on.

So as life rolled on and I set up my own business in the 80s I began publishing more widely, meeting authors from an increasing variety of spiritual disciplines; high church Anglicans as well as evangelical Protestants, liberal theologians, Catholics, Muslims, Buddhists, Sufis, moving on to a wide spectrum of New Age teachers, from acupuncturists to witches (and in my own very limited experience, the more tolerant and pluralist their beliefs, the nicer the people concerned are – fundamentalists, in which whatever branch of religion or politics you're talking about, are usually the worst). My original coworkers might see this as the slow slide to hell. I'm more inclined to see myself as something of an instinctive conservative and a slow starter, just beginning to learn. And I've learnt something from all of them.

Most of the couple of hundred or so books a year we publish now aren't in the area of religion, and of those that are about half are on paganism (which makes a kind of sense to me – after all, it's by far the oldest religious tradition, alongside which Christianity is scarcely a blip; it's based on a respect for Nature, which we're all going to have to adopt if civilization is going to survive; it's decentralized to the point where you can pretty much make up your own gods and goddesses, but then that's what we've always been doing anyway...). I still think of myself as Christian, though most Christians would probably call me a panentheist (the belief that God pervades everything and extends beyond space and time), or even on the Devil's side. I don't know Jesus personally any more in the way I once thought I did. I can't quote chapters of the Bible from memory like I used to. It's the words of Jesus that are important for me today, rather than the later teaching *about* him. He seems to me to offer an alternative vision of the world, one that has as little to do with the Bible-thumping mentality as it has to do with the materialist, secular mindset (let alone the worst kinds of Christianity which manage to combine both – like the prosperity gospel – or its overlapping New Age equivalent, the Law of Attraction; they're pretty similar – you can have anything you want if you believe in it enough; if you don't get it, you're not believing hard enough, or handing over enough cash). A vision of giving rather than getting; one which celebrates the weak rather than the strong; one which sees God in hands and hearts rather than temples and doctrine; a God who can be found anywhere, at any time, who is bigger than we can possibly imagine. I believe (I try and preserve my naivety, or I'll die of cynicism) it would really make a difference if we could follow it.

I just think of God now as more of a way (early Jewish Christians referred to themselves as "The Way") and less of a "person," in whose image we're made (or vice versa). I believe that a view of life based around God rather than self or science –

but which includes both these – is not only credible and possible, it's the best way of living, and is essential to our future well-being, even our survival. The teaching of Jesus expresses this as well as any other, perhaps better.

But its essential themes are common to all good religion. This takes me to what I see as the real religious question today. It's not so much whether religious beliefs are "true" or "false"; whether God (one or many) exists or not – and if you've read this far you're probably not 100% certain either way yourself; or which religion gets it most right. Those questions are significant, but nothing like as much as the one of which beliefs are "good" or "bad." Beliefs in religion are essentially no different to beliefs in the political, economic and social spheres. They can bring people together, helping them create decent, fair societies, in right balance with each other and with nature, or they can support exploitative power structures, oppressing the many in favor of the few. They can appeal to our better natures or encourage the worst. And in some respects the history of civilization itself is the story of which religious beliefs (or, rather, which traditions within them) have the upper hand. So in unravelling that we need to go behind the claims and counter claims; the ins and outs of this doctrine or that; the "did it happen this way or not?" events of the last few thousand years and more. To understand good religion and why it's still relevant we need to get back to basics, to answering some fundamental questions.

For example: Why do we believe in the first place?

It usually helps to start with definitions. We've got so cocooned in our little religious and cultural boxes (Christian, Muslim, pagan, atheist, or whatever) that we've forgotten what "religion" means. There are two meanings of the Latin *religio*, the root of "religion." The first most people hold in common, the second is where we start to differ.

The first meaning of *religio* is "relationship." The ties that bind us, the bonds we have a duty to uphold, like the "ligaments" that hold our bodies together. There's a common, universal and ancient thread in religious tradition that takes us back to when "relationship" began. It says that once we were content. We didn't worry. We lived in what is described in different traditions as the Age of Perfection, the Krita Yuga, the Garden of Eden, the Eternal Springtime, and so on, in innocence. We were at one with nature, because we *were* nature. We didn't know good and evil. We couldn't mess up. We couldn't even *think*.

So far, so good; most people would agree with this. At some point in our history, whether 100,000 or 7 million years ago (lowest and highest estimates, depending in part on how many species of "Homo" you include), we became "self-aware." Armadillos specialize in body armor, cheetahs in speed, this is our own specialty, it's what we "do." We began to watch ourselves "living." We divided the world into "me" and "it." We made a conscious choice to eat the apple (or not), to have sex (or not). We learnt how to manipulate things, changing them for new uses (the world's oldest known worked wooden implement, the Clacton spear, in the Natural History Museum in London, was fashioned over 420,000 years ago, and stone points used for hunting go back more than half a million years – we've been killing animals or people for a heck of a long time). Like Adam in the Garden of Eden (Genesis 2:20 – the foundational myth for our current predicament) we began naming them, and talking to each other. So on the one hand we began to enjoy the fruits of self-awareness, of communication, and love; on the other hand we learned the ashes of separation, uncertainty and the fear of death. Ever since then, since the "Fall," a metaphor for our birth of consciousness, we've been trying to put the two together again – the "me" and the "it," turning "it" into "you," figuring out how one should relate to the other, groping around the edges of our lives, looking for patterns, for explanations, wondering what's over the horizon.

We started asking the questions we still ask today: Why

can't we just be happy with what we've got? What is love really about? Can it survive death? Can anything? If not, what's the point? We've been investing in elaborate burial rituals and provisions to help the deceased into the next life for at least a hundred thousand years. Why is there anything at all? Is there a Big Truth? A God? Maybe we should shut up and relax. Accept things as they are. But if we could, and did, we'd still be up in the trees, chucking sticks at leopards.

Religion began as a response to the dilemmas that self-awareness created. For instance, rather than acting solely in the interests of the species, or the genetic pull of family, individuals could now override their biological programing and act in the interests of the self. By the way – killing, cheating, lying – these are "natural," with the first being the principle behind most forms of life, other than plants – you only live by eating something else – the second common amongst animals and birds; it's only the third, lying, that is unique to us, special to humans, because of our capacity to talk in complex sentences (lying is easy; it's telling the truth we have to work at; that's the tough part). But to act solely in the interests of the self is self-destructive for everyone in the longer term. Religions grew to connect us again with the larger whole, replacing our lost instinct. It's our "big idea" that ties us together; the one that stops the self from getting drunk on its new sense of power; a "larger truth." A solid religion creates structures that control the appetites of the self and encourages service and inspiration. The wisdom tradition of Homo sapiens sapiens ("sapiens" means "wise," which is very different from simply "clever," or "intelligent") – of relating to ourselves and the world around us wisely, of developing the vision of a good life and a moral code to frame it, of transcending our biology – this is what separates us from nature.

Christianity (and, to a lesser extent, Islam) is an oddball religion in this respect, because instead of focusing on how to live in harmony with our fellow creatures on the planet today it's traditionally, historically speaking, promised vast individual reward after you die. But more broadly speaking, across religion as a whole, in the first meaning of the word, it helps provide the framework for relating to each other, rituals for the key moments in life, for building societies. It's our means of defining and confronting what is good and bad, honed through tens of millennia of cooperation and stored in our genes. It gives us rituals to carry social engagement forwards, benchmarks to guide us, targets to aim for, stories to get us there, standards to judge ourselves and our societies by. If we didn't have religion, we'd need something close to it. And in the hole left in the twentieth century by the ebbing belief in God we've tried a number of different ideas, organizing ourselves around consumption (capitalism), production (communism), country (nationalism) and race (fascism). Maybe the jury is still out, but these ideas don't seem to have worked.

Of course that's an oversimplification (as is this book) – these ideas have always been around. As far as capitalism goes, joint-stock companies go back to the Tang dynasty in China over a thousand years ago. The first Christians practiced a form of communism (Acts 2:44), though of course that didn't last. Nationalist sentiments go back centuries. Few societies have pushed racial segregation as far as the USA from the eighteenth century onwards (in that period, the world's largest apartheid state to have existed), even though we know that "race," biologically speaking, is simply the reaction of the skin over sufficient time to sunlight, and there's only a 0.1% genetic difference between humans. You can argue that fascism, broadly interpreted as institutionalized supremacy and bigotry, classifying some groups as subhuman, has been the dominant culture since the first settlements. And so on. But only the twentieth century has showcased all these ideologies in such extreme form at the same time in a particular region.

Maybe the reason they don't work is because they're all based on "us," rather than the "other." They lack respect for a sense of the "sacred" (for the moment, let's call it God for short), which is the second meaning of *religio*. In this view, developing good relationships is not just a personal, moral issue, it's a universal one, an absolute. It's the meaning behind everything. Religion is about acknowledging it, bowing to it. Losing that screaming bit in your head that insists "it should be all about me."

We may describe this God as an idea of eternal perfection, or a spirit, or in human form, or, as Christian tradition starts to say from the fourth century AD onwards with its new version of the trinity (gods commonly appear in threes – more in chapter 37), as somehow all three at once; or in any of thousands of other ways. Each suggests that values are more than our invention. They're rooted in something that's bigger and more important than ourselves, a next level up, something that's beyond our control, which we can't twist to our advantage. To put it in terms of practical relationships, there are higher values that we can't compromise on, for which we're prepared to sacrifice more than seems rational.

This is more controversial. Why put yourself out for something you can't see? But the "sacred" has been with us so long it may even be something hardwired into the brain, that makes us human. It's even what the word "human" means. It probably originates from the Arabic *hu*, meaning spirit, or God; and the Sanskrit *manah*, or mind. We think that we are what we have become because we are essentially spiritual beings, minds seeking God, whatever those terms might signify. For tens of thousands of years we've practiced this search in religion, and more recently have described it in philosophy, the (sometimes obsessive) pursuit of knowledge. Religion is usually preferred to philosophy because it engages the heart, even the body, as well as the mind. It offers the medicine as well as the diagnosis. It describes what we have in here as well as how we relate to what's out there.

Religion is primary. So much so that most deeply religious cultures don't even have a word for it. For them, to explain why they're "religious" would be like trying to explain why they breathe. Reading, writing, math, science, these are secondary. They're what we have to go to school for. They're relatively new on the human scene. We have a hunger for the meaning that we describe in religion, for the stories that bind us together, that tell us where we came from and where we're going, that explain how we should relate to each other and the world around us, like we have a hunger for food and relationship. Indeed in most religions these are linked together in sacrifice and ritual meals. Communion, eating the flesh of another to partake of its spirit, is the most ancient and widespread of all religious practices, which most Christians today still follow, either literally (a priest changes the bread into the body of Christ – churches vary as to which point in the sacrament the change occurs) or metaphorically, depending on the denomination. And theology is to religion like cookery is to eating, like love is to sex. We've been doing it ever since our remote ancestors came down from the trees and started burying their dead.

If God did not exist He would have to be invented.
Voltaire (eighteenth century AD)

2. Why Religion Is Fundamental

The purpose of words is to carry ideas. When the ideas are grasped, the words are forgotten. Where can I find a man who has forgotten words? He is the one I would like to talk to.
Chuang Tzu (fourth century BC)

But do we really need God/gods today to bind our relationships, when we have marriage and music, laws and police, democracies and global institutions? Why do we still return to this ancient idea? And after all, why should human life have "meaning," any more than a tree has "meaning"? Surely spiritual experiences (undeniable) are simply a part of our general psychology, a by-product of our ability to think rationally, to look for cause and effect. If we throw a stone, we see the splash. So if we see lightning, we invent a god who must be throwing it. That's the persuasive argument that religion is just anthropocentric, projecting our wishes and fantasies on to the world around us. Now that we've grown up we know better than this, and our religious genes are no more relevant than the male nipple.

Sometimes it's the young who turn to God (or politics) through idealism; they feel there's more to life than their parents let on. There must be a hidden pattern that makes sense of everything (I've been there – thinking that my committed evangelical Christian parents were not really evangelical enough). Or the middle-aged do so through frustration at not reaching their dreams; they begin to see themselves as they used to see their parents. Or the old because they need new ones; the end is coming like a train and they wonder if there isn't something beyond extinction. After all, the laws in physics and math are timeless; why should life itself be finite? Dissatisfaction, the thought that we're being pushed around the edges of life rather than enjoying its center, is a powerful force that leads to belief.

Fear can do it still faster. Nothing prompts agonized questioning as much as imminent death, whether of a partner or our own. There aren't many complete atheists in a plane falling out of the sky.

(In my evangelical proselytizing days I would ask people at airports, "If this plane falls out of the sky, where would you spend eternity?" The best put-down was, "I really don't mind, friend, so long as it's not with you.") At the very least, confronting the reality of death can make us think about life and what we really value.

This may all seem a bit over the top. For those of you who don't have any kind of feeling for religion at all, I'm just trying to convey something of the intensity which it can reach. Obviously, we can live well without formal religion, or religion of any kind – that's common. In the better-functioning societies of today, like some of the European countries, particularly in Scandinavia, it plays a much lesser role than it used to. In part, I'd suggest, because in those societies good religious principles have been absorbed into the mainstream – it's just the difficult, ancient "creeds" they've abandoned. But the idea first mooted a couple of centuries ago, and common 50 years ago, that these beliefs would die off has proved an illusion. Around the world, overall, belief in God – and religion in general – flourishes, for good or bad. And I doubt there are many, religious or not, who don't recognize some kind of "scale" of experience, in terms of relationships with others or the world, and wonder if there isn't some kind of blueprint for it somewhere.

"Materialism," whether by that you mean anything from consumerism as the main principle of a good life, or simply a scientific understanding of how we came to be as we are, is not a compelling answer for many. For some, sure. I admire people who can live a good life in contentment, without the props of religion, or drugs, or alcohol, or the aphrodisiac of power. But we mostly have a sense that there's more to life, that it could be "better," that it has a "point." Partly, it's the positive wells we draw on that keep us coming back to it. There's a "state of flow"; the sheer delight at being alive, at the amazingly intricate beauty of nature. It could be experiencing the unity of the crowd at a soccer match, or a rock concert, or enjoying an extreme sport. These experiences can be just emotional. But then there are the peak experiences, described by Abraham Maslow as "the moments of highest happiness and fulfillment." There's the wonder of a discovery, there's gratitude at being loved, and at the power of love to change ourselves and others. And love – it's not something that science can describe, or give you an equation for; but life without it – it's one-dimensional.

A newborn baby, a dying friend, a walk in the woods, maybe even in a church – those often empty shells of the faith we used to have – at times most of us feel the pull of something, of being connected to a whole that embraces our little selves, that is in some sense absolutely "good." Maybe even a sense of awe, that pinnacle of consciousness, where we see ourselves in something else, or indeed lose all sense of distinction, when the boundaries dissolve. We might describe it as God, variously emphasizing the loving aspect, or the beautiful, or the true, or simply as a mystery that we can touch the edges of but can't know. These experiences might even lead to a state of self-transcendence. Sometimes, maybe just once or twice in a lifetime, we might have a breakthrough moment so strange and wonderful that nothing is ever quite the same again (and I'm not counting LSD trips here, though they can work in the same way; and ingesting entheogens could well be the oldest stimulus to religious experience, much as mind-altering practices like dancing, meditation, fasting, chanting, speaking in tongues, etc., are still part of the general tool-kit). We might even redefine the priorities in our lives. After all, the world is over there, and it's astonishing. We're here, and we're the only starting point we have. Surely we're related. If there's a meaning behind it we want to know, to be part of it.

And in so far as we're rational creatures we need a reason for living and a framework to live by. Rules are useful for that. And life is more than rules and logic. Hope would be a nice thing too. Religion is a way of enabling it to come at will, rather than just on occasion. Perhaps even leading to "plateau experience" – the province of saints and mystics who reportedly live in it all the time.

And what most religions agree on, if you look at it broadly, is that when you strip away everything that we tend to think of as constituting our lives – our possessions, home, health, friends, family, even our daily sense of self, the bundle of nerves and emotions that get us through the day – we get down to who we really are, and find there's something there. We're more than a bundle of molecules, more than science has yet described. If you dig deep enough there's a spark, a spirit, rather than nothing. There's "me." Some describe this as the "soul." Connecting with it brings us back to Eden, to the time before we realized we were naked, and invented clothes and fashion, work and worry, religion and psychology. We find we're back in touch with the world. The problems fall away, and nothing could be other or better than it is. We might even see the true nature of consciousness as eternal rather than transient. That love is real. That life is more energy than matter, force fields rather than flesh. That underneath the appearance all is essentially one.

Many say they encounter a force, which most characterize as loving and healing; many personalize it as a deity, which sustains and informs this world, nudging it every moment toward life rather than chaos.

There is no more powerful feeling on earth. Millions of talented, wealthy, beautiful people have given up ambition, money, and sex for religion. They even still do. It's not just for the uneducated, the ill, or the oppressed. It can be the assurance of being saved and loved, reconciled with yourself and the world. The moments when you know prayers have been answered, even of foreknowledge. Maybe it's the times when you are caught up in worship, when the veil between this world and the next, between yourself and God, splits. It can bring healing, opening up innermost thoughts, bringing to light childhood problems and clearing them. The experience of time, space and nature can be changed by it. The presence of God can be the defining point around which the world turns. We can actually love ourselves because we are part of a greater love. This then spills over into a love for others. It makes sense of everything. It's better than drugs, and without the downside. It can bring us peace: sometimes even happiness.

Depending on the channel they've found, some phrase it as reaching for God up there, others as God reaching down to us, others as finding God in here, others as going beyond the idea of God. The voice of God speaking out of the hurricane, the roaring fire, or the still quiet, the voice of reason or conscience, or no voice at all. But all describe the experience as a feeling of coming home, of being welcomed to our true state; a moment that wraps up past, present, and future, self and other, in an explosion of understanding and awed contentment, a "oneness."

Why we believe in God (of whatever kind) is easy to see. We always have done. It's a bridge over the abyss – the foreknowledge of our own death – the light at the end of the tunnel. It takes our uncertainties and fears and turns them around, enabling us to believe that what happens was meant to happen, and will turn out for the good. It's what drives us, makes us believe that love is more than sex, relationship more than advantage. That there's a "whole" we can be part of, where life makes sense. That even death might not be the end. We're even prepared to die ourselves for a cause as causes can make life worth living. If we can't, if life has no cause, no purpose, we think of it as having no meaning, no "worth." It turns self-awareness into a blessing rather than a curse, enables us to love life rather than fear it.

Whether this is true or not, it "works," or we would have

given up on it thousands, hundreds of thousands of years ago. Evolution, the survival of the fittest, applies as much to ideas as to animals like us. Alcoholics are more likely to be persuaded to give up drinking by acknowledging the "Higher Power" of the AA 12-Step Program than by being lectured at by doctors. Parents do not lessen their grief by thinking of their dead child as rotting flesh, but by believing their spirits might touch again. We're more likely to act in the interests of others if we can believe in love as a universal principle in life than if we see it as a self-gratifying fiction. We're more likely to be happy if we believe creation is basically good, and joyful, and continuous than if we think of it (rationally) as random, painful, and meaningless. A universe of billions of galaxies and black holes, destined for extinction, without a single particle of love, intention or spirit anywhere, which at the quantum level is absurd, an inhuman monstrosity, no meaning – apart from the meaning we bring to it, the stories we tell, the relationships we develop – okay, that may be the reality. We don't know, and probably never will. But even a fiction of salvation is better than a despairing suicide, if you're looking for something extra to get you through the day.

Atheists won't completely win the argument on the ground in another thousand years, because what they offer is not enough for everyone. Religion can support you when you have nothing, can give you something to reach for when you have everything. Indeed sometimes the more we have the more we realize there's never enough, and it's not what we really want anyway. In its purest form, it's the ultimate democratic way of thinking, asking the same kind of questions and exerting the same kind of power over a millionaire in her New England Hamptons' mansion as over a dying Neolithic clan leader clothed in wolf skins and huddled by a cave fire. In between it covers the lot – from birth to death, fear to hope, guilt to joy, from poor people to rich, happy to sad. In a vast and complicated world, religion gives us reference points, explaining who and where we are, and what we should do. What kind of priorities we should give our lives, and how we should live together.

And there's a point that every religion agrees on – that the key to understanding is in surrender, acceptance, rather than taking up a sword and battling through life for your own self-interest. Most of us have learned to let go with a partner in the interests of a deeper relationship: religion is about letting go of the world. The trick of doing it, of having faith (believing beyond the evidence) that the world makes a deeper kind of sense, comes with knowing for yourself where that point is, where faith is credible. Where you can make the jump. Where you can let go, and believe the unknown will take care of you. I think that's what "faith" is. It's believing hopefully. We do this all the time, every day, in relationships, trusting people that they will build on what we've developed rather than beat us up or cook us for supper. It's what being human is about – having faith, risking love, making deeper connections. The trick of having faith that the world is one of love and meaning without switching off your brain seems to be a question of knowing for yourself where that point is. It's different for everyone, and the average position changes through the centuries in different cultures, religions, and traditions within those religions – none more so than in Christianity; you can be saved by works (James 2:21-24); by faith alone (Galatians 2:16); only by helping the poor and needy (Matthew 25:34-46); by baptism (Mark 16:16); only if you endure to the end (Mark 13:13); just by believing (John 3:16); by keeping the law (Romans 2:13); by being born of water and of the Spirit (John 3:5); by eating the flesh of Jesus and drinking his blood (John 6:53-54); and so on… dozens of them, frequently contradicting each other (eg: in Romans 10:13 you can be saved by calling on the name of the Lord, but in Matthew 7:21-23 you won't necessarily be); some passages say that you can never lose your salvation while others say you can – it's a Babel of confusion, although of course that's not God's fault, it's yours (1

Corinthians 14:33).

We're all uncertain, if we have any sense, and there's no divine blueprint to help us out. We can ignore religion, like staying single, or join one, recognizing that it's never going to be perfect, any more than any other relationship can be. But there's a point where you have to commit, to make a decision. The point changes through your own life. This is my attempt to sketch where it is for me. Mindfulness, if you can manage it, is staying focused on where the point makes sense. Wisdom is thinking and acting out of that awareness. Salvation, or enlightenment, or reconciliation, or awakening, or peak experience (there are hundreds of ways of describing it), happens in the realization that the point is everything, the doorway through which you leave behind yourself and reconnect with life as it is rather than the little bit of it we can see.

It is the heart which experiences God, and not the reason.
Pascal (seventeenth century AD)

3. But Which Religion?

Faith is to believe what you do not see, and the reward of this faith is to see what you believe.
Augustine (fifth century AD)

Letting go and living in the love of God, or however you describe it – that sounds great, but it's easier said than done. For the average individual in the West, each of us consuming (in terms of the energy used in everything we have and do) on average a hundred times more than our grandparents eight times removed did at the turn of the nineteenth century, and escalating at ever faster rates, it's probably harder than at any other time in history. We've got so much more to let go of. As this is a book for novices in matters of religion, written by one, let me come right out and say I've never really managed it; which is why I'll either spend a long time in purgatory (if I'm lucky) or come back as a bug (choose your religion). Maybe I've just never really got the hang of it. And maybe it's not necessary. Maybe we're better off without it. This is for those who can't quite escape the feeling that it's important in some way.

You often hear preachers/gurus today paraphrasing Augustine's quote at the top of the chapter along the lines of (if you read underneath them): "Fake it until you make it." But the harder I try to believe in a God "out there" the more He seems a function of my own efforts. The more believers shout that He exists the more ephemeral He seems to be – why should any self-respecting God need that kind of help? Why would He command us, whoever He is, to worship Him? With the risk of eternal punishment if we don't? Is He that desperate for validation? On the other hand, however much I try to practice Eastern traditions, or the Christian *via negativa*, and lose the "self," there's always that niggling voice: "I'm still here, silly," which I can't quite lose. I've never been completely bowled over and turned into a different kind of person (not that's lasted, anyway). Equally, I've never quite lost the feeling that life without any sense of the sacred is a gray and shabby affair. Revelation keeps popping its head around the corner, but reason always pokes its eye out.

The main problem is *how* we can know we see or hear God. That we're not just talking with ourselves. I see publishing proposals every week from people who believe God (or angels, or Devas, or whoever) has spoken to them. Many of our authors believe they have had direct experiences of God. Some would dispute that most others really have had a genuine experience (I try and avoid those). They can't have done, because it's not the same as theirs. But what criteria do we use for accepting some as "real" (if we do) and others not? Aren't all these authors either encountering something "real" in some strange way or all a bit mad themselves?

Religion relies on personal experience for its validity: "I know it's true, because this happened to me." But that's entirely subjective. At any moment, around the world, you could eavesdrop on millions of worshippers praying to God/gods/spirits. But you'll never hear Him/Her/them talking back. As Shakespeare puts it in *Henry IV, Part 1*:

> **GLENDOWER**
> *I can call spirits from the vasty deep.*
> **HOTSPUR**
> *Why, so can I, or so can any man,*
> *But will they come when you do call for them?*

And why should our experience be equally valid for others who experience differently? What if they lead to contradictory beliefs? There are at least 100,000 distinct pictures of the divine world that we've developed in our history. And the pattern is really far more diverse, by factors of ten. There are for instance over 30,000 denominations in Christianity alone, about one for each verse in the Bible, and that's in a comparatively centralized and creedal religion (reflecting the difficulty of extracting a single message from the Bible – comparable numbers of sects in Islam and Judaism are around a hundred).

Many religions might appeal to sacred scriptures as the source of their authority, as divinely given, but that only shifts the problem along. Why follow one rather than another when they all claim to be true (actually, more often than not, they don't, that's a label some of the new religions like Christianity have claimed as they became formalized into authoritarian structures)? In the library of sacred scripture for instance the Bible is a single book (think of a large room with shelves all around the walls, floor to ceiling, curated on the basis of merit – and the Bible is one – or a fuzzy collection of some – amongst thousands). It's not the oldest, or the newest. Its authorship is less certain than most. It's not the best written, or the most coherent. It's far from the most inspired, or original, or moral. Only those whose knowledge of the rest of the library is limited or nonexistent claim otherwise.

Their arguments are tedious. For instance, Jesus must be the Son of God because he told me so, or the Bible says he was/is, or because he fulfils the prophecies of the Old Testament, or because it's the only explanation of the commitment of the followers, the power of the Gospels, the rapid spread of the faith, the coherence of the text, etc., all circular arguments, none of which stand up to a few minutes serious examination. Muslims use exactly the same arguments for Muhammad. They're of equal merit. Or perhaps Muslims have the better of it. Take the last point for instance. The *Qur'an* is vastly more coherent than the Bible, with a clearer message (though it was written to be recited, as poetry – it comes across in English translations as both repetitive and random), dictated by the angel Gabriel to Muhammad in the most extraordinarily beautiful Arabic, in a white-hot heat over 20 years, rather than, as with the Bible, by dozens of authors from different cultures, in different languages, even from different faiths, spread over a thousand miles and a thousand years, with another thousand years of debate about which of them should be included (which has never been agreed around all the Churches). If you wanted to make a rational choice on which monotheistic religion to follow, Islam makes more sense than Christianity, which split God into different entities when it was adopted by the pagan Roman Empire as the official religion, to accommodate its own polytheism. And it generates a level of sustained prayer and devotion across the whole community that puts Christianity in the shade.

There's nothing "sacred" or "true" about religions themselves. They're as much human constructions as schools, governments and ideologies. You can judge them, vote for them, like you do for political parties (or not). There are many options. If the Abrahamic religions (Judaism, Christianity and Islam) with their harsh desert God don't work for you, and you're looking for an intelligently conceived monotheistic religion that makes few demands on credulity and focuses on good practice in this life, then Sikhism is a good bet. The youngest and fifth largest of the major religions, it rejects religious monopoly, puts practice above creed, and focuses on truthfulness, honesty, self-control and purity. Sounds good.

And of course monotheism is a recent development, followed by some just in the most recent fraction of 1% of our time on earth. We might describe Hinduism as being the most successful religion on our planet today in terms of being followed by the largest proportion of the world's population over the last few thousand years. Some scholars say that it's the cradle of many of the others, including the monotheistic religions, much as our Western languages have developed from Sanskrit. Those inclined to mysticism might claim that the central Hindu teaching of *advaita*, of all things being one, is at the root of all good religion. Others claim that in its exploration of consciousness it developed sophisticated views of the unity of matter and mind millennia ago that science is only just beginning to appreciate. The most revered of their classics, the *Bhagavad Gita* ("Song of the Beloved"), written around the fifth century BC, is one of the earliest attempt we have to arrive at a fully comprehensive view of existence. The setting is a battlefield that symbolizes life itself. As the dialogue ripples out into deeper subjects a whole philosophy of life unfolds. It's a work of deep wisdom and tolerance. As Krishna says, "Whoever with true devotion worships any deity, in him I deepen that devotion; and through it he fulfills his desire" (7:21).

But this doesn't necessarily mean Hinduism can work for everyone. It's hard for Westerners to embrace the idea of 350 million or so gods (oddly enough very similar to the number of angels that medieval monks believed existed) rather than one, of duty rather than love at the top of the moral equation. And whereas organized Christianity was corrupted by empire and power, Hinduism's rich philosophical heritage was corrupted by the organized caste system. It is pluralist on a broad scale, but separation is locked in socially. We're conditioned by our past, our present, and they are rare individuals who can determine for themselves quite different futures.

This book has "God" in the title, for convenience, but of course good religion does not need "God," or "gods," at all – and the ultimate divine in Hinduism, Brahman-Atman, is not really a God, in the sense of being individual or personal. Buddhism is increasingly the religion of choice for many in the West (reincarnation is making a comeback) and does not see the divine as a "being" in any sense of the word. It prefers terms like the void, or non-being, or nothingness. Originally an offshoot of Hinduism, it developed different forms as it spread; first into Theravada (Sri Lanka) and Mahayana (Tibet), then with further offshoots like Madhyamika, Tantric, Vajrayana and Zen. It then got a further boost when the Chinese invasion of Tibet in 1951 scattered Buddhist teachers around the world in much the same way as the Roman destruction of Jerusalem in AD 70 scattered Jews and Christians. Historically, it's generally been the most peaceable and contemplative of the major religions. It seems the most intellectually rigorous, being based on reason rather than revelation, in some respects closer to philosophy. From the Buddha onwards, its leaders have stressed the need to test teaching against your own experience, rather than taking sacred scriptures literally, on trust, like the more primitive religions do. It focuses on the processes of the mind rather than what the mind thinks it sees. Through meditation, we gradually reduce the sense of self, clearing the mind of its junk. I struggle with it, but practices like *raja* yoga or *vipassana* meditation have been shown to lower blood pressure, slow metabolism and produce increasingly coherent brainwave patterns. Buddhism floats free of dependence on history and miracle much as Christianity freed Roman religion (or tried to, initially) from dependence on deities in the sky and statues representing them on earth. As in Christianity, after the Buddha's death his followers did introduce gods, saints, hell, etc., with rituals and complex theologies to lock believers into a particular system, trying to turn it into yet another organized religion. But Buddhism at its best is always about escaping such mental constraints and containers.

Still, it's difficult for most of us, after centuries of competitive individualism in the West, to take on board the insignificance, or nonexistence, of the self. With the ingrained perception that sins are something you can repent of, and get wiped from the record, the idea that they come back, through karma, to determine your status in your next incarnation is a tough one. In some respects it's a wonderful idea, based on older beliefs about the endless recycling of birth and death, a vista of renewal and many lives rather than the burden of a single one, and indeed was part of the official teaching of the Early Church (after all, Jesus rose from the dead in a different form), till it was denounced as heretical at the Second Council of Constantinople in AD 553. But if people are more enlightened than dogs why are so many of them nastier? And how does a dog, or a bug, make a choice to do good or evil? Or a tiger show compassion? The fact that meditation helps well-being doesn't mean that reincarnation is "true," any more than praying to Jesus and believing that he's answering somehow "proves" the Resurrection. The idea of time as circular rather than a line, the endless recycling of life, where there is no real progress, no leading up to a dramatic Judgment Day, or no acceptance that we could actually make the world better (or worse), is perhaps the hardest of all, though it seems a highly moral one; much more so than that of a moment's repentance bringing eternal salvation. After all, if we knew we were going to be reborn into this world, we might think twice about spoiling it. If we're one of the lucky few earning thousands or even a million dollars a day, we might bear in mind the millions on zero-hour contracts, or with no employment at all, when our positions might be reversed in the next life.

But hell, there are so many great religions out there. Of course, they all have their dark sides, none more so than Christianity, with its vision of Heaven for the few and Hell for the many. But for instance Taoism at times seems closer to the teaching of Jesus than does Christianity itself; a good Taoist has few demands and doesn't exercise power over others. Its vision of the world as determined by principles of balance and order offers an attractive alternative to one ruled by gods. The *Tao Te Ching* is perhaps the wisest book ever written. Its opening sentence is, "The Tao that can be told is not the eternal Tao." Words cannot define the Tao, or God, you can only come to it through the silent stillness inside you. You are not your thoughts, that's mostly mind-clutter, you are the one thinking them, being aware of them. It's not easy understanding that. Imagine the struggle a chimp would have if it tried to think of itself as "me." Now imagine yourself as not being "you." Try thinking for a moment of your name, the letters, as a label you've been given, and go deeper. It's a foundational way of thinking in many of the major religious traditions.

Then there's Confucianism, which demonstrates a stronger commitment to the wider social unit and the principle of good government than most other religions have started to get their heads around (indeed, Christianity, starting with its shift in the fifth century AD to forbidding marriages between cousins in favor of marriages between comparative strangers has led to atomized family units and weak clans). Maybe the success of the Chinese Empire over thousands of years, as a relatively peaceful, nonaggressive, inventive, well-functioning social unit, has something to do with their religion. (And I'm well aware that these are *very* relative terms; but, broadly speaking, the Chinese still live in China; they haven't, for instance, colonized North America, which they had the capacity to do; a century earlier than Columbus, Admiral Zheng He from China was roaming the oceans with a fleet of 300, and men numbering tens of thousands, in ships 30 times the size of Columbus' largest three boats, with his 90 sailors). More broadly, perhaps the communitarian, more equal and mutually supportive societies of the East are better placed to cope with pandemics, hence the huge discrepancies in the infection and death rates related to COVID between East and West.

Another is Shinto; the most ancient, beautiful, and simple of all the major religions practiced today, close to paganism and just as diverse. And you have the still older tribal religions, like that of the Aborigines, which have an imaginative power, fusing the soul and the landscape, past, present, and future, that for some dwarfs our own tinkering with the world of spirit.

And if you were to give religions a "moral score" – Jainism would surely come out on top. It's one of the oldest organized religions, with Parsha, the twenty-third leader (the first we know of as a historical person), living around the eighth century BC, way before Buddha, Confucius etc., let alone latecomers like Jesus and Muhammad. It's the most demanding one on earth, the Mount Everest of them all in terms of disciplined lifestyle and moral awareness, and has still less room for any idea of God. Its first principle is that the highest duty is not to harm anything living, including through thought and speech – it makes "wokeism," the left-wing attempt to purify the world of wrong thought and action, look tame. Never mind the brutalities of factory farming, they'll do their best to avoid stepping on an ant (serious adepts wear face masks to avoid swallowing insects, anticipating COVID precautions by many millennia). Its second principle, "many-sidedness," is that truth and reality are complex; reality can be experienced, but never fully expressed through language. And so on. If the world could somehow convert overnight to Jainism, most of our problems would be over. The coming climate crisis would be resolved. We would stop eating meat, protect Nature, cut harmful emissions and bring the world back into balance again. Politicians would be judged on how truthful they are. It sounds impossible... particularly today... many Western politicians wouldn't pass the first hurdle... but there are around five million Jainists in the world.

God has no religion
Gandhi (twentieth century AD)

4. How We Believe

Man makes religion; religion does not make man. Religion is indeed man's self-consciousness and self-awareness so long as he has not found himself or lost himself again.
Karl Marx (nineteenth century AD)

These religions and many others have enormously rich, varied, and complex traditions, literatures, and rituals. This is not to suggest that the grass is greener on the other side of the hill, but only the ignorant or foolish say the resources of spiritual and social capital of these religions are less than those of Christianity. No regular Christian event comes close, for instance, to the two to four million Muslims who take the pilgrimage every year to the Black Stone of the Kaaba (they should go at least once in their lives) for the summer Hajj, let alone the 70 million who at the start of this millennium crowded to the Kumbh Mela festival on the sacred River Ganges. And all of them seem, from a historical point of view, to have been less aggressive and damaging than Christianity (and to a lesser extent Islam), with its focus on a single divine savior, rather than many or none, and its insistence that the entire world believes in Him, indeed that the future of humanity depends on it – the more pluralist religions tend to have less of a compulsion to convert and conquer. I find it hard nowadays to take seriously any Christian theologian/evangelist/minister (or atheist) who talks/writes as if Christianity is the only "proper" religion that has ever existed. It's just an example of the exclusive/ignorance ratio – the less individuals know about other religions and sacred scriptures the easier it is to believe theirs is the only true one.

Actually, placed in this broader context, Christianity is a rather odd religion. It has frequently turned itself inside out and upside down – which is perhaps why it has survived – you can read pretty much anything you like into it, depending on which tradition you tap into. The bulk of its sacred books are taken from a different religion altogether (though it rather crudely gave them all equal status, which they don't have in Judaism, and messed around with the order, ending with the minor Malachi, to leave the impression that there's something still hanging out there, waiting for future fulfillment). It even implies that Jews can't really understand their own scriptures because they have to be interpreted in the light of the New Testament. Starting as a cult within Judaism, it soon changed to persecuting Jews, in history's longest-running one-sided feud. It's monotheistic, but also polytheistic, with three divine beings in the Trinity (plus a raft of others, like the Devil, and various godlets of different angelic rank, sanctified saints, and so on). It's philosophical, with God as the First Mover, the uncaused Creator, but the identification of one human (Jesus) with God is more akin to folk religion. It's as superstitious as any, and centers on the biggest blood sacrifice ever offered a deity. God is a person, but also ineffable. Jesus is fully God but also fully man. A circle can be a square, or black can be white, from one minute to the next.

After a long, shaky start, it's now the most widespread, but has lost most of its original heartlands to Islam. Its founder, Jesus, preached loving your neighbor as yourself, but the largest number of adherents today are in regions of the world which Christian empires forcibly colonized and/or depopulated (more in chapter 39). Actually, it effectively has two founders – alongside Jesus there's also Paul, who Jews see as the founder, who elevated the wandering preacher of zen-like parables into a cosmic figure of redemption. It's a strange mix of rational and magical thinking, generally based on uncertain premises. Of course to some extent all religions are, but only Christianity has a supernatural event like the Resurrection at the core of its theology (at least nowadays, in its dumbed-down form, though it wasn't that way for the first Christians, more in chapter 31).

Which in itself is a bit confusing, because the world wasn't saved by his sacrifice on the cross, which is why the teaching developed that he had to come back some day to finish what he started. But we're still waiting.

More than any other, it suffers from DID, Dissociative Identity Disorder, promoting a God of love on the one hand, but on the other hand condemning the vast majority of humanity to eternal torture (or just till this earth ends, in a few billion years? Or till the universe ends, in umpteen trillions of years? – the teaching is not clear here; our own judicial sentencing is far more precise), on the grounds that our natural state is depravity rather than, say, just unconscious, unaware, or unenlightened.

Perhaps the oddest thing is that no Christians try to follow the Bible, because it would be impossible. Nobody (including Jews) follows the 600+ laws in the Old Testament. Christians say that Jesus brought a "New Covenant" to replace the old, but then the overarching theme of the parables and his teaching in the gospels is the association of wealth with evil (more in chapter 25). I've yet to meet a Christian who has given all her money away.

So how should we think of different religions now? Why follow one rather than another? If we're open to truth and honest to God we know that the advances in knowledge, civilized societies, religious achievements from the communal to the individual, have been scattered all over the world in place and time. Qualities like faith, insight, intelligence, and sincerity are universal. We're a global village now. Truth is not tribal, or national. We're all migrants, ever since we left Africa 60,000 or so years ago. Our aliens are from other planets, no longer from other countries, however much contemporary demagogues try to demonize refugees and immigrants.

But the thing is, even if everyone in the world decided they could believe in the same God and saw Him in the same way, even if we only had one sacred book, one temple, one church, and had done for the last 10,000 years; even if there were no atheists, no heretics, no believers in other religions; that wouldn't prove anything about whether God is really "there" or not. Everybody could be wrong. We don't, for instance (or at least most of us don't, though there are many millions of animists, pagans and Shintoists who think otherwise), believe there are real spirits in trees and stones any longer, even though everyone in the world believed that for tens, perhaps even hundreds of thousands of years. And any doctor will tell you that the brain can believe anything, even when the evidence of the senses contradicts it. None of us sees "straight." We deceive ourselves. We all feel we have right and logic on our side. It's in our makeup. We all fantasize, hope and fear. We fall into love, believe it's forever, fall out of love, and then do it again.

Our minds are "recursive systems," in the language of cognitive psychology. We not only watch ourselves "doing." We think about what we're doing, and then we think about what we're thinking about. We shape our thoughts into ideas and images and ideologies. Then we analyze, and change them. We know there is no eternal, ideal perfection; we know, on our level of existence at least, that life is muddled, subjective, that we're not even physically the same as we were yesterday, with every one of the 50 trillion or so cells in our bodies being replaced every seven years or so. Many on the spiritual journey have had the experience of peeling back layers of the mind, like an onion, and wondered: "What could I be thinking about if I could stop thinking? If I could get myself out of the way and just approach God? Or if I could somehow peel back all the layers, might there be nothing in the middle? And no God?" And the fear is that if we peel back too many layers we lose all sense of who we might be.

Some psychiatrists even suggest that schizophrenia (and there are more schizophrenics in Western Europe than regular churchgoers) is not due to a lack of rationality, but too much of it. We can't bear too much reality, even if we could see it.

All we think of as valuable and real is like a dream dimly remembered in the morning. We can't even be certain of what we see with our eyes, let alone what god we pray to in our heads. Bees, dogs, us, we all see the world differently; our limited and very different senses can take in only a small spectrum. Interpreting what we see is something different again. People who have been blind from birth and recover their sight don't see cars, trees, houses, but a confusing jumble. Making sense of this is a process we learn. As newborns, we are helpless. We have an instinct to bond with people, to register responses and react in a way which benefits us. As we age we begin to exercise control over what we see by interpreting it. We build up layers of meaning, making symbols and images, imagining one thing in terms of another. For which we need help. The very few instances on record of abandoned children being brought up in the wild, without any human contact, suggest that if you don't grow up in a network of relationships, you can't grow up at all. When they come back into society, they can't form attachments, can't even learn to speak. Donald Winnicott in the twentieth century spoke of the young child developing its experience of being alive and real in mind and body by internalizing the love and care of its mother, so it becomes an inner presence, enabling further love and growth. As the philosopher Hannah Arendt elaborated later, as you grow, moving away from your parents, to be alone becomes a "two-in-one" condition. Winnicott described it as the True and False Self, much as Sigmund Freud had described it as the Ego and the Id, or Carl Jung and Carl Rogers the Real and Ideal Self. Eckhart Tolle, more recently, has reinterpreted it in spiritual terms as the egoic mind on the one hand and the conscious self on the other – the "real" you of the present moment. Whatever – it's not difficult to have a personal relationship with an ideal or perfect person in your head, a "tulpa," an imaginary friend for adults, whether Jesus or Shiva, any more than it is to have one with your self. You already have it. Indeed, it can be easier than having to deal with flesh and blood people, with their emotional and mental patterns different to your own, particularly when from other cultures.

As we age we continue to create identities at many levels. We've learned to search for fellow minds, and we look for signs of them everywhere. We see figures in the curtain design, or in clouds. Animal shapes in the trees. We look for causality, read patterns into events to make them better or worse than they really are. We lie for our own benefit, or even for that of others. We find reasons to be nice to people we don't like. Experience is as much our perception of reality, interpreted in our heads, as the thing itself. The Vedantic philosophers figured this out five millennia ago (and influenced key European philosophers of the modern age like Schopenhauer when their works were made available in translation in the nineteenth century), calling the illusion of reality that we see *maya*.

This ability to project our imaginations on to the world around us and shape it to our desires has turned into our cumulative wisdom, instinctive and cultural, taking on myriad different shapes along the chain, handed down through the generations. Out of it in the last 70,000 years or so we've produced art, music, religion, politics, everything that makes us what we are. The "self" doesn't figure all this out on its own. It's created out of our collective definitions of what matters, which we inherit, and make our own.

At an individual level the relation of the "me" in here and the "world" out there forms an image in our brains. Some neurologists believe they've identified the part of it, nicknamed the "God-spot," that sifts incoming data to enable us to distinguish between the two. (Similarly, some evolutionary psychologists suggest that beliefs in supreme beings are so widespread that they're hardwired into the brain.) At times circumstances lead to moments of transcendence when the sense of "me" disappears. These can be occasioned by our own efforts, as in worship, meditation, fasting, through drugs, entheogenic plants, in dance, self-mutilation, sex – if you're lucky. Music can also help achieve this, as can nature, love, art... religion simply makes a habit of it. Believing in God is a way of relating, a disciplined way of defining the space (or lack of it) between ourselves and the world. If you live in Washington or Tehran you probably see God as "out there," a reality outside our heads, with a gulf in between, which we can only cross with His help. If you live in Paris or Peking you probably see this God as an illusion, and focus on the reality we think we can see, or that we can find within ourselves.

There's no universal spiritual logic to all this. We don't even have this "God-spot" equally. In some individuals the capacity is strong, in others weak. Some are driven to understand, others uninterested. Maybe they're better off. It's a mixed blessing. Saints and prophets, like great musicians and artists, are often on the borderline of breakdown, or over it. It's inherited, and not completely under our conscious control; epileptics for instance can suffer from it severely; or it can be triggered by electrical impulses. But God-spot or not, it's not hard to see how God, the embodiment of love (or, in some cases, evil), can also become an inner companion, like the love inherited from a parent. One easier to talk to, more "real," than our neighbors, or even family.

We know today from scans that the changes in brain patterns produced by these beliefs are the same across all cultures and faiths. In other words, experiencing Krishna, or God, or Allah, or Odin, or Pan, or any of the other thousands or millions of gods, amounts to the same thing as far as the brain is concerned. To say, "I believe my religion alone is true," is about as intelligent as saying, "I believe my local football/baseball team is incomparably better than any other – past, present or future." No religious experience is more "real" than another, any more than it's more real to love one person rather than another. Otherwise we would all love the same person, believe the same way. The questions are more whether we've found the right person to love, and the one who loves us. Whether we have a religion that feels true for us, and whether it's a good one. Whether we can move forward in relationship, or whether we're still stuck on the fence.

Religion is nothing special. It's not something you do on Sundays, or in quiet times. It's not something you can separate from loving, or living. It's not different from washing the dishes, or dreaming at night. It's not either "real" or "imaginary." Both God as reality and imagination are just different ways of coming to terms with the polarization of the world into "me" and "it" that came with self-awareness. Maybe there's just matter, and religion is a way of seeing it as miracle. Maybe it is a miracle. Some see it that way, others don't. Maybe it's like whether you see the glass as half empty or half full. Maybe it depends on whether you're an intuitive or analytic thinker (intuitive thinkers are more likely to believe in God, in conspiracy theories, and to get sums wrong). It's our response to life that determines what it means for us, rather than some unprovable definition of life itself. And for some, defining their lives as in the hands of God enables them to live better ones. We turn what we see into stories, and imagine better endings. We then act them out; we become what we create. That's what our lives are. The self is not a "thing," but a process, a creation, trailing clouds of memory and potential. Religion is like art, with our own lives as the medium. It's why most of the world's great art has a religious dimension. It inspires us in a way that atheism, nihilism, existentialism, consumerism, have never managed, other than the odd sparkle.

We shape the world we see; the world shapes us. Religion describes the relationship. Believers see God as the measure of it. But we're on uncertain ground here, to be entered with trepidation, shoes and hats off. No one can really describe it for anyone else. Beliefs can lead you to the river, but they can't make you drink. And at the riverbank they look the same. They can all be equally persuasive, and equally fragile. Christians in Montana might believe in Jesus materializing through walls (Luke 24:36) and see him appear to them. Animists in Burma see ghosts doing the same. The Uduk in Sudan experience ghosts reading their minds. Every culture on earth has their equivalents. All these figures are "real" for those concerned. Saying one is real and the others imaginary is chickening out. Saying they're all imaginary doesn't help us understand why we see them. If we want to hold on to our own dreams with integrity we should tread lightly on those of others.

The images we see, the voices we hear, are "real" in the way that responses to art and music, beauty and love are real. Also to ugliness and evil – the brain takes no prisoners, and there's a lot of scary stuff lurking around the sludge at the bottom. It doesn't discriminate on our behalf. We "choose" our experiences. Religion is about the choices we make. And it operates in the mind's borders, drawing on our strongest emotions, our wildest fears and hopes. Making sense of them with the discipline of words channels nonsense and fantasy into inspiration and guidance. It allows others to evaluate their worth, and maybe share the experience. But the worst thing we can do is take ourselves too seriously, the voices in our heads or the words on the page too literally (I suspect many who talk, preach or write extensively about religion are damaged goods in some way – and I include myself in that – the Christian conviction of original sin can stay with you even after the sense of salvation through grace has gone). Did God for instance really tell Abraham to tie up his son and cut his throat on a windy hilltop (Genesis 22:2-9)? If He spoke like that to us wouldn't we sooner think we'd gone nuts and go to a psychiatrist than do what He said? If Abraham tried it

47

today wouldn't we arrest him for a particularly brutal and appalling attempt at child-murder; view his religion as a sick and dangerous cult; lock him up and throw away the key?

He who knows does not speak;
He who speaks does not know.
Lao Tzu (sixth century BC)

5. Good And Bad Beliefs

*Like the bee gathering honey from different flowers, the wise man
accepts the essence of different Scriptures and sees only the good in
all religions.*
Srimad Bhagavatam (sixth century AD)

All religions look equally bizarre from the outside. It's not
difficult to see how we came to believe differently, how we
even came to believe the impossible and imagine it rational, the
immoral and imagine it good. If you repeat new understanding
often enough it is laid down as a pattern in the brain to be found
more readily again. Over time new insight becomes tradition,
part of the way the community thinks. Tradition then becomes
expectation. Tell yourself over and over again for instance
that you're a sinner and you begin to believe it. Practice ritual
confession and it becomes necessary for your mental health.
Whatever it is that you believe or hope you see you can only
interpret it in the expected way.

Over time we encounter the deity we've been taught to
expect. In every spiritual experience, vision, dream, near-death
experience, the God we see takes the forms we're familiar with.
All beliefs are learned. They're not written in our DNA. We inherit
our beliefs from our parents, they from theirs – Christianity has
been around for enough generations – a hundred or so – to affect
the very way we think, whatever we believe now. For instance,
we see our personal rights as being of first importance. This
arises from the notion of a relationship with a personal God,
which gained a huge impetus from Protestantism in the sixteenth
century and onwards. By contrast, in Hinduism your personal
rights are secondary to your place in the caste system. We believe
in our power to radically change the direction of our lives, to
seize the day, arising from the idea of making an instant decision

to follow Christ. In Buddhism change happens in increments over hundreds of reincarnations, not suddenly. We think of the "self" as something separate, that's "me." We Westerners exist in our heads, emotional, calculating and solitary. We can't live in the same way as animist peoples who experience all nature as sacred and interconnected. Being stoned out of your head is not the same thing. And so on. This is a reason why we're not venturing far on to the territory of other religions here. It's hard enough to make sense of your own inheritance without having to get under the skin of a different culture. Very few of us have the time or energy for that. We can learn from other religions and societies, speeding up the continuous process of cultural osmosis, but we can't change who we are.

Which is why if a good Christian had been born in Saudi Arabia he or she would be a good Muslim today. It's called "imprinting." Real personal judgment plays a small role. Individual conversions from one religion to another are comparatively rare, and, short of economic or military persuasion, usually cancel each other out numerically (and as has been pointed out many times, conversion experiences are essentially the same, psychologically, in all religions). For good reasons... organized religions protect their turf, and penalties for leaving your faith are often severe. If you're a Bible-believing Christian, for instance, and your son, daughter, wife or friend suggest following a different God (let alone no God at all!) you should have them battered to death, and throw the first stones yourself (Deuteronomy 13:6-10).

Sure, traditions are important. Living together without them would be impossible, we'd be lost, all at daggers-drawn. After all, an individual who thinks he alone has the truth is defined as mad. If she gets a few friends together who think the same, they have a cult. Add in a few states and a few generations, and when it gets up to around a million followers we call it a religion. There are over 150 religions today with a million or more followers. Incidentally, in the history of religion Christianity is a slow starter. It's tough to figure out these kinds of numbers at a distance, but it looks like it took several centuries to get to a million followers. It then jumped to around ten million in the fourth century AD when it became the official religion of the Roman Empire (you had no choice but to sign up, unless you were prepared to die, along with your family), and then collapsed, along with the Empire, taking another millennium to get back to ten million. In its first few centuries Islam grew over ten times as fast, stretching from the Atlantic to the Pacific.

But there is nothing "definitive" about tradition. Religions can evolve through time to the point where they not only might seem unrecognizable to the first followers but teach the opposite of what the founder intended, much like all human inventions – "gunpowder" for instance originally had nothing to do with guns, it was developed by Taoists in China for use in medicine, in the ninth century AD, but within another century was being used in war. And even within different religions you can trace the changing patterns of understanding. A few centuries ago virtually all Christians believed that witches rode through the sky on broomsticks; that prophets could do the same in chariots (2 Kings 2:11); that Jesus rose through it to heaven (Luke 24:51 – it was a common belief at the time, that noteworthy people ascended to heaven). It's taken the successive centuries for each of these beliefs to turn from accepted fact to metaphor or fiction.

Different traditions within a particular religion also think in different ways. So Catholics for instance might see a miracle in a statue weeping blood. Eastern Orthodox, with their tradition of disallowing statues, see it in stigmata, the imprint of Christ's suffering on the flesh. More commercially-minded Protestants, who see both these thousand-year-old traditions as mere superstition, see it in the opportune arrival of cash, or a new job. There's never real, objective evidence. Where one sees miracle the other sees fakery, or coincidence, or hallucination. The intensity of the expectation creates at least the belief of change if not the reality.

Believers overestimate the evident truth of their particular religion. There's no difference in *kind* between the miraculous birth of Jesus or Krishna; the levitation of Jesus (for example, Matthew 14:25) or the Buddha; the empty stone tomb of Jesus or Mithras; the ascended Jesus or Ascended Master (see chapter 41). If you want to believe in one, fair enough. But the difference in terms of "evidence" between them is less than you think. And insisting on the absolute truth of one and dismissing the others is plain mean-spirited. For instance, the divine Vishnu descending himself into the womb of Devaki and being born as her son, Krishna, seems no less credible than God (rather than a boyfriend) somehow planting sperm in the Virgin Mary.

But, equally, nonbelievers, and in particular most journalists and politicians, even historians, tend to underestimate the impact of religion as a whole. As organized religion is marginal to the lives of many in the West, in Europe at least, they read this indifference back into the past, and into cultures different from theirs. But it will still be flourishing when all of our recorded history so far just amounts to the first chapter of our adventures. It's extraordinarily powerful.

Religion pictures the biggest life we can imagine, covering our beginnings and endings, our most beautiful dreams, and our worst nightmares. So, by definition, it includes everything. We've pictured a multitude of heavens and hells, angels and monsters. Gods that are the embodiment of righteousness and justice, like the God of the later Old Testament prophets; and gods that rejoice in mountains of skulls and flayed human skins, like their contemporary Assyrian god Ashur; or gods that enjoy nothing more than the taste of human hearts and livers, like the Aztec god Huitzilopochtli (though the earlier version of God in the Old Testament is sometimes not far from this; and in some respects the God of the New Testament is worse – however much savagery, rape, slavery and genocide the Hebrews/Israelites are commanded to inflict on others, and themselves, the idea of eternal torture for unbelievers only comes in the New Testament – polls variously put the number of Americans who believe in a physical hell at between 50% and 85% of the population, though there's actually very little about it in the Bible, where several very different cultural traditions are lumped together in translation as "hell" – Sheol, Hades, Gehenna and Tartarus).

Religion can comfort or terrify like nothing else on earth. It can transform your life or blow your mind away. It can start wars and sustain them for centuries; depopulate continents (see chapter 39 if that seems like exaggeration). Or it can lead to the most extraordinary and inspiring stories of lives devoted to the well-being of other people.

We end up with a mixed bag, just like we have haute cuisine and junk food; art and rubbish. A good part of the history of humankind has been the struggle of the good to rise above the bad – which is going to be more relevant to the survival of civilization over the coming decades than at any other time in history. Good religion is about exploring and strengthening the bonds that tie us with each other and the world we live in, to make it a better and holier place. It's difficult because relationship is difficult. Having a close relationship with anybody or anything means giving up something of your own self-interest. Seeing something as sacred involves putting it at a higher level than yourself. So it stresses service rather than mastery, self-control rather than gratification, humility rather than pride. Subordinating your own interests to a larger good. It's about morality.

Then there's bad religion, which divides: "My leader or view or bit of the world is sacred, yours isn't. The Holy Spirit is a Christian spirit; other spirits are evil. The words I hear in the night, the comfort in the day, the healing, these are the voices and actions of God; yours are of the devil." That's the easy kind (which is why it usually wins over the good). It points out differences between people rather than their common humanity. It strengthens hierarchies, divides along lines of gender and race, worships wealth and power, rather than working for social justice for everyone. It bottles up the grace of God and puts the stopper on, rather than spreading it around. It can lead us to lay waste to the good around us. It's anti-human rather than humane.

Of all the world religions, for instance, it's only Christianity, and its successor, Islam, which condemn people to eternal damnation. It's one of the reasons the Chinese rejected the Jesuit missions in the seventeenth century. Xu Dashou, a Ming scholar who came close to converting to Christianity, but finally rejected it, said of their teaching: "The books of the Barbarians say: if you have done good throughout your life but have not made yourself agreeable to the Master of Heaven, all your goodness will have been in vain. If you have done evil all your life but for one single instant did make yourself agreeable to the Master of Heaven, all the evil you have done will immediately be absolved."

Xu hits the nail on the head. If Hitler had repented in the last moments of his life, and then been shot by the approaching Russians, good orthodox Christians should believe that he went to heaven, and that the millions of Jews he gassed went to hell. It's as irrational and immoral a teaching as you can find anywhere in the history of world religion (more about how it developed, in the first centuries AD, in chapter 33).

And if the world is about to end anyway, and if precipitating it will bring God to earth, then in the eyes of fundamentalists – why bother to be good? Why bother to look after what we have? Why waste time on love? What's the point of planning for the benefit of generations further down the line, of living sustainably (a key theme in the Old Testament)? For the fundamentalists of all religions, "peace" is a delusion. It would prove them wrong. For them, God's agenda is for supremacy, for conflict, for holocaust, for the extermination of all except the few saved. This is the religion of the emperors, the Aztecs, the Nazis, a religion that consumes its own base in the form of real people. It's the triumph of the ancient Sun God, bent on destroying the moderating gods of moon and rain, turning the kingdom of God into an inferno; self-destructive, and evil.

It's often justified by appeal to a particular revelation, scripture or tradition. But then there are so many of them. It's not difficult to believe in this god, or that god, out of the 100,000 or so to choose from (or hundreds of millions, if you want to look at it more broadly), or to think that you have the answer and everyone else is wrong. It's a form of religious racism, though there isn't really a word for it. It's the worst kind of "ism" there is. To tyrants, narcissists and schizophrenics it comes naturally. Trying to understand where we really are in the web of relationships, but holding that in tension with an awareness of the limitations of our own perspective, that's surely the better path. Good religion is based on relationship and life; fundamentalism, in any religion, on separation and death.

It's down to us. We, with the help of our parents, peers, communities, choose how we see God. And of course we don't have to see Him at all. Believing in God is not compulsory. There was no one at your birth saying, "We'll only let you live if you believe in God." Equally, there's no one when you die saying, "Because you haven't believed you'll now be tortured in hell forever." That's a religion for playground bullies to preach and the fearful to practice.

All organized religions have a tendency to turn options into absolutes. They can make it difficult to believe what could come naturally. They can deny knowledge, or even love. At their worst they can promote the opposite, where lies plus hatred equal evil, or illusion. And we're suckers for that because, given half a chance, we'll believe anything. And if it works to our personal advantage so much the better. And there's nothing quite so self-interested to believe as "you have won the lottery of eternity, and are now going to heaven." And it's in the nature of religion and churches to keep inventing more obscure and exotic beliefs, more selfish beliefs, until there's a collective cry of, "We can't believe this anymore."

Let's ignore bad religion for the moment. Believing in God is not difficult in itself. The basics are simpler than riding a bike. You realize you're an insignificant speck of life with a confused medley of loves and hates and noise in your head. That there's a wonderful world out there, which is informed by a purpose greater than you can imagine. Step one.

You put the two together. Step two.

You let yourself go. Step three.

You then live your life in this light rather than for the interests of your self. Step four.

It may take you 5 minutes, 5 years or 50 to get there, or 5,000 more lives in other traditions, but that doesn't matter, as long as you make a start.

Believing this has been as much a part of our humanity as being born and dying. Religions describe this process differently. Some emphasize the "world out there," that of truth; others how we relate to it, the world "in here," that of love. Ultimately, as all good religion recognizes, they come to the same thing, because each is shaped by the other.

To put it another way, we have minds that want to know, and hearts that want to love. The mind and heart together make up what we think of as the soul. Truth plus love equals happiness. Truth without love is arid. Love without truth, fantasy. Certainty in truth or love makes one the enemy of the other. Everyone draws their own line, leaning this way or that. In what is now a global village we need to draw a wide circle, one that includes everyone. If our vision excludes most people, putting them outside the circle of salvation, it's probably not true, and certainly not loving. It then doesn't deserve to last, and it won't. And if pushed to describe God, about half of all believers will shape the answer in general terms around truth, and half around love (more on this in chapter 48). They're surely both right. Truth is the aim of our journey. Our beliefs, our lives, should incorporate what we know to be true. It's the principle we follow. Love is the measure of how far we've traveled. It's the basis of our practice. For Christians, God is our best understanding of both. Jesus is our best example. The supreme one we have in life and words of finding truth through love. He shows the way. And we try to follow.

Some will say that this is all fancy. Others that our failure to see the spiritual more clearly simply reflects our primitive stage of evolution. We're still more apes than angels. Maybe we'll never know. Maybe, anyway, it doesn't really matter one way or the other. Because the practice of religion is mostly about living life on earth in the light of this bigger vision. It's about translating imagination into fact, about making us better people, and the world a better place. And in what became known, eventually, as Christianity, the supposed founder, Jesus, seems to say as clearly as anyone that it's not the kind of spiritual experience you have that matters, let alone what kind of God you believe in or not, but what you do with it. All the good visitations or prayers in the world don't add up to the effect of good action, and we're all capable of that, however rarely we manage it. Which will bring us back later to the lost opportunity that Christianity represents.

I believe in God, but not as one thing, not as an old man in the sky. I believe that what people call God is something in all of us. I believe that what Jesus and Muhammad and Buddha and all the rest said was right. It's just that the translations have gone wrong.
John Lennon (twentieth century AD)

6. How Beliefs Change

And who is so stupid as to imagine that God planted a garden in Eden eastward, and put in it a tree of life, which could be seen and felt?
Origen (third century AD, one of the key Early Church Fathers)

We believe because we always have done. Because it works. It's the way we relate. "How" or "what" we believe in is more difficult. We can't measure what goes on in our heads like we can measure the outside world. So many of us tend to assume that people who see God are either fantasizing (if we're atheists or agnostics) or that their thoughts are true and good and those of everyone else wrong or evil (if we're believers).

Obviously, there's a strain in religion that can infantilize people. Gaslighting, for instance, a form of psychological manipulation making people doubt their rationality, or even their sanity, is common in Christianity, as in all religions. God frequently uses it in the Bible – "For as the heavens are higher than the earth, so are my ways higher than your ways, and my thoughts than your thoughts" (Isaiah 55:9). Jesus presses for a child-like faith (Matthew 19:4). Paul praises foolishness (1 Corinthians 1:20-22). Augustine puts faith before reason, "there is nothing more wholesome in the Catholic Church than using authority before argument" (*Of the Morals of the Catholic Church*).

But credible, good religious belief acknowledges that it's not trying to describe the world in the same way as science does. It tells a story. In living a good life we interpret the world we see by the better one we imagine. In doing so we can make the real world better, we can make a difference. Better to have faith and suspend the rational mind than to think straight, see nothing, and have no faith, hope, or love.

Jesus started a religion by telling stories – parables – which are more about how to think than what to believe. For his later followers that wasn't enough, and over the centuries they added creeds and doctrines. And over the millennia we've lost the plot, we've forgotten the point. Christianity has stopped making public sense.

For instance the village community where I've lived for forty years is not particularly academic, and certainly not radical. It's fairly literate and conservative, inclined to treat a thousand-year-old institution like the local Parish Church as sympathetically as possible. Regular churchgoers might number 2% or so, with another one or two percent traveling to other denominational churches – and at Christmas, or Easter, that could be multiplied a few times. But I doubt that more than one in a hundred can wholly identify with "orthodox" Christian teaching (whatever that means; I'm no expert in theology, orthodox or otherwise; I struggle with words like "transubstantiation," generally being more concerned with getting through the day without fouling up than learning another language; but then it seems to me that all the great spiritual teachers used pretty simple language, or nobody would have bothered to listen). Suggest to any of them that they should pray "The Sinner's Prayer" (also called "The Consecration Prayer" or "The Salvation Prayer" – not that it appears anywhere in the Bible) – and they'd probably think you'd gone off your trolley.

I realize this is not so true of North America and other parts of the world, but Christianity is now essentially a private concern (at its best – but its increasingly vocal support around the world for populists and demagogues tends to put it in the "any religion but this one" kind of category for many spiritually-minded people) and its serious practice in Western Europe involves only a few.

Today we look to anthropologists to tell us how we got here. Biologists tell us what we're made of. Historians and psychiatrists explain why we think as we do. Scientists explore the edges of time, space, and matter. They all have something real to say. Novelists and playwrights take care of the imagination, and give us our stories of today, the ones that explore where and who we are, how we relate. Theology, the "science of God," if you go back a few centuries, used to account for the bulk of publishing. It's now a small subsection lost somewhere between history and philosophy on bookstore shelves, if it's there at all. It inspires little else, where it used to inspire everything. How did it get to this point of irrelevance?

The stories we tell change over time. Religion ceases to be credible when the institutions that have grown up around it hang on to a story for too long. It's happened tens of thousands of times through history. It's seen most clearly in lesser-known religions. They have narrow beginnings and stay narrow. They fade as the world moves on, the followers die off. Their gods of wood rot, stone sinks back into the earth. World religions (though any "religion" is a tentative notion, "world religions" even more so), like Christianity, for instance, currently followed by more people than any other to date, reflect the collision of cultures, of one way of thinking being illuminated and enlarged by another, in this case the Hebrew and the Greek. They evolve more than others. Their definitions of the eternal, the universal, change with our definitions of what time and space are, according to the culture of the time.

Hebrew religion and Greek philosophy, the Church and a classical education: these formed the culture of the Western world. And going back – halfway through the first millennium BC – both Hebrews and Greeks believed in a physical sky god, with penis and clothes, holding court. The Hebrews called Him Yahweh, and the Greeks Zeus. In Job, for instance (a short novel written somewhere around the sixth century BC), God chats with his various sons and courtiers, asking one of them, Satan (not yet a separate force of evil), what he's been up to (Job 1:6-

12) – clearly, He's not yet omniscient – and Satan replies:

Going to and fro in the earth, and walking up and down in it.

It's all quite casual, as if he'd popped out for a cigarette. The two of them decide to run a bet on how far God's favorite servant on earth can be tormented and still remain faithful. God wins, sort of, and finishes the book boasting:

Where wert thou when I laid the foundations of the earth? Declare, if thou has understanding. Who hath laid the measures thereof, if thou knowest? Or who hath stretched the line up on it? Whereupon are the foundations thereof fastened? Or who laid the cornerstone thereof; when the morning stars sang together, and all the sons of God shouted for joy?

It's sublime language (at least it is in the Authorized, King James, Version. I gather it's great in Hebrew as well). And the unknown Hebrew writer turned this Babylonian story (and the first verse tells us that Job is not even a Hebrew, but from the land of Uz) into one of the world's great meditations on suffering and purpose, which, like Shakespeare, can be read in quite different ways. The Old Testament has many wonderful passages (as well as many that are not). If you want to curse or praise, top yourself or jump with joy, there's little to compare with the Psalms.

But it's a bit spoilt for us today when we realize He didn't know what He was talking about. As a world-view the Hebrew one was already past its sell-by date. If God had taken the trouble to go hiking, like Satan, He could have learnt some answers from the Greeks, a few hundred miles away. In Greece, a series of brilliant thinkers had already, when Job was written, started to develop a different way of looking at life, observing and measuring the world, and experimenting on it. Today we call what they did "science."

Thales in the sixth century BC has been described as the world's first scientist, and his successors laid the foundations for 2,500 years of discovery. Euclid's *Elements* (fourth century BC) remained the mathematician's Bible up till the twentieth century, when deep space conditions and added dimensions came into the frame.

Eratosthenes could have given God the "measures" of the earth; he calculated its diameter to within 75 miles of the true figure (7,923 miles) by measuring the angle of sunlight down different wells (he also calculated the tilt of the earth's axis and the distance from the earth to the sun). Aristarchus could have told Him that the earth didn't have cornerstones, it wasn't built like a house, that it wasn't even flat, but a sphere that circled the sun. The Greek achievements were amazing. Epicurus left us stunning letters reflecting on the infinity of the universe, the nature of our senses, our soul, of language, of religion and society, and the happy life. Democritus has been described as the father of modern science – "Sweet is sweet, bitter is bitter, hot is hot, cold is cold, color is color; but in truth there are only atoms and the void." And we could go on and on. In the sixth to second centuries BC the Greeks developed the first complete world literature, the most beautiful buildings ever, astonishing sculpture, the beginnings of democracy. Our philosophy, the process of understanding through reason, goes back to them (as well as the idea of God as an infinite, omniscient, only necessary reality, which fed into the Christian understanding of Him). We've scarcely had an original thought since Plato (and he used to complain about the ignorance of the Greeks compared to the Egyptians).

The Greeks weren't perfect, and their legacy was not all positive. It could be argued that Plato's metaphysics missed essential truths that some older societies took for granted, and that science is rediscovering today. For instance that body and mind/soul are not separate, but interdependent; that the genius of humankind lies in each person's creativity; that consciousness is more than rational thought, and that in looking at the world we change it. Plato set us on the search for the True, the Good and the Beautiful, but believed in demons as much as anyone, and that lower types of humans deserved domination. But in terms of understanding the physical world and describing it, and also the mental/spiritual, they were in a different class to the Hebrews.

Today we act on a daily basis like Greeks (at least most readers of this book are likely to – though polls consistently suggest that a quarter of Americans still believe the sun circles the earth), but pray like Hebrews. Christians may no longer think of God as a king living in the sky, but still accept the underlying thrust of the story, that there is a God who thinks like we do, we are made for Him, the universe exists because of this, and He still intervenes on earth in the same kind of way. What the Church teaches today is still recognizably part of the same world-view.

So how did these different frames of reference merge, especially when in the first few centuries BC the two cultures were antagonistic? The attempted imposition of Greek culture on to the Jewish by the successors of the Greek Alexandrian Empire led to the lengthy and bitter Maccabean wars. They (or at least the hardliners) despised each other.

Both peoples were absorbed into the Roman Empire. The Romans were more interested in getting from A to B than in where Z was. Like most successful empires they assimilated beliefs rather than imposed them. They inherited much of Greek culture and philosophy. Christianity, as an offshoot of Jewish religion, began to spread through the Empire in the first century AD. By the end of the second century leading Christians, known today as the Church Fathers (like Origen, quoted at the beginning of the chapter), were investing huge amounts of time and energy in constructing a belief system that rejected the primitive thinking expressed in much of what eventually came to be called the Old Testament, reconciling the best of Jewish and Greek thought, enabling the new cult to make sense to the wider Mediterranean world.

The Western half of the Empire later collapsed into the Dark Ages, and the light of civilization in this part of the world was restored during the Golden Age of Islam (ninth to twelfth centuries) by the Umayyad in Spain, the Fatimids in Egypt, the Abbasids in Mesopotamia. It's from them that we got useful things like surgical instruments, hard soap, fountain pens, checks, coffee and crankshafts. The first university was founded in Morocco in AD 859 (by a woman!), the first manned glider flew in AD 875. In the twelfth century, by pillaging some of these more advanced societies (in a series of jihad-like invasions known as the Crusades), the Christian barbarians of the north (relatively speaking) began to recover the knowledge of the ancient world. This was a serious challenge to the Christian scholars of the time. Rather than measuring themselves against local pagan customs, they became acquainted with the independent and often humanist thinking of Greek and Latin scholars, playwrights and poets. They had to up their game, and make Christianity intellectually respectable. This led to a further synthesis of Greek and Christian thinking, and the beginning of Christian apologetics, particularly in the theology of Albertus Magnus and Aquinas in the thirteenth century, who developed the classical idea of God by which we know Him today (he also taught that the height of heavenly pleasure was being able to view all the people being tortured in hell). The Renaissance followed, and by the sixteenth century we were catching up with a picture of the universe that had started to take shape a couple of millennia earlier, which was then developed in the Enlightenment.

Of course this is overly simplistic. As far as Christian understanding goes, we've generally gone backwards rather than forwards. For instance, most of the Church Fathers interpreted scripture allegorically rather than literally. Many even in the Middle Ages had a more sophisticated idea of God than many Christians today. By the fourteenth century Gregory Palamas, one of the most influential theologians of the late Byzantine period, was talking about God as "in His essence absolutely unknowable." Even a savage, virulent Protestant reformer like John Calvin in the sixteenth century considered some Old Testament ideas about the world "baby talk." And during the Enlightenment scientists saw themselves as exploring the majesty of God's creation rather than taking Him out of the picture. Though even the greatest scientist who ever lived, Isaac Newton, who in an era that believed in witchcraft and sorcery modeled the math of the universe, spent far more time trying to unravel the secrets of Revelation, and alchemy, rather than gravity.

So knowledge and achievement can regress as well as progress (let alone standards of living, inequity, civilization itself, etc.). In the sixth century BC the Greeks and others were considering the possibility of a world without gods, predicting eclipses of the sun accurately, and speculating on the earth as a ball whizzing through space. In one of the great Greek stone theaters, the 15,000-strong audience could hear the character Talthybius singing in *Hecuba*:

> *Do we, holding that the gods exist*
> *Deceive ourselves with unsubstantial dreams*
> *And lies, while random careless chance and change*
> *Alone control the world?*

When Euripides was writing this, in the fifth century BC (and for most of Christendom he would have been burnt at the stake for doing so), one of his 95 or so plays, there were half a million hand-written volumes in the Great Library of Alexandria alone, and nearly every city in the ancient Mediterranean world had at least one library, quite apart from private collections. Run forward a couple of millennia till the time the Europeans caught up with China and were about to enter the age of print, and there were only 30,000 volumes in the whole of Christendom. Not one of them saw the earth as other than the center of the universe.

In recent centuries science has advanced too fast for the Church to keep pace, and our views have polarized. The picture of the world it gives us is centuries, millennia, out of date. The Church fought against astronomy in the seventeenth century, geology in the eighteenth, biology in the nineteenth, psychology in the twentieth, even, bizarrely, against a better understanding of its own sacred texts. The Vatican took 400 years to admit, in 1992, twenty years after men walked on the moon and after a commission managed to spend ten years looking at the evidence, that it might have "misunderstood" Galileo, and hasn't offered an apology yet. And that's progressive compared with large sections of today's evangelical community. Look at the chat forums like Quora, or denominational mission statements and creeds. The level of ignorance on show is hard to credit.

This is probably unfair to the unknown writer of Job, and to the many Christians who don't take it literally and see it as a parable, and maybe even a subversive one at that. You could argue that the Book of Job challenges, rightly, the idea that God's blessing brings wealth, or even that He will be on your side if you are faithful to Him – that idea of God makes Him just another gambler up in the sky playing your life as a lottery – the book isn't trying to say anything about how the world was made. And Christians no longer think of God as a king living in the sky. But they do still tend to believe that the underlying thrust of the story is true. There is a God who thinks as we do. We are made for Him, and the universe exists because of this. God still intervenes on earth in the same kind of way. What the Church teaches today is still recognizably part of the same world-view.

Which leads to a problem. Because what the head cannot believe the heart cannot worship.

The fact that an opinion has been widely held is no evidence whatever that it is not utterly absurd.
Bertrand Russell (twentieth century AD)

7. Childish Beliefs

*The electromagnetic quantum vacuum is a form of light. It is an
underlying sea of energy that permeates every tiny volume of space,
from the emptiest intergalactic void to the depths of the Earth, the
Sun, or our own bodies. In this sense, our world of matter is like the
visible foam atop a very deep ocean of light.*
Bernard Haisch (astrophysicist, twentieth century AD)

Traditionally, religion involved the "great minds," the thinkers
and seekers of their age. Those who wanted to explore the
known universe, to make sense of it, to find our place in it.
Today, Christianity, in the form it's frequently practiced, is more
for the poorly educated, wannabe authoritarians, those selfishly
wrapped up in questions of personal salvation, or children.

Not that I think children should be taught religion. Or,
rather, at least, not Christianity – to be told at a young age that
you're basically already a failed human being, in original sin,
is a form of mental abuse. But all childish beliefs once made
sense. We can see the world is flat, it's obvious. Life is fickle
and dangerous, run by capricious gods, so sacrifice will appease
them. Things often go wrong for no apparent reason, so clearly
there are demonic forces in the world working against us, and
we need the right spells and rituals to defeat them. For instance,
fungus-type things, whether it's mold on walls or a skin disease
like leprosy, can be cured by sprinkling the blood of birds
seven times throughout the house (Leviticus 14:49-53). But our
understanding changes as, individually and collectively, over
lifetimes, centuries, millennia, we learn more. We grow up.

Many Christians though are on a diverging path from modern
common sense. It's easy to see why – if Jesus didn't really ascend
from the earth like a space rocket, why believe he physically rose
from the dead? If hell is not a burning lake of fire, why should

heaven be a real place? If the Devil is not a real, personal entity, why should God be? Once you start to unravel the threads it's hard to know where to stop, or how to knit them together again differently.

So we have two contradictory stories today. To describe what I mean, have a look at the greatest story of all, the story of our beginnings.

To understand ourselves we want to know who our parents were, the family history; we're interested in what makes us the nation and race we are. We want to work out what made us human, and we trace our origins back through history, biology, chemistry, all the way back down to physics. And the question at the beginning is the same for all of us. Were we planned, and loved, or an accident, the result of meaningless encounters?

We want to believe the first. God created the universe: if not, we're orphans. At the beginning of the twentieth century Oxford and Cambridge University Presses were still printing the accepted dates in their Bibles. There are variations of year, day and month, but 4004 BC comes close, if you work out the biblical chronology (Archbishop Ussher in the seventeenth century was the most precise, pinpointing it according to the biblical evidence to 6pm on 22 October in that year).

In perhaps the most conspicuous example of mass willful stupidity since civilization began, around half the people in the world (the majority of Christians and Muslims) still broadly accept this date, because the books of Moses (sacred to both religions, as well as Judaism) can't be wrong.

The drive to a literal reading of the scriptures is strongest in the Muslim world. At first sight that's odd, as a millennium ago Muslims were far ahead of Christendom in science and learning (which is why for instance today though we write in Roman letters we count in Arabic numerals rather than Roman – I, II, III, IV etc… in Roman numerals I'm writing this in the year MMXIX). But their fundamentalism has a harder edge. Muslims place scripture on a higher plane than Christians do, so it hurts them more when it's undermined. For them the very shape of the words is sacred. They were literally dictated by God. If you want to worship Allah properly you should do so in Arabic, whereas Christians positively encourage new translations in both English and other languages (despite the conviction of some that God really does speak in English, and only in the King James Version of it, at that).

It all depends on where you're starting from. Everyone is to the left of someone else in how literally they interpret scripture, all suspicious about the rigidity of those on one side and the heresy of those on the other. Most Christians/Muslims for example no longer accept the Hebrew view (a cosmology which they adopted from the Egyptian and Babylonian empires) that the earth is a flat disc (there are 14 references to that in the Old Testament), about the size of Brazil, with Sheol underneath. It is fixed, "immoveable and firm" (Psalm 93:1). But a surprising number do – around one in six Americans for instance (and people seem to be getting dumber; amongst millennials, people aged 18-24, it's one in three). The scriptures after all are "infallible," or "inerrant" (which mean pretty much the same; the Bible doesn't say everything that is right, but it doesn't say anything wrong either). In 1993 Sheik Abd al-Aziz ibn Baaz, the supreme religious authority in Saudi Arabia, declared in one of their many medieval fatwas (something like a papal encyclical) that anyone who believes the world is round is an atheist and should be punished (the penalty for atheism in many parts of the Muslim world is death, as it used to be in Christendom).

It seems daft to most of us today to think of the earth as flat, in a universe of several levels. If you drill for oil you don't disturb the underground spirits (1 Samuel 28:14). If you set off in an airplane you end up where you started, a couple of days later, with jet lag. Very few Christians take the biblical world-view literally in every respect.

But thinking of the earth as flat is no more daft in terms of modern knowledge than thinking of it as a few thousand years old. Today no reputable geologist would accept a biblical account of how the earth was formed (or, to be more precise, Gallup polls suggest that even in the USA the number of earth and life scientists who accept creationism is under 0.1% – far fewer, statistically speaking, than the number who are likely to be mentally ill, let alone incompetent). No biologist would dispute the broad processes or the approximate timeframe of evolution; the questions are on whether it's gradual or punctuated, how it started and what drives it. No anthropologist would agree that people emerged "ready-made." But even in the expensively-educated USA, Gallup polls over the last 20 years consistently show that nearly half of the population believe that God created man in his present form in the last 10,000 years (I've been on forums where the majority seem to believe that not only the earth itself but the universe as well is only 6 or 7,000 years old); 40% believe that man has evolved, but God guided the process; under 10% believe that God has had no direct involvement. Two-thirds think "creationism" more likely than "evolution." Creationist Christians (including its rebranding as "Intelligent Design") are in the majority, if you count them worldwide. (Buddhists, by the way, are more inclined in general to accept evolution, and anything that science tells us.) A large proportion of the Christian Church increasingly puts superstition before science. The more that modern scholarship shows up the shallowness of their biblical understanding, the more shrill they get, spreading conspiracy theories, claiming victimhood, supporting political authoritarianism and retreating into a fundamentalist groupthink bunker from which Jesus will rescue them when the End Times arrive. It's an example of the handicap principle, which applies to all religious and political cults – the more absurd the position becomes, the more followers will double down on it, to demonstrate loyalty to the cause.

More "mainstream" (minority) Christians shake their heads sadly at this kind of knowledge-denial. How can a modern society effectively function and produce the scientists and engineers we need to solve our increasing problems if half the population is brainwashed into accepting a world-view that was scarcely credible back in the Bronze Age?

But even most of these minority Christians, who generally accept the overwhelming scientific consensus, still accept the events framed by this ancient world-view, where God opens trapdoors in heaven to throw thunder and lightning, shouts down to earth, sends doves or messengers. Jesus for instance came from heaven to earth as a baby, went down into the underworld (as Acts 2:31 implies and the later creeds affirm) and rose through the sky back to heaven. They would even say it's necessary to believe this to be a Christian. Some only accept part of the journey as real, other parts as metaphorical. For instance, he didn't really rise through the sky to heaven – that's a metaphor – but he certainly rose from the dead. That's literal – that happened, even if the others didn't (more on this in chapter 29). But they're all batting off the same base. The creationists are just being more consistent.

It's a credit to the power of religion that educated people today still feel impelled to take these stories literally. The Hebrews were an undistinguished nomadic tribe (if they existed at all, some scholars doubt it) of the Middle Bronze Age, scratching a living on the margins of the great Persian and Egyptian civilizations. They couldn't write (a later development for them), let alone do science. So when counting the years backwards they confined themselves to a genealogy you could keep in your head if you multiply the average lifespan by a factor of ten or so. The average lifespan of the ten generations from Adam to Noah in the Jewish Bible is 857 years. The nine generations from Noah's son Shem to Abraham reaches a more modest 333. We know from tombs of the period in Jericho (which was a walled town from at least

8000 BC onwards) that most people died before the age of 35. A few lived as long as we do, but a century or so really is the limit.

To step back a moment, of all our ancient scriptures the Bible is one of the hardest to reconcile with a scientific account of how the world came to be. The "Hymn of Creation" in the *Rig Veda* for instance adopts a much subtler, questioning approach, and doesn't assume that humankind is the center of the universal purpose. It's ironic that of all the calendars available, the modern scientific Christian West has based its chronology on one of the world's least accurate. In contrast, the Persians for instance believed the world was created 500,000 years ago rather than 6,000. Farther east, in India, each Day of Brahma, each breath of the Creator, is reckoned at 4.32 million years, which improves on the Judaic/Christian traditional view by three factors of ten (and indeed the cyclical theory of the universe is still a credible competitor to the inflationary one). Sometimes it's a case of the older the religion the wiser, which is what every religion declares to its rebellious cults.

And it's not just that these stories are harmless, sometimes they get nasty. In the Old Testament for instance God enables Joshua to stop the sun and moon and put the universe on hold so that the Hebrews had enough daylight to finish slaughtering the Amorites, whose lands they were invading and daughters raping (Joshua 10:13 – I puzzled over this one even as a youngster – wouldn't it have been easier just to send angels to zap the Amorites than to stop the sun? Did it then have to go faster around the earth to start the next day at the usual time? We know today that if the sun did stop and the earth stopped spinning even for a second everything on it would be swept into space).

It surely must stagger even the most conservative Christian mind to take this seriously for a moment. At the beginning of the twentieth century astronomers thought our galaxy *was* the universe. We know now that the universe is so big as to be beyond

73

our comprehension, with several hundred *billion* galaxies. If you think of the space covered by the earth circling the sun as the dot at the end of this sentence you would have to drop it into the Atlantic Ocean to get an idea of the size of our galaxy. You would have to reduce the galaxy to a similar dot and drop it into the ocean again to get an idea of the size of the universe. There are thousands of stars with their circling planets for every grain of sand on every beach on earth. The idea that there is a God who would bring this to a juddering halt to aid mass-rape and murder on our planet is insane. Today we would be petitioning the UN to impose sanctions on the Hebrews, send in peacemakers. We would put the leaders on trial for war crimes. We would wonder at their delusions of grandeur.

And we don't know what, if anything, lies beyond the cosmological horizon. There could be a "multiverse," bigger than our universe by millions of powers of 10, and in 11 or more dimensions. It's hard to believe that all this was created for us, for life on earth, present or future, let alone for one tiny group of murderous nomads on this planet a few thousand years ago.

We can't square the God of the Hebrews with what we know today, however much refined by tradition. Something has to give. Good religion looks forward, shaping our future to better ends, not backwards, glorifying past evil. In holding on to the Hebrew God of scripture we've diminished Him. The Church has driven God to the margins, while our world-view has moved on. And even the Hebrew God was bigger in some respects than our God today. "God" after all is just a relatively recent three-letter word with Germanic roots meaning "good" as opposed to "evil." The Semitic words for God ("Semitic" is now obsolete as a racial term but is still used for a group of related languages) in the first millennium BC: *Elat* (Old Canaanite), *Elohim* (Hebrew), *Alaha* (Aramaic), *Allah* (Arabic) come from roots better translated as "One" or "All." They understood that God does as much evil as good, if not more (in Exodus 32:14 for instance God "repented of the evil which he thought to do unto his people") – as many early Christians recognized, which is why they saw Him as a junior God, with Jesus coming from the High God above Him (more in chapter 34). Our current version of God as a vaguely benevolent (though generally ineffective, or at least inscrutable), undemanding spirit somewhere is a much reduced, tame version.

The Old Testament authors looked at the night sky and saw the greatness of God in the heavens. They imagined the greatest God they could. We still can, because we still feel the same way. We still look wonderingly up at the stars, if we're fortunate enough to be able to see them, through today's air pollution. We still try to look around the corner, to see what might be coming down the line, in hope or, more usually, with anxiety. We still invest in the idea that someone else, or a government, or a charismatic leader, or a God, will see us through. We still want to understand the big picture, find meaning and purpose in life, even if we understand there's no off-the-shelf answer, and it's something we each need to create for ourselves. Of course we can live as if our own concerns and couplings are all that matters. What religion suggests is that that is not just a life unexamined, but a life unrealized. But times change. The Hebrews had some deep insights into our behavior and how we relate to God. But they imagined Him in their own terms. None of us can do otherwise, which is why we all describe Him so differently.

The Hebrews believed in a God who was not only in our image (or the other way around), but was "personal" to them. That wasn't difficult when a horse and rider could cross all the land in the known universe in a few weeks, when heaven could be seen with the naked eye, and God could physically shout down from it and be heard. The heavens cuddled the earth like a warm blanket. It's not difficult to have a close relationship with a God like that. It's hard to avoid Him.

Today we see the world differently. The heavens are not cuddly. They're remote, dark, empty, fierce, beyond our imagining. Individual jets of light hundreds of light-years long shoot at nearly the speed of light from black holes with a mass equivalent to billions of our suns. And humans have only existed on this microscopically small speck of a planet (we're only just getting to the point where we can find planets circling stars in our own galaxy, let alone the billions of others) for the relative blink of an eyelid. Literally – if the period of the universe's existence is scaled down to a single day, the earth forms in the late afternoon; complex life arrives after 11pm, and God first appears to Moses in a burning bush around a tenth of a second before midnight. Isn't this like an ant telling us the world was created for its benefit? And above all, the heavens are vast. They're so vast that the idea they were created so we could cozy up to God, the kind of God who had trouble finding Adam and Eve in the garden, walking in the cool of the day because the noonday sun was too hot (Genesis 3:8-9) leaves a wry smile.

The God we can believe in today, if there is one, is the biggest we can imagine. Not just twice but millions of times bigger, on the kind of scale that the universe we know today is bigger than the one the Hebrews knew. He includes the gods of the Hebrews and Amorites, the Greeks and Romans, the Inuit and the Aztecs, the snows and the sun. Those that have disappeared, and those that are to come. He's a God for all of us, at every moment, a heartbeat away.

God lies ahead. I convince myself and constantly repeat to myself that: He depends on us. It is through us that God is achieved.
Andre Gide (twentieth century AD)

Part II

How Credible Is Religion?

8. Why Religion Is For Grown-Ups

God is the expression of the intelligent universe.
Kahlil Gibran (twentieth century AD)

Across the unimaginably vast size and time of the universe, through processes we are just beginning to understand, matter has accumulated into galaxies, stars, planets, and on at least one of these – chemical reactions have somehow led to life, even intelligent life (sort of). But given enough time, New York will be a mound of rubble. Mount Everest will be a sandy beach. The energy of the universe moves towards disorder. It's a fundamental, universal law – the second law of thermodynamics. It's true of our lives, our societies, cultures, nations. It's true of religions, humanity, the planet, of the universe itself.

We expend energy defying entropy, whether that's in individual and social relationships, creating art, appreciating beauty, working, being charitable, trying to do our best. We even look for meaning and purpose in the world and universe as a whole, for eternal truths that give us a reason for being here. For a meaning that will outlast our own speck of time, or (more usually) at least help us get through the time we have. We've told each other lots of stories about this. But can any of them be credible in a world of science rather than superstition?

It's been one of the privileges of my job to come across more inspiring accounts of the individual experience of God than most people. I wish we could publish more of them. So I don't mean to insult anyone's beliefs. But let's try to call the shots straight. There are no laws or truths of religion that can be measured with a ruler, or seen under a microscope. We're talking in different categories.

As far as "evidence" in the strict sense of the word goes – something that would stand up in a modern court – religious experience amounts to zero. Legally, it's hearsay. Evidence needs corroboration by independent witnesses, forensic examination if it's material, the possibility of repeat performance. Miracles are ruled out, by definition.

As far as "proof" goes there have been a number of experiments under rigorous conditions into questions such as whether prayer helps people get better (though none as yet on the equally widely-held corollary, from a historical point of view at least, that cursing them can make them ill), but the results are inconclusive. Some say that they prove it, others that they don't, but the $1 million prize on offer for proving any aspect of the paranormal, on any scale, goes uncollected every year.

You can make a good argument that most religion is a comfort blanket for adults who can't grow up, who don't want to take on responsibility for the world as it is, for themselves as they are. You can argue that the world really *is* one of magic and miracle, but you have to shift the perspectives of the argument. I've felt enough, seen enough, heard enough, to believe that it's possible. Mind does affect matter, even if it's just our own bodies. The heat somehow generated by a faith-healer's hands really can have an effect, sometimes; synchronicity (coincidences beyond what we would accept as coincidence) does seem to happen, sometimes. But you can't legislate for it, repeat it, or describe it in terms that make sense in medicine or science. And you can't overstate it. The success rate of faith healing, for example, is roughly 10%, no more than might be explained by natural remission and placebo effects (the placebo effect is still not really understood – it's repeatable, measurable, but something more is going on than just having faith that your doctor or medicine is going to make you better). The odds of a miraculous cure at Lourdes are far less. The Roman Catholic Church has accepted about 65 healing claims as genuine out of the 150 million or so people who have visited the shrine over the last century and a half. And, of course, these seeming-miracles happen equally across all religions and cultures.

How far the mind can affect things at a distance, change the course of events, or how far that's just reading meanings into what happens, I don't know. If everyone prayed intensely at the same time for a meteor to be moved off a collision course with the earth, would it have any effect? Could a pebble be moved an inch? I guess not. It's never been done, anyway, not in a way that can be "proved," photographed or videoed. Which is not to say it's not worth praying together. In that kind of concentrated agreement, focused on a higher purpose, we could maybe achieve a few other things, like getting rid of world hunger, or terrorism, or nuclear weapons; providing everyone on the planet with a decent education, basic health care, clean water, toilets, decent roofs over their heads, access to the Internet – any one of which would be a good start, and affordable, and help everyone else as well, if the will to do it was there.

When religion ignores science it's on the way to irrelevance. When it contradicts it, it's superstition. But then it doesn't have to do either. It plays a different kind of role. It refreshes the parts science doesn't reach. They both come from the same kinds of promptings, the same questionings. Good science is prompted by curiosity, and knows it's always open to later correction, or rather expansion, in that there's going to be a bigger truth out there which explains more, without denying the benefit of what's already been done. Good religion is the same. It's prompted by questioning, and perhaps fear, but its central element is doubt (certainty in religion invariably makes it go toxic). It knows that there's a bigger truth out there, a bigger mystery. God is not a cartoon-like figure we can pin down in a few sentences, or prayers. And they can work together. Science tells us how to get to the moon, but doesn't tell us why we want to go there. Even the battiest religion can help us get through the day better than knowing everything there is to know about evolutionary theory. And good religion is informed by science, much as science has been informed by religion. Science without religion or morality is the fast road to hell. Religion without reason, likewise.

But then literal "truth" is not the primary question. It may not even be a useful one to bother much about, if you're short on time. Good and evil may be fictions we create, whilst nature is indifferent. But at the very least they're *our* fictions, and we live in the world we create. And maybe fictions have a way of turning into fact if you trust them.

And of course you can even have Christianity without miracle and magic, like the Quaker tradition, which sees miracles as unnecessary, or even unhelpful. Many believers say that you can leave the supernatural out of it, even that there is no supernature, no God.

Maybe these positions are mutually exclusive, but I don't see it that way. Some want to take their scriptures literally, and believe there is a God "up there" in heaven, sending messengers or family to earth. Others take this (or some of it) as metaphor, and believe in God "out there," outside physical space/time, somehow off the edge of the universe (not that it has one, which can make the whole idea of God "out there" difficult to get your head around today; or, if you reckon it does, then God must somehow be retreating at a billion miles per hour, which is the rate at which the universe is expanding). Others see Him more as "in here," in the ultimate relationship between self and non-self; the beginning of the road rather than the end of it. That's how it seems to me that Jesus describes the kingdom of God. We find our images to latch on to, but in themselves they're not important.

But here's a diversion for a chapter or two. Is the idea of a "God" or some absolute truth or reality out there or in here somewhere utterly implausible? Does the world feel sacred because it *is* sacred? Perhaps it's a meaningless question. Meanings are just what we make them, what we read in the stars, write in books. There's no evidence for anything else. But then there's no evidence for something as fundamental to our experience as consciousness either, apart from the fact that we know we have it and see the results. "I think, therefore I am," as Descartes said back in the seventeenth century. But how do we think?

Scientifically-speaking, consciousness and God are as slippery as each other. You can turn over every molecule in the universe and not find God (or love, or justice, or anything that matters to us). Equally, you can turn over every molecule in the brain and not find consciousness (or anything to do with your "self"). We still have no real idea what it is, or how it works. We don't need it – we've known for a century that enormously complex psychological processes can be wholly unconscious. As far as anybody knows, anything that our minds do, as far as ordinary living goes, they could do just as well as if they weren't conscious.

We don't need consciousness. We don't need God either. Stars explode, galaxies form, life develops, termites build their cathedrals, all without knowledge of God.

But we know we're here. We can enjoy it. We can revel in the existence of our self, and of others. Maybe there's an equivalent perception one level up, of a universal self, of God, which we can equally enjoy, if we can get there.

Millions of words are written every year on whether there's some kind of Platonic reality, maybe a God; whether mathematical truths would exist even if there were no universe for them to be applied in; whether the mind is identical with the brain or whether it extends into a "field" of consciousness. And you just end up with a headache. After a few thousand years we're not much closer to agreement.

Neither side is as conclusive as either thinks. The argument that religion is fantasy is impossible to refute. But equally the materialistic, reductionist one, that we're nothing more than the molecules and neurons that make us up, is impossible to prove. After all, each level of description is more than the sum of its parts. Matter is more than molecules. Life is more than matter. Brain is more than life. Mind seems to be more than brain (disputed). More keeps coming from less. The seemingly impossible keeps happening. Life *did* emerge from molten rock, humans from a common ancestor with the monkeys, cathedrals from quarries. Why shouldn't there be a spirit that is more than mind? Perhaps we're just on the borderline between the two, like a nematode worm between plant and animal, or a chimp on the shimmering edge of self-consciousness. Perhaps when there is sufficient mind it "emerges" into another level of complexity like all the other levels do? Why not look positively forward to the next step? If we don't, it's not going to be there.

I believe it's possible to reconcile science and religion if you're open-minded in both. By all means, lean one way or the other. If you take a rationalist point of view you may be more attracted to a religion that doesn't depend on miracle. You don't have to hurt your brain and deny everything you learnt at school.

To take an example of this, let's go back to the creation stories of the last chapter, seemingly impossible to believe today. Good theologians, rather than propagandists in the Vatican, or Tehran, or the Bible Belt, say we should read them because they express brilliantly in story form the belief that the world was created for a purpose. That we are here for a reason. If we can't see that, then life is meaningless and let's party or murder as we please, let's do what we can get away with. There's no one to tell us off.

And of course, it's not just the Genesis stories. They echo the oral myths of indigenous societies around the world, still handed down today from the Inuit in Alaska to the Aborigines in Australia, about how we came to be self-aware through language. About how the universe is there in so far as we see it, and see it looking back at us. Consciousness brings life to the void. The world, the landscape, people, are all sung or spoken into existence. The origin of existence is the Word, the creative act, the ultimate definition. God speaks out of His eternal silence and the Word takes on the flesh of creation. It's words that make us, and everything we see (without words, we can't talk, we can't create meaning). In the greatest and oldest religious texts we know of, the *Vedas*, which were probably begun in the fourth millennium BC with the canon being fixed after 1000 BC, half a millennium and more before the Old Testament started to be written down, the words are part of the fabric of the universe, existing before time itself. In the *Prashna Upanishad* they create the universe at the beginning of each cycle of existence. There's a pale reflection of this in the first verse of the Gospel of John:

> *In the beginning was the Word, and the Word was with God, and the word was God.*

Religion is not just art, it's literature. Religion is not about taking these texts literally, it's about understanding why they're written as they are. We come back to our two meanings of the word. At one level *religio* is our gift to ourselves, the framework we create to live as if our lives mattered, to function without despairing, to give a name to our collective journey. And at the level of "sacred" we sometimes put God in charge because every bus needs a driver. Most religious believers in the world aren't bothered whether it's literally "true" or not, in the sense that that's not a particularly meaningful question. "Life" is "true," and life is what we make it. That's the human path. If facts were what counted we'd have concentrated on claws and teeth rather than brains and imagination. We'd have got tougher rather than softer. We know what we are, the question is what we are going to do about it, what we are going to be. And a religious understanding of this is that life is not about survival of the fittest. It's about taking care of each other, collectively. Growing together.

This may sound stupid to atheists, and to any scientist who sees life in terms of its constituent, measurable parts. But it's the way we all *feel*. It's why adults hang on to the idea of God even when churches describe Him in ways children find stupid. In every moment of life we're conscious of affecting things, albeit in tiny ways: no one lives as if their lives are totally random. We believe that we can make connections, develop friendships, find love, meaning, and indeed in doing so change ourselves, other people, and the world for the better. Our world seems small and friendly (some of the time anyway, on a local scale), not vast, alien, and incomprehensible. What counts is the purpose and effort we bring to things. The relationships we develop, the good we do, the love we enjoy, the art we create, the photos we take, the choices we make, the footprints we leave behind. If this is illusion, we all vote for it.

And as far as I can work out, the fact that we can do this doesn't fit into physical laws. Free will is not accounted for by cause and effect. However far down you analyze the emotional and chemical and genetic activity behind every thought and action, however far our muscles seem to react before we tell them what to do (by milliseconds, but this seems to be the case), there comes a point where we turn probability into fact, where we change what might happen. This is what our "self" is, our will, our conscience, our "soul," that nonphysical essence of who we are, that we've been trying to describe since records began, that indeterminate and troubled space between our genes and God. And it's still as crucial as ever. If mind is equal to brain activity and can be measured, explained, accounted for in terms of our genetic makeup and environmental influences, then we're not responsible for what happens. So religion is not for children, or grown-ups who want to believe like children, when they should know better. It's for people who want to be responsible, and are prepared to be responsible for others. It's a serious matter; the ultimate one – where we figure out what kind of person we want to be.

Is there no God, then, but at best an absentee God, sitting idle, ever since the first Sabbath, at the outside of His universe?
Thomas Carlyle (nineteenth century AD)

9. Could God Be There?

I want to know how God created this world. I want to know his thoughts. The rest are details... In the view of such harmony in the cosmos which I, with my limited human mind, am able to recognize, there are yet people who say there is no God. But what makes me really angry is that they quote me for support for such views... The religion of the future will be a cosmic religion.
Albert Einstein (twentieth century AD)

The idea that you can "prove" the existence of God died in the eighteenth century with the philosopher Kant. Arguing about it is futile. It's like arguing whether 0 exists (first developed out of the teaching on emptiness around the third century AD in India and called *sunya*, which spread to us through Persia). It's a concept, like God, perhaps even like free will, that we've invented; and, like them, perhaps too useful to easily lose.

On its own terms, atheism makes complete sense. Any beliefs we have can be seen as constructs of our imagination and our culture. But then is this a bad thing? We need the help of our imagination to get through the day as best we can, as enjoyably as we can. We're not wholly rational beings. But then the universe doesn't seem to be entirely rational either. Maybe in matching an irrational self with an irrational world we can glimpse a deeper level of reality, which we call God. This is a sketchy look at the possibility of a purpose present in creation.

More cosmologists today believe in God than biologists, though not necessarily in the form of a personal deity. It's a question of perspective. Biologists deal with life on earth, and we know in principle pretty much all that has happened on the way, apart from the pretty basic questions of how it started in the first place and what drives it. On the cosmological scale it's different. Our feeling of control vanishes. Though we can "see" from one end of the universe to the other and back to a few milliseconds from the beginning, we can't even account for 95% of what has to be there, according to physics as we understand it, which is why we call it Dark Energy and Dark Matter. It's not that it's too small or too far away for microscopes or telescopes to see it, it's in a form that we don't understand, that we don't even know how to search for. What we know is still very little. Cosmologists are prepared to accept that the universe is more open-ended and mysterious than we can possibly imagine. That there is a further, final "truth out there" to be discovered, and always may be.

It's true we have this impossibly vast universe, in which our planet and solar system are the tiniest of invisible specks. We know today it's taken four billion or so years for life on earth to slowly develop, through several mass extinctions, to produce human beings as one of the trillions of possible outcomes. We live in the wafer-thin atmosphere of the planet, crawling about on its surface like bacteria in cling-film around an apple, orbiting a third-generation star. But, the religion of "the sacred" says, the fact that we're here is a miracle. It could only have happened because it was meant to be.

How it happened is generally agreed. Around 12 to 15 billion years ago the universe existed as an unimaginably small point, one of an infinity of virtual particles, in a foamy mass of wormholes, smaller than physics can measure (about 0.01 of a meter with another 34 zeroes before the 1). Maybe they were "naked singularities," a mathematical point with no dimensions at all. Maybe they existed in up to ten or more dimensions. With one of them, within a billionth of a billionth of a billionth of a second, repulsive gravity caused it to expand in three dimensions in a "Big Bang" into an area perhaps vastly larger than what we can see today, to create the physical universe of matter that we know (though the Big Bang has its problems and is not definitive, but then nothing ever is in science – something religion could learn from).

That's so strange that anything else is possible. Nothing else can be as surprising. The question many wrestle with is how we get from this unimaginably colossal "explosion" to our fragile life on earth. The second law of thermodynamics (the rule that order decays into disorder) would suggest that the Big Bang should have resulted in almost anything other than an ordered universe. It's been calculated that if it had differed in strength by only 1 part in 10 to the power of 60 the universe as we know it could not have existed. That's the rough equivalent of firing a bullet from one end of the universe to the other and hitting a dime. This is called the "flatness" problem. There are others that make it hard to understand how the universe can be as it is, like the horizon and the singularity problems.

There's a raft of similar remote coincidences where, if variables had been fractionally different, the universe as we know it would not have been possible. Similar astronomical odds accumulate with the emergence of our planet and its life forms. We live on a knife edge of probability, poised between huge uncertainties and impossible odds. "The ultimate purpose of life, mind and human striving: to deploy energy and information to fight back the tide of entropy and carve out refuges of beneficial order," as Steven Pinker says. Perhaps what is true of us is true of the universe as well. For some scientists the inescapable conclusion is that there is an element of cosmic design. Sure, it's just the old teleological argument (which goes back to the ancient Greeks) dressed up for today, but it's still forceful. And you can put forward similar arguments for the relevance of the ontological and the epistemological (arguments from being and knowing). Maybe the universe is designed for life, or is self-designing, in the same kind of way that the earth might be. This theory says that the earth evolves in the direction of life. Perhaps the universe does too. With hindsight James Lovelock, who proposed the Gaia theory, may be seen as significant to our way of thinking today as Aquinas was eight centuries ago.

I don't know which is right, and I guess you can think either way, the universe as purposeful down to the tiniest molecular event, or utterly random. Or somewhere in between. No one knows. And it doesn't really matter. Most atheists and believers are not really that far apart. Atheists might say that everything is meaningless and random, but we can carve out of this our tiny portion of awareness where we can live and create and love. Believers might say that the universe is one of consciousness and purpose and love, and we can join in this awareness and find a reason to live. Both can be equally creative and loving. In the statistics of depression and suicide there's no difference between them. In his search for a myth for our time, Jung expresses it well – *Human consciousness created objective existence and meaning, and man found his indispensable place in the great process of being.*

At the largest scale of the universe the idea of a purpose, of a "God" in some form, is a possibility, however remote. Most scientists assume the universe is random rather than purposeful in the sense of being directed. Organizing principles don't amount to purpose, still less to a personal deity. And purpose is hard enough to define, impossible to measure or prove. Because out of the trillion possible outcomes of the Big Bang we could just happen to be in the one that "worked." One sperm in a few million on any ejaculation might make it, the others don't. The fact that we're here to see what has happened is just that, a fact. It's absurd to suggest that there's anything more to it than that.

But it can seem equally absurd that the awesome odds against there being anything at all aren't countered by a force of some kind that turns the potential of becoming into being. And if it's there, if it exists at all, it must work through the universe at all levels.

It sure is hard though to see ourselves as the point of all this, as the Church describes it, to believe in a God who waits for about 15 billion years for the purpose of the universe to begin with the creation of humankind. Who then intervenes sporadically through one microscopically small tribe in one locality for a thousand years or so, and is likely to come in judgment any time soon. Perhaps, honestly, He's not particularly interested in us. Perhaps He has a different purpose that He is seeing through to the end game. Perhaps if we take religion in the sense of "belonging" and "sacred" seriously enough we'll still be around in 10 billion years, when the stars start disappearing, to find out. And if not, then the universe and its purpose roll on without us.

Anyway, let's jump for a minute from the biggest to the smallest (physically, we're roughly halfway ourselves between the impossibly big and the impossibly small). Here we go to things as small in relation to us as the universe is large. Atoms themselves, like the universe, are mostly empty space – if you think of the nucleus of the atom as a marble in the middle of a stadium, the protons that form its shape are the size of gnats whizzing around the perimeter. So much space that if you took it all out of everyone the world's population could fit into a matchbox. Leucippus first proposed the idea of the atom as the smallest indivisible thing moving through empty space in the fifth century BC. We had to wait till the twentieth century to get much further, and find out that they are divisible, indeed little worlds of their own. The particles that in turn make up atoms are also little worlds of their own, and here we get down into a world that's even more difficult to get your head around, that of quantum physics.

There's a further twist here, as far as science goes. It's not only that we can't see the world straight and true, it's apparent that the world isn't "straight and true" either. It may not be measurable. It may not even be there without an observer to see it. Just as it takes two to love, it takes two to exist. A subject and an object to make a "fact."

At this level of smallness there's a widespread acceptance amongst scientists of certain principles that relate to the problem of measurement. This was first expressed in Heisenberg's Uncertainty Principle, which says that a particle can be in different places at the same time. When you see it it's a point, when you don't it's a wave of probability.

There are many attempts at explaining this. One that some quantum physicists stump for is the "many worlds" interpretation. Every time a particle seems to be in two places at once it is indeed just that, but in a separate universe, so you end up with an infinity of different universes that have split off from every particle event. Which would seem to provide an impossible number of different universes. But no more impossible than imagining the universe as it is now crammed into a dot smaller than anything physics can measure. Another, more popular suggestion is the "super string" theory. This suggests that the universe is made of wave patterns of near infinite length, though these waves are mathematical constructions in many dimensions rather than "things." The nature of the waves is such that they cancel out everywhere except in one tiny region, and it's there that the quantum "thing" materializes. So everything is in a sense everywhere but manifests itself at one particular point, which is where you (or the experiment) look for it. There are half a dozen of these string theories, for example, M-theory, which says they're all true.

Then there's the Holographic Principle, which suggests that physics is not after all a description of the world as it is, a description of matter, because there is no matter. The matter is really energy. The energy is really information. Maybe the universe is trying to tell us something. Maybe it's God who is real, the point where the deluded known and the illusory unknown meet, and we just struggle to see Him straight.

Related to this is the Exclusion Principle, which suggests that all particles are still in some way connected. Affect one, and you affect another simultaneously at the other end of the universe. How this can happen when nothing can apparently travel faster than the speed of light, is not known. But in some ways the universe still behaves as if it is an indivisible speck. The quantum state stands outside the "now" as well as the "here." Quantum units have no mass, know no distance or time. They somehow encode the probabilities of all possible events. Everything that has ever happened and will be already exists in these patterns. We're a cog in a vast machine, but standing at the crossroads of multiple paths, every one of which we could take, every possibility of which has been foreseen. Everything follows from everything else.

Some scientists are suggesting that there may be a form of "proto-consciousness" or "intelligent information" that's inherent in everything, as much a fundamental property of matter as is mass. And, after all, in some senses we're made of information ourselves, in the form of the 3.5 billion letters of DNA in each of our trillions of cells (though that's probably overly mixing up a model with reality). Bell's theorem suggests that there's no such thing as objective reality, and that consciousness is in some way coequal with matter in its formation. What we see becomes "real." Reality lies in the relation between the two. Complexity and chaos theory add weight to this, suggesting that beyond matter and energy there are patterns of information that we don't yet know about.

Some writers (not always scientists) have picked up on these new insights in science, and ancient ones in religion (the idea of the conscious unity of everything fascinated the Greeks: Anaxagoras, Plato, Seneca, the Stoics, all spoke of the "mind which rules over all things"; Philo, a contemporary of Jesus, a Jew living in Alexandria, combined the best of Greek and Jewish ideas into the first systematic theology, and saw the logos as the "tiller by which the pilot of the universe steers all things" – God as a universal principle in the kind of way we think of gravity today) to suggest that the world we live in might be no less interconnected than the quantum world. After all, it's hard to have a principle true at one scale and not another. So synchronicity might be "real." Some claim that this "zero point field" explains everything from cell communication to homeopathy and extrasensory perception, from flocking schools of fish to miraculous healing. There's an energy flowing through everything that we can't define but grasp at in terms varying from ley lines to chakras, and can touch through ESP or prayer.

This takes us into more speculative, seemingly absurd areas. But there's an increasing amount of evidence from respected medical sources, with no religious agenda, that people can be brought back to life hours after the patient (and the brain) have been pronounced dead. Which implies that consciousness, the "mind," is not dependent on activity in the brain. A few hours is not like years, or forever, but I think there's something that could be open-ended, though perhaps that's faith talking. But there's a vast literature on near-death experiences, or actual-death experiences, which isn't just related to oxygen supply and neural activity. And it's hard to get into issues in physics like retrocausality, where the present influences the past and the future influences the present, with tachyon particles traveling backwards in time, traversable wormholes and quantum tunneling, and action that happens faster than light, without acknowledging that, at least hypothetically, the universe itself is somehow alive, in ways we are not close to understanding.

The stream of knowledge is heading towards a non-mechanical reality; the Universe begins to look more like a great thought than like a great machine. Mind no longer appears to be an accidental intruder into the realm of matter... we ought rather to hail it as the creator and governor of the realm of matter.
Sir James Jeans (astronomer, physicist, mathematician, twentieth century AD)

10. The Universe As God?

Gazing through 240,000 miles of space towards the stars and the planet from which I had come, I suddenly experienced the Universe as intelligent, loving, harmonious. The presence of divinity became almost palpable, and I knew that life in the universe was not just an accident based on random processes.

Edgar Mitchell (astronaut, twentieth century AD)

I'm pretty ignorant in physics, my interests are more in the humanities; all I know is from general reading, from respected scientists. I don't subscribe to the "quantum theory proves that anything can be true" line of thought, which so many publishing proposals we get seem to follow (and which we turn down). But there are some in every generation who think they've discovered everything there is to be found, that history has finished, science has ended, and they're always wrong, just like believers who think they have the complete answer to everything. The only thing we can reasonably be sure of is that what we now think of as the weird edge of science is maybe just the beginning of our next steps in understanding.

A unified theory which reconciles the theory of relativity (dealing with cosmological events that are bigger than us by a multiple of zeroes) with quantum physics (similar numbers of zeroes going in the opposite direction) has yet to be found. Most scientists accept that the laws of physics that we have now will be superseded in years to come, much as relativity superseded gravity – or, rather, included it in a broader picture – that's the way science works. Many think we will never understand the universe, even that the fundamental laws of physics could change through time and space. Gravitons and particles might replace leptons and quarks as the interesting units (but this is some way ahead – for instance theory might predict gravitons must be there, rather like the Higgs boson, but they're impossibly too small to "find"). To speculate further, perhaps we'll come to see the speed of light as a threshold to something different rather than an absolute limit. The world of matter that we experience might be one small part of our new equation. Maybe, on the side of our physical existence, we live in the world of particles, but on the cognitive side of our being, we live in the world of waves. Perhaps the world of consciousness, of choice and purpose will come to be seen as vastly larger, 99% of what there is rather than 1% or zero. And if anything can travel faster than the speed of light it's likely to be thought. Religion describes it as the Word, the Logos, the principle of reason. God, the final answer, beyond which nothing can be known, nothing exists, talking to Himself, the ultimate conversational loop.

And perhaps at the quantum level choice determines time as much as position. Perhaps there is ultimately no clear distinction between random events, choice and the acts of God. They're all part of the description of the picture. Accepting this is a process common to many religions. We make sense of the circumstances that seem to dictate our lives through assimilating them. In the sense that we have responded to events, we have chosen who we are. When we can say "yes" to our existence, and don't regret a single moment of it, good or bad, past and future, and can see it as "one," we have reached enlightenment.

Maybe we're just thinking anthropomorphically here, like the ancient Egyptians, who read divinity into the sun, declaring it to be Ra, who is renewed every night by spending time with Osiris, the Lord of the Dead. In practice, on a daily basis we think of our existence as the reality, and everything else, whether dreams or God or waves of probability, as increasingly unreal shadows. But the old stories, all those ancient, deluded religious ones, suggest that it might be the other way round. Maybe they were on to something, in their own way. Today science suggests that our world could be a peephole of fragile consciousness through which we can see an infinitely richer, multidimensional one. Time running backwards, different versions of ourselves existing simultaneously, aliens and galaxies made of invisible matter, trillions of universes at the end of our fingertips – these are all theoretical possibilities in the world of modern cosmology and quantum physics.

You can believe you're in the only real universe for you and that everyone else is in a different one; that you live forever and it's only other people who die. Or that you die many times in your life, shifting to a different timeline on each occasion. Or that you're a "Boltzmann brain," spontaneously created, floating for a trillionth of a second in the near-eternal void. It's perfectly respectable amongst top astrophysicists today to speculate that we're in the only universe there is but it's one that's "learning" rather than "evolving," in the same way that machine learning algorithms do – it has no goal in mind but "looks" for regions of stability, creating the laws of physics in the process. Or that we're all virtual reality simulations of an infinitely powerful computer, that there could be billions of these simulations and we'll never know whether we're real or not. It's not that dissimilar in some respects from the Grand Omnipotent Deity of the Salafis or Calvinists. Or the idea of some Buddhists that the universe is a projection of the mind. Push a physicist on the implications of quantum theory, and she might accept that consciousness has a better claim to existence than objective reality. The universe is only there because it's being looked at, being brought into definite existence, out of all the alternative possibilities. The laws are as they are because of our own existence.

Maybe this is all too subjective, making claims about a universal perspective which is inaccessible to us. But nearly half a millennia after Galileo upended our world-view by showing that the earth wasn't the center of the universe, some are back to thinking that in some respects perhaps we could be. So it's not difficult to believe in God in the twenty-first century as a possibility; in some ways it's easier than at any other time in history. It's just the idea of believing in one version of Him as the Absolute and Only Truth that's hard.

This is all irrelevant to the practice of religion. That's a question of how you want to live, not what you know. But if you worry about who God is and where He might be it suggests the beginnings of an answer. Medieval theologians turned mental somersaults trying to make sense of how the supernatural worked in nature, down to how many angels could fit on the head of a pin. They'd love to be around today. You can speculate forever, almost anything could be "right." A central Hindu insight for instance is that when consciousness is focused it contracts, and the ultimate alpha and omega point is one of pure consciousness. Maybe we'll come to see God as the original "point" of consciousness, the ultimate singularity, splitting Himself into relationships. Too small to measure, too big to understand. A vast, many-layered tapestry in which all of life is but a single bright thread. To make a huge jump, maybe we'll see the collective choices of all the bits in the universe as His scattered consciousness, making up His "mind," *Brahman*, to which all our actions and thoughts, our share of this consciousness, *atman*, contribute in tiny measure. This, after all, is what Schrodinger thought. He was a Nobel Prize-winning physicist whose equations laid the foundations of quantum mechanics, and is best-known for the paradox of Schrodinger's cat, which he developed in discussion with Einstein (a thought-experiment where a cat can be simultaneously alive and dead). In *What is Life?* he reworks the *Upanishads*:

> I – I in the widest meaning of the word, that is to say, every conscious mind that ever said or felt "I" – am the person, if any, who controls "the motion of the atoms" according to the Laws of Nature.

We don't know how we link up with this God. But then we have little idea how consciousness works in our brains, or even how life started in the first place. Let alone what triggered the Big Bang, or why there is something rather than nothing. We know little more about the mind of God than the bacteria that make up the bulk of our bodies know about us. But there is something weird going on here. There are about 100 billion or so neurons which create brain activity. Each of these ends in a little bunch of feelers, like coral polyps. The gaps between these feelers are called synapses. Chemicals called neurotransmitters transmit nervous impulses between them. The number of possible pathways between the synapses of the brain exceeds the number of atoms in the universe. The gap between them, about a millionth of a centimeter, approaches the atomic scale, where quantum uncertainty comes into play. In other words, our brains operate at the level of quantum particles where reality is "created" by the observer, where electron-tunneling can take place.

To "will" would then be to select from the quantum states that appear, the different possibilities that run through the brain. We could be "choosing" our reality. Somewhere, down in the depths of the mind, remote from us as God is, the real action of the universe is taking place. In every nanosecond billions of connections in our own brains are being made that have never been made before, that are different from anything that has ever happened in the universe. Each of us is a miracle on legs, changing every moment. Somehow out of all this we can think, create, and love. Or hate and destroy. Religion is the thread of sanity we weave into our tapestry of probabilities to create peace and happiness rather than mayhem and murder.

It's not so very inconceivable that we are ourselves part of the process of creation, one membrane out of trillions. Or that perhaps, at some level, we can "link up" with a universal mind. Maybe we live within it, our thoughts dreamed into form by mind, a ripple on the ocean of consciousness. When we die our borrowed bodily forms return to the recycling machine of nature, the atoms of which we're made refashioning themselves again into earth, minerals, plants, and people. Our fragments of consciousness return to the background energy-state of the universe, which we variously describe as Dharmakaya, or God, or Tao, or Brahman, or the fundamental equation, or Noumenon, or Reality, or the Absolute, or Primary Energy, or simply the sea of "things that might be." This is the only thing that is "One," that doesn't change because it includes all possible changes: "I am that I am" (Exodus 3:14), or "The one 'I am' at the heart of creation" (*Shvetashvatara Upanishad*).

It's no coincidence that all the great religions lean in this direction. It's hard to go to the funeral of someone you've loved and not feel that this must be in some way true, that something of what we are exists outside time and space. Maybe it's wishful thinking. Maybe if you're a left-brained, rational kind of person you're inclined to dismiss it. Maybe if you're a right-brained, living-in-the-moment kind of person you're inclined to believe it. It doesn't matter. It's a possibility, if you want to act on it. The experience of God can be described as the form we give to our relationship with the "other," the definition we give the point where our deepest desires are returned with interest. And in so far as we need a model it's a better one for today than a king in the sky. He is the line we draw at the limits of our capacity for understanding, for emotion, and wonder. We carve out our meanings from the apparently indifferent rock face of existence, and assume there is a rock there that we call God.

And since creation is continuous, since the universe never "stops," maybe God is still developing. He is the original point of energy from which matter is formed, which in turn gives rise to life, to consciousness, which in turn creates energy, completing the circle. Not a being, but Being itself, the "ground of everything," which some Buddhists and Christian theologians describe in pretty much the same way. Our brains are spiders' webs of molecules with the stability and lifespan of summer mist, fleetingly grasping at fragments of this consciousness, much as our bodies are passing hosts for bacteria and genes, before we pass on to wormfood.

But if God is a process, how did the universe begin in the first place? If the form that reality takes has to await the participation of an observer, how can anything exist before the observer is there to see it? This where we have to take an imaginative leap out of the four dimensions of space and time that we live in.

Imagine an eye with a long stalk in the form of a loop, with the eyeball looking back at its own beginning; or the best-known Taoist symbol, the Yin-Yang. That, in the world of quantum physics, may be the most credible explanation of how the universe came to be. Perhaps consciousness is something created by its own workings that has already happened. Religion is simply our attempt to realize where we are before we get there, and it's by doing so that we arrive. It is the practice and growth of consciousness, the universe's way of thinking about itself. Religion is not anti-evolution ("Creationism" is a sad joke, a declaration of personal ignorance about science, the Bible, and life itself) – it *is* evolution. Darwin is the St. Paul of our time. Gaia is our new Mother Goddess. God was not there at the beginning, but He is there at the end, and in the end is our beginning.

I regard consciousness as fundamental, matter is derived from consciousness. Everything that we talk about, everything that we regard as existing, postulates consciousness. There is no matter as such; it only exists by virtue of a force bringing the particle to vibration and holding it together in a minute solar system; we must assume behind this force the existence of a conscious and intelligent mind. The mind is the matrix of all matter.
Max Planck (the originator of quantum theory, Nobel Prize winner, twentieth century AD)

11. The Bigger Picture

*Many years ago when an adored dog died, a great friend, a bishop,
said to me, "You must always remember that, as far as the Bible is
concerned, God only threw the humans out of Paradise."*
Bruce Foyle (twenty-first century AD)

How big is God today? How does He work? Religion in a broad
sense is credible. It's based on the idea that consciousness plays
a role in the universe, and always has done. Mind and matter are
two sides of a coin, a reflection of each other, an idea for which
the Church burnt Giordano Bruno at the stake in 1600 AD (a
brilliant sixteenth century Dominican friar, and mathematician,
called by some the founder of modern philosophy, he also
proposed that the stars were distant suns with their own planets,
perhaps even with their own life; that the universe was infinite,
with no center; clearly, such heretical thinking meant he had to
be fried to death).

God creates consciousness, consciousness creates God.
God is the universal consciousness working through life, the
shorthand we variously use for our experience of the world as
meaningful, beautiful, loving, and true. Materialism, reductionist
philosophies, are for people who want to give themselves a hard
time, who look for the lowest possible common denominator.
But there's not much point in arguing about it, in the limited
sense of whether someone or something called God exists or not.
If He doesn't, you're wasting your breath. If He does, He doesn't
need your help.

The key religious question is what you decide to relate to.
And here we get back to the difference between good and bad
religion. It's pretty much the same as good and bad personal
relationships. Much religion is self-obsessed. It was the way I
used to figure it. I was driven by particular verses. As a teenager

I was a "watchman unto the house of Israel" (Ezekiel 3:17-18), caught up in the ego trip of "I'm so sinful," followed by "I'm so saved, hallelujah!" I believed, when running the Christian Union in my last year of Secondary School, if I didn't convert my fellow-students their destiny in hell was on my shoulders – what a dickhead! (My humble, scraping apologies to anyone concerned who happens to stumble across this.) Scattered around the shores and islands of old empires you have thousands of Christian sects today, from Evangelicals several times removed from everyone else in purity of doctrine, to Voodoo worshippers and cargo cults, all convinced that their picture of God is alone true, that if they don't follow it the bottom of their world will fall out. (An example of a recent "cargo cult" today is that of the Kastom people on the island of Tanna, in Vanuatu, in the Pacific; they believed that the son of a mountain spirit traveled to a distant land, married a powerful woman, and would in time return to them – on small islands, in the middle of the vast ocean, gods or salvation are always likely to come from somewhere else. Even prior to Queen Elizabeth visiting there, with her husband Prince Philip, back in 1974, they considered him a divine being. The visit confirmed it – and why not? – it was "real," far more self-evident than the reappearance of Jesus after the crucifixion.)

That's sad religion. But then mainstream Christianity itself looks cultish today. It centers on a belief that the Son of God came to earth 2,000 years ago to save humankind. It's why so many Christians claim that the world is only a few thousand years old. The salvation history that the Church teaches is written from that understanding.

But religion is probably at least as old as language, and connected with it. It's then that we gained the ability to learn from each other, rather than having to increase the size of our brains in order to progress. That's when we started to talk about how we relate, to start loving relationships, to respect the relationships we had with the world around us. And as we learned to communicate in more complex ways through language, our bodies adapted to run down animals over long distances and throw spears, to hunt in packs. We started to make choices, to trust other people, even to consciously self-sacrifice for the common good.

Today we have fossil skull shapes of where our larynx would have been that suggest that we were speaking 200,000 years ago. We could have been speaking since we separated from the chimps, millions of years ago. Anthropologists argue over whether there's evidence for drawing and sculpture that dates to 100,000 or more than 250,000 years. Every decade or so it gets pushed back another 10,000 years.

This helps put the claims of particular religions in perspective. Christianity for instance has been practiced for less than 1% of that time, during most of which it's been followed by 1 to 10% of the world population. But surely God is not so forgetful that he waited for 10,000 or so *generations* before sending His Son to save humankind, threatening to come back any day in judgment. Even if we go back only to our immediate ancestors who developed our "modern" culture, from whom we are indistinguishable in every way, and whose genetic tree we can trace in our bodies back to the mitochondrial "Eve," the entire Christian experience barely registers.

Our understanding of the love of God today needs to be bigger as much as our picture of the universe is bigger.

For instance, what about the other species of Homo who have disappeared? Just 300,000 years ago there were at least nine of them walking on the earth simultaneously, including ourselves. Didn't God love them? To take an example, anthropologists have recovered 500 skeletons of Neanderthal man (Homo sapiens neanderthalensis), the latest dating to 34,000 BC (estimates of the ages of fossils are accurate to around 10%). In anthropological terms that's like yesterday. Their brains may have been larger than ours, around 1.8 liters to our 1.4 (disputed). They came out of Africa hundreds of thousands of years earlier than we did, and over that time developed a stronger and tougher body than ours, designed to cope with the cold climate. They cared for their sick and wounded (the anthropologist Margaret Mead called "a healed femur" the first sign of civilization), and buried their dead with ritual and ceremony, covering them with flowers, placing stones and antlers around the graves, and may have played music. They stitched clothes, carried spears, produced jewelry and pictures with manganese pigments, and probably went seafaring through the Mediterranean. Most anthropologists say we probably killed them off, whether through warfare or disease or both. The most recent discovery of a new hominid only happened this century, of Homo floresiensis, on the island of Flores in Indonesia, where over a million years they had evolved into dwarfs, as frequently happens on islands across different species, a process called "insular dwarfism" (in contrast to, say, Homo heidelbergensis, who in one period, as the grassland savannahs of Africa expanded, grew to an average height of seven feet). Like Homo erectus, who was using fire over a million years ago (couldn't have survived on the plains at night without it), they traveled in boats, or rafts (or they couldn't have got there). We probably killed them off as well, as their disappearance around 40,000 years ago coincides with the arrival of our immediate ancestors. But Homo erectus probably believed in an afterlife, in the burials at Choukoutien outside Peking they built houses, worked wood, threw spears, drank from bowls. You can't do that without the capacity for abstract thought, the ability to conceive the idea that reality lies elsewhere, beyond this life, a "religious sense." This is why religion in some form will always be with us. It's part of self-awareness. Religious belief involves defining what the "self" is, and is not. The practice of religion is transcending it.

There's a score or so of other Homo cousins we've discovered in the last half-century, most of whom trod the earth for longer than we have (and it's hard to see us surviving as long as they did – indeed, it's thought today that we nearly went extinct 70,000 years ago, after the Toba supervolcanic eruption, which brought the population of Homo sapiens down to around five to ten thousand individuals).

God must have been in the frame for them too, surely? You don't stop loving children because they turned out a bit differently than the way you wanted them to? But they would have described Him differently. For instance, the ultimate religious act in most traditions of Homo sapiens has been to sacrifice an individual for the common good, to drink his/her blood and eat their flesh (the ghostly descendant of this practice survives in Holy Communion: "Take, eat; this is my body," Matthew 26:26). But if it had been Homo robustus (vegetarians who dug for roots rather than omnivorous scavengers like ourselves, who will eat pretty much anything nowadays, however bad for us, apart from the nutritious insects that probably formed a good proportion of our diet in times past) who had survived rather than Homo sapiens, there would have been a quite different idea of how to please God. We eat and sacrifice flesh and see God's offering of His Son as a lamb. So lamb is high on the menu. Unfortunately they take up a lot of space, being grazers on lush grass, like cattle, which is why we've become more dependent on chicken, and to a lesser extent pork, compared to the Hebrews (nomadic wanderers over poor pasture, more suited to goats). But maybe Homo robustus would have seen Him as a plant. Which seems more logical. Predators eat other mammals, but, by definition, the vast majority live on plants, so we're all dependent on them. Our religion is shaped by our biology, by our stomachs, even before culture has its say.

We can keep extending the circle of creation with which God is involved. For instance, we're closer to chimps genetically than gorillas are, than two species of clams are to each other. Your hand is a chimp's hand (though with only a quarter or so of the strength). And so are every bone and nerve in your body. We still have the goose pimples which raised our now nonexistent fur against cold and enemies. For the first weeks of life our embryos are indistinguishable. Chimps recognize themselves in mirrors, can make sentences with sign or computer language, have prodigious memories, feel happy, sad, and may mourn their dead, perform primeval rain dances in response to thunder and lightning. Like them, we still prefer to sleep upstairs for security. They dream like us, like all mammals, maybe even reptiles. Anthropologists generally agree that the key distinguishing feature of Homo sapiens is not our brain, or intelligence, or moral awareness, or soul, or even our sense of humor, but our posture. Standing on two legs came first, the increase in brain size came later. Or, more probably, they developed together.

Most people who work closely with them say it's hard to see any fundamental difference between the three species of homo around today – ourselves (Homo sapiens sapiens), Common chimps (Homo troglodytes) and Bonobos (Homo paniscus). Our development of technology and culture over the last million years disguises our much longer period of similarity. It's a question of degree. And as we're the ones driving the others to extinction, perhaps we don't hold the moral high ground. There are only about 200,000 chimps left now. They're gradually being killed off to satisfy our demands for more exotic restaurant menus, for "bush meat." We're eating them off the planet.

Apart from our taking the seemingly suicidal step of walking on two legs, increasing our visibility to predators, in favor of becoming more sociable killing machines, Common chimps and human beings have developed along similar lines – we might have the iPhones, but in all the important respects of sex and social organization we're the same. The Bonobos, who split off later than us, developed differently. You can make a case for their having a potentially superior morality. Their family groups are led by females who maintain their position by sex rather than force. Fighting is rare. Killing animals for food, as both we and chimps do, unknown.

What if we had learned from the Bonobos rather than the Common chimps? Our society could have been more peaceable, more "moral." Sex would be initiated by the female to reconcile and reward rather than by the male to express right and power. Our popes, priests, and presidents would be female. God would be Mother. Joseph would be a eunuch rather than Mary a virgin. Jesus would have been a daughter. The Bonobos would probably have been better at managing one of the main problems confronting the earth today – our over-breeding. Climate change might not have become so much of an issue. We wouldn't be wrecking the topsoil (about 60 years of it left) so we can eat meat and live comfortably in hot and cold climates, turning the oceans into watery deserts, polluting the atmosphere.

We might be no more the favored species of Homo than the Jews the favored people – just equally deluded. The more we dominate nature, and the more powerful an image we have of ourselves, the more powerful our image of God needs to be. The worse we become, the more we destroy, and the more sinful we feel, the holier a God we imagine, and the bigger the churches need to be. We like going into cathedrals, as tourists rather than worshippers – "this is so impressive…" – but the sheer size of them, the wealth of the treasures they hold, is generally in proportion to the degree of institutionalized slavery in the feudal system they represent; the direct pillage of other cultures; or the guilt-ridden legacies of barons salving their consciences at the end of their life, buying salvation – like the great national museums of the nineteenth century being established on the back of slaves and cotton.

Maybe Christianity works best for bad people. In a hundred or two years' time perhaps we'll all look back on our habits of owning and eating our animal relations – any creatures with faces – with the same kind of distaste that we now have when we view slavery and cannibalism. "Did we really behave like that?"

There's a joke about a man and his dog who had both died in a car accident. They were walking along a road and came to a high marble wall. In the center was a tall mother-of-pearl gate that glowed in the sunlight. Behind it was a golden street.

The man and his dog walked toward the gate. As the traveler got closer, he saw a man at a desk. "Excuse me, where are we?" he asked.

"This is heaven, sir," the gatekeeper replied.

"Wow! Great! Would you happen to have some water?" the man asked.

"Of course, sir. Come right in, and I'll have some ice water brought right up." The gatekeeper gestured, and the gate began to open.

The traveler pointed to his dog. "Can my friend come in, too?" he asked.

"I'm sorry, sir, but we don't accept pets."

The man thought a moment and then turned back toward the road and continued to walk the way he had been going.

After a while he came to a dirt road that led through a farm gate. There was no fence. As the traveler approached he saw a man in a chair, reading.

"Excuse me!" he called. "Do you have any water?"

"Yeah, sure, there's a pump over there. Come on in."

"How about my friend here?" The traveler gestured to the dog.

"There should be a bowl by the pump."

They went through the gate, and sure enough, there was an old-fashioned pump with a bowl beside it. The traveler filled the bowl and took a long drink. Then he pumped some water for the dog.

"What do you call this place?" the traveler asked.

"This is heaven," was the answer.

"That's odd," the traveler said. "The man down the road said that was heaven, too."

"Oh, you mean the place with the gold street and pearly gates? Nope, that's hell."

Said the traveler, "Doesn't it make you mad for them to use your name like that?"

"No. I can see how you might think so, but we're just happy that they screen out the folks who'll leave their best friends behind."

I sometimes think that God, in creating man, overestimated his ability.
Oscar Wilde

12. Is God Good?

Learn to look with an equal eye upon all beings, seeing the one self in all.
Srimad Bhagavatam (sixth century AD)

Interestingly, a little diversion here, once upon a time most Christians thought this way, in terms of a wider circle of creation, and respecting their fellow creatures. In the first few centuries missionaries took Christianity into the Western reaches of the Roman Empire where, under the influence of Greek philosophy and state control, and assimilating pagan trappings and ideas, it changed into the religion we know today. But missionaries also went East. Here, in India and China, they encountered societies far more sophisticated and literate than those to be found in Europe after the fall of Rome. The first recorded use of the Christian calendar anywhere in the world is in China, in AD 641, and one of the earliest printed books in the world, now in the British Museum, is a copy of what is probably a Chinese Christian calendar. It's dated AD 877, over half a millennium before printing was "invented" in Europe, with Gutenberg. And Christians in the East followed a policy of nonviolence, not just toward people (like the first Christians in the West also did, before it became the official religion of the Roman Empire, when massacring people over minor theological points became a godly thing to do) but to all living things. Vegetarianism was obligatory. Maybe the Eastern Christians got it more right than the Western ones. The kingdom of God is not just for us, in the West, today. God, and our interpretations of Him, could be bigger than we think.

In the seventh to ninth centuries followers of the "Religion of the Light," as it came to be called, may have outnumbered

Christians in the West two or threefold to one, with churches in most Chinese cities, and cathedrals even in remote Tibet. But they were largely destroyed by first the Muslim and then the Mongol onslaughts, much as the English church nearly disappeared under the Viking invasions of the eighth to tenth centuries. Only traces of them survive. The liturgy of the Eucharist that the Nestorian Church in India still uses, for example, *The Anaphora of the Apostles Addai and Mari*, is the oldest in use anywhere.

We can keep extending our circle of creation indefinitely. I used to look at Egyptian or Indian images of their gods and think, "Gross! How could anyone be as stupid as to think God looks like that (the monkey god Hanuman for instance)!" But for most of history, before we had the technology to easily kill fierce animals and dominate creation, we had seen gods in their image rather than ours – or a mix of the two – half human, half animal/ fish/bird; and of course it's still a dominant form in parts of the world. There are still traces of it in the Old Testament.

Sure, God is easier to understand, easier to talk to, if we think of Him in our image, as a "person." It's hard to ask for forgiveness from a dolphin (though let's not get too sentimental, they seem to be as intelligent in many respects as we are, but perhaps more prone to gang rape and murder for pleasure), or love an abstraction. We make God personal and as physical as we need Him to be. Statues, creeds, rituals, sacraments, scriptures, sacred places – they all help to focus our thoughts outside our selves. But assuming that God really is anything like us – sometimes loving, sometimes vengeful and petty – or only interested in us is like thinking parrots must be human because they can speak English (or whatever language you're trying to get them to repeat something in).

And why shouldn't we widen the circle further? Expanding our circles of coexistence and empathy is what religion is about. It's not just other human fossils and chimps we're connected to. For several hundred thousand years our ancestors saw life as the purpose, rather than people. It's all sacred and interconnected. We're part of everything else.

They were right. We know now that all life descends from a common ancestor that lived around four billion years ago. Biology shows us how interconnected we are. It can follow the evolution of our bodies over this period. The first circulatory system of our aquatic ancestors was seawater. So our blood is still salty, combining elements of sodium, potassium, and calcium in the same proportions. Our skeletons are still hardened with lime. We can trace the development of self-awareness in our own brains, from the reptilian at the stem to the mammalian at the top. We're part of a community of life, a twig in a forest. Nature is so connected that, incredible as it may seem, every time we breathe we take in about a thousand million molecules that the Buddha breathed out.

If, as monotheists say, we are made in the image of God, then God can't be less than this. He is not just the cerebral bit of our brain, with some kind of magical body and superpowers attached. God cannot be just our God, He reflects the whole kaleidoscope, wearing a myriad of forms. From cells making pairs, to green shoots in the desert, through to the sacrament of sex, He is the irrepressible drive to life. In India it's seen as a form of cosmic energy called *prani*, farther east it's *chi*. There's no word to describe this in Christian theology as God is generally seen as separate from creation, though the Cambridge Platonists like Ralph Cudworth in the seventeenth century came close.

Think of it this way; small gods live in trees or temples or on mountaintops, or in the pages of a book. They concern themselves with the interests of an individual, or tribe, or species. They need priests and bureaucrats to translate their demands, to measure them out and keep a percentage. A universal God is just that. Concerned with all of life, with the universe, impartially working through every molecule, every atom in a universe 50 billion trillion miles across. It makes more sense. There's no "point" in life at which matter becomes conscious, at which animals turn into humans, at which we begin to sin, at which God gets involved with life on earth to remedy a problem of His making. We can't even define "life" itself, let alone create it. The categories we give it – species/phyla, animal/vegetable/mineral, mind/body/spirit – these are not "real." What we see now is that there is no absolute dividing line between body and brain, brain and mind, mind and consciousness, consciousness and spirit. Every society, every religion, draws these lines differently, at different times. Christianity itself has variously disputed whether children, or women, or slaves, or colored people have souls. We still differ as to when an individual life begins. If there is a clear line anywhere in biology (relatively) it's between bacteria and all other life forms. "Soul" is bigger than we think. Boundaries are as much openings as barriers. From the first division of cells in the primeval sea onwards they exist not to enclose us, but to enable more complex exchanges of information. We find ourselves through sharing connections with everything else. Half of all species are parasites. 90% of the living cells in our bodies are bacteria. It's difficult for us to get this, in the West.

However, this is not just a pagan or New Age idea but is central to Middle Eastern thought, and provides the context in which Jesus taught. Modern scholarship suggests that Aramaic, the Persian lingua franca across much of the region, which Jesus spoke, doesn't draw clear distinctions between "self," "neighbor," and source of life or "God." Unifying them in a comprehensive pattern of belief and behavior was the wellspring of many religious traditions in the area, and has perhaps continued most clearly in Sufism. And they all draw on the way we all used to think for most of our history, when we saw the Mother Earth as an interconnected web of life, ourselves included; a literal Tree of Life (like the one in Genesis 3:22 of which God was afraid that if

Adam ate the fruit He would be facing competition), embracing everything, including matter and spirit, body and soul.

So why not believe in God as always active, always present, in every birth and death and every falling leaf, in every chemical reaction since the beginning of time, as the architect of all life, all creation, the whole universe, rather than last week's odd-job decorator, intervening very occasionally through single individuals? He really does notice the death of a sparrow (not that He's going to do anything about it). Let's think of God as everything outside our sense of self.

And that's millions of times more than we can see, but that will do to start with. It's a theme of the *Gospel of Thomas*, perhaps the first of the gospels to be written:

Jesus said: "It is I who am the light which is above them all. It is I who am the All. From me did the All come forth, and unto me did the All extend. Split a piece of wood, and I am there. Lift up the stone, and you will find me there."

It's not so much we who are living, controlling and deciding, as life being lived through us. And after a few billion years of trial and error, of building layers of complexity till awareness emerges and sees the light, He is now looking around at what He's created and saying, "Yes, indeed it's good." The world is beautiful and true. It dazzles and astonishes. It's amazing every moment that it's here at all. We're incredibly privileged to be here to share it. If we have a problem with life, we've made it. The world doesn't have it, and we're not as important as we like to think. The butterfly is as significant as we are. The difference is, we have the pleasure of being aware of it.

But why should the world be good? It often doesn't seem that way. Ask almost anyone up till a few thousand years ago whether gods/God/spirits were "good" or not, and they would probably have laughed. What a strange idea! What's "good" about seeing your mother suffering a painful, drawn-out death? One child starving to death, another eaten by lions? Gods are capricious and cruel by nature. The world can be nurturing, beautiful and wonderful, sure. And in the Christian tradition and many others our experience of God is often phrased as encountering an overwhelming sense of beauty, love, and light. But the world can also seem pointless, destructive and mad. Why should God, if anything resembling that exists, be anything more than an impersonal force? Or one of darkness, evil, and death? The world of nature, of which we are a part, is not wasteful, as everything is eaten by something else, but it's certainly not compassionate. No "morality" there. The idea of a benevolent, all powerful and omniscient God seems like a contradiction in terms. As Darwin (whose own doubts about God were more moral than intellectual) wrote:

> I cannot persuade myself that a benificient & omnipotent God would have designedly created the Ichneumonidae with the express intent of their feeding within the living bodies of caterpillars, or that cats should play with mice.

And if that's not enough, all the pain of all the trillions of creatures eaten alive on the planet since life began will pale into insignificance beside the sufferings of hell – the most morally offensive, evil religious teaching on the planet.

Maybe the Semitic view of God as both good and evil, of the Eastern one as embracing everything there is, is closer to the truth. But perhaps the purpose working through creation really is a positive, "good" one. This is impossible to say, because we can only speak of what we know. And what we know we've helped determine. But travel back in your mind's path, if you can, to how you used to be as a child. Your memories of your "self," if you can recover them, are likely to be good ones. We like who we are, at least who we were. Now imagine a journey back to our direct ancestors, rat-like rodents. We can trace our similarities; for instance, both rats and humans still have a common fear of snakes, dating from when their ancestors pursued ours in tunnels under the feet of the dinosaurs. We still mimic a snake's "Shh..." as a warning to children. And young rats that are regularly and gently stroked with a brush function better as adults. Being "loved" makes them more relaxed and comfortable. They can actually work out problems better. Their brains get more wired up. This works with mammals, not with reptiles. All furry animals are vastly more intelligent than scaly ones. It's taken a lot of scientific experiments to prove what every pet-lover instinctively knows.

We're no different. Good relationships develop communication skills, which in turn lead to greater understanding and more complex responses to situations. At birth, our brains are relatively unwired, prioritized to keep the heart and lungs going. The next few years are a dialogue between brain and surroundings, with the child taking on the culture of parents and others. We become part of the collective nervous system, programed to learn from each other, bond and share with each other. Children from loving, secure homes grow up with more confidence in their abilities than children from violent or broken ones. As these children acquire greater sensitivity to shades of meaning they find it easier to develop symbols that summarize and convey attitudes. The frontal part of the brain, where we reason and choose, is not fully wired up till the teens or even twenties. Which is why the Jesuits and all Churches, and schools, try to get indoctrination in early. And over millions of years and dead ends, wrong turnings, communication grows the brain, in a virtuous circle. A more complex brain enables deeper love, which in turn spurs the search for meaning. If life forms more developed than human beings exist they are likely to be more loving forms, or they would have destroyed each other (or so we hope). So, logically, if there is a highest life form we call God who created the universe He is likely to be creative and loving rather than destructive, or He would consume Himself. "In the Beginning arose love," as the *Rig Veda* claims.

"Love" is not the right word for this process, and altruism is no better. English is a more limited language than many in dealing with these ideas, with one word for consciousness for instance whereas Hindi has dozens, and all language is inadequate anyway. We don't really know what this process is, when it began, what it might become. This is where science shades into religion, where we live by faith that it's what we think of as love that makes the world go round. Imagine it for the moment as simply the highest form of self-awareness that we know of. It has emerged, over a vast period of time, from cooperative relationships, right back to the first parasites. Somehow, early multicellular life developed digestive tracts, spines, binary systems for propulsion and seeing, and they've evolved over hundreds of millions of years into us – falling in love, writing poems about it.

Love is the point at which cooperation turns into more than sharing out of self-interest, becomes valuing another for his/her own sake. We go beyond need, possession, addiction, desire. We value the bonds that enable us to strengthen and deepen that love – honesty, loyalty, faithfulness, and others. In loving God the understanding that we can love everything breaks through, which is why it can be so overwhelming. Indeed, it can be so in part because, as a whole, our society, including the Church, is so irreligious. God is not found there. So it comes as something new. We feel loved in return by the whole rather than the particular. We experience a love, or sense of connection, that is complete, unchanging, unconditional. A shorthand rule for all good religion – for any comment, statement or belief, try replacing the word "God" with "love." If it then doesn't make sense, it's wrong.

We make gods in our image, and our images change. One of

the great insights of the Protestant Reformers in the sixteenth century was that our salvation was not to be bought by money, or by virtue of the sacraments. Perhaps our equivalent perception today is that God, however we describe Him, is not only interested in us. Perhaps He is too big for us to know. He had His doubts about the Hebrews, was often thinking about wiping them out, maybe He still has doubts about us. Perhaps the intended purpose of creation is another million years away, or a billion. Perhaps it won't be realized till the universe ends. Perhaps we're grasping for something that is too far beyond us.

Maybe, for believers, the interesting question is not so much which God we believe in, or whether we have the right religion, as whether we have the right "soul" in the first place. Great idea, but, sorry, wrong species. Perhaps Neanderthal man was more religious than we are. Perhaps God is in their image rather than ours – after all, they were around for at least twice the time we're likely to be. Perhaps God is not particularly bothered whether He is more properly honored in Texas or Tashkent, by white or black, Christian or Confucian, Homo sapiens or Homo erectus. Perhaps with us it was more a case of, "This is a nasty new lot of homos, let's expel them. I'll give them a chance – kill some animals and stitch skins for clothes, to give them the idea, then block the entrance with armed guards, and stop them getting back in and ruining everything" (Genesis 3:23-24).

Perhaps Genesis is more deeply true than we imagine. Perhaps we are all the race of Cain, and have killed off our brothers, related species like Homo neanderthalis, cursed by our genes to fight to the finish. We're only intermittently able to grasp the principle that good religion is based on love and life rather than separation and death, on relationship and respect rather than power and glory. The Jeremiahs and Ezekiels of our time, the prophets of today, are those telling us to repent of what we're doing to the rest of creation and change our ways, or we as a species won't make it through.

Many religions picture a situation where we are the center of the universal purpose, because we put ourselves first. But cosmologists often point out that if you condense the history of the universe down to a year, the whole history of human civilization would take up a few seconds. To a mayfly, born in the morning and dying in the evening, life is eternal summer on a riverbank. If one of them could think, it might reckon the world was made this way, for its benefit. We're no wiser. Multicellular life goes back around 500 million years, mammals around 100 million. But we're not the end-product of evolution, we're barely at the beginning. The evolution of life on earth has most of its time to run, unless we destroy it all.

This is all tough to imagine. You stand on the beach, see the waves rolling in, and it seems like however long you stand there, they'll carry on rolling in forever. But 10,000 years ago, you could either have been standing on top of a hill, in the same spot, or drowning. 100 million years ago, and that spot could have been at the top of a mountain, or the bottom of an ocean. There's time to change.

And here's a thought that millions are starting to accept and spread. Perhaps we're just on the edge of the next level up. We're puzzled creatures, caught in the dim twilight zone between self and universal consciousness, much as our primate cousins are in the zone of dawning self-consciousness. We're a step on the way to the creatures God wants us to be, not the end-product. Multiples of 10 often seem to be harbingers of a new level of complexity. A dog for instance has 10 to the power of 9 neurons in the brain. Self-awareness seems to develop at our level, around 10 to the power of 10, or 100 billion, which is around the number of stars in our galaxy, or the number of people who have ever lived. Maybe there's a next level beyond awareness of the individual self, to the collective self, and on up to an awareness of the world as spirit rather than matter, purpose rather than molecules. Maybe in another million or so years natural or artificial evolution could raise the number of neurons in our brain to 10 to the power of 11. Why not?

Is there any reason in theory why we shouldn't evolve toward a level of consciousness as different from the one we enjoy now as ours is from that of our pet dog? Maybe it will be a different type of consciousness, and self-awareness is a disease, as Kierkegaard suggested, that will one day destroy its host. Perhaps one day we can recover a more archetypal kind of consciousness, of the kind Jung was searching for.

If not in a million years, then maybe in 10 million? The humble hedgehog has been around far longer than that. 100 million? There are at least a couple of billion years to go, before the planet is uninhabitable (by any life form – for us, it's more likely to be measured in centuries). And then there's another few billion years to go before the sun burns out and takes our planet with it – indeed, it's uncanny how most of the great religious traditions, whether in the Americas, Africa, Asia or Europe, see the world ending in fire, even in lands of snow and glaciers like Iceland where Fenrir consumes the sun in the *Edda* (but then they do have volcanoes).

So how far from dog to God? Everything that exists (in this universe at least) is on a line of relationship. Maybe 10 to the power of 12 neurons? 20? 72 (the number of atoms it contains)?

God is our name for the last generalization to which we can arrive.
Ralph Waldo Emerson (nineteenth century AD)

13. Why Good Religions Are The Same

There is only one religion, though there are a hundred versions of it.
George Bernard Shaw (twentieth century AD)

God should be the biggest we can imagine Him to be, but we've made Him too small. We've cut Him up into thousands of stories, as in the Tower of Babel, talking of different gods. Different religions don't represent different truths, they're just the clothes of our spirit, and beliefs the cut of the cloth. And they change with fashion, like the clergy haircut – the "tonsure" became compulsory in the Middle Ages. Imagining gods is as easy as designing dresses, which is why we have so many.

As we probe our common experience, talk over our fears and hopes, forms take shape and flesh. That figure of Woden will keep the wolves from the door. The prayer flags will flutter our thoughts to heaven. The words of a mantra or the Lord's Prayer will pierce the veil. We carve our creations into wood or words and worship them. Faith says our creations represent something real. It says there are moments of honesty that we can reach about ourselves and our intentions, where we can say, "Yes, this *is* true." We step outside our skins for a moment, and tap into the universal current of intention. With practice we can do it at will.

But we're just gadflies on this universal river. A good faith is aware of its failings, that all our images of God are just that, images. But then image, creation, is at the heart of everything. It's all there is. Without it we wouldn't be here talking about it. A good faith says we're not, as atheists or humanists would say, the highest known form of consciousness so everything beyond that is make-believe. It says we've only just started on the road to a consciousness that cumulatively ends up as the creative force behind the universe. Our finest, most beautiful attempts to describe this are the first fumbling of children realizing that they're alive, that they can talk, interact, create. It's not that there's a void beyond our horizon of self-awareness, but that this is a journey without a horizon. We just happen to be aware of the point we're on – as we're aware of our point in time – and can occasionally see a little way forward. Nonbelievers and believers can agree on where we are. The question is whether we're going anywhere.

We have these tens of thousands of different beliefs about God, and most of them can be described as secondary, as significant as a hemline, and as susceptible to change. But there are certain core differences between good religious ideas that are less easy to explain. Different religions approach God from opposite ends of the "me" and "it," "in here" and "out there" spectrum. Over thousands of years they've sharpened their definitions. The first leads to monism, the other to theism.

Monism teaches that there are no separate gods out there, that all reality is one, and you find it within yourself. The main example is Buddhism. Theism, on the other hand, externalizes God and then prays and worships Him/Her/Them. The clearest example of this today is Islam, which means "submission to the one God."

The two seem poles apart, like north and south, good and evil. But it's not so difficult to see them as different approaches to the same end if, referring back to chapter 10, reality is found in the relation between the observer and observed rather than the subject and object. There is no "thing" called "good" or "evil." The Hebrews saw both as aspects of the same divine reality, as did Jesus (Matthew 5:43-45). Our experience of God is the same. He can be subjective or objective. It depends on how you're looking.

This is hard to understand, but so is quantum physics, and surely whoever God might be He's more mysterious and wonderful than that. We have a membrane of skin that mostly separates our insides from out, but there is no such clear distinction between what we think and what we see. Matter, consciousness, imagination, purpose, God – we slice the pie in different ways. We poke around here and there, looking for an easy answer. But no two people can see God in the same way. We don't even see other people in the same way. Some individuals seem admirable to some and hateful to others, whether it's a family, community or at a national level. Our brains are different. We all generate our own pictures, dream our own dreams, respond differently to those of others, succeed and foul up in our own ways.

The problem with theism is that it tends to push God out to the heavens as a remote, separate figure it can be hard to believe in. The problem with monism is that it tends to make Him or ourselves indistinguishable from the world around us. The extraordinary appeal of Christianity over two millennia has been to combine the best of both worlds by having a transcendent God who incarnates Himself into matter, in the form of one individual. Its weakness is that it muddles the two different approaches to God, reducing spirit to flesh. Its major, frequently bloody, internal disputes, which took many centuries to resolve (not that they ever really have been), have accordingly centered on how far Jesus is one or the other.

In practice of course all the major religions embrace elements of both theism and monism. A monistic tradition like Buddhism for instance also has its theistic elements, particularly in the Amida and Theravada traditions, with prayer to and worship of the Buddha. Hinduism is something of a mixture in that the *Upanishads*, the sacred scriptures at the heart of the religion, are monistic, with their core teaching of *advaita*, or "there are not two things." In daily life, though, most Hindus behave like theists, offering sacrifices and prayers to Shiva, Vishnu, and other gods. Indeed in the tradition of *bhakti yoga* a theistic belief in God is seen as an easier, more enjoyable path for those who need that kind of help in surrendering their ego. It's a devotional step on the way to *jnani*, or final understanding, to accepting that "I" is nothing other than a glimmer in the eye of God.

Similarly in theistic religions you have the mystics for whom everything – the dualities of inner and outer, self and other, good and evil – resolves into God alone. In Judaism the writings of Zohar in the thirteenth century, which see the soul as an expression of God, are a good example. In Islam this tradition is represented most strongly by the Sufis, particularly Ibn al-'Arabi of the same period, who preached powerfully on the oneness of Being. The great Sufi leader Hallaj went further and was crucified for saying that everyone is God.

As with Judaism and Islam, Christianity has mystics with a monistic vision like Meister Eckhart, Hildegard of Bingen, Mechtild of Magdeburg, Julian of Norwich, and others. It has to be mentioned, though, that as in the Muslim tradition, Christian mystics who have pursued the "inner light," outside the forms of the organized Church, have often been persecuted by the establishment. The Church has preferred to make saints of legendary figures, bureaucrats and charlatans rather than mystics.

Contemplative branches of Christianity like the Quakers stress the inner light rather than the external forms. The Dazzling Darkness of Christian mysticism, the *via negativa*, is not far from the Way that is Nameless (Taoism), the experience that is beyond language (Zen), the state Buddha describes as Absolute Emptiness, where the mind is void of everything except pure consciousness. Indeed if God is pure consciousness, and consciousness is all there is, it's hard to see how any degrees of difference between Him and us might be established. God as Everything or Nothing? All religions stitch a framework of thought and ritual that leads to one of these conclusions if pursued rigorously, and one is simply the mirror of the other.

The mystics in each tradition have essentially the same teaching. So do those at the more theistic end. There is little difference between Christian fundamentalists, Islamic Salafis and Jewish conservatives who insist most clearly on a God "out there." The words are changed – the Bible for the *Qur'an,* or Allah for God – but the literal reading of each is the same, overriding the lessons of history and the teaching of compassion. Perhaps a general truth is that an intense focus on the religious experience often leads to a situation where the "god without" becomes hard to distinguish from the "god within." It's perhaps the greatest tension of the religious life – do you find yourself, or God? What's the difference?

I used to be heavily involved as a teenager with an evangelical para-church organization called the Navigators. For a confused adolescent, it supplied context, comradeship, direction, much like being a member of a street gang, or the Hitler Youth. We were the shock troops of God's Army. The military analogies were often made explicit. I remember a week-long Bible study and leadership conference where the climax at the end was an all-night prayer session, in the manner that a medieval squire underwent in church before taking his vows the next day and being knighted. Praying for a few minutes, or even an hour or so, was one thing. But all night? How much is there to say? And how do you actually know you're hearing the voice of God rather than your own? It's not like anyone else in the room could hear Him talking to you. I couldn't make the cut. Later I came across one of the wonderful Sufi poets, Rumi, whose words back in the thirteenth century summed up my experience:

So what do I have to do to get you to admit who is speaking?
Admit it and change everything!
This is your own voice echoing off the walls of God.

Both traditions have their dangers. Mystics can suffer depression and madness in confusing themselves with God (there's the story of a devout English soldier who was hanged for heresy in the seventeenth century; he was asked at his trial why he claimed to be God, and his answer went something like – "One night I stayed up praying, and by the early morning I realized there was no one else with me in the room. I was praying to myself. So I must be God"). Conservative theists are prone to take their God so literally they are prepared to condemn and murder people who disagree with them. Much of it might simply come down to the way you think. Conservatives might be more attracted to the "prophetic" tradition of rooting truth in historical events. They like hard creeds, logic, hymns, mountains. Liberals might prefer the "mystic" tradition of seeing truth as timeless. They're more attracted to consensus, mystics, Palestrina, the sea. Add your own qualities. There's room for all of them. Some have had happy experiences of both monistic and theistic traditions, and say they are not dissimilar. We can reach a stage of desperation about ourselves and the human condition, or an overwhelming sense of its beauty or mystery, which is then crystallized into a Higher Being, or God. Or we can progress through stages of enlightenment where we realize that we are part of Being, which includes all desperation, beauty, and mystery. Ultimately it's meaningless to draw too much of a distinction between them. Our brains can't process these concepts without relevant sensory information, which in this case, by definition, doesn't exist, since God is not a "thing." And at the deepest level of reality we know, that of the quantum world, reality does not exist independently from the act of observing it. If we do not see God, He is not there. If we do, He is.

This is not to say that all pictures of God are of equal value. But they're cultural and personal. To claim them as uniquely true is meaningless. The disputes between different Protestant sects over who is saved and who is not seem mad today, the differences between Protestants and Catholics inconsequential.

The fact that they gave rise to so much suffering, including the longest, bloodiest war in Europe, the Thirty Years' War, which halved the population of swathes of what is now Germany, is a monument to our bigotry. The fact that the differences are still important remains a monument to our arrogance. The differences between Christianity and other religions are matters of interpretation.

Perhaps we can simply accept each other, even learn from each other.

For example, to take two seemingly conflicting viewpoints, Christians say that God is personal and that to find salvation we reconcile a personal self with a personal God. Buddhists say that neither we nor God are personal because neither exist. Reconciling nothing with nothing makes for enlightenment. In the Christian experience of salvation you make a huge choice. You wrestle your soul to the throne of God's judgment and lay it at His feet. You give up your ego's demands, your own claims, in joyful abandon, and experience an astonishing peace of mind. In the Buddhist experience of enlightenment you realize there is no choice to be made. You have no soul, no ego, there is no God, no claims from Him on you or you on anything else. You go beyond them all in joyful abandon and experience an astonishing peace of mind.

Who's right? It makes no difference. The brain patterns produced by both Christianity and Buddhism are the same. The advice on how to live is similar. One emphasizes the outer path of forgiveness, the other, the inner. Wisdom and compassion are the twin pillars of both. Prayer and meditation work equally well. Both exist as working possibilities, as aspects of a larger whole, of something we have little knowledge about. We're playing mind games. We'll never know if they're real or not. Faith is living as if they are. Good religion is holding the two in tension, the outer journey and the inner.

We need to understand our separateness before we can be

reconciled. We need to practice love before we can understand what it means to be loved. In giving love we create the potential for love to be returned. To the extent that we know and love ourselves we are known and loved. God is love. By believing in a God of love we bring Him into life.

If you dig deep enough into Buddhism and Christianity you may find they both have their origins in the ideas first formulated, as far as we know, way back in 5000 BC, and earlier, by the Rishis of the great Vedic civilization of the Sarasvati valley in India, that we share the same consciousness, the same "I." We are joined in one spirit (1 Corinthians 6:17). The material and spiritual are two sides of a coin. If for a moment we forget politics, the play of personality, the noise of the self, the demands of religion, and reach into the quiet space within us, we find God. And then the world is one.

In today's universe, as described by science, we are all part of the continuum of life. What is true of the material is also true of time. Since Einstein we know that time is not an absolute, but just one of four dimensions through which we move. It's a function of gravity. Time does not matter, and in moments of profound experience does not exist. Reality is eternity, "a great ring of pure and endless light," as the seventeenth century metaphysical poet Henry Vaughan (one of my favorites) puts it. There's no dividing line between this moment and the last, or the next. All exist in an equally real sense, now. And there's no clear distinction between this world and the next, between us and God. To ask, "Did God create man, or man create God?" is like asking which came first, the grass or the grazing animals, the chicken or the egg. They developed together. Life is a process. The line may curve, swing around corners, it might even zigzag, through successive mass extinctions. But it has never completely stopped and started again. Not on our planet anyway. Reality is not sliced like salami. It includes what we create, even what we think, what we dream. In the bigger picture there is no time.

There is no space. There is no matter. There is only light. Reality is "one," which is why the experience of "oneness" is at the heart of religion. You are not alone.

The Christian of the future will be a mystic or will not exist at all.
Karl Rahner (twentieth century AD)

Part III

How We Became Christian

14. How To Read The Bible

We pick out a text here and there to make it serve our turn, whereas if we take it all together, and consider what went before and what followed after we should find it meant no such thing.
John Selden (seventeenth century AD)

To sum up where we've got to. Religion matters. It bonds us to each other and the world around us. We're all related, the universe is relationship. Spirit and matter are codes we use to describe relationship at different levels. Our definitions vary through culture and time. Ignorance and arrogance lead us to assume that the tradition we happen to be in at a particular point in time is the universal truth for everyone at all times. Every now and again we need to disentangle the good from the bad, rethink what's worth retaining, and what we should leave behind.

In the rest of the book we look in more detail at how the Christian religion developed, where it went wrong, and why the teaching of Jesus still matters today. Not just for ourselves – whether one individual is "saved" or not, out of the 100 billion or so people who have lived on the planet, is not really a "universal" issue – but for our collective future. For the next few chapters we focus on how its mother religion, described in what we know as the Old Testament, developed.

For this we need to grapple with the Bible. I'm going to be referring to it a lot here, so it seems fair to explain how I approach it.

Even if you have no sympathy for religion, it's worth knowing something about it. It's by far and away the world's most influential book, with over 100 million printed each year, though the scholarly consensus today is that the Old Testament doesn't preserve any information of historical value that we don't have from more reliable sources, and the New Testament has little more. It's the collection of sacred documents we happen to have ended up with, through a long sequence of accidents, violence, inspiration, and debate. Large tracts are only of specialist or historical value, and indeed weren't read on a regular basis by the Israelites themselves. The texts mix contemporary events with dimly-remembered history and law, legend and chronicle, myth and prophecy, as often as not assimilated from other traditions. The first stories of Adam and Eve, the Tree of Knowledge, Garden of Eden, Noah, are all adapted from earlier epics like that of *Gilgamesh*, the first story we know of, which had been written down up to a thousand years earlier, and had still older origins, setting the pattern for all the greatest of myths, that deal with our fear of death and extinction. These stories were transmitted orally, as performance art, becoming more magical and elaborate along the way. Their sources are as distant from the time of the Hebrews as the Hebrews themselves are from us. Some of the Psalms and parts of Proverbs are taken from Egyptian writings, praising very different gods. Ecclesiastes seems more inspired by the skeptical philosophy of the Greeks than the Hebrew idea of God. The Song of Solomon is erotic poetry included because the compilers mistakenly thought it was by Solomon (perhaps a natural assumption, given his love of women, including his 700 wives and 300 concubines (1 Kings 11:3) – most of the Old Testament heroes, from Moses, Abraham and Jacob onwards, have multiple wives, often supplemented with slave-wives, or concubines; it's only a couple of millennia or so later that the Church starts to enforce monogamy, for its financial benefit). Ruth, Esther and Daniel were written as fiction and understood as such before making it into the canon. The Acts of the Apostles is now seen by scholars as largely fiction, as far as events go (and sometimes contradict the letters of Paul). And so on.

It doesn't really matter though – historically-speaking, for most Christians, the Bible hasn't been significant. For the first few centuries AD it didn't even exist, as such. For a millennia after that it was only available in Latin, which most people (including priests) couldn't read, even if they were literate (which most weren't). It wasn't till the nineteenth century that it became affordable for the average family. It was rituals and sacraments that were important on a daily basis. It was very much in the interests of the Church to interpret and mediate the Bible. The clergy walked in lockstep with the kings, who ruled by divine right, and in tandem they controlled the bulk of the wealth and the minds of the people. So the Bible, for them, was a problem. Quite apart from the evil actions of all the main Old Testament characters, including God Himself (the lies of Abraham, deceptions of Jacob, theft by Rachel, savagery of Moses and so on...) it's a subversive book. Kings are overthrown, the Prophets call for justice, Jesus preaches on the evils of wealth, forgiving your enemy and turning the other cheek. As the priest John Ball said, who helped lead the Peasants' Revolt in 1381:

When Adam delved and Eve span, who was then the gentleman? From the beginning all men by nature were created alike, and our bondage or servitude came in by the unjust oppression of naughty men.

The King and Archbishop had him hanged, drawn and quartered (it was a nasty death, you get cut down from the hanging noose when you're still just about alive, then disemboweled, emasculated, then beheaded, and your body chopped up to be sent to different parts of the country as a warning). Possession of an unlicensed English Bible (which first appeared at this time, the Wycliffe Bible) became punishable by death.

Today we're at the other extreme. As a whole, the Church Fathers tended to interpret scripture allegorically rather than literally. In the eighteenth century came the Enlightenment – the general idea that we could use reason to understand what's going on, and determine our values and objectives, rather than accept divinely-ordained truth as authoritative in every aspect of our lives, whether that was administered through kings or the church. Critical analysis of the Bible began. Deists like Benjamin Franklin and Thomas Jefferson were key figures in founding the USA (Jefferson even produced his own version of the gospels, removing miracles, the supernatural and the Resurrection). The Great Awakenings of the eighteenth century were in part a reaction against these trends, taking the Bible as word-for-word inspired by God. Out of the Revivals, in one of the most regressive developments in Christianity, in the nineteenth century Charles Hodge, Robert Dabney and James Thornwell founded modern evangelicalism and the fantastical doctrine of biblical inerrancy. In part, to justify slavery, which they saw the Bible supporting as "some of the plainest declarations of the Word of God" (Presbyterian General Assembly Report 1845) – in which, of course, they were right. So now millions of people invest a lot of time "studying" the Bible, individually or in groups, as if it were a single, coherent, divinely-given text. Ritual and the sacraments are now incidental to most non-Catholics, the Bible is central.

The trouble is, in each decade our knowledge about the Bible itself increases, as does our understanding of all the relevant areas of history, archaeology, cosmology, phenomenology, neurology and so on. Today, taking the Bible literally just makes it difficult for rational people with even a minimal education to take Christianity seriously. It's the literary equivalent of believing the earth is flat. Best to start off reading the Bible in terms of legend and myth, hagiography and poetry, memoir and fiction, like many Christians did in the first few centuries, looking for the underlying meanings and the life lessons. Then you can be pleasantly surprised when it sometimes aligns with history.

But I do take the Bible seriously, if not literally. How to read it comes under the category of "hermeneutics." The word, appropriately enough, has its origins in "Hermes," the Greek's messenger of the gods. Considered to have invented speech, he was also a liar, trickster and thief; as speech can be true, false or ambiguous (the principles, or lack of them, behind claims of "fake news," were figured out a long time ago).

Take an easy one, for instance, the story of Noah's Ark. On the spectrum from some adherence to fact, all the way to fabrication, where does it fit in?

It provides material for innumerable illustrated books for children – in my career I confess to having published lots of them, from chunky board books for toddlers upwards, without really thinking what it was about (the sales were very attractive – we sold hundreds of thousands – you could always do well around the world with another full-color Noah's Ark story) – drowning almost everyone on earth. And at the time fundamentalists date the story to, the world population would have been around 30 million, and a lot of children and babies.

I feel guilty about it today (I guess this book is a partial attempt to make up for it). It didn't really occur to me that adults would still be taking it literally. So what's the point of this horrible story today? Okay, it's a nice explanation for children of how rainbows happened (not so appropriate for them to read the bit about Noah cursing his son Canaan because he saw him naked when passed out with drink), but is it worth reading now? Why would we want to hear about a God who gets so upset that Noah seems to be the only person on earth who pays Him attention that He wants to kill off everything alive, let alone believe in such a monster?

It's an incredible story, in every sense of the word. It's prefaced by an obscure reference to the giant Nephilim. According to Numbers 13:33, they later inhabited Canaan when the Hebrews arrived there after the Exodus – no explanation of how they survived the flood; clearly, we're in mermaid and unicorn territory here (unless it's a *really* ancient ancestral memory of hybrid humans/Neanderthals, from the Neanderthals' point of view, as they were shorter – Israel was one of the places where F1 hybridization took place):

> *The Nephilim were on the earth in those days – and also afterward – when the sons of God went to the daughters of humans and had children by them. They were the heroes of old, men of renown. And God saw that the wickedness of man was great in the earth, and that every imagination of the thoughts of his heart was only evil continually. And it repented the Lord that he had made man on the earth, and it grieved him at his heart. And the Lord said, I will destroy man who I have created from the face of the earth, both man, and beast, and the creeping thing, and the fowls of the air; for it repenteth me that I have made them.*

Simply on a literal reading, it illustrates a constant theme in the Bible – that God makes mistakes. He repents. But it's impossible to take literally. We know there have been dozens of minor life extinctions before, and five major ones – respectively 440 million, 365 million, 250 million, 210 million and 65 million years ago. We can see the climate changes in ice cores, the fossil deposits in the mud and rocks, the impact of volcanoes and meteorites, etc. It's inconceivable that there could have been a worldwide flood, with water covering the mountains, a sixth extinction level event, embracing virtually all life, within the last few thousand years, leaving no trace. Nobody with any credibility in geology, climatology, paleontology, anthropology, biology, taxonomy, history, archaeology and so on, would give it a moment's thought.

The story itself is incoherent, because there are two of them woven together here, which is why at one point the animals come in two by two, and at another point it's seven pairs of every clean animal, one of every unclean animal, and seven pairs of birds – and the difference between clean and unclean, according to the Bible's own chronology, wasn't developed till a millennia later, after the Exodus. In Genesis 7:17 the flood lasts 40 days, a few verses later it's 150, with another few months till the waters abated. And how would Noah have collected creatures from other parts of the world – like kangaroos from Australia, or sloths from South America – and fitted them in? It's one of the most popular topics on Christian online forums. "How did Noah manage to collect kangaroos from Australia, and sloths from South America? Easy; the earth was one continent back then" (without considering that continental drift began around two hundred million years ago – if it had all happened since the time of Noah there would be nothing growing or standing on the planet, the earth would be moving too fast under our feet).

We don't even know today how many species there are – probably somewhere around 10 million, some say it could be anything up to a trillion – shake any tree in the Amazonian rainforest and new species fall out. What did they all eat? Indeed, what did they all eat when they came out of the Ark, when all the vegetation would have perished? And where did the water needed to cover the earth and its mountains come from? Literally speaking, it's a nonsense.

But many, perhaps most Christians, do believe it happened. The world's most expensive "folly" (in the strict sense of the word; a private, very expensive construction for which there is no conceivable good purpose) is in Kentucky, a supposedly to-scale wooden replica of the Ark. It cost about $100 million to build, over half a dozen years, using 1,000 Amish carpenters, and 100 tons of steel to accommodate building regulations (Noah must have been a pretty fit, even superhuman 600-year-old to have built the same boat). A museum alongside tries to explain what happened to the dinosaurs who were on it, and why they aren't around today. If it wasn't for the damage done by brainwashing children into believing this nonsense it would surely be a very expensive joke.

But when I say it's an incredible story in many ways, I mean it. It's a Hebrew variation on *Gilgamesh* (again, the first story we know of, written down up to a thousand years earlier, with still older origins), which they adapted to fit their beliefs. In *Gilgamesh* Enlil decides to destroy the world because the humans are making too much noise (!) – in the biblical version the writers posit a more wrathful, judgmental God. There are also other Mesopotamian flood stories, which are part of the few hundred flood stories around the world. Why are they so common?

Suggestions are made, for instance, that the Mesopotamian flood stories draw on folk memories of a regional flood when the Mediterranean broke through at the Strait of Bosporus to form the Black Sea, possibly around 7,000 BC. But it's not a necessary hypothesis. Most people lived around water – seas, lakes and rivers. They relied on water for trading routes, fishing and food, as well as water for crops and drinking. Before the era of banks and dams, breakwaters and culverts, flooding was a common, major natural disaster, alongside famine and disease. People believed that there was an ocean of water above the firm canopy of the sky, a few hundred yards up in the air, which at times trickled down as rain through the holes (stars). It's a world where, in the Bible, animals talk, chariots drive across the sky, iron floats. There was a sea of water underneath the ground, which occasionally bubbled up as springs. It was logical reasoning, for the times. Visiting travelers and traders would talk of vast oceans, places of storms and chaos, giant waves and leviathans. With no distinction between the natural and the supernatural, the elders would craft their stories over the campfire, passing them on to the next generation, of how the gods in heaven got angry and sent floods to punish the hubris and wickedness of men, which is why they had to be placated with sacrifice and worshipped.

People processed what happened to them by telling stories. That's how they made sense of events. Noah's Ark is a fascinating insight into that process, into the shared cultural history of the times. I think it's something we still need to do, something we can learn from.

When I occasionally post on online forums about the Bible I'm often accused of not having read it, or making fun of it. But I see the story of Noah's Ark as a fundamental one for us today, more relevant than at any time since it was written. Much as the Hebrews changed the Mesopotamian flood story to suit their times and culture, making it relevant for them, we can do the same today.

God gives Noah warning of what He is going to do:

And God said unto Noah, The end of all flesh is come before me; for the earth is filled with violence through them; and, behold, I will destroy them with the earth.

Like other gods of the time He's human writ large; frequently erratic, jealous and angry. Besides, what did He expect when He expelled Adam and Eve from Eden, cursing the ground to make life hard for them? Thanks and praise? He holds up a mirror to us.

But violence is not just between people, it's what we do to creation. To all life. Only around 4% or so of animal biomass now, for instance, is "wild." The rest of it is domesticated (apart from the 1% or so that we account for), often caged, often in appalling conditions, slaughtered for our use. And at the moment we're exterminating species at a fantastic rate, some say tens of thousands a year, others, hundreds of thousands. Humankind has upped the average extinction rate by a hundred- to a thousand-fold, leading to the kind of mass destruction of life that the planet hasn't seen since the dinosaurs disappeared 65 million years ago, racing us into the Sixth Great Extinction. The history of life over the last few billion years suggests that any one of them could hold the key to the future.

We can be more precise about the warnings we get from

scientists. The overall global temperature has risen 2.12 degrees F. since the late nineteenth century, with the recent years being the warmest, and the amount of carbon dioxide in the atmosphere has increased by 30% over the last 50 years. The temperature of the top 300 feet of the oceans has risen by 0.6 degrees, and acidity of surface waters has increased by 30%. 500 billion tons of ice in Greenland and Antarctica are being lost every year, and glaciers are retreating almost everywhere. Global sea levels rose eight inches in the last century, accelerating every year. Arctic sea ice is declining, extreme weather events involving high temperatures and intense rainfall increasing. Mass migration of species from the equatorial region is already happening.

We don't need God to wipe out life from earth, we're headed to doing a pretty good job of it ourselves, at least as far as we're concerned, in terms of our own survival. Even when you forget about the likelihood of nuclear holocaust (which is a bit like the Garden of Eden scenario; given enough time, somebody is going to eat the fruit, press the button, inevitably). Noah did his best to save what life he could. God is not going to help us. We need to do the same as Noah, he's a role model. The earth itself is an ark, the only one we have.

Perhaps the future is elsewhere, and this planet really is as utterly insignificant as it appears to be. Think of the umpteen trillions of planets there probably are in the universe, and how rapidly consciousness has evolved on earth in the last few million years or so. There may be millions of life forms elsewhere who would see us as barely out of the slime stage. If life is not unique to earth, then, if we survive, we should be preparing ourselves to confront another image of God that is unlike any of our own.

We probably won't know in our lifetimes. We've only just got to the point of being able to tell that there are indeed planets around nearby stars, and that most of the 100 billion stars in our galaxy probably have them. It will probably be decades before we're able to view them through telescopes. But if out of all the billions of planets in the universe in the "goldilocks zone" (right kind of distance from a suitable star) only the earth supports life, then life itself is "religious" in the highest possible sense. Every form of life on the planet relates to every other. Every one of them is "sacred." Our pagan ancestors had it right. Any religion that doesn't see this isn't worth the name, doesn't even match up to a comprehensive dictionary definition of what "religion" is. Looking after the one earth we have is fundamental to good religion.

Noah's Ark is a myth. Myths don't give you facts, they talk about their meaning, and what we should do about them. So I read this story as an urgent message for our times. Ironically, it's Bible-believing Christians who don't see it that way, who make up a lot of the climate-change deniers. Taking the Bible literally, they read it wrong. They miss both the real story and the message.

The earth we abuse and the living things we kill will, in the end, take their revenge; for in exploiting their presence we are diminishing our future.
Marya Mannes (twentieth century AD)

15. How Myths Are Constructed

Truth did not come into the world naked, but it came in types and images. We will not receive it any other way.
Gospel of Philip (third century AD)

Christians tend to think of God, the teaching in the Old Testament about Him, and the Old Testament itself, along with the New, as something unchanging, everlasting, as though one book after another was slotted into the planned frame like pouring concrete into a mold. But it would be more accurate to compare the Bible with the mud houses and towns of ancient times. Every generation extends, develops and rebuilds its houses. After millennia you get "tells" – the mounds rising from the plain – which indicate different layers of occupation, one on the top of the other. In the view of modern scholars the image of God in the Old Testament is built up in the same way. The authors, like all artists, were taking their material and shaping it into new forms. Far from revealing an unchanging God, the Old Testament gives us the clearest example in religious literature of how we change Him according to our needs and desires. The God of the Old Testament is so much richer, complex, multidimensional, simply more *interesting* than the omnipotent, omniscient God that Christian tradition tries to make Him out to be.

I'm going to try and keep the book simple, and as short as I can, so we'll have to cherry-pick; but to begin at the beginning...

If I'm asked, "Do you believe in God?" – it gets complicated pretty early on – "Which God?" The second verse, in the first chapter of the Bible, immediately raises questions. The spirit of God here which sweeps over the waters is female, *ruach*, a Persian word. And in Genesis 1:27 God creates man in his image, "male and female," in other words – hermaphroditic? Creators were often described that way, and that's how the Church Fathers like Clement and Origen saw Him. Bisexuality was normative when the Bible was written, and in the Roman Empire.

Cosmologically-speaking, we know today the account is absurd, with the earth being created on day three, and in Genesis 1:16-17 the sun, moon and all the other stars are placed in the firmament above the earth (and obviously God didn't really "rest" on the seventh day – it's not like He had to put His feet up and read the newspaper, watch some TV; there were several hundred billions of galaxies to create, trillions of stars etc.). Then there's a surprise because in Genesis 2:4 the story starts again with: "These are the generations of the heavens and the earth." Creation here takes one day rather than six. The construction of the earth is different, and man comes before the trees, birds and animals rather than later. Here, God is physical rather than a spirit. He walks in the garden like a man, in the cool of the day, avoiding the heat of the sun, calling out for Adam and Eve because He doesn't know where they are. This second God is a lesser being than the exalted God of the first story, and the details of His creation are correspondingly downgraded. Whereas the first account ends with the creation of humanity, the second begins with it. He doesn't create man in His image, but out of earth, and then plants a garden for the man to live in and look after (the attempt to place it at the headwaters of the four rivers doesn't actually work – they don't meet there). When this God realizes Adam will be lonely, He anaesthetizes him and creates a woman from one of his ribs (the story doesn't explain why we still have pairs of ribs), rather than creating the man and woman together as in the first story. The Hebrew word for Eve is "chava," from "chayim," meaning "life." She is the mother of life, whereas Adam is just earth, or "dirt."

Presumably they're vegetarian, because there's no death in the garden, and God only allows the eating of meat after the

Flood (Genesis 9:1-4). He says to the couple that they will die if they eat the fruit of the tree of knowledge of good and evil (presumably He also says the same to chimpanzees, parakeets etc., though how they're all – particularly Adam and Eve – going to know it's wrong to pick the fruit of the knowledge of good and evil before they know what wrong is, that's not clear). There's a serpent in the garden who urges them to go ahead and eat, saying it won't kill them, "Your eyes shall be opened, and ye shall be as gods, knowing good and evil." The serpent is right. Adam eats the fruit but lives till he's 930. He and Eve realize they are naked and hide.

The serpent is actually one of the most interesting divinities in the Bible. The symbol on the pharaoh's forehead, he's been interpreted by the Church as the Devil tempting Eve, but is one of our oldest religious characters, seen as a god in his own right in many religions, often associated with healing, wisdom and immortality – more significant for most of history than God Himself. He was widely worshipped in Canaan and around the world – and still is; in India for instance the serpent goddess Kundalini is the creative power in the universe, representing the divine feminine, and can be accessed at the base of your spine through Mantra, Tantra, Asanas or meditation. He is still the emblem of medicine, and many traditions are still fascinated by him, like the snake-handling churches of the Ozarks in the USA. Gnostics saw him as a serpent God. Indeed, he was worshipped by the Hebrews, may even have been their main god for centuries – Moses plants a serpent rod in the wilderness so the Hebrews can look on it and be healed (Numbers 21:4-9). The rod is given a name, Nehushtan, and is worshipped by the Israelites (increasingly the term used for the Hebrews as they settled in Canaan) for several hundred years before King Hezekiah breaks it in the eighth century BC (2 Kings 18:4). So in the Genesis 2 and 3 version of the story, written around this time, the serpent, once present in the Temple in Jerusalem as the great Brazen Serpent, is now cursed by God, condemned to crawl on its belly and eat dust (Genesis 3:14).

This second God, as skilled a tailor as He is a surgeon, makes clothing for the two out of animal skins. He feels threatened because the man and woman have upgraded their status to equal His own and drives them away, before they can taste the fruit of the tree of life, leaving angels (junior divinities) with flaming swords at the entrance in the east wall (it's not clear how much of a wall it was, or why Adam and Eve couldn't just nip around to the west and climb back in). This time He's not pleased with what He created (Genesis 6:5-6).

Why many Christian teachers persist in saying there is no contradiction in the Bible is hard to understand. There are hundreds, thousands. Genesis is not unusual. Jewish and Christian scholars have been through all kinds of mental hoops to explain why there are two different stories here. In the early eighteenth century a German minister suggested the obvious reason – they were written by two different people at different times. Chapter 1 is from the "Priestly" source, written around the sixth century BC, when the Israelites called God Elohim, but were developing a more sophisticated idea of Him as spirit, under Persian influence. Its depiction of God as female spirit (1:2) doesn't occur again anywhere else in the Hebrew Bible, but is common in Persian literature. The second version of the story in chapters 2 and 3 comes from a couple of hundred years earlier, around the time of King Hezekiah, from the "Jahwist" source, involving a different God, Yahweh (or, more accurately, YHWH). A third writer combined the two sometime in the fifth century BC – both traditions were by then so well established that neither could be left out.

Both Gods are present in Christianity today. There's the Almighty who created the world and saw it as good, but has remained largely absent since, leaving it to its own devices. There's also the more human, personal God who intervenes, taking sides and answering petitions, bringing the right weather, judging and condemning. It's hard to believe in both at the same time.

But of course this isn't a specifically Christian, or even Jewish/Christian, story. The plot details of both are drawn from Mesopotamian myth, and go back thousands of years earlier to the Sumerian cylinder seals, animist beliefs, and they're found in the rituals and art of ancient people from around the world. Every culture has a creation myth, usually involving deities, humans or human-like figures, and speaking animals or reptiles like the snake in Eden. And the basic theme of a deity creating order (good) out of chaos (bad), shaping the formless void, is common religious currency around the world (the Christian article of faith that God created "ex nihilo," from nothing, didn't emerge till the third century AD).

So... we're already into four versions of divinity in the first few verses of the Bible; the almighty creator of the universe, a female spirit, a physical God walking in a garden who doesn't know what's going on, and a divine snake (there are shades of others too, but let's stop there).

Incidentally, the feminine never wholly disappears. For instance, another female Persian goddess or demon called Lilith hovers offstage. She's mentioned in Isaiah 34:14-15 ("screech owl" in the King James Version is *lilith* in the Hebrew), and survives in a separate Hebrew tradition as Adam's first wife. Her children are referred to as "*lilim*" (Numbers 6:26). Rather than being created from Adam's rib she emerges from his unconsciousness when he is in a deep sleep and wakes him up. In later Gnostic tradition she is seen as independent and even superior to Adam, with her favored sexual position being on top rather than underneath. How different life might have been for billions of Jewish, Christian, and Muslim women if Lilith rather than Eve had made it into Genesis. Just trying to imagine it shows the power these stories still have in our own culture and psyche, however remote the later church teaching may seem.

Goddess worship amongst the Hebrews diminishes as their religion becomes more patriarchal, though passages like Jeremiah 44 suggest that it remained popular, with many worshipping the "Queen of Heaven," generally thought to be Astarte, the goddess of war, fertility and sexual love, the chief goddess of the Phoenicians and Canaanites (Solomon built temples in her honor). The Mother Goddess recovers some prominence amongst the first-century Christians, in non-canonical gospels like the *Gospel of Thomas*, the *Gospel of the Hebrews*, the *Apocryphon of John* and the *Gospel of Philip*. Later, in the Christian tradition, Mary, the mother of Jesus, becomes a goddess in all but name. Many of the Early Church Fathers regarded the Virgin Birth as an unhelpful superstition, and Mary as irrelevant, but the idea grew in importance as the years went by. In AD 431 at the council of Ephesus, the city of the virgin huntress Diana, she was given the title "God-bearer." By the twelfth century she was seen as miraculously conceived by her mother Anne, who became the center of a further cult. The idea of her having sex was so horrible for the Church that bizarre traditions arose, like the theory that she conceived through the ear rather than the vagina. Sex, symbolism, relics, all combine in the Middle Ages to produce beliefs and behavior that we now think of as utterly weird, as in the story that Catherine of Siena had the foreskin of Jesus as her wedding ring.

Her semidivine status strengthens even in modern times. In 1835 Pope Pius IX (a deeply unpleasant, arrogant, anti-democratic and anti-Semitic individual, so unpopular that when he died the people of Rome tried to throw his coffin into the River Tiber) made it an article of faith for all Catholics to believe in the Immaculate Conception (like Jesus, she never sinned). In 1950 Pope Pius XII pushed the nonsense even further with the Bodily Assumption (like Jesus, when she died she was transported bodily direct to heaven), etc. After all, if Jesus' father was divine, why not his mother also? Pope John Paul II promoted the cult of Mary at every opportunity. In 1987 he wrote in *Redemptoris Mater* that Mary "preserved her virginity intact." Not only is she too pure to have had sex with her husband but the process of birth itself is defiling, so Candlemas celebrates her purification from that (despite the fact that the gospels are clear Jesus had at least five brothers and several sisters – Matthew 1:25, Mark 6:3 – some try to interpret these as cousins or stepchildren, but there are no grounds for doing so other than trying to detach Jesus from the messy business of being human).

It may seem extraordinary that in the twentieth century the Church should still be inventing even more ridiculous things to believe, but there you have it (and, to be honest, it's a logical development – after all, if Jesus had been born in the normal way, then he would have been born with Original Sin, and so couldn't have been the Son of God; though then Mary would also have to have been born sinless, rather than simply not sinning during her life, and so on back to Eve – turtles all the way down). In this Mary was probably fulfilling the needs that male-dominated monotheistic religions often fail to satisfy. If it were possible to track the focus of devotion down the centuries she has probably been more significant for the majority of Christians than Jesus.

Anyway, back to the topic – I introduce this Creation myth here because it's fundamental to the way we think today. We have this new masculine (broadly speaking) God who creates heaven and earth, replacing the Mother Goddess who for tens of thousands of years previously *was* heaven and earth. And the Garden of Eden and expulsion of Adam and Eve become the key plank of Christian theology in the centuries after the death of Jesus. Without the Fall, there was no need for Jesus to be sacrificed on the cross to redeem humanity from the Original Sin of eating the fruit of knowledge. So orthodox Christianity is based on this myth. For the Jews, it wasn't really significant. The story is not referred to again in the Old Testament. For them, it illustrates a widely-held belief around many cultures and religions, that in some ways we were better off before we became self-aware. God created man in His spiritual rather than physical image, so humans are in some sense "divine." Expulsion from the Garden is simply a lesson that humans, despite their divine spark, have to live with the consequences of their decisions, in a way that other animals don't. And many early Christians saw Jesus as coming to remind us of our divine nature, not to save us from our sinful one.

There were no poor and no rich; there was no need to labor, because all that me required was obtained by the power of will; the chief virtue was the abandonment of all worldly desires. The Krita Yuga was without disease; there was no lessening with the years; there was no hatred or vanity, or evil thought, no sorrow, no fear. All mankind could attain to supreme blessedness.
Mahabharata

16. From Mother God To Father God

Buy the truth and sell it not.
Proverbs 23:23 (c. fifth century BC)

To move from myth to ethnoarchaeology – there may only have been a few small family groups of Homo sapiens, initially – DNA samples suggest that all people alive today descend from no more than half a dozen women. Numbers would have fluctuated over the years with the climate. Around 100,000 years ago the Ice Age caused North Africa to become colder and drier, and water levels fell, opening up land bridges. After a few previous abortive attempts, around 60,000 years ago our ancestors started to spread out into the wider world, as previous species of Homo had done before them. Geneticists think there may only have been 1-10,000 of them. Today we would certainly be classifying them as an "endangered" species. But they were as rational, intelligent, as superstitious as we are, probably taller than us and healthier, with paint on their faces, spears in their hands, and spirits in their heads. Spirits were everywhere. The world was alive for them, animate. In many indigenous languages today more words are verbs rather than nouns. Everything has its own spirit, its own identity. A "beach" need not be a noun, but what happens when water meets sand. Life was a process, rather than a collection of "things." Which, after all, is the way we know things are – the sand on the beach is ground rock, which was once magma in a volcano, which was once the dust of exploding stars. They were in tune with the rhythms of nature, reading its signs to a degree almost incomprehensible to us today.

They sat around the fire at night wondering where we came from, imagining better futures, even afterlives, being reunited with their ancestors; interpreting dreams, telling fantastical stories with endless variations and subplots; preparing for worse times, hoping for better. They painted the animals that supported them in ochre on the cave walls, adding their handprints, developing rituals to control the movements of their prey. They crafted works that demonstrated their mastery of creation, finding meaning, triumphing over the here and now, over the uncertainties of short lives, leaving something for their descendants to remember them by, and something to take with them to the next life. As Picasso reportedly said when visiting the caves at Lascaux – "we've learned nothing." They saw life as good, but were aware of its dangers. They worshipped the spirits of life and death, leaving offerings to placate them, to ask for protection from the wolves and bears, from famine and flood, thunder and lightning. As Petronius, a Roman courtier almost contemporary with Jesus, puts it – "It is fear that first brought gods into the world." Religion was the original one-stop shop for all of life's questions.

Were they cooperative or aggressive? Would they welcome a stranger, or kill them? Without a time machine, we don't know. Opinion is divided. A rough consensus would be that in Paleolithic hunter-gathering times there would have been little to fight over, and the population density was too low. Each life was likely to have been valuable. There's some evidence that they supported the disabled, even if they couldn't contribute to the survival of the group. They were almost certainly egalitarian, with few individual possessions – they had to carry everything with them as they moved.

Some say that large-scale violence probably didn't come till later, when tribes had to compete over resources and defend land. There's evidence of brutal massacres from around 10,000 years ago. Though then there's the period of old civilization in Europe, from around 6,000 to 2,000 BC – the incredible temples in Malta, the stone circles and graves like Stonehenge, Newgrange, Skara Brae, Carnac – these were built over generations, drawing in labor from tens, hundreds of miles around, across tribes –

through cooperation rather than coercion. What is beyond doubt is that war became more frequent – indeed, even a defining characteristic of life – as city and nation states grew.

It's the age-old question – are we good or bad? It's one of the oldest debates, on the nature of humanity. Did we need civilization to temper our inherent brutality and propensity to kill, or is it the organized structures and accumulated wealth of civilizations that continually lead us to war? What do we think of ourselves, today? Human nature hasn't changed in the last thousand or two generations. Maybe it's down to us as societies to decide which we want to be.

The first wanderers from Africa weren't particularly aiming to get anywhere – they had no maps, and moved on average a mile a year, a few dozen miles per generation, following opportunities and food, occasionally coming into contact with earlier species of Homo, who had left Africa hundreds of thousands of years earlier – fighting them, interbreeding, or both (around 2% of DNA in non-African populations today is inherited from Homo neanderthalensis). As they spread, even physical characteristics changed, over time – different facial structure, eyes, different digestive systems (the ability to drink milk into adulthood is confined to a minority of the world's population whose ancestors lived by dairy farming), different color skin, like "white," in some northern areas (less sunlight, so lighter skin allows you to absorb more vitamin D – and might also make you more prone to cancer; everything in evolution is a trade-off). As they reached different parts of the globe their societies, cultures and beliefs also diverged, naturally. Worshipping a sun god doesn't make the same kind of sense in Alaska as in Mexico. Much as Christianity would look different if the Romans had executed criminals rather than crucifying them – could we have worshipped a headless Jesus, like Chinnamasta is worshipped in India or Xingtian in China? Could the resurrection still have happened, if Jesus didn't have a head, rather than just holes in his feet and a wound in his side? Religions are shaped by geography as well as culture and biology. But the oldest concept we find of God all around the world is as a prodigiously fertile Mother. Obviously... if you want to think of God in terms of gender, seeing Her as Mother makes better sense than Father. Males don't have wombs; and biologically speaking, we now know that at conception the female chromosome is produced first, the male chromosome is added later (the Genesis story gets it the wrong way around; Eve should have been created first). So the world was seen as the Great Mother, the womb of everything, embracing the heavens, earth and underworld, life and death. Rain – essential to life – dropped from her breasts, the clouds. She gave her body, the earth, to feed the crops. As Goddess of the underworld she sent the spring and rivers.

Fertility symbols (Venuses) go back at least 30,000 years (about 1,500 generations), one figurine (Berekhat Ram) has even been claimed as 250,000 years old (about 12,000 generations). But despite the prominence of the Virgin Mary and the resurgence of the goddess in New Age literature today most of us are more familiar with the idea of God as Father. Historians generally agree, in very broad outline, that this concept developed as societies became more complex and hierarchical, with stronger authority figures ruling them. Around 12,000 BC the earth's weather warmed by several degrees, and the population exploded. Small family units turned into bands of 50-100. Larger numbers probably led to over-hunting, and food shortages. Some animals were domesticated, and some hunter-gatherers changed into pastoral nomads, shepherding their food source around with them in the form of livestock, rather than having to search for it afresh every day. Some, perhaps first around the Caucasus, or more widely around the Middle East, figured how to "plant" food in the ground, domesticating wheat, leading to crops, around which grew villages, bringing the gods of the seasons and weather. The wild plants and animals of the area were particularly suited to this, but over the next couple of thousand years broadly the same social, economic and religious patterns developed all around the world, from Peru to New Guinea.

Out of the villages, came towns. Farmers pushed out foragers. Property was handed down through the generations, leading to ancestor cults. Cities developed, which had to be protected. The biblical Jericho was surrounded with a rampart 12,000 years ago. They enabled the accumulation of wealth and power, leading to kingship, class, rule and more elaborate fortifications, and to the increasing division of labor, specialized functions, and to male dominance. "Natural" religion gave way to "organized" religion. It bound larger groups together, creating rituals and ceremonies to strengthen allegiance to the tribe. The more heartfelt the devotion, the stronger and hence safer the group. Kings came to be seen either as gods (in Egypt) or as ruling by divine right (in Mesopotamia). Their sons became sons of god. Power, class, and divinity became inextricably linked, to the degree that it's only in the last couple of centuries that we've managed to separate them in our thinking (and in practice, through various revolutions in Europe).

As cities enlarged the extent of land and people under their control, enabled by the horse and wheel to plunder more widely, and turned into states of a million or so people, more complex hierarchies of gods emerged to reflect increasing power. Wealth increasingly became concentrated in the hands of a few. With diets being less varied, and many being worked to death, average height decreased. Disease, due to living in close proximity to more domesticated animals, began to spread (a reason why, when, several thousand years later, the Europeans spread around the globe, they carried infectious disease with them, and contaminated the indigenous peoples, rather than the other way around – horses for instance are easier to domesticate than zebras, wolves easier than jackals). Hard work, extreme inequality and constant war became the new normal. With advancing civilization kings turned into emperors, leading to the idea in very recent times, 3,000 to 5,000 years ago, of henotheism – one god holding absolute power over the others. Competing, violent gods began to reflect the politics of the new warring empires. So sky gods became more powerful. The first male sky god that we know of is Dyaus Pitar of the Hindu *Vedas*, which through various incarnations ended up as the Greek Zeus and Roman Jupiter and our own "Father in heaven" in Latin – Deus (all European and Semitic languages – with the exception of Basque – can be traced back to a common Proto-Indo-European language that survives in archaic Sanskrit).

This took thousands of years, and the process was never complete – the Egyptian Isis, for instance, the universal Mother Goddess, was worshipped in temples all over the Roman Empire. But as we lost a sense of interconnectedness with the earth it lost its sacred nature. Rather than being the Mother of life, the Garden of Eden, it became a place of exile; *cursed is the ground for thy sake; in sorrow shalt thou eat of it all the days of the life* (Genesis 3:17). Divinity was pushed up into the heavens. Spirits of nature became angels in the sky. The process was accelerated when around 5,000 years ago, maybe much earlier, words began to be translated into writing. Writing has been described as the second most important thing that's happened on the planet, the first time since the arrival of DNA that information could be stored and retrieved. We could not only reflect on our thoughts, but build on those of others. We developed a "written culture." For the first half a millennia, it was mostly used by kings and priests to count and track their wealth and slaves. But over time, like data capture and digital surveillance today, it massively increased the power of the elite, to rule. Empires were built on the ability to send written commands, rather than having to travel hundreds or thousands of miles personally to persuade someone. But people found new uses for it – by 2500 BC the Egyptians had libraries; with stories, poetry, prayers, religious plays, and books on medicine, mathematics, along with census lists and tax registers. A few hundred miles away in Sumeria, a couple of centuries earlier, books of temple hymns are credited to the first named author in literature, a woman named Enheduana. And after tens, hundreds of millennia of expressing religious insight through dreams, trance, divination, signs and singing, people began to shape the words describing our experience of spirit into pictures, then letters. Put religion and writing together and you have an extraordinarily powerful new force in shaping the way we think and live. Speech is transient, fleeting. But if it can be put on papyrus, it has power, it need never "pass away," as the Bible puts it. If it was written down, it was beyond debate, beyond argument, it was "true" (one reason why Socrates, for instance, one of the founders of Western philosophy, and the first moral philosopher, was suspicious of it, and didn't write anything down himself – much better to converse back and forth to come to an understanding of the truth rather than just read one side of the story). Most Christians and Muslims still think this way, about the Bible or the *Qur'an*. Writing made possible the idea of a single god, with an enforceable code (as in the stone tablets of the Ten Commandments), rather than a plurality of divinities for different people. Instead of gods being everywhere, the spirits of different places, with limited influence, living in an eternal present, they could be given a "story" with a beginning and end. Religion got itself a "history"; the world is imperfect because God has a plan which has still to come to fruition. The story could even be given a sacred status, and handed down through the generations as "The Word of God." Judaism, Christianity, Islam – they would not exist without writing. Their followers are, literally, all "People of the Book."

This is nowhere expressed better than in Genesis, the world's most influential story. For tens, hundreds of thousands of years we understood that we share this earth with other living things, plants and animals, and that we're all part of the web of life. But no, there's this new understanding, much like kings and emperors have power over people, people are given dominion by God over nature. It's there for our use. We're no longer wandering the earth as nomads, following the shorelines and rivers and the weather, foraging for what we can get. We should have more, indeed, once upon a time we used to have it – with everything under our control, everything knowing its place, the perfect garden, with no need to work, food on tap.

Like the many other stories of the region which they draw on, the Genesis stories were revolutionary in their time. They reflected this new, widespread understanding around the world that humans could shape nature as they wanted. So God Himself becomes vaguely human, rather than a force of nature, or of place. We began to believe that we could talk to God directly, and so also of course that He could talk back. He started to communicate through words of power and truth rather than visible manifestations on earth – extremes of weather, or graven statues. The Hebrews, Greeks, Hindus (and most people) all came to believe that gods and people were related. So naturally they had the same desires and were often visiting the earth from the sky or underworld, particularly for extra sex. They raped, kidnapped or fell in love (or did all three) with the prettiest girls. The children of such crossbreeding were usually male, often larger and stronger than other children. In Genesis 6:2-4, for example, the sons of God copulate with the daughters of earth to produce giants. Blue eyes, representing the sky, were also a common feature of these children. In Hindu stories the children of such partnerships could be blue all over.

The majority of the world's population today believe that God exclusively revealed Himself to humankind in written words of different scriptures. God wrote them Himself, or communicated them to authors so directly that even if the authors wrote in their own styles they couldn't say anything He didn't want them to say. It's similar to people believing today that spirits communicate through channeling, automatic writing, or Ouija boards.

"Revelation" has nothing to do with scripture as such. It best describes the moments of collective inspiration, expressed in particular texts, when new insights shift our common perspective. The point of revelations, much like scientific discoveries, is that they are always being improved upon. The most conservative positions on the Bible or the Church are simply the most conservative ones in society. There's nothing necessarily "religious" or "Christian" about them. Indeed Christians often take the low moral ground, reading the Bible through the lens of the social prejudices of the time. Or worse – by taking the Bible literally. As late as 1866 the Vatican defended slavery as part of natural and divine law. The conservative church is often a generation behind the rest of society in its moral position, a couple of generations behind its humanist opponents. You see the same happening today with disputes over how to treat LGBT people, whether women can be priests and have authority over men, what control can they have over their bodies – though sections of the Church at least have reluctantly shifted their position more than in Islam.

But it could have been worse. The trouble is, the early Old Testament reflects the primitive social thinking of a tribal nomadic people of 3,000 years ago. They had the same kind of loves and hates as us; and like us they were often paranoid, vicious, fearful and ignorant. Carrying out the 600 plus laws of the books of Moses would involve murdering or casting out most people with a job in a modern society, not just homosexuals (though verses taken to apply to this are far more ambiguous than most modern readings suggest – the Bible says nothing about faithful, monogamous, same-sex relationships) and adulterers, or women who have sex before marriage (Deuteronomy 22:13-21 – of course the same doesn't apply to men), but hairdressers

(Leviticus 19:27), farmers (Leviticus 19:19), restaurateurs (Leviticus 11:10), footballers (Leviticus 11:6-8), bankers, and dozens of others – today there would be no one left to throw the stones. I'm not suggesting the Laws of Moses are uniquely bad, they're paralleled in the *Laws of Manu* in Hinduism, and reflect the concerns and attitudes of many of their contemporaries. But they're not for today. If you want to take scripture as infallible rather than think the issues through, then join the Taliban. Even better, the Khmer Rouge. Pol Pot and the horrors of the Cambodian killing fields would be the logical result of taking the Bible literally.

Revelations are the aberration of faith; they are an amusement that spoils simplicity in relation to God. They distract the soul and makes it swerve from its directness in relation to God. Special illuminations, auditions, prophecies and the rest are marks of weakness in a soul that cannot support the assaults of temptation or of anxiety about the future and God's judgement upon it.
J. J. Olier (seventeenth century AD)

17. The Shepherds' God

Now religion in the hands of self, or corrupt nature, serves only to discover vices of a worse kind than in nature left to itself. Hence are all the passions of religious men, which burn in a worse flame than passions only employed about worldly matters; pride, self-exaltation, hatred and persecution, under a cloak of religious zeal, will sanctify actions which nature, left to itself, would be ashamed to own.

William Law (eighteenth century AD)

We degrade the Old Testament by ascribing it to divine dictation, to some form of magic. At the human level it's fascinating enough. It's the most extraordinary record in world literature of a single people's experience and understanding of God as it changes over a millennium. It records the transition from a local god on earth – a transactional religion where sufficient sacrifice of food and life is reciprocated by the god's protection – through a savage warrior God (there are a thousand verses describing his violent actions) to a universal God of love, worshipped in the heart and mind. It plumbs the heights and depths of our experience of life, of pleasure and pain, happiness and despair. That's why it's still worth reading. So if you find the Bible inspiring try paying the same kind of attention to other sacred scriptures. If you find it boring or irrelevant, just turn it around in your head. Think of it as a "work in progress," maybe 10% revelation, 90% description and error. We can read it to learn how the Hebrews got God wrong, not right, and how they learned along the way from their mistakes.

But reading the Old Testament today is not easy. The cultural gap between us and the nomadic Hebrews is vast. Most Christians find it hard enough to relate to the faith of Muslims, who worship the same single God, though under a different name, and live in the same century, the same city. Another difficulty is that the events it purports to describe were written down half a millennia or more after they maybe happened.

For instance, we monotheists (Jews, Christians, Muslims) date our understanding of the one God back to Abraham, a Hebrew. The Hebrews, *Habiru*, were probably not a defined race. The term has connotations of mercenary, robber. Some Old Testament specialists say Abraham was a Chaldean shepherd who left Ur in Mesopotamia roughly around 1400 BC (there are no dates in the Bible; though the Hebrews did have a calendar – during the Exile they adopted the Babylonian months – but they seemed to have relied more on ancestral lists, which are often repeated with many variations, changed to suit different audiences). Others say he could have been a tribal chieftain of the Amorite people, or a Canaanite holy man, or a literary invention of many centuries later. A few biblical scholars say the Hebrews and Israelites were entirely separate peoples. The general consensus is that they were a breakaway Canaanite group, with the earliest speaking that language, following its customs and religion, who moved from the coastal cities into the poorer hill country of the Cis-Jordan.

Whichever... there are definitive 500-1,000 page books on the history of civilization being published nowadays without the Hebrews/Israelites/Jews even being mentioned, they were insignificant at the time. Linking the two great civilizations of Mesopotamia and Egypt back in the second millennium BC was the Fertile Crescent – a band of habitable land that stretched in a great arc from the Tigris and Euphrates Rivers, up to what is now south Turkey, and down the coast to Egypt, skirting the Arabian desert. In those days, as its name suggests, this land was full of fertile valleys and wooded hills, though even back then over-irrigation was reducing yields in the river valleys of Persia. Further deforestation and overgrazing by goats has turned it into the barren landscape that much of it is today.

This is where the Bible stories take place. They're based on journeys around this arc. To simplify enormously (and assuming these people existed, more on that later), based on the biblical texts, and the few scraps of evidence we can pick up from elsewhere – Abraham left Ur, in Mesopotamia, down in the right-hand side of the Fertile Crescent, to the left-hand side, to Canaan/Palestine, around 1400 BC. His immediate descendants moved further on into Egypt, because they were starving. A few hundred years later, they managed to leave Egypt, and reoccupied or conquered Canaan. Over a period of time (Chronicles, Judges, Kings) they established the nation of Israel, which could have been a significant regional player for a century or so. But in the sixth century BC it was destroyed, and the people were forcibly transplanted back to the other end of the Fertile Crescent, in Babylon. In the fourth century BC, a group (under Nehemiah) was allowed to return, to Canaan. So much of the story of this book – it's set in that landscape, swinging back and forth, like a pendulum, through different cultures and languages, crossing several thousand miles each time (if you follow the trade routes available back then rather than the distance between airports).

We'll never know if Abraham was a real person or not, there simply isn't enough information. Dates for his proposed life vary over a 1,000-year period, the distance between us and the Norman conquest of England, and his historical existence as an individual is no more certain than that of King Arthur and his Knights of the Round Table.

But the interesting thing about Abraham's story is what it tells about the gods of a pre-urban, pre-agricultural society of nomadic people. Their god doesn't even have a clear name of his own. English translations gloss over the different names of God as "God" or "Lord." But Abraham's god is described in the Hebrew of the Old Testament as El, with variations such as El Elyon, El Olam, El Shaddai, El Berit. He's the name of the highest god of the Canaanites, and present in many Middle Eastern religions.

This is why words beginning or ending in "el" in the Bible and the Middle East are so common. The most obvious of course is "Israel" itself, which some scholars think is a compound of the Egyptian gods Isis and Ra with El, others prefer "strength of El," others think it's "wrestled with God," referring to Jacob's night-long fight with Him in Genesis 32:24 (it's an interesting episode; Jacob defeats God, and it probably originates from an early tale of the moon god defeating the sun god, which is why it has to end at daybreak, so the sun can rise; wrestling matches between gods also occur in Babylonian and Hindu mythology).

El is also referred to over 1,500 times in the Old Testament in the plural as "Elohim." He is to the elohim something like the fairy king is to the fairies; for them the main god among many. He's not special to Abraham, He's not significantly different from the gods of his neighbors. He speaks in dreams to local kings as well as to Abraham and Jacob. He's recognized as a god by the pagan priest Melchizedek (Genesis 14:18-24) whose own god Abraham also recognizes. He's not all-powerful (Genesis 19:22). Like the other gods in a region where elder sons became a threat to the father, He favored younger sons (such as Abel, Isaac, Jacob, Joseph, David, in the various Bible stories).

He's a low-maintenance kind of god, a nomad's god, carried around with the luggage, of the kind Rachel could steal from Laban (Genesis 31:17-35) and hide in the camel's saddle, after Jacob has cheated him of cattle. He doesn't demand temples or priests. He's for pastoralists, advising on the direction of travel, where to graze the flocks, on domestic issues, family relationships. He needs feeding and honoring like any other guest. He's the kind of god that has been around for tens of millennia, and still is in many parts of the world. He still plays a large part in the lives of Christians, who ask him for advice and confirmation on their decisions in life, such as where to live, who to marry, and to intervene on their behalf or that of others. He also of course helps with the main issue in the lives of the people of biblical times, when crops were uncertain and infant mortality rates high, that of fertility, promising successful reproduction – an aspect of His powers that we've rather forgotten about today. Indeed He's an unusually powerful fertility god: though Abraham is childless from his seed will come a great nation (Genesis 12:2). It's such an ambitious promise (particularly as he and Sarah are apparently over 90) that Abraham wants guarantees. So they bind themselves together in a covenant, in much the same way as people do in a legal document (Genesis 17:1-14). The covenant is confirmed in the act of circumcision. This was a common practice in the Middle East, particularly with the Assyrians, and all over the world, from Pacific islanders to Aztecs. Its origins are uncertain, but probably have to do with the sacrifice of the first piece of flesh after copulation to insure good growth for the next year's crops.

If you want to take Abraham literally, as a historical figure, he's not an attractive character. He's in the old tradition of the trickster, even twisting fate and his god to his advantage. He prostitutes his wife (who is also his half-sister) "at every place, whither we shall come" (Genesis 12:11-20; 20:1-18), much to the disgust of his hosts when they find out that the two are married (he also has two slave-wives, Hagar and Keturah). Even by the Bible's own account, the moral standards of neighboring tribes are frequently better than those of the Hebrews. This doesn't seem to worry El, who is not a "moral" god in the sense that we understand God and morality today. He backs Abraham up by sending plagues and threatening death to those he has deceived, whilst rewarding Abraham's pimping with prosperity.

Up to this point Abraham has been making reasonable arrangements with his neighbors, like taking his herds in a different direction from his nephew, Lot, to avoid conflict over grazing. But now he wants more. El promises Abraham and his descendants the land of Canaan, but doesn't ask the people in Canaan to leave the land first, so setting the scene for thousands of years of trouble, a conflict that still makes the news every year.

Abraham becomes the shepherd's nightmare, the guy who won't cooperate, who wants it all for himself. He worships a god who reflects his own interests rather than the powers of nature, common to the time, that affect everyone alike. El becomes the god of Abraham alone, "mine," a tribal god who even divides families down the middle: "Yet I loved Jacob, and I hated Esau" (Malachi 1:2-3). He represents the worst kind of religion, where personal material or spiritual gain come above common decency, morality, even parental instinct. A god of individual greed rather than collective responsibility. His spiritual followers today are the Muslim terrorists, Jewish Zionists, Christian fundamentalists, American evangelicals, who all believe in the same god of Abraham, believe they have his ear, and (like Abraham himself) put a higher value on their creed, or their country, or their money, than the lives of children.

Not many people today read the Abraham story in this way, though many of the early Christians did (see chapter 34). Many Jews take it literally: the story is what it says it is. God gave Abraham this land, they are his descendants, so the land is theirs. God says so. Some Christians today agree with this and support the US Government in its $4 billion a year subsidy of the Israeli army. Some Christians look for other meanings, more suitable to their own times and circumstances. The Dutch Boers for instance, trekking into the African interior, saw it as a story for them: God was giving them the land they saw before them. From this and other Bible passages the Dutch Reformed Church developed the doctrine of apartheid.

More liberal Christians today (increasingly few, in the decades-long dumbing down of Christianity in the popular mind) look for less aggressive interpretations. For instance, they might say, Abraham wasn't really a bad guy. And El wasn't really going to let him cut his son's throat, whatever his wife

Sarah thought about it. The story isn't to be taken literally, it represents Abraham's understanding of a new idea of God, one who *doesn't* demand human sacrifice, at least, not any longer. God identifies with the victim, not the oppressors. And in the New Testament it's clear that God now cares for all people, not just the Hebrews, and later He's seen as even offering His own Son as the scapegoat for the sins of humankind.

We all read the idea of God that we want to believe in back into the text. All we know for sure is that the three great monotheistic religions trace their history (and in the case of Jews and Muslims their race) back to Abraham. If he existed, he was the most influential person in history. No conflict has been so enduring and bitter as the one the Bible credits him with starting. No idea in history has been as powerful as the one that the one God of the entire universe will spend "time" on your personal affairs, to your advantage, intervening in the processes of life on earth for your benefit. Over half the people in the world today (Jews, Christians, Muslims) believe in Abraham's new personal God. They read the promises to Abraham as applicable to them, whether it's of land, wealth, or salvation.

With Abraham's more immediate descendants the scene shifts from Canaan to Egypt for the great story of the Exodus.

Those who talk of the Bible as "a monument of English prose" are merely admiring it as a monument over the grave of Christianity.
T. S. Eliot (twentieth century AD)

18. The Warriors' God

O daughter of Babylon, who art to be destroyed; happy shall he be that rewardeth thee as thou hast served us. Happy shall he be, that taketh and dasheth thy little ones against the stones.
Psalm 137:8-9 (c. sixth century BC)

The most interesting question in the Old Testament, and perhaps in Christianity as a whole, given the significance of the kind of God we believe in, is: "How exactly does the minor but ambitious tribal El turn into the ferocious and ruthless battle-leader Yahweh, who then becomes the moral and almighty universal God?"

("Yahweh" is a guess, as biblical Hebrew has no vowels; "Jehovah" is also common, and "J" is a prevalent letter – Jacob, Jews, Jerusalem, Jesus, Joshua, etc. – but "J" isn't a sound that Hebrew contains. Some scholars now prefer "Yahowah," and, in Hebrew, Jesus would probably be more accurately translated as "Yehoshua," or, in everyday language, "Yaho." Though it's hard to see that catching on – "I have a personal relationship with Yaho" – doesn't quite have the same ring to it. The Syrian Christian church, perhaps the oldest, tends to preserve the Aramaic form of Jesus – "Isho.")

Like the cunning and commanding Aeneas in the *Aeneid*, the equivalent Exodus story for the Romans, Moses dominates the Exodus. Again, whether he actually existed, whether the Hebrews were ever in Egypt, are much disputed, with a vast literature on the subject. The main problem is that, apart from the Old Testament, there is no mention of the Hebrews in the hundreds of thousands of clay tablet records of the period, or any evidence of them in the millions of archaeological sites around the main rivers like the Nile, Euphrates and Tigris. The population of Egypt at the time was around three to four million.

Their records were so detailed and precise we know of *single* slaves escaping from their masters. The biblical account numbers the Hebrews as between one and two million (by the time you count in women, children, etc.). It's inconceivable that such a population movement could have happened without a recorded trace in Egypt or any of the neighboring countries (let alone the murderous plagues, and the loss of the pharaoh and his army, which would have threatened the very survival of Egyptian society). There's no sign of them in Sinai, just over a hundred miles wide (if the biblical numbers are correct the front of the column would have left Sinai before the rear entered it), and back then a virtually unpopulated desert region, though traces of Bedouin encampments survive from 5000 BC, well before the Exodus. Spending 40 years there (another magical number) is nonsense. It's folklore. And when it comes to something like the stone tablets of the Ten Commandments – nobody has ever seen them (what we usually think of as the "Ten Commandments," those in Exodus 20, are not described as such; that honor is given to the different commandments in Exodus 34:1-28, like "Thou shall not seethe a kid in its mother's milk"). And would an omnipotent God really write them on stone using His (callused?) finger (Deuteronomy 9:10)? In contrast, the commandments of Hammurabi, on which they draw, inscribed half a millennia or so earlier on black basalt, you can see in the Louvre Museum in Paris.

Some Christian scholars say there could be a factual basis for the stories, maybe there was a series of such migrations out of Egypt over a period of centuries, which are conflated or most vividly expressed in this particular story, though none would claim it happened as described. But virtually all serious historians say it never happened. The trouble is, whereas the Garden of Eden is easy to treat as myth, the Exodus is claimed as history and is the base of what follows, which means that the Bible and *Qur'an* are founded on myth. But, like with Abraham, what we're interested in here is not so much whether or not the stories actually happened, but what they tell us about the God the Hebrews believed in.

Moses sees God differently from Abraham. He may even be a different God altogether. El has now taken on the majesty of the higher gods – the ones like Zeus who the Greeks believed would burn you into ashes if you saw his true form. Whereas El would pop in for supper with Abraham, dirty and hungry (Genesis 18:4-8) and wrestle all night with Jacob (Genesis 32:22-32), Moses has to wear a veil so that his compatriots aren't blinded by the glory of God reflected in His face, after he's caught a glimpse of His backside (Exodus 33:18-23).

Where did this new powerful God come from? If the Hebrews were in Egypt it was probably between 1400 and 1200 BC. They could have been one of many enslaved populations. The first mention of Israel comes in 1209 BC, when the pharaoh left the land "wasted." During this period the Egyptians had developed the idea of one all-powerful Sun God to reflect the glory of the pharaohs – the earliest recorded monotheistic religion. Aton, the Creator of the Universe, was worshipped as the only God by Amenhotep IV around the year 1360 BC. Sigmund Freud popularized the theory that the Hebrews plagiarized the one Supreme Being from the Egyptians, since developed by scholars into the theory that the Hebrews were a group of Aton worshippers fleeing the persecution that followed Amenhotep's death.

Another theory is that Moses adopted Him in some form from the polar opposite, the moon god worshipped by the Midianites, another of the many nomadic tribes in the region. Moses lived most of his life with them and married the daughter of the high priest (Exodus 2:16-3:1). (It's a bit troubling that then, when he led the Hebrews out of Egypt, he was so keen to slaughter all the Midianites, except for the virgins – but perhaps he hadn't got on well with his father-in-law.) There are many other theories.

Alternatively, more conservative scholars suggest that after a virtual absence from hominid history for a few million years or so God decided the time was right to enter the human stage. At least in a small kind of way, for setting fire to a bush in the desert to catch the attention of Moses so He could speak to him, an outcast from a tribe no one else had heard of or bothered to mention.

But whoever He is, it's not yet the Almighty we're familiar with today. Some of the miracles that God does through Moses, the pharaoh's magicians can also do (Exodus 7:8-13). It's a question of degree, not nature, more a question of: "I'm a better magician than you are" – so at God's command Aaron turns his staff into a snake, but then so do pharaoh's magicians (the same happens centuries later with Elijah; he can call down fire from heaven, the priests of Baal can't, so they can be killed). And He doesn't seem all that familiar or friendly to the Hebrews either. Moses' view of God seems to be more one of war and death than fertility and life, the more common kind of deity, represented by the bull of their ancestors, which they believed had delivered them from Egypt (Exodus 32:4; translated into English in Genesis 49:24 as "the mighty God of Jacob"; bull worship continues through the centuries in the Northern Kingdom of Israel – 1 Kings 12:28; divine bulls, representing morality, are a common feature of ancient religions, traces of which can still be seen today in the bullrings of Spain). The Hebrews are so uncertain of this new God which Moses has laid on them that Yahweh wants to massacre them all for their lack of commitment, sparing Moses alone (Exodus 32:9-10), but Moses persuades Him to change His mind because it would encourage their joint enemies, the Egyptians. It's hard to see where Moses stops and Yahweh begins. Yahweh repents, but Moses then acts on His behalf, calling on his elite guard, the loyal sons of Levi, to "slay every man his brother, and every man his companion, and every man his neighbor" (Exodus 32:27), which they do, killing 3,000.

The Book of Leviticus follows Exodus as an extensive interlude, with rules largely about what foods are "clean" to eat, and what are "unclean." They're pointless, do not follow any dietary or health logic, and no Christians follow them today. They were just a means for the priests to browbeat the people. It's a common development. In the same period the Hindus obsessed to an even greater degree with correct daily performance for different castes, as represented in the *Laws of Manu*. The Egyptians obsessed with the rituals to take the soul on its afterlife journey, following the *Book of the Dead*. Today the Church obsesses in the same kind of way over sex – marriage, homosexuality and the place of women – all of which the Bible largely ignores. Nothing gets the Church as worked up as issues relating to transgender. Marriage for the Hebrews tended to be confined to the family, to keep property intact – a cousin was ideal; Leviticus 18 prohibits a number of sexual relationships, though in practice many of them happen in the Bible without undue comment, as with Abraham and his half-sibling wife. But sex in general, with multiple wives, concubines (sex slaves) was encouraged – numbers of children (and most probably died in the first couple of years) were needed to pick crops and fight. The writers and compilers of the Old Testament would have been mystified by Christianity today, and not seen that they had anything in common.

The Book of Numbers picks up the thread of the story. After a year at Mount Sinai, the Hebrews set out again with their "Ark," in which God is now living, having left His mountain home. The people soon complain about the catering that God and Moses provide, but are answered with plagues; dissent is silenced with leprosy. They get to Canaan but spies sent out to survey the land come back disheartened because of the military strength of the people living there. God wants to destroy the people yet again for their lack of faith but Moses reminds Him about how jubilant their enemies would be, so God sends another plague instead.

The Hebrews realize they've saddled themselves with a

tyrant-priest, and rebel. Nomadic tribes, after all, tend to govern themselves through consultation and kinship ties. One of the world's first recorded attempts at participatory government ends in mass-murder when the earth opens and swallows the leaders with their women and children, taking them all down into Sheol (the underground – there's no conception yet of heaven and hell). The morning after, there's another rebellion, leaving 14,700 dead (Numbers 16). Further rebellions and plagues follow: 24,000 are killed when some of the men start having sex with the local Moabite women (Numbers 25:1-15). The deaths only stop when an offending couple are caught in the act and speared through. The ringleaders are rounded up and hanged in the sun.

The climax of Numbers comes in chapter 31. This may be the first example in writing and practice of the "holy war" ideology, later to become institutionalized in Islam as one aspect of Jihad, and to find expression in Christianity through the Crusades. Some detailed instructions on how to wage such a war are given, including ritual cleansing before battle (Joshua 3:5); abstinence from sex (2 Samuel 11:11); rules of engagement are provided in Deuteronomy 20 – as in, regarding local tribes, "thou shalt save alive nothing that breatheth," but for "very far off cities of other nations" – "smite every male... But the women, and the little ones, and the cattle... shalt thou take unto thyself." There was probably more in The Book of the Wars of Yahweh, referred to in Numbers 21:14, but this has been lost (there are many books referenced in the Old Testament that have been lost to history, like the Book of Jasher, the Book of Shemaiah the Prophet, Visions of Iddo the Seer, etc. There are also books that were once taken as canonical but now aren't, like The Book of Jubilees, The Book of Noah and The Book of Giants – an expansion of the biblical narrative on giants in Genesis 6:1-4).

The Hebrews have been unfaithful again – doubly so, first with the Midianite women and then being attracted to worshipping their competing tribal God, Peor. So they get the plague, but blame the Midianites for leading them astray. (As a footnote, most gods around this time were gods of "place," rather than "people," and many lived on mountaintops. Peor is named after Mount Peor – or vice versa. It's not clear where the Hebrews thought their new God lived – "Deuteronomist" says Mount Horeb, the mountain of the sun; the other main thread of the Old Testament – the "Priestly Source" – says Mount Sinai, which is probably named after the Sumerian goddess of the moon, Sin.)

Anyway, the Lord, through Moses, instructs the Israelites to slay all the Midianites. They kill all the males, but Moses is angry with them for sparing the rest, so he orders them to go back and murder all the boys and women, except for the virgins, 32,000 of them, who no doubt they can keep for rape (Numbers 31:15-18) – see for instance Deuteronomy 21:10-13; 22:28-29, etc.; God encourages kidnapping and forced sex. (And as far as the "me too" movement goes, if women dress themselves up to look attractive, with make-up and high heels, He's quite prepared to sexually molest them Himself, in the usual manner of patriarchal deities – Isaiah 3:16-17.)

God's word? Really? I went through a phase of rereading the whole Bible every year when I was younger. I must have read many verses like this many times over, without it ever occurring to me that Moses, if he lived, must have been a psychopath (I've come to adopt a very simplistic rule of thumb that the more committed a Christian is to the literal Word of God, the less they've really listened to what they're saying, and the less they know about the Bible itself).

Time and again Yahweh (or Moses) wants to go over the top and kill. Even when a man is found gathering sticks on the Sabbath, and the people aren't sure what punishment should fit the crime, Yahweh commands that he be stoned to death (Numbers 15:32-36). The continual complaint from them both is that the people aren't brutal enough in their treatment of their enemies (let alone their own people). It's not as if this was inevitably the culture of the period. The drama of poetry like the *Iliad* (written at roughly the same time) lies in the sympathy with which the Greek poet treats the Trojans, particularly their hero, Hector, whose death is the poem's tragic centerpiece. Similarly, Aeschylus imagines the Greek defeat of the Persians through the eyes of the Persian women left at home. Throughout this period you can find better morality (and much better language) in the writings and gods of "pagan" cultures than in the pages of the Old Testament, as many early Gentile Christians were later ready to point out (more in chapter 34).

These chapters are so rarely read nowadays that we forget what a brutal God this is; mad, bad and dangerous to know. We shake our heads wonderingly at the leaders people are prepared to follow today, but we only need to read our own sacred texts, or look at our own recent history, to see how easily we can approve of genocide, or turn a blind eye to it. El hadn't thought what to do with the people already in Canaan. He promised Abraham the land without being prepared to follow through. The second time around Yahweh knows. He will "blot them out," and dictates His military strategy to Moses for doing so (Exodus 23:29-30). Again, there's no evidence for this invasion. The Canaanites appear to have already been pushed out by tribes coming from the north, the same movement of peoples that gave rise to the tales of Homer describing the same period; the *Iliad* and the *Odyssey*. The usurpers were the Phoenicians, with their God Baal.

The difference between El and Yahweh can be summed up in the different treatments of Abraham and Jephthah. El lets Abraham off the sacrifice of Isaac. Yahweh gives Jephthah, the Judge of Israel, no such help. He has to kill his daughter and burn her as an offering to God (which in this case He accepts – Judges 11), because he promised God that he would sacrifice the first person he met coming out of his house if He gave him victory over the Ammonites.

After the Hebrews settle in Canaan they appear to give up on Yahweh, this nasty God of terror and war. Warrior desert gods for barbarian invaders are not much use in helping crops grow. As happens time and again through history, the invaders settle down, start intermarrying, adopt the customs and beliefs of the tribes around them; honoring their gods, ploughing the land, going down the usual route of kingship, taxes, with the art of writing becoming a necessary adjunct to record the transactions. This is again a disputed subject, but for the Bible reader it is made clear when in 621 BC, several centuries later, King Josiah (640-609 BC), son of David, the sixteenth king of Judah, described in the Bible as righteous, sends his secretary to the Temple to collect taxes. The high priest Hilkiah gives him an old book he's just found buried in the Temple somewhere among the cast-offs. They believe this to be all or part of the "book of the law" written by Moses (2 Kings 22:8) and Josiah realizes that for centuries they have been worshipping the wrong gods and have forgotten about the God of the Exodus (whichever one that was). He tells the people to celebrate a Passover feast and the writer of Kings adds: "Surely there was not holden such a passover from the days of the judges that judged Israel, nor in all the days of the kings of Israel, nor of the kings of Judah" (2 Kings 23:22).

Josiah starts a campaign to cleanse the kingdom. He destroys all the pagan altars and throws out the foreign statues and idolatrous clutter from the Temple, gets rid of the cult prostitutes and slaughters the priests. From here on the worship of Yahweh seems to predominate amongst the Israelites, though the next four kings "did what was evil in the sight of the Lord."

In all of the stories in all the sacred books of the world religions these episodes are among the least enlightening, the most barbaric. There are four reactions of Bible-believing Christians to them. The majority just ignore them, wish them away. Some double down, saying that the victims deserved everything they got. They were all wrong/evil. Many turn to agnosticism or atheism – one reason why surveys suggest that atheists know the Bible better than Christians. There's a fourth way, which many of the early Christians understood – they see that, like Moses, we all make God into who we want, a reflection of ourselves, good and evil. But we can turn bad gods into good ones.

Properly read, the Bible is the most potent force for atheism ever conceived.
Isaac Asimov (twentieth century AD)

19. The Captives' God

Talk as much philosophy as you please, worship as many gods as you like, observe all ceremonies, sing devoted praises to any number of divine beings – liberation never comes, even at the end of a hundred aeons, without the realization of the Oneness of Self.
Shankara (eighth century AD)

So if the Hebrew King Josiah hadn't heard of the one God of Abraham and Moses, when did monotheism (one God) rather than henotheism (one god amongst many) really take root among the Hebrews? It's much debated, but the overwhelming current consensus is that it didn't develop till after the Exile. Most of the so-called Books of Moses are reckoned to date between the eighth and ninth centuries BC, hundreds of years after Moses, possibly as late as the sixth century BC. In the Ten Commandments, there's no sense that God is the only god, He's just a jealous one (Exodus 34:14):

For thou shalt worship no other god: for the Lord, whose name is Jealous, is a jealous God.

Indeed a thread running through Judaism and the Old Testament is that there's the "Seen God" who talks face to face with people (as in Exodus 33:11) and the "Unseen God" who you couldn't see without being blasted (Exodus 33:20). And then there's a dual narrative running through Judges, Samuel, Kings and Chronicles. On the one hand, the later scribes record the doings of the men of God. On the other, there's the almost buried but frequent acknowledgement that "the high places [the foreign altars] were not taken away" (2 Chronicles 15:17). The oldest Hebrew inscription that exists, the Moabite stone, makes reference to the god Chemosh. Saul names one of his sons after

the Phoenician god Baal, as does his son Jonathan. And much of
the book of Hosea is about changing allegiances: "For I will take
away the names of Baalim out of her mouth, and they shall no
more be remembered by their name" (Hosea 2:17). In Psalm 82
it's clear that God is not alone in the heavens:

God presides in the great assembly;
He gives judgment amongst the "gods":
How long will you defend the unjust
And show partiality to the wicked?

There's the continuing thread, also, that the Hebrews don't
deserve to have this God to themselves, and that He hedges His
bets, supporting other peoples as well: *Are ye not as children of*
the Ethiopians unto me, O children of Israel? saith the LORD. Have
not I brought up Israel out of the land of Egypt? And the Philistines
from Caphtor, and the Syrians from Kir? (Amos 9:7). I guess our
equivalent today would be along the lines of: "Why are you so
sure you've got me right? Don't you understand that I also work
with and through Muslims, Buddhists, and every other people?
And it's the refugees that need saving now, not you?"

The generally accepted overall picture amongst the specialist
historians, rather than Jewish/Christian/Muslim scholars, is that
Yahweh was originally a child of El, god of the sun, and perhaps
had a mother, Asherah, goddess of the moon (in the Hittite
tradition Yahweh is briefly married to His mother, and an early
Hebrew inscription found at Kuntillet Ajrud refers to Asherah
as the wife of Yahweh). He is one of many children. Baal (the
god of rain and fertility) is one of His brothers. Another, who He
frequently battles with, is Yam, the seven-headed sea dragon,
the god of storms and destruction, mentioned in Job 9:8 and
Psalm 74:14. We make gods in our image, so they tend to come
with families. The impulse to duplicate relationships on earth
in the heavens is so strong that the early Church began to think

Jesus must be God's son, though they didn't go as far as giving God a wife.

The name Yahweh is first given to El at the beginning of the First Book of Samuel, where it means "Lord of hosts," suggesting that He is now the supreme High God, displacing El, ruler of the elohim. The Hebrews (increasingly called Israelites, a nation with a capital and approximate borders) begin to adopt him as local to themselves. By the seventh century BC there's no question for them as to who is in power: Yahweh guides and controls the elohim (Deuteronomy 33:2) and uses the stars in battle (Judges 5:20). By the fifth century BC, El and the elohim have largely disappeared and only Yahweh is left. The old stories, in which God is one of many, with many names, went through their final compilation and editing as late as the fourth century BC. The writers retrospectively ascribed the grand deeds of their legendary ancestors to their worship of the one God, Yahweh.

The main motor of this change is the Exile, an event that most historians regard as historical, in contrast to the Exodus.

We're skipping vast chunks of history here... all the fun stuff about Elijah and Elisha, Gideon, David, Solomon (the last ruler of both the Israelite kingdoms and perhaps the most interesting character – built temples to Astarte the goddess of sex, and others) and so on... We haven't touched on the development of Abraham's simple pastoralist religion of superstition, sacrifice and circumcision, through the Ark of the Covenant and the Tabernacle to the Temple religion with it hundreds of laws, High Priest and thousands of lesser priests. You could drop the history of the USA from its founding to the present day into this period and not see it, at the rate we're going, but so much of this territory is uncertain. There's no real consensus on whether these people existed, or whether Jerusalem was a small village or the capital of a kingdom – though there is a single reference to the House of David on the Tel Dan Stele which was discovered in 1993. The first non-biblical historical reference to the Hebrews/

Israelites is to a defeat that King Ahab manages to inflict on the Assyrians, in alliance with the Kings of Damascus, at Qarqar in 853 BC.

But we have to move on... one of the things we do know, though, is that the first event to be mentioned both in the Bible itself (2 Kings 17:1-6) *and* elsewhere is in 722 BC when Assyrian records tell of the conquest of the Northern Kingdom of Israel. This is where we start to get into real "history," rather than folklore, legend and myth. We do know that the Assyrians were brutal conquerors, putting the early Israelites in the shade (though they didn't sacrifice their own children). Yahweh wasn't actually savage enough. The Assyrians didn't just kill people, they would intimidate the inhabitants of a city they were besieging by bringing forward captives from the last campaign, impaling them on spears around the walls, or skinning them alive, or sticking hooks into their flesh and dragging them to death behind chariots. The Israelites might not have fared this badly – their God was irrelevant to the Assyrians, but apparently they were valued as skillful musicians and chariot drivers. Ten of the twelve tribes were carried into captivity and disappear from the record, leading to later fantasies that they could be found in Africa, or America, or any other unexplored territory. The southern tribes of Benjamin and Judah were left to carry on the nation. During the following century the Babylonian Empire replaced the Assyrian. In 586 BC Nebuchadnezzar, the Babylonian monarch, destroyed Jerusalem and carried the remaining Israelites of the Southern Kingdom off to captivity, back to the land that Abraham had been called to leave a millennium or so earlier (this wasn't unique to the Hebrews/Israelites, since the first Empire of Akkad under King Sargon, around 2300 BC, violence and war, genocide and moving populations around, had been endemic).

The religion had already been changing. The prophet Ezekiel, for instance, was one of those carted from Jerusalem to Babylon. He blamed the Exile on the rich, the powerful, the shepherds who were only interested feeding themselves rather than their sheep. But now it took another step-change. They were now one of many minor races shuttled around within the Babylonian Empire. They had lost the land and the Temple. Their religion had to change, fast. Yahweh is no longer relevant as god of "place," living in the Temple. He, and the Israelites, are now homeless. The all-conquering war God, now defeated, is dropped, and the religion is slowly transformed into one whose purpose is to preserve national identity through ritual and law. It became important to preserve the stories of the tribe before they were forgotten. So they had to be written down on scrolls, and that's the origin of the Old Testament. Some parts of the Pentateuch could have been written earlier, but the bulk of it was written during the Exile or later. It was in this period of exile that the Israelites forged the religion of survival that later enabled them to keep going despite the destruction of Jerusalem by the Romans in AD 70, their consequent dispersal and 2,000 years of wandering, down to the last century.

One of the flourishing areas of biblical studies today involves the attempt to trace the origins of different sections of the Old Testament and to work out when they were put together, and by who. All scholars, conservative and liberal, accept that the process of revision and reinterpretation of the existing material whilst pulling it together was continuous and lengthy. The gaps and joins still show. Different writers describe events in different ways, reflecting changing beliefs and agendas. For instance, in 2 Samuel 24:1-2, written before the Exile, David's decision to take a census is said to be due to God's anger with his people. But in 1 Chronicles 21:1, written after the Exile, the inspiration comes from Satan.

Overall, they were largely in exile in Babylon for about seven generations. It's a crucial period. They couldn't help but be influenced by the society in which they lived, much as early nineteenth-century Polish, German, Greek, Swedish, Italian, etc. immigrants to the USA have, over a similar period, now become part of that culture. Anthropologists say it doesn't take more than two or three generations to be pretty much completely assimilated into the culture you've entered.

While they were there the Babylonian hierarchy of Empire was replaced, in 539 BC, by the Persian, and the exiles adopted the Persian Aramaic as their first language (the one Jesus and his disciples later spoke). Thereafter Hebrew was confined to temple ritual and law (until it was picked up again in the early centuries AD), much as had by then occurred with Sanskrit in India and would later happen with Latin in Europe.

The Persians created a vast Empire stretching from Libya to the border of India. They followed the ancient religion of Zoroastrianism, the world's first major one, inherited from the Medes, several empires earlier, and already had their own sacred books, the *Zend Avesta*, now mostly lost. Zoroaster was born to a virgin, Dughdova, who conceived him by a shaft of light. The priests were called Magi, and the later wise men who came from the East to the birthplace of Jesus were probably seen as such – Zoroastrianism was still flourishing then. The Magi had been studying the stars for thousands of years – the world's first observatory, the Temple of Belus, is believed to have been established in 2350 BC. They introduced the zodiac, dividing it into 360 degrees, and the Sabbath, the full moon day, the *shabbatum*.

Persian religion was more sophisticated than the carrot and stick religion of the Israelites, where being faithful to the right tribal God was rewarded with goats, sheep, wives, concubines and slaves. They asked the kinds of questions we ask today: Why should good people suffer and innocent children die? Zoroaster answered that, rather than many gods, there were only two. There is one true, wholly good God, Ahura Mazda (*Ahura* means "lord," as does the Hebrew *Adonai*). His creation of the world is ongoing – we participate in bringing him into being by performing good deeds. Later comes his evil brother Ahriman, god of lies and darkness, who fights against him, and rules for 7,000 years (it makes some psychological sense, reflecting the choices we all make between good and evil). But in the end he will be defeated, because good is superior to evil. So there's only one real deity, because eventually there will be only one moral value – the world will be entirely good. All of us have immortal souls. It is our duty to love and worship Ahura, show compassion to all living things, and do as we would be done by. It makes some sense of the world as well – it's surely not logically possible for God to be omnipotent, omniscient and all-benevolent, at the same time, given the world as we know it. There's a spanner in the works somewhere.

The similarities between Persian beliefs and the later Israelite religion aren't in dispute, just the interpretation. Some Christian scholars sensible enough to realize that religions do actually influence each other (how could Christianity have developed, for instance, without Judaism?) might say: "Okay, there are common threads, but the Israelite religion is inspired, with the Holy Spirit revealing the truth to humankind, whilst the Persian religion is not."

But historians would say that this is putting the cart before the horse. The Israelites' god was a minor, relatively unknown one, occupying a tiny corner of what is now the Middle East, competing with hundreds of other tribal gods. The Persian religion came first and was overwhelmingly more important in the first two millennia BC, influencing all others over an area of several thousand square miles. The influences were all one way. And they were overwhelmingly positive ones. The Holy Spirit itself comes from the Persian Spenta Mainyu, through whom Ahura Mazda fights the cosmic battle. The equally widespread, common Israelite idea of a God particular to a single tribe (or family, village, or city) who could do both good and evil, change his mind twice a day, and give help in battle, slowly changed under Persian influence into a holy, just God. The Israelites stopped sacrificing children, evil came to be embodied separately in Satan, the Israelites' version of Ahriman, and by the time the New Testament was written had begun to take on flesh. Along with God and Satan came other Persian ideas like life after death, heaven and hell, resurrection and the judgment of the dead.

To take an example of the change in beliefs: there is for instance no sense of heaven and hell in Hebrew/Israelite tradition prior to the Exile. There was no judgment of the dead. There was nothing basically wrong with this life. Indeed, many verses suggest there is no afterlife, eg; "For the living know that they shall die: but the dead know not any thing, neither have they any more a reward; for the memory of them is forgotten" (Ecclesiastes 9:5). Blessings for the Hebrew patriarchs are counted by the number of years you've lived, the number of goats you've reared or stolen. It's why the two major themes of the psalms are unfairness and desertion by God. The psalmist demands and pleads for justice now. There's no sense of justice to come, now is all there is (for example, Psalm 6:5). They have a sense of heaven a few hundred feet up in the air, but it's not a place where people go as a reward for a good life, but where the gods live. After death, people go down as shadows to the underworld, Sheol, a state of near nonexistence. This is another universal belief, a similar place to the Greek Hades or the Norse underworld ruled by the goddess Hel, from which we get our "hell" (the word that's used in some modern translations for several different ideas in the Old Testament, blurring their meaning – Ezekiel 31:14; Isaiah 22:13; 1 Kings 2:1-2). A few outstanding individuals, like Elijah, are treated specially and rise up through the sky in a chariot of fire to join the gods in heaven (2 Kings 2:11). But even key biblical figures like the prophet Samuel, called by God to create a kingdom for the Israelites, appointing Saul as the first monarch, end up in Sheol, as grisly underground ghosts (1 Samuel 28; the witch of Endor raises Samuel's shade here to give advice to Saul). There are about 60 references in the Old Testament to the dying, both righteous and unrighteous, going to Sheol, "the land of gloom and deep darkness," none to anyone going to heaven or hell. Even in the time of Jesus the Jews were split on these ideas – the Sadducees (very roughly speaking, the priests) and mainstream Judaism could not reconcile hell with a loving God, so considered that souls beyond redemption simply ceased to exist. Whereas Pharisees believed in spirits, angels, resurrection and the afterlife.

Their ideas had developed in the Exile. Zoroastrian teaching said that the dead will be brought back to life with newly-resurrected bodies. The final prophet (to be born around AD 2341), the world savior, born of the seed of a prophet and a virgin mother, will overcome disease and death in a last cataclysmic battle. A great judgment will follow, with metals turning into rivers of molten liquid, valleys and hills being leveled, and the coming of the kingdom. Wrongs and rights will be sorted. Justice will be given to all. The seven archangels of Zoroastrianism turned into the seven (a universally magical figure, which crops up repeatedly in Revelation) of Jewish tradition, resurfacing in the Dead Sea Scrolls and still seen in the seven-branched menorah (candlestick). These ideas fed into Islam as well as Christianity, and influenced Hinduism and Buddhism.

Nebuchadnezzar's successor eased the hardships of the captivity and many of the exiles were assimilated into Babylonian culture, as we can see from the book of Daniel, but others longed for home. The last Babylonian ruler, Nabonidus, was overthrown by the Persian emperor Cyrus, who allowed those who wished to return to Jerusalem (a Zoroastrian, he was tolerant of all religions within his empire). But with no walls left to defend them only a minority appear to have taken advantage of this. The local population in Israel was now down to around

30,000, and they seem to have adopted the beliefs and practices of their neighbors. They made a start on rebuilding the Temple but were opposed by the locals (Ezra 3:3), mostly people from other nations who had been resettled in the land by the Babylonians. These people, who followed a syncretistic religion, later became known as the Samaritans. They created a rival temple on Mount Gerizim and followed their own version of the five books of Moses. They still sacrifice in the same way today, and may be closer to the religion of Abraham than the Jews, not being so contaminated by the Persian influence.

A determined effort to rebuild the walls of Jerusalem was made a hundred years later under the reign of Artaxerxes I. By this time many of those of Israelite descent in Babylon and other centers of the Empire were enjoying lives of some comfort and prosperity. Nehemiah, a trusted royal servant, was even given an escort of army officers and cavalry (Nehemiah 2:9) to take a group back to Jerusalem.

Here, for the first time, the Bible joins the mainstream history of the region, maybe 1,000 years after the time of Abraham, about 445 BC. We're still only talking about tiny fragments of information, but their historicity is confirmed by non-biblical writings. Nehemiah had the resources and authority to rebuild, and Ezra, described as priest, scribe, and descendant of Aaron (Ezra 7:1-6), had the spiritual authority to teach. He took with him, and may well have had a hand in composing, the larger part of the Old Testament that we have today. Ezra assembled the "men, women, and all who were able to understand" in front of the Water Gate in Jerusalem and read to them "the Book of the Law of Moses which the Lord (Yahweh) had commanded for Israel" (Nehemiah 8:1-3). A fortnight later, they celebrated the Feast of the Tabernacles in memory of the 40 years supposedly spent wandering in the small Sinai Peninsula after the escape from Egypt. The Hebrews began to draw together in weekly meetings to read the scriptures. They became known as the first

"People of the Book."

This is where the Hebrew Bible, the *Tanakh*, ends, with the book of Nehemiah, with the land restored to them and the temple and city walls rebuilt. Most scholars date the return of this party of Israelites to Jerusalem as the moment when the Jewish religion really came into being, and it's from now that most historians talk of the "Jews" as an identifiable body of people. In the fourth century BC many of the Old Testament stories went through their final compilation and editing. The writers retrospectively ascribed the grand deeds of their legendary ancestors to their worship of the one God, Yahweh. The God we know and love today has arrived.

Thy word is a lamp unto my feet, and a light unto my path.
Psalms (fifth to first centuries BC)

20. Time Out

Men never do evil so completely and cheerfully as when they do it from religious conviction.
Pascal (seventeenth century AD)

My apologies for going on for so long about the Old Testament, but this is our heritage. These old stories from a small Canaanite tribe have helped make us who we are. But we can step back for a moment. The enforced "time out" in Babylon that eventually led to the creation of Judaism, Christianity, and Islam is worth putting into a wider perspective. Then, as now, beliefs (however strongly held at the time) were tenuous, provisional ideas that washed across cultures, geography and time. That's one reason why the Old Testament is so interesting. It was compiled in a period that may have been uniquely creative in the cultural history of humankind.

By the fifth century BC we're roughly halfway through the story of civilization, if you date the beginning from when we developed complex social structures around major city/nation states; a fraction of 1% of the time we've been on earth, and the coming of Jesus as the Son of God is still half a millennium away in the future. Rulers had taken on the qualities of gods, and the gods themselves had correspondingly been pushed from earth up to the heavens. The idea of absolute power, represented in the heavens by monotheism, was widely current. But there were also contrary trends. There was a new literate class across the Old World – in places like Athens, which had rejected the idea of godlike kingship, and put its trust in the idea of policies being decided through talking about them rather than submitting to diktats from above – maybe as many one in ten Athenians could read. People were not just looking skeptically at the older religions that celebrated survival and promoted fertility, they began to rebel against the idea of bowing the knee to absolute power at all, whether in the earth or the heavens. They saw the concentration of power and wealth in the political and economic structures of their day, and the identification of these structures with divinity, treating most of the population as animals, as compromised and corrupt. For them (hopefully, there are always going to be some) religion became more a matter of inner development. They saw the potential for salvation as being within each individual, rather than being achieved through obedience, sacrifice and worship. The idea of "universal spirituality" and rules of personal conduct applicable to everyone became significant. "What does it mean to have a worthwhile life as an individual?" Some, particularly in Greece and China, even began to see gods as the products of human imagination rather than real beings, with man as the measure of all things. The question of what is "real" became central to reflective thought, leading to philosophy. With an absence of local gods on earth, who you could relate to more directly, pessimism about the body, the world and this life increased. The idea that there is a better world out there, of which this is just a shadow, began to take shape. Our bodies may be stuck in this world, but through meditation and insight we could access the transcendental dimension of reality that lies beyond it. By the time of Jesus, the question of how to be redeemed from a fallen world and enjoy the real one was the concern of dozens if not hundreds of schools and cults: Greek, Egyptian, Jewish, Persian, and many others.

It's hard to underestimate the extent to which the way we think today was shaped around this time. A long-lived Marco Polo in the fifth century BC on a pilgrimage across the Old World could have started from his home in Italy (not that there was a country called that, in the sense that we understand countries today – Italy has only existed as a sovereign state for a century and a half) with Pythagoras, the West's first great mystic, who realizes that the nature of the universe can be expressed in math, teaching reincarnation (or the Eternal Return) and the sanctity of all life. Then across the Adriatic Sea in Greece he could have sat at the feet of Socrates and Heraclitus as they teach their vision of the Supreme Good, before moving on to the Middle East where the Old Testament is taking its final shape, and Jeremiah (in Palestine) and Ezekiel (in Babylon) are talking of a holy, just God to whom we are individually responsible – the currents of thinking in the Axial Age are central to what became Judaism. 2,500 miles away in India there's Buddha's experience of Nirvana and the first readings of the *Upanishads*, as well as Mahavira's religion of nonviolence to all living things. And a further 2,500 miles away to the east, in China, Confucius and Lao Tzu are teaching the philosophy of the good and virtuous life, with human principles at the center. We would struggle to find a comparable group from the last two millennia. In that respect it's been downhill ever since – spiritual growth and the accumulation of wealth and power always seem to be in inverse proportion.

All these traditions are "major" today. We're most likely to find what is good and valuable in them by focusing on what they have in common. At the heart of each is the question of knowing and being yourself, the moment of understanding when our inner beings touch the universal law, described as Dharma, God, Torah, Tao, Nirvana, Ren, Katon or whatever. In so far as there was a God, He was transcendent, ineffable. What mattered was the way you lived in relation to Him, other people and all other life. This loving relationship came to be phrased and felt differently over the generations in different parts of the world; they emphasized different aspects of how to live truthful and holy lives, and where salvation lies.

For example, the Eastern religions of Confucianism and Taoism tend to look to the past. To find our right place in life we align ourselves with the spirit and wisdom of our ancestors. Two key religions originating in the Indian subcontinent, Hinduism and Buddhism, look for it in the present moment – that's how we free ourselves from the cycle of time and the world's illusions. The Middle Eastern, monotheistic religion of Judaism, and its later offshoots, Christianity and Islam, place it in the future. Our past and present may be hopeless but God's plan is for all creation to be redeemed. The Eastern and Indian religions led to the wisdom tradition, emphasizing the interior search. The monotheistic religions developed the prophetic tradition, emphasizing relationships with others and changing society. The particular genius of Jesus (through understanding local threads, he would have had little idea of what had been going on here, around the world) was to combine the two.

But they all overlap. All say that understanding our past is crucial to understanding our present. All have traditions that place some form of salvation in the future, whether that of Jesus, Buddha Maitreya, Krishna, or the Zoroastrian Saoshyans, with the literal-minded in each tradition and generation fixing one date or another to frighten or thrill us. But all say there are values outside of ourselves, outside society, embedded in creation itself. To find happiness we realize them in our lives. The deepest happiness we can find is in the present moment, living fully right now, with the past forgiven and the future secured.

Each religion is colored by the culture it arises from and the circumstances of the founder. In the case of Buddhism, for instance, its founder was an aristocrat from an ascetic tradition dissatisfied with the sensual life of court, seeking true happiness and enlightenment. The later Christianity began among a poor group within a marginal people who had been mostly under foreign rule for centuries and looked for future salvation. Each has millions, even billions of followers today who find some salvation, enlightenment, peace, fulfillment in their own traditions. They feel they understand themselves, their role in the world, hear the voice of creation itself speaking to them, and redefine the focus of their lives from the "self" to "God" or "other." There are thousands of accounts in print of lives being transformed, and with the alteration of a few words it's often hard to tell in which religious tradition the experience took place.

The simplest summary of all their teaching on how to live the good life is the Golden Rule: *And as ye would that men should do to you, do ye also to them likewise* (Luke 6:31, see also Matthew 7:12, etc.) – the antithesis of the beliefs that had grown up around kings and emperors, and around the Gods of Abraham and Moses. Live ethically, renounce desire, treat others as yourself. We tend to identify this with Jesus, due to general ignorance of other religions, but it was a frequent theme in Judaism. Rabbi Hillel, a near contemporary of Jesus, used much the same language, and managed it without reference to God. Confucius had based his philosophy on it 500 years earlier. His key concept is *ren*, "the love of man" (*Analects XII*, 22). The basic Buddhist precept is that you should consider all beings as like yourself. The same ideas are central to Jainism and Islam. And all the great spiritual leaders say that relationship is more than a social benefit, it's at the core of life, the reason we came to be here. It's simple, direct, and if you follow it you can't go too wrong. Indeed, it's probably fair to say that it's the oldest and most fundamental law in the social development of Homo sapiens, ever since we began talking to each other. Gods, in their best incarnations, are simply the invisible witnesses we create to discourage transgressions of group norms. Psychology experiments show that if you think someone might be watching, you behave better.

The winnowing process of the last few thousand years has developed this as the central commandment, with an associated range of virtues like self-control, moderation, service, generosity, faithfulness, and so on. It's what being a good Christian, or a good Muslim, or Buddhist, or whoever, is all about. It's all that matters. Everything else – the details of which God or not you happen to believe in – and how you happen to describe Him or Her – is secondary. That's the starting point of good religion. If you can't accept the principle of loving your neighbor as yourself, whatever class or gender or color they are, then – however often you attend a church/synagogue/mosque/temple, whatever particular doctrines you believe – your religion, in effect, means nothing. It's probably just shoring up prejudice.

It's probably no accident that it was around the fifth century BC that "science" also made huge strides. In the last few centuries science has stormed ahead again, but religious ideas and language haven't essentially altered in the last few thousand years. We're still reading the same books. Just, usually, the wrong ones. The kind of biblical commentaries that mostly analyze one verse against others, on the assumption that because God wrote or inspired them all there is a single, comprehensive message to be found in the disparate collection of texts we decided made up the Holy Bible, have no value (and I've read a lot of them). That's why the twenty-first century may be one to match the fifth century BC – religions have a lot of catching up to do.

It is only in the microscope that our life looks so big. It is an indivisible point, drawn out and magnified by the powerful lenses of time and space.
Schopenhauer

21. The Prophets' God

Man's highest and last parting occurs when, for God's sake, he takes leave of God.
Meister Eckhart (thirteenth century AD)

Back to the Israelites, this change in their God from a local tribal deity to an omnipotent sky God, who then becomes increasingly abstract and withdrawn from the affairs of humankind, can be traced in broad outline in the Old Testament. The stories you might remember from childhood are mostly in the first part. In Genesis and Exodus God walks on the earth, chats with Adam and Eve, wrestles with Jacob, talks with Moses on Mount Sinai. In Judges, Samuel and Chronicles He's up in heaven but speaks directly from there. But of the 41 kings of Israel Yahweh speaks only to the second and third. From events we guess at being dated at around 1000 BC and earlier there's 1,000 years of the Old Testament story still to be told, and He doesn't appear so directly again, becoming a God more of vision than event. He "hides his face," a phrase used increasingly in the major and minor prophets. And for many Christians, the prophets are less interesting – God doesn't seem to be around much, and as for the miracles – instead of Moses parting the Red Sea, for instance, Elijah refills a jar of oil that never empties. Disney isn't going to make a film out of that.

It's the best recorded, most drawn-out disappearance of a God in history. Much of the power of the Psalms is in their reflection on why He does this, and on how we can survive without Him. In Esther, where the Jews are saved from being massacred by a woman who is the wife of the Persian King Ahasuerus, God is not mentioned at all. The story is about the power of the Persian rulers over the Jews, not the power of God over the enemies of the Jews. (Ahasuerus, incidentally, is better known in history as

Xerxes, whose defeat by the Greeks was one of the great turning-points in European history.)

The simplest, most obvious explanation of why God disengages Himself from direct involvement is that it is a function of distance. The further away something is in time and space the easier it is to believe. In the UK, when we look back over a similar period of more than a millennium we have our stories of Arthur and Excalibur, Merlin and his magic powers, which were widely credited up to modern times. Once we get into the area of reliable records less is left to the imagination. When the Jews (maybe Ezra) compiled and wrote down the old tales they incorporated the magical, but as they got closer to their own time, they wrote what they knew had happened. That translates, as it always does, into mundane politics rather than miracles. They were adjusting their faith to suit the reality of the times.

But there's also a deeper issue at play here. Previously, Hebrew and Israelite religion had been pluralist, variously adopting different regional gods. Under Persian influence God came to be seen as One, but the Jewish experience led them to see God as uninvolved, as separate from nature, as pre-existent. The Creator, rather than part of creation, became immaterial, and unfathomable. In a world of successive humiliations and defeats by an unending succession of emperors and tyrants, a bigger God was needed, rather than a local tribal one. A God who was above every king on earth, who could turn every setback to good, even if it wasn't going to happen in this life.

Obedience to the warrior God hadn't saved the Israelites from being slaughtered and exiled first by the Assyrians and then the Babylonians. And as the centuries after the Exile moved on it became apparent that being faithful to the Law didn't work either. Israel was still oppressed by its enemies, and never regained its independence, despite huge efforts, particularly during the time of the Maccabees. And this gave rise to a new thread of writing – the apocalyptic literature – like that of Daniel.

The Jews developed the theory that the earth as a whole had grown so wicked that it was past saving. God would therefore destroy it, letting only a faithful survive – an idea which came to dominate Christianity.

So revelation slows, and ends. By the time we get to Jesus the Jews had no doubt that there were inspired scriptures, but they had fuzzy edges. Some Jews thought the writings of Moses were the only authoritative scriptures; others, all the books in the Greek Septuagint translation; yet others only the books originally written in Hebrew. So when Jesus refers to scripture it's not even necessarily scripture that is now in the Old Testament (for example, John 7:38).

The Old Testament itself wasn't given its current form in Judaism until a couple of generations after the death of Jesus, when the destruction of Jerusalem in AD 70 scattered the Jews (and the Jewish Christians). The response of the Jews was similar to that during the Exile. Having again lost their Temple and their homeland they turned to the holy writings to keep their faith and identity alive. The surviving scholars came together at the Academy of Jamnia, near Jaffa in modern Israel, under Rabbi Jochanan ben Zakkai, and in AD 90-100 at the synod of Jamnia, decided which books would go into the Hebrew Bible. The text itself was not finally agreed till the seventh and eighth centuries AD.

Between the time of Ezra and the destruction of Jerusalem in AD 70 there had emerged a substantial body of Jewish writing. Some of this writing was included in the Septuagint but was not accepted as canonical at Jamnia, and so does not appear in the Hebrew Bible. The Roman Catholic Church, following the Septuagint, includes in its Old Testament canon twelve books which are not in the Hebrew or Protestant Bibles. Called "deuterocanonical" by Roman Catholics and "Old Testament Apocrypha" by Protestants, these twelve books are – *Ecclesiasticus, Tobit, Susanna,* a *Letter of Jeremiah, Judith, Baruch, The Song of the*

Three Children, Bel and the Dragon, 1 and 2 Maccabees, additions to *Esther* and *The Wisdom of Solomon*.

But the Jews perhaps sensibly always regarded Rabbinic commentary (the *Talmud*) as having nearly equal status. Most religions have a similar approach. The Hindu have their sacred texts, *shruti*, and the commentaries, *smriti*. The title of the greatest work in the East, the *I Ching*, means "classic" and "warp"; it's the warp upon which the weft of the commentaries is written. Christians, on the other hand, with their lack of authoritative commentaries, have to reinvent the wheel of interpretation in each generation, going back to square one every time.

So, getting back to the Old Testament, what's its relevance for non-Jews? These chapters have so far given a lopsided view of the Old Testament. Undeniably there's a strong thread that describes God as an average physical deity, built like us, with the characteristic morals of contemporary kings and emperors, a preference for particular perfumes (Exodus 30:34-37), frequently perverse, deceiving His own prophets (Ezekiel 14:9-10). He's also represented in the usual terms of a weather god, thundering through the devouring fire of Zoroastrian tradition, hail and earthquake (for example, Psalm 68:7-8). He's also at times a jealous God, a bigoted, racist, murdering, evil kind of a God that you wouldn't wish on your enemy. We no longer want a God that encourages us to hate our enemies and God's "with perfect hatred" (Psalm 139:22), approves kidnapping and rape (if the girl is beautiful enough; Deuteronomy 21:10-13), condones human sacrifice (Leviticus 26:29), and threatens us with cannibalizing our children if we don't follow all the barbaric tribal laws (Leviticus 26:28):

> Then I will walk contrary unto you also in fury; and I, even I, will chastise you seven times for your sins. And ye shall eat the flesh of your sons, and the flesh of your daughters shall ye eat.

God Himself says He doesn't change (Malachi 3:6) but of course He does. As the Old Testament moves on God becomes less anthropomorphic and polytheistic, and more sympathetic ideas come to predominate. He takes on the high moral standards of Ahura Mazda. It is in many ways more interesting than the first half, though it doesn't have the good stories. The idea of God changes again. He broadens and deepens. Many of the themes and narratives of the first part are common to many cultures (and plagiarized from them), but there's little to compare in world literature with the suffering expressed in Lamentations, the cries of the prophets. The awareness develops that there's no short, quick answer to injustice and agony. God comes to be an expression of our hope rather than our might. He's found in our despair and weakness. He identifies with our suffering rather than our victories. God becomes a loving Father rather than a warlord, as first seen in the Song of Hannah (1 Samuel 2). There's the compassionate God of the prophets, the idea of God as the embodiment of moral holiness. This is stronger in the latter part of the Old Testament (and in the Gospels) than in any other religious literature.

The question throughout the Old Testament is not so much whether God exists or not, that was taken for granted, by everyone. It's more what kind of God was necessary for the times. He can be seen as developing from a "primitive" God of dance and music, war and slaughter, through the period of highly organized sacrifice in the Temple, to the focus of the prophets on an interior God, one seeking a repentant heart rather than the sacrifice of pigeons and goats. Various traditions of Hinduism go through the same process in the same period.

Some Christian writers explain this by saying that God only reveals Himself to people in so far as they can understand Him. The understanding develops through the Old Testament and into the New, and we move from a God of anger and violence to a God of love and justice. This rather misses the point that the

God of the Revelation to John at the end of the New Testament regresses to Old Testament behavior, slaughtering humankind wholesale like the God of Noah – even worse, promises to torment most of mankind in Hell forever, which doesn't come up in the Old Testament, where you may be punished on earth for your wickedness, but not after you die. But in any case, why not take this thought further? We can continue to change our idea of Him. We can build on the growing perception through the Old Testament that God is not a mighty warrior who we expect to defeat our enemies, to justify our worship of Him, but a universal God of unconditional love.

Most Christians still retain the Jewish idea of God as a Spirit separate from us who (in the Christian view) incarnated Himself into an individual on earth. Though slowly edging out of sight in the Old Testament He explodes back into the world in the New, appearing as a baby rather than locking Himself in an ark or temple. But maybe if there is this God of all relationships in the universe who acts out of purpose and love, who is the God of all consciousness, He does indeed disappear as we realize Him into being, because God is not an idol, but consciousness itself. The disappearing God of the Old Testament suggests that as we grow up we find that God's choice is our choice, His love is our love. In the Old Testament God gradually becomes not so much a deity telling us *how* to behave but the embodiment of the way we *should* behave. He's not yet a universal god, but becomes more abstract, removed further from Earth. By the time of Amos (eighth century BC) some Jews evidently see Him as rejecting the earlier picture of Himself as an almighty ego in the sky demanding worship and sacrifice in the Temple like the neighboring idols. He becomes a principle of justice:

I hate, I despise your feast days,
and I will not smell in your solemn assemblies...
Take thou away from me the noise of thy songs;

for I will not hear the melody of thy viols.
But let judgment run down as waters,
and righteousness as a mighty stream.
Amos (5:21-24)

In many ways the Judaism that had developed by the first century AD was more attractive than the Christianity that later grew out of it. It was concerned with how we lead our lives, how we treat each other, with social fairness, with the heritage we leave our children. It had become in parts at least a religion of community and forgiveness. Following many centuries of oppression the prophets tried to imagine a better kind of life, a kingdom of God where oppression did not rule. When God called the prophets they replied, "I am here." They knew, of course, or thought they did, that God knew they were there. They were showing their commitment, to step up to the new project.

The time was ripe for a prophet who would spell out the implications of this new thinking, who would see God in people, in the way we live, revealed in action from the heart rather than in laws issued from a God up there.

One of the forerunners was John the Baptist, who saw that the collective rites of the Jewish people were no longer sufficient for purification, and that the work had to be done individually. It was taken further by Jesus, who didn't seem too bothered about rituals like baptism (he never baptized anybody) but asked individuals to commit themselves to a new kind of life. But he did not drop out of the sky with a new message, he was a product of the times, like we all are, a credit to Judaism, challenging his contemporaries to continue changing their idea of God.

The new covenant Jesus taught, the fulfillment of the law, replaces for Christians the one made with Abraham and his descendants that kicks off the Hebrew story. The promise of land to Abraham is not relevant to us today, any more than is Solomon's Temple. In the new covenant God is no longer an objective deity but is shared, entering our inner life. We move from the gods of stone and wood, through the written descriptions and images of God, to God-consciousness. The people of the Land, who became the people of the Book, are to become the people of Spirit.

It's summed up in Jeremiah 31:31, 33 (see also Jeremiah 31:34; Joel 2:28):

> *Behold, the days are coming, saith the LORD, that I will make a new covenant with the house of Israel… After those days, saith the LORD, I will put my law in their inward parts, and write it in their hearts; and will be their God, and they shall be my people.*

Jesus fulfills the Old Testament in the sense that he symbolizes God becoming embodied as humankind, as truly self-aware, to the point where the distinction between self and God disappear (which is not to suggest that the Old Testament prophesies his coming – he's not mentioned there once, however indirectly).

This is what the Old Testament (unintentionally) has been leading up to, and Jesus was the greatest of the prophets, too radical for most, including the Jews themselves and the future Christian Church, which largely stripped out his teaching and reversed it back into a religion of blood sacrifice, coercion and conquest. In perhaps the greatest of all historical ironies, his teaching against the evils of wealth and social injustice were turned upside down, and continue to be so today in the conservative and fundamentalist churches. He became an instrument for the system he hated. Maybe we can take it further and say with Nietzsche in the nineteenth century that the search for truth has killed God. We can take the words of Jesus on the cross: "My God, my God, why hast thou forsaken me?" (Matthew 27:46) as a metaphor for our own experience of God. In so far as we kill others, we kill Him. If we don't realize Him in our lives, He's not there. It's only through redeeming our image of Him that we can redeem ourselves.

> *God is indeed a jealous God –*
> *He cannot bear to see*
> *That we would rather not with Him*
> *But with each other play.*
> Emily Dickinson (nineteenth century AD)

Part IV

A New Religion?

22. The New Prophet

Happiness is the only good; the time to be happy is now, the place to be happy is here, the way to be happy is to make others so.
Robert Ingersoll (nineteenth century AD)

We're about halfway through the story of written religion, and with the New Testament we reach home ground, a mere 80 or so generations ago. We come to the life of one of thousands of religious reformers, one who has perhaps had more impact than any other on the way we think today (though probably not in the way he intended). The academic consensus is that he was a historical figure, but that virtually nothing can be known about him for sure. He's one of the few religious founders for instance for whom we don't have a record of his words in the language he spoke. The bulk of Christian scholarship, in trying to work out the exact meaning of the Greek text in the Gospels (both Paul and the gospel writers, generations later, wrote in Greek), is chasing the wrong camel, as he spoke in Aramaic. It's a language that depends on inflection rather than a root grammatical system like Greek. "Body" and "spirit" can be the same thing, depending on emphasis. "Father" is not about gender, need not even be parenthood, but could imply universal creation. Even the Greek is often uncertain – "eternal" for instance doesn't necessarily refer to time, it could just indicate a supreme quality. "Eternal Life" could mean "Abundant Life." Then there's the question of which early manuscripts are the definitive ones. As early as 1707 John Mill published a Greek New Testament that showed 30,000 different available readings from the 100 manuscripts at his disposal – we now know of 57,000 different ones with little idea which are closest to the lost originals.

It's not just the language we're uncertain of. As an individual, there's little to go on. If we met him, would we like him? There's no way of knowing. Perhaps he was a religious crank, a wild-eyed, scary-looking guy. It's unlikely he came out of the desert looking like a film star after six weeks of no food, no washing and confrontations with devils (an episode reminiscent of shamanic initiation, as is the Passion of Jesus and his descent to the underworld). Even allowing for later additions to the text, we have to accept he was a fanatic. Many of his followers left him when talked about them eating his flesh and drinking his blood (John 6:52-66). Some thought he was crackers (John 10:20). Others, that he was too disreputable to be a Jew, and must be a Samaritan (John 8:48). At one point, his own family thought he was mad (Mark 3:21-25). His own brothers didn't believe in him (John 7:5) – he had four of them, and sisters, probably three or more (Mark 6:3) – though apparently none of these were divine in the kind of way Jesus was later claimed to be. The many verses where Jesus seems to attack our (and the Jewish) idea of family values are accepted as authentic by the vast majority of scholars. Why would his followers choose to invent such ugly words? "For I am come to set a man at variance against his father, and the daughter against her mother, and the daughter-in-law against her mother-in-law. And a man's foes shall they be of his own household" (Matthew 10:35-36; see also, Matthew 23:9; Mark 3:31-35; 6:4; Luke 9:59-62; 14:26; John 2:4, etc.). There are too many curses in the gospels for us to argue they bear no relation to what Jesus said. He may have been a harsh, uncompromising character who generated more fear and dislike than love (though he says nothing about the two main concerns of modern evangelical churches – abortion and homosexuality). His understanding was limited to that of the time, like taking biblical characters such as Adam and Moses as real people (for instance Mark 10:6), and drowning all life on earth apart from those in the ark as the right thing for God to do (Matthew 24:37).

On the other hand, his teaching is the most uncompromising there has been on the themes of love, service, justice and equality.

In reading the gospels he also comes across as witty, emotional, passionate, and particularly enjoyed the company of women, welcoming them as disciples and friends, particularly Mary Magdalene. He was open to everyone, taking pains to include those that Jewish society excluded – a tax collector, prostitute, lepers, Roman enemies, the Samaritan woman, the woman caught in adultery, etc. He drew an immediate group around him of a couple of dozen people, and their lives were so changed by being in his company that after his death they came to believe that his spirit was still living with them. They wanted to share the joy and fullness they still felt in his presence with others. They began to develop the "gospel," the "good news," which is that though the world might seem like it's ruled by forces of death and destruction, it's actually love that wins out in the end.

Whichever, if he came today it's unlikely he would look like a soulful shepherd. The gospels give us no clues, other than he was pretty much physically indistinguishable from everyone else, so perhaps his equivalent today would be a textile worker in a Thai sweatshop, or a small Colombian farmer. We'd possibly hear about him after he'd been murdered by the military. He certainly wouldn't have got a visa to enter the USA today – born in the Middle East, dark skinned, no job, no money, homeless, a refugee, troublemaker and persistent lawbreaker.

There are no contemporary accounts of him at all. A couple of generations after his death there are two mentions of him in *Antiquities of the Jews*, by Josephus (virtually all scholars believe the more detailed one was inserted by later Christians), which really doesn't mean anything – I know I had a great-great-grandfather called Jethro, for instance, but that doesn't provide any grounds for believing that he performed miracles simply because my father said he could. Besides, Josephus reports several individuals claiming to be the Messiah. Perhaps they believed it of themselves, it doesn't mean that Josephus believed it of them (they couldn't *all* be the Messiah). Hypnogogic hallucinations are common, let alone mental illness.

He doesn't seem to have been noticed at the time. A biographer in the modern sense of the word wouldn't have a single "fact" to go on. If you've been brought up in the Christian faith, one of the most difficult but necessary things to get your head around is that the Christian Church not only messed with the order of the books in the Old Testament, to give the impression there's a further fulfillment to come, but it's also been a bit sneaky with the order in the New Testament. The impression it gives, in the current sequence, is that the four gospels are like "biographies," coming first; and the letters of Paul, James, John, etc. are commentaries on that. In truth, it's the other way around. The first references to Jesus, in Paul's letters, speak of him more as a spiritual channel to God than a real person of recent memory. There's no mention in them of Galilee, Nazareth, Jerusalem, or virtually anything he said or did. The Gospels come after Paul's letters, a couple of generations later – all scholars, conservative or not, are agreed on this. They are interpretations of his life, made by faith communities in the light of what they had come to believe about him (this is where scholars begin to differ). Their provenance is unknown. No records of their authorship are attached to them till the late second century AD.

It's not that the Gospels are necessarily all "invented" stories. But we have to take evidence as we find it. The Jews had little more concept of "history" than they had of science. As with science, it was the Greeks who developed the idea of "history," through the first "historians," people like Thucydides and Herodotus back in the fifth century BC. They had an idea of "objectivity." Prior to that time, in the epics of Homer, for instance, as in the Old Testament, events were driven by the fickle gods. But Herodotus traveled around the Mediterranean sifting facts, looking critically at legends, rejecting the improbable, the contradictory, putting forward alternative possible narratives. The gods are largely absent. In Thucydides there's no reliance on divine events at all.

A couple of the later Bible authors who wrote in the Greek style – the author of 1 Maccabees and the (possibly Gentile) author of Luke, for example – were influenced by this approach, but as a whole the world-view of the Jews was different. The Gospels are today known as "foundation documents," written for the instruction of a spiritual community. Similar in their aims to the *Rule of the Community* and the *Covenant of Damascus* written for the guidance of the Essene Dead Sea community. There's no explanation of how the information came to be there, they're not written in the style of: "This is how we know." It's more like: "Have you heard this one?" Angels appear to Mary, Joseph, Zechariah, and the Devil confronts Jesus, but how do the writers know this? How do they "know" that Jesus prayed with intense agony in the Garden of Gethsemane, sweating blood, just before his arrest? The disciples were asleep, and didn't speak to him again. Jesus needed a Boswell to his Johnson, to write down what he said, but there was no one there to do it.

The whole structure that the Christian Church built up in the first few centuries after Jesus' death, as far as the gospels can be read as a historical record from our viewpoint today – it's a bit like someone saying now – "I know someone who's found these interesting books, English translations of something written in Mandarin on scrolls in Hunan, China, back in the nineteenth century. Who the authors are – that's a mystery, but they claim to be recording the words of a teacher who spoke in Sherpa, and lived a few generations earlier in Tibet, but nothing is known about him." Familiarity with the text disguises our remoteness from its source.

To make a comparison with Buddhism; soon after Buddha's death the first Buddhist council was called to corroborate his teaching (the *sutras*) and check the wording. His words were recited by a close companion, Ananda, to a group of 500 disciples who made their corrections and gave their approval. The words were handed down orally for nearly 200 years till the third council wrote them down. We can be reasonably sure that there is a close correspondence to what he said. There's no comparable assurance with the gospels.

This isn't the place to get into all the detail, read the theologians for yourself. The proper ones, that is. There are no serious scholars working in reputable institutions who say that Jesus spoke every word attributed to him and every event happened in the way the Gospels say. There are thousands of "Bible teachers" who do say this. They tend to work out of the colleges of the American Bible Belt, and they have their equivalents in the seminaries of Iran, or the monasteries of Tibet. It's like insisting that Earth was created a few thousand years ago, while ignoring the geology underneath your feet, the evidence in the libraries, the ruins of older cities, fossils, the cosmology of the Solar System, pretty much everything we know about life.

The serious output is enormous, millions of words a year. It's all speculative. Much of it revolves not so much around whether Jesus actually said these words or those, out of the 60,000 or so recorded (half in the canonical Gospels, the others in the non-canonical) – actually, he likely said about a quarter, with another quarter being probable – but whether he lived at all, and if he did whether we can really know anything about him for sure. The vast area of doubt allows every kind of theory to flourish, from the serious (for example, that he's a fictional version of his brother James) to the bizarre (arrived from space). Conservative arguments that the weight of later Christian documentation and Gospel manuscripts suggests that his historical existence is more certain than that of, say, Julius Caesar or Alexander the Great, are simple nonsense. The historical evidence for the existence of both those figures is overwhelming. But in any case that doesn't mean we accept them to be divine simply because their followers believed them to be so. Nobody worships them today.

The majority of scholars accept that there is a historical Jesus behind the stories. The likelihood is that Jesus lived, but didn't think of himself as divine. He was a charismatic religious preacher, healer and leader who wanted to bring people closer to God. His teaching had much in common with that of the Stoics, Essenes and other groups. We shouldn't strive for success on earth but invest in helping the poor. Live for today, as if there might be no tomorrow, with our destiny in the afterlife in the balance. Be aware that it's our heart and mind that God judges, not our adherence to particular rituals or beliefs. He was scandalized by the wealth of the Temple authorities and the injustices of his society, and came to believe that in some way he represented the true Israel, that he could bring about a spiritual kingdom on earth. He may have felt that his death could help bring this about. If so, he failed.

For many Christians it's their personal experience of the Jesus who lives for them that's important, not his teaching on this or that issue. For over twenty centuries he's been made into a kind of Hamlet of the spirit world, focusing our anxieties about death and perhaps an afterlife, our ambivalence about "self" and "other," body and soul, ourselves and God. He's fulfilled a multitude of roles, from revolutionary to messiah, ruler to servant, lover to friend, judge to savior. He is strong, but aware of weakness. Self-sufficient, but lonely. Judgmental but loving. He is meek but angry. He reconciles but divides. Following his teaching is easy but all-consuming. Out of all these contradictions devotional writers create the character they want. Many Christians journey from one image to another, interpreting him differently according to their own changing experience of life.

None of it really matters, anyway. Tell Confucians or Taoists that Confucius or Lao Tzu may not have existed (possible) and it probably won't make a scrap of difference to the way they think and live. We overestimate the contribution of individuals to events, or traditions, or beliefs. It makes us feel better, to have someone to emulate, to look up to. It makes it easier to remember the words if we can visualize a person speaking them. We need a picture. But it's the words that count.

It is the customary fate of new truths to begin as heresies and end as superstitions.
Thomas Henry Huxley (nineteenth century AD)

23. Yet Another Virgin Birth

To assert that the earth revolves around the sun is as erroneous as to claim that Jesus was not born of a virgin.
Cardinal Robert Bellarmine, at the trial of Galileo (seventeenth century AD)

For many Christians the Old Testament has some great stories of faith, but much of it is dull, at times a bit embarrassing, or even incredible. The New Testament, on the other hand, is the real meat, the heart of the message. And it's all true. After all, it's "gospel."

But it's not really any easier to read. Take the first book for instance, Matthew. It almost certainly wasn't written by Matthew the disciple of Jesus – the name was added later in the second century, with no evidence behind the choice. The scholarly consensus is that it was written around AD 70-110, with the majority tightening it up to AD 80-90. There are many reasons for this – an instance is the prophecy of the Great Tribulation in Matthew 18, which in verse 34 Jesus says will come in the lifetime of his listeners. This refers to the sack of Jerusalem by the Roman army in AD 70, with the consequent death of a good proportion of the population and the scattering of the rest. So Matthew is putting the words of a prophecy into Jesus' mouth that had already been fulfilled by the time he came to write the book.

Most scholars (taking them across all traditions, Jewish, as well as secular and Christian) see his gospel as a later theological construct rather than fact. It's not difficult to see how and why it takes the shape it does. At the time he wrote the Jews were throwing the Christians out of the synagogues, and the cult was fighting for survival as a strand of Judaism. It's dominated by the debate between the Jewish and early Christian communities as to whether or not Jesus fulfilled the scriptures. Matthew's 60-plus references to the Old Testament are there for that purpose. So the first seventeen verses provide a fanciful genealogy linking Jesus back through some Israelite kings to Abraham (and it's different to the genealogy provided by Luke, whose audience was a more Gentile one, and so he traces it all the way back to Adam, father of all). Then, in verse 18, we have the Virgin Birth.

We know Matthew was writing hagiography rather than biography because we can see him doing it. For instance, writing in Greek, he claims in verse 23 that Jesus was born of a virgin to fulfill an Old Testament prophecy. In the original Old Testament Hebrew "almah" simply means "young woman." After the Exile the Hebrew books had been translated into Persian Aramaic, and then in the third century BC they were translated from that into Greek, called the Septuagint, where "almah" becomes "parthenos," which meant "virgin." But that's not in the original. There's a different, specific word for a virgin, "bitullah," which isn't used here.

The difficulties increase when you see Luke writing a different version of the Virgin Birth story. He has the census, which Matthew doesn't seem to have heard of (and which didn't happen, at least not Empire-wide). He has the shepherds, but not the wise men, and gets the dates of Quirinius wrong. Luke's story has a domestic tone, a Christmas-card sweetness, whereas Matthew's has messages from angels, a miraculous moving star, a jealous king frightened for this throne, wise men paying homage with expensive presents, massacres (which didn't happen; Josephus was anxious to cover Herod with as much mud as he could, and doesn't mention it), night flights and escape across borders.

It gets more difficult still when you think of where the Virgin Birth is *not* mentioned. You would think that the miracle at the heart of the Incarnation would have a major place in the New Testament. But Jesus himself never refers to it. The first New

Testament books to be written, and indeed the bulk of it, are by Paul, who doesn't mention it either. Indeed, quite the opposite; in Galatians 4 he describes Jesus as "made of a woman," not "made of a virgin."

The simple answer here is that it's a story that needs a certain distance from the source to be credible. Paul and Mark (who wrote the preceding gospel to Matthew and Luke, using sophisticated storytelling techniques to develop character and conflict) were too close in time to the life of Jesus, and the story simply wasn't around, or wasn't believed. Matthew and Luke are writing when there's no one around to refute the story, and are writing for Gentiles, for Greek-speaking audiences, more prepared than the Jews to accept accounts of remote miracles, and they put it in, one of many legends about Jesus current at the time. John (or the writer of the Gospel of John) is writing later still, with a more developed theology of the Incarnation of the Word, and has no need of the more fanciful elements. He simply ignores it, along with many other tall tales of Jesus' early life that haven't made this collection of Gospels.

At this point, can you be so sure it happened? It's not that modern scholars start from a position of atheism. Most have a high respect for the Bible and what it means to our culture today. Otherwise they wouldn't bother to enter what is an overcrowded field. Doubt about how literally you can take the Bible is kick-started by the logic of the texts themselves. But let's come at it from a different angle, that of common sense. Imagine yourself into Joseph's situation. We find ourselves in a common human problem. You discover your teenage fiancée is pregnant. She hasn't told you, but the evidence is there to see. (Joseph "found" Mary to be pregnant; Mary didn't tell him till it was too obvious to conceal, or didn't tell him at all.) You haven't had sex with her yourself, and believed her to be a virgin. You ask her how it happened, and she says as a result of a dream. You might think she is lying, or mentally disturbed. You certainly don't believe her. What really happened?

Here's one possibility. Perhaps Mary really believed God had impregnated her. Perhaps she had sex and didn't know what was happening, translating this experience into a divine event. Perhaps she was the village idiot. Perhaps she was raped, scared out of her wits, and invented the story out of fear. Perhaps she had enjoyable sex with someone and lied about it. The penalty for having sex outside marriage was death by stoning. Girls are still murdered by their families today in remote hilltop and desert communities in Pakistan, and in British towns, for having sex outside marriage, willing or not.

Or here's the strongest possibility. Maybe it didn't happen in any of those ways. Maybe it was an ordinary marriage ("Is not this Jesus, the son of Joseph, whose father and mother we know?" John 6:42) – an ordinary legitimate birth, and the story was added later.

Some desperately extreme arguments are put forward to suggest a virgin birth is a physical possibility – it occurs naturally in about one in a thousand species – perhaps this was a one-off occurrence. But as far as we know, a virgin birth for humans is impossible.

So could it have been a miracle? In theory, if you believe such things. But the difficulty in accepting miracles lies in getting to the point where that seems the most likely (or only) explanation. When a woman today says, "I was raped by aliens from a flying saucer," we don't take it too seriously. But this has the supportive evidence of 3.7 million Americans who claim to have been abducted by UFOs. As many as 25 million have claimed to have flown through the air without mechanical assistance (Roper poll, 1992). The majority are perfectly sane, intelligent people. Most of the memories are "recalled" later, sometimes under hypnosis. The psychological word for this is "confabulation," the unconscious mixing of fantasy with reality to the extent that the individual cannot distinguish between them.

So if we don't believe the evidence of millions of Americans today who can be interviewed, why should we believe the reported words of a village girl in the ancient Middle East 2,000 years ago who we can't talk to? There are no witnesses and no first-hand evidence. No doctor or lab reports. Mary doesn't speak to us directly in the Bible, nor does Joseph. We don't know how many people the report went through before it was written down. What we do know is that the people of that time believed differently from us; gods coming to earth and mating with women or raping them, virgin births, these were part of the mental landscape. Anyone of significance was prone to having a virgin birth and exalted as a god. It wasn't just a common belief among Romans. The same stories were told of Greek gods and satyrs, or Arabian djinni, Celtic dusii, Hindu bhuts, Samoan hotua poro, various demons good and bad, "powers of the air." Why should we credit this one and not the others? It's a male sex fantasy.

So we start with an impossible event, for which there's no direct evidence. Both the circumstantial evidence of the times and the "hearsay on hearsay" contradictory nature of the stories within the Bible itself suggest it never happened. If God tried to bring a paternity suit he wouldn't stand the remotest chance of success. Still convinced it's true?

So little trouble do men take in the search for truth: so suddenly do they accept whatever comes first to hand.
Thucydides (fifth century BC)

24. The Kingdom Of God

Religion is a defense against the experience of God.
Carl Jung (nineteenth century AD)

So why bother with Jesus today? It's not the miracles that made him significant, then or now. In his time miracle workers were as common as wise women and witches in the villages of medieval Europe, or along the River Ganges today. It's what he said that makes him significant, and still does. People who accept the status quo don't change anything, don't found religions.

Not that Jesus actually intended to found a new religion – we can be almost certain of that. He insists that he wants to fulfill the law, not replace it (eg: Matthew 5:17). He's clear in the Gospels that his message is to the Jews only (eg: Matthew 15:24). There are verses that read differently, like Matthew 28:19 – "Go ye therefore, and teach all nations." But faced with this contradiction, it makes sense to say that the latter were added later when the faith was already spreading amongst Gentiles, having been rejected by the Jews. And besides, there was no such thing as "nations" in the way we understand the word today.

He gives many reasons, "mission statements," for his life's purpose. He has come to disrupt, to heal, to serve, to announce the kingdom and invite people in (the kingdom on earth and in heaven are used interchangeably), to bring light and proclaim liberty, to bring God's message and the Lord's favor, to bring good news to the poor, and so on. The one thing he *doesn't* say is what has become the main plank of most Christian theology and practice – that he came on earth to die on a cross as payment for our sins. That's Paul's later interpretation. There's no "altar call" in the gospels.

Jesus simply doesn't talk in terms of founding a new religion. Nazareth, Jesus' home town, was a morning's walk from

Tiberias. This was a large, bustling city on the shore of Lake Galilee which Herod Antipas had built and which he made his capital. Jesus must have been aware of the multiplicity of beliefs that jostled for space in every corner of the Roman Empire in the first century AD. He doesn't mention one of them. He never says to the worshippers of Zeus, Osiris, Mithras, Ra, Mercury, Diana, Isis, Adonis, Attis, the apostates, agnostics, Epicureans, "You're going the wrong way. You believe in the wrong God. I've come to put you right."

He never describes God, except in relation to ourselves, individually. He never tries to convert anyone to the God he believes in. As an evangelist, he doesn't impress. The fact that the Roman centurion and the Syro-Phoenician woman and the others whose daughters/friends/servants he heals believe differently from him is not an issue. It's how you act that counts, where your heart is. Love and faith are the bottom line, not faith in one god or another.

As someone who makes Julius Caesar or Alexander the Great seem relatively insignificant, you would expect him to have something new to say, to be upsetting. And perhaps what Jesus had to say was worth the disciples putting up with him as a person, with the way he ripped apart their livelihoods and families. What was it?

We don't really know whether he was more of a prophet or a healer, a rebel or a priest, an Essene or would-be Messiah. We don't even know what he believed. The creeds are a centuries-later invention. The closest Jesus comes to one is the Lord's Prayer. After a year (or three, depending on which gospel you follow) of being with him night and day, his own disciples had little idea what he was about. Their incomprehension is a constant theme in the gospels. The crucifixion and resurrection take them by surprise. Religions aren't as clear-cut as we like to make them.

What we do know is that he was a great storyteller. And those who doubt the historicity of much of what he said and reportedly did all agree that we come closest to his words when we read the parables. They're a world away from Greek philosophy or Rabbinic theology. Galilee in those days was a fertile place of fields and scattered villages, and the parables draw on the imagery of the countryside around. The countryside comes alive in his stories: wildflowers, weeds amongst the crops, wheat to be separated from the chaff, fig trees and grapevines, ripe harvests, the farmer with his seed, baking bread, fishing with nets. It's a world away from the later theology of Paul, or the Greek philosophy of the time. It's utterly different from the bombast of revelation and apocalypse, common currency back then. It's all based in real life, in the way ordinary people worked. To put it in contemporary terms, he's talking in the language of Uber drivers and Amazon warehouse workers. Of commuters on the rat race, and those who have dropped out. Of those on welfare benefits, as much as hedge fund managers.

Like Zen or Sufi tales they're mostly in the form of paradox and riddles. They ask questions rather than give answers. It's true of all great teachers. They don't tell you what to think, they prompt you to think for yourself; to think differently, unconventionally. And the really big questions – they're always bigger than the answers, and will still be standing when everyone has had their say. Because there is no answer. But in the meantime, they can prompt you to rethink how you live. And the questions that Jesus kept asking– they turn the contemporary understanding of life upside down, as much now as then.

And what scholars also agree on is that at the heart of the parables is the kingdom of God. At the age of 30, the ritual age of spiritual maturity in Zoroastrianism and many other religions, Jesus set out to preach it. "Repent: for the kingdom of heaven/ God is at hand" (Matthew 4:17; Mark 1:14). It's not in the distant future, it's here now.

That still doesn't make it easy to be sure of what the parables are, let alone what they mean. The same parables are treated differently in different Gospels, with different emphases, different styles, and the later writer of the Gospel of John scarcely includes any. Mark's parables tend to be ones of nature, set in the world of the villages. Some of them have an allegorical meaning, like the parables of the sower and the fig tree. Luke avoids allegory, even when repeating one of Mark's parables. He lets the meaning look after itself, and focuses on Jesus' teaching on prayer or the dangers of wealth. Matthew uses allegory and emphasizes the teaching on hell, which hardly occurs in Luke.

The "kingdom" is mentioned over 50 times in Matthew, for instance, but John, probably a couple of generations later, doesn't mention it all. Rejected by the Jews, Kingdom teaching was even less likely to appeal to the ruling Romans, so it was edited out. The Church has rarely discussed it since. Both Catholic and Protestant branches have consistently persecuted people down the centuries who tried to take this teaching seriously.

But in looking at the whole rather than focusing on particular verses it's possible to get an idea of what Jesus was on about. Though obviously we only have a tiny fraction of his speech, the most memorable words. Even if you include the non-canonical gospels, everything he said, including duplication and later additions, would only have taken a couple of days. It's the most slender of foundations on which to build a religion, if we want to go back to the source, but it's all we have to work with.

The parables illuminate different aspects of the "Two Great Commandments" of Matthew 22:36-40 and elsewhere:

Master, which is the great commandment in the law? Jesus said unto him, Thou shalt love the Lord thy God with all thy heart, and with all thy soul, and with all thy mind. This is the first and great commandment. And the second is like unto it, Thou shalt love thy neighbour as thyself. On these two commandments hang all the law and the prophets.

The second is "like unto it," not inferior. If you don't love your neighbor (anyone) as yourself, you don't love God. Love, like justice, is a virtuous circle, not a one-way track. It's in giving that we receive. The subject of almost all the 65 or so of them is the kingdom of God, and how you have to be ready for it. It's the "economy" of true Christianity, the forgotten heart of the message. It has little to do with what we think of as Christianity today. There's no theology. It's not "consider the creeds," but "consider the lilies."

The most common theme is that the kingdom is worth everything (Matthew 13:44-46), but it's free. It's always open for you (Matthew 20:1-16). Indeed it seeks you out. It will grow and take over (like the mustard seed, Mark 4:30-32). It's not incremental, a question of doing a little bit better, it's a different way of living (Luke 5:36-39). It's turning to a new reality (Mark 1:14-15; Matthew 4:17). Jesus is not here to restore a lost state of union with God but to show the one you already have. "You are the light of the world" (Matthew 5:14). It's more a question of recognition than of choice.

Life is not a burden, a shadow from which we need to escape, from which God will redeem us. It's a gift, a grace. It's a feast, a wedding (Matthew 22:1-14), a celebration. Your true nature is not a material one, subject to time and decay, or a sinful one, but an ever-present innocent spirit. Love, joy, and peace: these are your virtues, this is how you are, if you can realize it. So live openly and freely. Live like the flowers do, without a care. Be aware of the beauty around you. They don't worry about tomorrow, or how many of them there are, or whether they're looking their best, they just do it. Live in the present moment. Enjoy it. Now is all that counts (Matthew 6:25-34; 10:29-31; Luke 12:22-34). Now is all there is. If you acknowledge this gift, saying thank you for what you want, you'll find you have it. If you believe you have it, you will. Belief is creative. It can move mountains (Matthew 17:20-21). Anything you ask for you'll get (Mark 11:24). There's no mystery, no hidden truth. You are free to ask for and imagine anything. If two or more believe the same thing, and ask for it, the power is multiplied exponentially (Matthew 18:19). The universal Father wants you to have everything.

The kingdom is not for the few, it's for everyone. It ignores the distinctions that scarred Jewish society, indeed defined it. Jesus reaches out to those who God has cursed, like the disabled and blind (Leviticus 21:18-20). He mixes happily with prostitutes, the hated tax collectors, even lepers, who everyone believed must have committed the most terrible sins and were strictly segregated. He goes further: every individual is of supreme worth (Matthew 20:30-34; Luke 15:4-7). It's what you are in yourself that matters, made in the image of God, not how you look, what your family is, what your race or gender is, what you believe, what you think of yourself. It doesn't matter if you're ill, poor, or criminal (Luke 14:16-24; 19:1-10). The Jews (along with virtually everyone in the first-century world) saw tolerance as weakness, open-mindedness as sin. God blessed distinctions, and rewarded those who practiced them. The more you gained and the more powerful you were, the closer you were to God. He gave you a hard time if He was displeased with you. But the kingdom of God Jesus described is the reverse of theirs and ours. Those who are ahead in the social exchange have more they need to lose. They're still trapped in the race for gain, for self-esteem. The more you have, the farther from God you are (Luke 14:16-24). The first will be last, the last first (Luke 14:7-11; 18:10-14). It's those who suffer now who will be blessed (Matthew 5:3-12). God is embodied in the powerless, not the powerful. It's not the fittest, or cleverest, or wealthiest who get to the kingdom, it's the sick. How we treat them is a measure of our own soul's health. We're all weak, it's the soil in which we grow. We must treat them as God has treated us. And it's the children. They are innocent, and innocent of judging others. Be like them, be happy, no need to justify it, no need to join the rat race. And it's the poor. They have not exploited others. And it's reciprocal.

Forgive people what they owe you (Matthew 18:23-35). The more forgiveness, the more love in return (Luke 7:41-43). It seems not too far from the law of returns, called karma in the East. If we can forgive unconditionally we receive unconditional forgiveness. You have to forget calculation, the measurement of benefit to yourself. It's in giving that we are blessed, through giving love that we receive it. Loving your neighbor is a given (Luke 10:25-27), but this is not enough.

Go out of your way to help everyone you can. When it comes to separating the sheep from the goats on Judgment Day, it's not what you've believed that is going to matter, but what you've done (Matthew 25:42-45):

> Then shall the King say unto them on his right hand, Come, ye blessed of my Father, inherit the kingdom prepared for you from the foundation of the world: For I was an hungred, and ye gave me meat: I was thirsty, and ye gave me drink: I was a stranger, and ye took me in: Naked, and ye clothed me: I was sick, and ye visited me: I was in prison, and ye came unto me. Then shall the righteous answer him, saying, Lord, when saw we thee an hungred, and fed thee? or thirsty, and gave thee drink? When saw we thee a stranger, and took thee in? or naked, and clothed thee? Or when saw we thee sick, or in prison, and came unto thee? And the King shall answer and say unto them, Verily I say unto you, Inasmuch as ye have done it unto one of the least of these my brethren, ye have done it unto me.

You must love your enemy too (Matthew 5:38-48; Luke 6:27-34; 10:28-37). If someone hits you, let them hit you again – though as the theologian Walter Wink points out, the meaning here is "if they backhand you, turn the other cheek." It's not cowardly submission, it's a refusal to be humiliated, a form of nonviolent resistance. Don't harbor injustice, hatred, bad feelings. In the eyes of God you are them. If you see yourself in a leper or your worst enemy you've understood. The key to the new attitude is giving up the "self." Free yourself even from all ties of obligation and family (Matthew 8:21-22). Forsake all that you have (Luke 14:33). Overcoming the world is not conquering it, but realizing that it doesn't matter. Lose yourself, become like a child, love for its own sake, and you can enter the kingdom (Mark 10:13-15; Matthew 16:24-25; Mark 8:34-36; Luke 9:23). Accept life as it is. Let the self die (John 12:24). When we lose it we dissolve into divinity. It's only when you can really give up everything you want, everything you think you are, that you understand who God is. Then there's no separation. We go beyond forms, beyond choice, and God takes over. We share His peace. Our true self, or divine self, the "I" that experiences, is inwards: "The kingdom of God is within you" (Luke 17:20-21). It's what all the great spiritual teachers say, in all traditions. Understand this, and you will live in the love of God, as Jesus does (John 14:21).

Freud called loving your enemy the most impossible commandment ever written. It outrages our sense of boundaries. But Jesus says there are no boundaries. God even loves the good and the evil in creation without distinction (Matthew 5:43-45). It's only when we realize this that we see the kingdom. It's only when we forget ourselves that we find God. Because God is to be found in everyone else. We can be happy in so far as everyone is happy. The kingdom is in the midst of us (Luke 17:21). We are in him, and he in us (John 17:21), we are all in each other. Everything created is a manifestation of God. There is not so much difference here from the central Hindu perception that "there are no others." The Jews regarded God with such reverence that they did not address Him by name. Jesus calls Him Abba, "Dad." We are all sons of God (John 20:17). We are all one (Matthew 25:40). We can never be separated (Matthew 28:20). Jesus models the way to live in conscious union with God (John 14:6). There really is no divide between Him and us, us and the world. Jesus is simply the mirror in which we can see ourselves. Is this the best you can do? Can you go further? In going further toward God we see Him coming toward us. When we realize this we no longer need divine beings "up above." Contrary to the experience of Moses, Micah, and dozens of others in the Old Testament, God is no longer "visible" (John 1:18; 5:37). The kingdom of God is "spread out on earth," and made real in ourselves, by forgetting ourselves (Mark 1:15; Luke 4:43; 17:21-23; Matthew 4:17). God is as much like our twin brother as He is like an almighty deity up in the sky. It doesn't matter which mountain you go to, to worship God (John 4:20-23), He's not "up there" anymore. He's "down here," "in here." In John 17:3 "eternal life" is not living in a fairy-tale palace in the sky after death, it's "knowing the one true God."

In other words, the kingdom is here, now. It's not some distant point in the future, or up in heaven. It's what we have. It's what we can make of it. Heaven is here, not up there, not in the future. The kingdom is not a place, but a relationship. And we're all in it together. If one of us is oppressed, or poor, or disturbed, we all are. And it escapes more exact definition because it comes across in the life and words of Jesus as not so much a "state" as an "attempt." The more closely we try defining it the more we end up with another set of boundaries that will need jumping. He's unstoppable in his pursuit of it. Family, disciples, Pharisees, Romans, none of them could persuade him out of it. It's not a search that can easily be mapped out in steps because it's internal. It's what you make of it. It's a process, not a formula. It challenges you in so far as you're open to being challenged. He never tried setting it down in writing. He never turned it into laws; laws are there to be broken. He didn't set up a community or suggest working arrangements for living together; he seems to have overturned whatever living arrangements he could find. There's no practical advice. There's no mission statement, no soundbite. It's just "go further." If you've given some of your money away, give it all away. If you've forgiven your enemy seven times, forgive him seventy-seven times. If he hits you, let him hit you again. There's no hedging of bets, no qualifications.

It's as demanding a teaching as any on earth. All our instincts say that living in an orderly society is a question of compromise. You give a bit, take a bit. The kingdom even offends the evolutionary logic of altruism – that cooperation works in the long run because if we help others they might one day help us, because cheats will be found out and punished. It asks us to shed all our instincts for self-preservation, developed over millions of years. Living in the present, not worrying about the future. Untying the laws that keep society sane and ordered. It asks us to abandon the rational mind, the main asset that distinguishes us from the animals, and instead just trust. Have faith. No matter how tough it gets. It's faith that makes us what we are. Faith and love. They can achieve the impossible. Live like a child of God with the stars in your head and the flowers at your feet. Give like a child of God who has everything and needs nothing. We all came into the world with nothing. We didn't choose our parents, our advantages. We're all responsible for each other. Believe like a child of God with complete faith in your fellow-children. And it will be true.

Is this all daft? Can we believe that basically we're more good than bad, that cooperating to create a peaceful, just world is possible? We go back to the beginning of this book. We need a big idea to make sense of the world we live in, to make it a better one, to provide a large enough incentive to act in the interest of everyone rather than ourselves. It's our recognition of the never-ending difference between what is and what could be that enables us to make things happen, and turn from indifference to love, from apathy to action, from animal to spirit. This is what the evolution of life and consciousness is about. There are no brick walls, glass ceilings, other than those we create for ourselves. There's no one stopping it, other than ourselves.

We start as insignificant. As individuals we all are. Jesus is no different from us. But we could have a great future together. The kingdom places the highest possible value on every individual life. Bringing them together in love creates the kingdom of God on earth. But we can't do it on our own. Just loving our neighbor isn't enough to get us going. We need to recognize that the demands of love and goodness are more than we can manage, and yet we have to imagine further. We need this bigger idea to aim for, the sacred ideal, this idea of truth and love that we call the kingdom of God, the idea of a larger, universal purpose that we call God, or we'll find ourselves in an evolutionary dead end. We'll die the death of a thousand wars and pollutants, till the crust of the planet we live on runs out of patience.

Jesus doesn't stand outside the tradition of great spiritual teaching down the ages, as some kind of divine interloper a couple of thousand years ago, but bang in the middle. At the heart of the experience of all religions is the feeling of reclaimed oneness with creation, both what we see and what we can't, of belonging to a whole that is both divine and beautiful, true and loving. And at the heart of his teaching is the ancient idea that God is in him, he is in God, we are all in God, God is in all of us; and the proof of the inner realization is measured by action in the world, giving ourselves unstintingly, singing our hearts out, patiently building the kingdom of God on earth brick by brick.

To sum it up, life is just what it is, and being a Christian is just a particular way of living it rather than looking for a different one. We're in the kingdom of God if only we could see it. It's not the next world that's important, but this one. Not the future, but now. Not the kind of beliefs we have about God, but the kind of people they help us to be.

It's not history that's important, it's the myth. History is just what has happened, where we've gone wrong. Crucifixion is what we do to others and may suffer ourselves – the loss of loved ones before their time, cancer, madness. It's the myth that matters, the expression of what we hope to be, resurrected in a brighter world. If we could really follow it, we would change our selves, and bring a better world about. But we can't seem to do it. We can manage it in pieces. Individuals can create it between themselves to some extent. Many of the best relationships are based on the idea of sacrificing your own interest for the benefit of your partner. And we can extend that to the family. Some saintly individuals manage to extend it further, to communities of the disabled, or the poor. But for most of us it's an ideal that rarely happens. But it's there though, as an idea.

Unlike the Buddha, Jesus' reasons for thinking as he did, how his thinking developed, have not been passed on to us in terms we can understand. It's the lost story of Christianity. But this idea of the kingdom is the key to his message. It's evidently not what the Jews were expecting. His disciples could never quite get the hang of it. Maybe Jesus himself didn't know where it was leading. Perhaps he had no plan, no purpose, and was going with the flow. All we know is that the material in the gospels that is most likely to have been said and enacted by him revolves around the kingdom of God. He may have believed that in giving up his own life he was helping to bring it about.

And that's the potential power of Christianity, the power of Jesus, today, that he taught again this wonderful idea that would make us all happy if only we could all take it on board at once. And it would have to embrace everyone, because humankind is one. But few of us can be the first to let go of what we have. We don't believe we have the courage, or the love. We're content, more or less, with the image we have, with the religion that tells us we're okay if we confess. The one we've inherited, absorbed from our peers, developed for our protection. We would feel stupid if we abandoned it. The kingdom is for the fools of this world.

Men will wrangle for religion, write for it, fight for it, die for it; anything but live for it.
Charles Caleb Colton (eighteenth century AD)

25. The Evil Of Wealth

When goodness grows weak,
When evil increases,
I make myself a body.
In every age I come back
To deliver the holy,
To destroy the sin of the sinner,
To establish righteousness.
Bhagavad Gita (second century BC)

The kingdom is what life should be like, what it could be like. It's what it is, if we could realize it. But we change the teaching. We corrupt the insight. We create new creeds and laws. Control turns into oppression. Inspiration turns into deceit. We drown in our own creations. Every now and again a teacher picks up the original manual and says: "This is how we're meant to do it. We're all on the same side. Love each other. Treat others as you would like to be treated." Then we sink again (after we've killed the teacher).

So what does the kingdom mean in practice? Can it still fire the imagination?

There are many aspects we could cover – repentance and forgiveness, freedom from the self and from time, equality and relationships, God and inner peace, nature and love. We could talk about health and healing, stress and well-being, the environment and community, oppression and justice, grace, gender and disability, war and peace, and much else. But this is a book of snapshots. Let's just look at one, which might seem a bit prosaic at first, what Jesus says about money.

For 95% and more of our history we haven't had money. Coins don't appear till the sixth century BC. We simply lived on what we could forage and hunt, or plant, and bartered. In the Old

Testament there are two main ways of thinking about money. Early on, in the nomadic wandering days, with each goat herder thinking of himself as good as any other, God gives wealth to those He favors. It's the measure of His approval. Many Christians still think this way, particularly those promoting the prosperity gospel. The other, which comes later with the prophets, when the nomads had settled down, started to own property, and people, got involved with commerce, trading, building temples and paying taxes, is that the wealth is not ours, it belongs to God and is for sharing. Every jubilee year we should redistribute it.

That, incidentally, is a rather bald, incredible statement. It may have been honored more in the breach than the observance, Jews certainly haven't followed it for many centuries now (and have generally been excluded from land ownership). But Leviticus 5:1-13 and other passages are clear. The land belongs to God, and every seven years should lie fallow (good agricultural practice, let it recover, look after it – apart from animal dung, they didn't have much in the way of fertilizer). Every seven years times seven, the fiftieth "Jubilee Year," society presses a reset button. All debts are written off, property is restored to the original owners, and slaves are freed (though the slave's wife and children were still owned by the master, and foreign slaves were never freed, they were inherited by the master's heirs – Leviticus 25:44-46).

Okay, there's some small print, there are ways of wriggling off the hook, lawyers have always been busy on behalf of the rich. But the intention is there, and in contemporary terms, that's still pretty mind-boggling. Socialist manifestos have nothing on it. Inheritance tax looks feeble. Personal fortunes, banks, companies – every fifty years, they'd pretty much disappear. Hard to see that being voted through as government policy.

Of course it's not just a Jewish idea. Societies have always faced the problem that returns from capital are greater than the rate of economic growth, leading to increasing inequality, until plague, war or revolution levels it out again – which always happens, or, logically, by now, one person or family would own everything on the planet. A thousand, two thousand years before the Old Testament prophets, Mesopotamian kings periodically cancelled all debts, as described in the Hittite *Song of Release*. Most of the old empires, though, institutionalized debt, leading to effective slavery. There's an example in Genesis 41: Joseph shows the Pharaoh how to store grain in the good years. When the Hebrews are suffering in the lean years they come to Egypt in search of food, and become indentured to the Pharaoh, leading to the slavery from which it takes them nearly half a millennium to escape, in the story of the Exodus.

And of course cooperation rather than control goes right back to the 95% of time we've lived in groups of a few dozen or hundred. People had to stick together, food had to be shared, if the families were going to survive. Back then, one or two individuals accumulating the bulk of the food and possessions – unimaginable. It's still the main purpose of good government, apart from defense (or should be) – to redistribute excess private wealth for the good of society as a whole, to build and improve the infrastructure, hospitals, schools, etc. that everyone depends on, and help those who can't help themselves.

But where does Jesus fit in? Let's take the Gospels literally for a moment, like good Christians should. In the first three Gospels, the earliest in the New Testament, there are about ten times as many verses on money as there are about going to the cross, or on sex and marriage/divorce. Around half the parables are on money and possessions. Which makes it surprising that the cross seems so significant in Christian teaching and money rarely covered. We've built up a lot of teaching *about* Jesus without paying the same kind of attention to what he *says*. Perhaps we just don't like it.

We might take the view that these verses on money aren't relevant now. We live in a democracy. We don't have slaves.

We're not under foreign rule, we're not oppressed. Society is fairer, most of us are middle class rather than poor, and we don't have numbers dying of starvation in our streets. But it's not just our neighbors down the road we should be thinking of. The world today is more of a global economic unit. Most of what we buy comes from abroad, as food and manufactured goods, or as raw materials to have value added, often by a multiple of several hundred times from cost to retail. We've exported our cheap labor and the associated hardships. Economically as well as spiritually, everyone is linked to everyone else.

In the time of Jesus, Palestine and every small region of the world was pretty much self-sufficient. Rome was very different, needing massive imports of grain, slaves and animals, etc. to keep the population fed and entertained, but overall the relative discrepancies in wealth between different regions and nations were close to zero. It remained this way for about 1,500 years until the Christian nations (successively the Portuguese, Spanish, Dutch, Russians, French, British, Germans, Italians) began their empire-building, plundering the resources of other countries (at the end of the eighteenth century, before the British took it over, the largest GNP in the world was that of India). Two hundred years ago the ratio of wealth between rich and poor countries had reached 4 to 1. Over the next century it rose to about 10 to 1. Today it's 60 to 1, and still increasing. Today it's we in the developed world who have the money, who are rich.

The overall percentages of rich to poor in the global economy are just as bad today as they were in Palestine in the first century AD. Then the top sixth of the population (governors and priests) owned around 60% of the wealth. Today, globally, the top sixth (that includes you, or you couldn't have paid for this book) control 80% and have an average income of $70 a day; 30% of the world's population live on less than $2 a day. The daily income of around half the people in the world wouldn't buy a cup of coffee in Starbucks. Four out of five people in the world live in substandard housing with no decent sanitation. One-third are malnourished, with no clean water. Every year around 10 million children die of starvation, many times more than that from preventable diseases, while 100 billion dollars of food gets thrown away in North America alone. Whereas many in the Third World can't find enough to eat, the main health problem in the First World is eating too much. For most people, life is not much different from 2,000 years ago.

The higher up the scale you go the worse it gets. Even within the United States, 10% average 10 times the income of the remaining 90%, the top 1% average 40 times more, and 0.1% average 200 times more. The richest 1% in the world earn more than the remaining 99%. Twenty-six individuals earn as much as half the rest of the world put together.

I'm not suggesting that it's the fault of the rich that they have so much – they're working within the framework of the society we've created. Money just generates money. The more you have, the more you get. Bill Gates became the richest person in the world way back in 1995, when he hit $10 billion. He's a great philanthropist, putting other very wealthy people to shame, if they had any. He has given away nearly $50 billion, but he still has $126 billion. It's an insane system. Neither am I suggesting that it's the fault of individuals in the West that much of the world is underdeveloped – most countries are poor because they have poor institutions, power is controlled by a few, and they run the countries for their benefit. But we voted for the policies that enabled the inequity within rich countries to happen. All the underdeveloped countries were effectively ruled by Western empires for most of the last two to three hundred years, and we plundered them, extracting resources, destroying local institutions and economies, leaving them with no social capital to build on.

So if Jesus were around today he would probably have had as much to say on money as he had then.

What are his words to the rich? He could have preached to them from the Old Testament, quoting verses like Deuteronomy 15:7:

If there be among you a poor man of one of thy brethren within any of thy gates in thy land which the Lord the God giveth thee, thou shalt not harden thine heart, nor shut thine hand from thy poor brother.

But he goes further, much further. Rich people cannot enter the kingdom of God, period. Christian commentators consistently water down the message by saying that it's the love of money he condemns, not money itself. But that's not there in the Gospels. It is by the time Paul writes to Timothy (1 Timothy 6:10), but Jesus doesn't sugar the pill like that. He never says: "Money's okay if you use it for good, if you give a portion to charity, if you don't let it rule you." He says if you have it, give it away (Luke 6:30). If you hang on to money you'll be corrupted; you don't understand how dangerous it is. There's no ambiguity here (eg: Matthew 6:24 – *No man can serve two masters: for either he will hate the one, and love the other; or else he will hold to the one, and despise the other. Ye cannot serve God and mammon*). You simply can't be rich and follow him in a world where there are poor people. If you really treated the poor as you would like to be treated, if you saw God in them as well as yourself, you couldn't be rich. You couldn't live with yourself.

The most vivid teaching is given in the parable of Lazarus (Luke 16:19-31), who is the only parable character to be given a name. He hopes for crumbs from the rich man's table. The rich man doesn't do anything wrong in the parable: he comes across as a decent enough guy, concerned about his family. He's just rich. After all, he'd earned his wealth, and it trickles down from the top to benefit everybody. No doubt Jesus' listeners thought, as we might, that Lazarus' poverty wasn't the fault of the rich man. Maybe the fault was even with Lazarus. Perhaps he should have found himself a job. If the rich man had given him more he would probably have gambled or drunk it away. But the condemnation of the rich man is absolute. He doesn't get a chance to repent. He doesn't even get a chance to warn his wealthy brothers of the burning fires of hell that are waiting for them.

Money is the acid in relationships, which are all that matter; both at a personal level – I've seen it in my own family – but also of course more broadly, more corrosively, through society as a whole, with a multiplier effect as distinctions increase. In case we haven't got the message, it's repeated many times. On judgment day the people God rejects are not the ones who aren't saved or born again, but those who haven't helped the poor, the ill, the prisoners, the strangers (Matthew 25:42-43, 45). There isn't a clearer message in the Gospels.

There's a sad irony here. The wealthy top sixth today largely live in North America and Europe. As 75% of Americans say they have made a personal commitment to Jesus Christ, the rich are mostly Christians. The majority in the world are like Lazarus, outside the gates.

If you're in the top sixth today, earning $25,000 or so a year (the average income of the West), there's little doubt about it; if you take the Gospels literally, you're damned. The confessions you've made, the time you've had with Jesus himself, even the numbers you've converted, are all irrelevant. The Western Christian Church is going wholesale to hell.

The Churches talk instead about individual salvation. But Jesus says nothing directly about going to the cross to save people from their sins. Most scholars see the few verses that obliquely point to that as later additions. Nor does he talk of setting up a church and sacraments through which people can be forgiven their sin. The doctrines of the Trinity, the divinity of the Holy Spirit, the dual nature of Christ, are not mentioned in the Bible. Capital Letter Doctrines are later interpretations by the Church formulated to define and control access to God. They are not words that relate to the way we all live. Indeed, they take away the responsibility for change from the individual and give it to God. These matters of sin and salvation have a role to play in the psychology of faith, but a secondary one. They're tools for improvement, not descriptions of the problem or the solution.

That's why the Church hasn't made a difference for the better in the last two millennia. On the spiritual insight and guidance that Jesus offered it reimposed the old, old religious role of propitiating the divine through sacrifice. And if you've ever seen an evangelical preacher whipping a congregation into frenzy over the "power of the blood" you can see the ancient practice of blood sacrifice still exerting its pull. The unique angle that the Church took was to turn the idea of sacrifice around and see it as a once-for-all event; and one which demanded nothing from us, other than acquiescence; no regular, respectful offering; but one that God has offered us. In the biggest conjuring trick in history, it made Jesus into the Son of God so that God was sacrificing Himself for humankind rather than man cutting and burning chickens and children to keep disaster, death and demons at bay.

Even if you were the most sinful of all
Sinners, you would cross over all evil
By the raft of knowledge alone.
Bhagavad Gita (second century BC)

26. Losing The Way

No one can be redeemed by another. No God and no saint is able to shield a man from the consequences of his evil doing. Every one of us must become his own redeemer.
Subhadra Bhikshu (nineteenth century AD)

Social justice is one of the dominant themes in the Bible, and Jesus brings it to the forefront, making it personal. Of course it's hard, if not impossible, to live on a Third-World income in the West (though, ironically, a country like the USA is so unequal within itself, with poor provision of public services, that an American teenager is on average going to die five years earlier than his peer in a country like Bangladesh). But that in itself is a judgment on the kind of global society that we've largely shaped. Because individual responses are not enough. A kingdom of God with a few individuals present is as meaningless as a heaven with a few saved souls. It's a contradiction in terms, because we're all in God, all one. A true kingdom response to the inequalities in the world would mean redefining what we mean by society. Rethinking the definition of money. We should think about abolishing altogether the idea of an economy based on debt and individual success. Get rid of "interest," which was morally condemned by most religions, including Islam, Christianity, and Judaism (with 14 condemnations in the Old Testament), up until around the sixteenth century.

Sure, there are plenty of arguments to say that life is getting better, capitalism is working, we're turning the corner, and the wealth will eventually trickle down. But the rich keep getting richer, in the USA and UK, with everyone else's income and life expectancy static or declining. The more we have, the less we want to share. The richer people are, in general, the meaner they are. The richer the nation, the less generous it is in giving aid (the USA is the meanest of all the developed nations). Where your treasure is, there will your heart be also.

Maybe we should think about creating a society where no one in the world has an income less than the current average of $9,000 a year. In modern parlance, "optimize the velocity of money and the circulation of value." Put crudely, in other words, a hundred people with $10,000 to spend bring more economic benefit to society as a whole than one person with $1,000,000 squirrelled away in offshore funds (add zeroes as you wish – the richest families have over $30 trillion stashed away there). Maybe we should be as wary of people who want excessive wealth as we are of those who want excessive power or sex at the expense of others. Tax millionaires more, and ban billionaires (currently, broadly speaking, the more money you have, the less you are likely to pay). Extend basic human rights to cover everything needed for a decent life, and extend them to the environment. Recover the Old Testament idea that decisions should be made for the benefit of the "seventh generation."

Would this simply involve redistributing wealth to people who haven't earned it? Maybe. But is the wealth of the West all down to honest hard labor anyway? To take an example from chapter 39, perhaps we should repay the 20 million or so kilos of gold and silver looted from Central America in the sixteenth and seventeenth centuries. At a rate of interest about half that we charge Third World countries today for debts incurred largely for the benefit of Western businesses (particularly arms manufacturers) the accumulated debt would run to several hundred digits and bankrupt every Western government many times over.

Of course this teaching is fantasy. To change like this is impossible. It goes against human nature. Difficult enough to make life work as it is without giving your hard-earned income to people you don't know, and who probably won't thank you for it. I couldn't do it. My home, where we've lived for forty

243

years and the kids have been born and raised, is my castle, the garden my sanctuary. My little boat, my escape. I'm not the stuff that real "disciples" are made of. Unlike Peter and Andrew, who Jesus called away from their nets to follow him, I'd just carry on with my fishing. "Wish you well, sir, a noble project, but beyond me."

Actually, most of what Jesus says, I've always kind of hoped that he didn't really mean it. That he was going over the top, to make a point. And he certainly uses rhetorical devices like hyperbole and irony. But the message seems to cut through all that. It *is* a simple one. It's radical. All religious founders are more radical than their later followers imagine possible. That surely is the point of the Gospels. Jesus went the whole way. He said better to try living the impossible than the immoral. If he was around today he would probably be saying that the first step in following him is to live on the global mean income, and give everything above that to those who have less. The degree to which Christians would think this to be absurd is the measure of the distance the Church has traveled from his teaching. All I know, is that in 60 plus years of some kind of engagement with Christianity, I've never heard a preacher/pastor/priest say anything like this. Homilies on how to be a better person, sure. Condemnation of sin and people who are sinners because of their lifestyle, or believe a slightly different creed, sure. Tithing, sometimes. But never, ever (other than from charlatans who want the money given to them) words like those in Matthew 19:16-22 (an episode also covered in Mark and Luke) to the rich young man who has done everything right:

> *If you want to be perfect, go, sell your possessions and give to the poor, and you will have treasure in heaven. Then come, follow me.*

After all, who would then pay their salaries (which generally accounts for half and more of all church revenues)? The words,

"For ye have the poor always with you" (Matthew 26:11), are not an excuse for neoliberal capitalism, they're a judgment, a curse.

The trouble is, we all want that bit extra for ourselves, to put more into our cupboard than into our neighbor's, to protect our own interests. We need more and more possessions, bigger houses to put them in. We need more space, more privacy, more technology, more money to pay for it all, and the merry-go-round spins faster and faster, while many starve to death, most suffer for want of a few dollars. "The world has enough for everyone's need, but not enough for everyone's greed," as Gandhi said. Maybe we'll give up a bit, but only if everyone else does too. Few are prepared to go out on a limb. And if we do it gets chopped off. Going to church is so much easier. We get saved, without really having to lose anything. Perhaps that's what Jesus meant by taking up your cross and following him. We really do have to be prepared to lose it all.

I used to decry the idea that Jesus was some kind of premature socialist or anarchist, but Marx's summary of communism: "From each according to his ability, to each according to his needs," effectively paraphrases Luke 3:11: "He that hath two coats let him impart to him that hath none: and he that hath meat, let him do likewise." And of course these terms weren't around then. Capitalism, in its modern form, is a recent innovation. Adam Smith, the "Father of Economics," doesn't mention the term in his definitive *The Wealth of Nations*, the first modern work of economics, published in 1776. The trade guilds that were the bedrock of European economies in the Middle Ages were more like trade unions. Merchants were entrepreneurs. The domination of the economy by corporations who have a legal obligation to maximize profits which can be returned to shareholders so they can trade shares, without any acknowledgement of other stakeholders or the public good and public services which they rely on, barely goes back more than a century. And the jury on that is still out – in a hundred or even fifty years' time maybe our grandchildren might be saying, "What the hell did that generation in charge from the 1980s to the 2030s think they were doing, consuming as if there was no tomorrow and resources were infinite? The world was relatively stable, they had the resources to change direction, and they blew it."

Modern capitalism is the antithesis of Jesus' teaching. Corporations have to grow to pay back their shareholders rather than contribute to the common good, so the economy has to grow. So people need to consume more, new markets have to be found and exploited, wages driven down, value extracted from real communities and delivered to the remote owners of the capital. It's turned the natural world, and the people in it, into units of money. Worse, actually, in that we don't cost in the exploitation of natural resources, destruction of the habitat, with the accompanying pollution and carbon release. We decide that Amazon.com, Inc. is worth a trillion dollars, but the Amazon itself, the lungs of the earth, nothing. So we can burn it down for cheap burgers. Rather than individual lives being priceless, every life, human or otherwise, has a price. Jeff Bezos is the richest individual in the world because (along with being a business genius) Amazon has nearly a million workers earning $15 or so an hour and it pays minimal tax. In some years he could give them each $100,000 and still be better off than he was the previous year.

Jesus was driven by a vision of the whole person, of the whole world, how we relate to each other and to God, rather by economics or politics. He saw that it's only when we have no vision for something better that we want to accumulate. If we knew we were going to die next month we'd look back and wish we'd given more of ourselves to others and invested in relationships rather than more expensive furniture. We'd spend the next weeks working out how best to give things away rather than getting more. And the vision Jesus had was to live as if now is all that matters, where the world and God are indivisible; where sickness, evil, space, and time itself are overcome by love. But to suggest that he had nothing to say about politics or economics, about how we should live together socially, is to miss the whole point of his teaching. Like admiring the styling of a car without realizing that its purpose is to get you somewhere. Like having several expensive cars when neighbors a few blocks away struggle to afford the bus fare.

The teaching is not unique to Jesus. Great teaching never is unique to one person. The Buddha underwent a greater degree of personal deprivation. Muhammad too lived an ascetic life. Giving up everything to go on the road with just a begging bowl is more a characteristic of Hindu teachers than Christian. But going further than you might think reasonable or possible in the cause of other people seems central to what Jesus was about. And again, we can only speculate on what he really said. But even scholars who doubt the existence of a real Jesus would put the teaching against the evils of wealth at the center of the "teaching of righteousness" out of which the first stories about him grew, and which the first Christians followed.

This teaching on money is not on the fringe of Christianity, the slightly uncomfortable, awkward teaching that's mentally consigned to the "irrelevant today" category, like the laws of Leviticus, but part of the bottom line. It's the modern emphasis on salvation without lifestyle sacrifice that's heretical. It's the prosperity gospel that influences so much evangelical Christian thinking and government practice that is satanic (along with its New Age equivalent, the Law of Attraction – it's easy to become a millionaire, just imagine it hard enough, and it will happen).

Of course others select different texts and come to different conclusions about Jesus. Most Jewish scholars see Jesus as an erratic but essentially orthodox Pharisaic leader, maybe teaching much the same as Hillel with a sprinkling of Essene thought.

Some Christians see him as a teacher of inner wisdom and enlightenment, with the kingdom being entirely spiritual. Most, on the other hand, see him as a kind of apocalyptic, universal superhero, who has risen from the dead and will return one day to rule the earth. More likely is that unconditional love was at the core of everything he said and did, with the second coming and judgment being written in later. This tradition may have come from John the Baptist (whose followers some of the disciples probably were) rather than Jesus.

But everyone finds something different. It's like trying to get a message out of Shakespeare. Maybe there is no "message." He was just living and speaking without the kinds of boundaries we hem ourselves in with. He really was completely open to God, to goodness, and life. And when you are, there's not really much more to say other than remain completely open. Treat others as you would want to be treated. Take it where it leads you.

It's fair to say that if this kind of kingdom really was at the heart of Jesus' teaching it was short-lived. The first disciples "had all things common; and sold their possessions and goods, and parted them to all men, as every man had need" (Acts 2:4-45). They lived as he taught (it's kind of ironic that many American Christians today see the "socialism" of the Democrats as the biggest threat facing their country, as if by European standards the Democrats weren't already a right-of-center party). But their successors grabbed the devil's temptations that Jesus had rejected, turning the kingdom of God into the kingdom of gold leaf, with the Church being the richest organization in the world over most of the last millennia rather than one of the poorest. For most of the last couple of thousand years it owned around a quarter of the land in Western Europe (in a period when wealth was measured in acres). One pope in the fourteenth century even declared it heretical to say that Jesus had been poor; despite that statement in Luke 9:58, one of the most challenging to our Western lifestyle today, particularly when it comes to our treatment of refugees and the homeless:

Foxes have holes, and birds of the air have nests; but the Son of man hath not where to lay his head.

Of course, there have always been individuals and movements in the Church trying to restore the original vision of simplicity, equality, oneness with creation, self-sacrifice for others – from attempts in the first centuries to start the first hospitals, through the Franciscan and Dominican orders down to the liberation theologians of the twentieth century. A stream of theologians down the centuries have condemned the love of money. But, overwhelmingly, in practice, the "Church" has been synonymous with wealth, and supported the oppressive power structures of the day. It soon lost sight of the "world" as the "kingdom," full of the presence of God, with every person, every relationship sacred, there to be realized and enjoyed. In the process of conquering the world Christians forgot about saving it. They turned it into a collection of individuals who could be converted one by one and pay their dues, with the Church as the turnstile clocking them in, much like the temple priests of Jerusalem grew fat on the sacrifices people brought to the altar. It's been heading off in the wrong direction ever since. Jesus would have disowned the religion the Church created, and would have been appalled at the idea that even one heretic had been tortured in his name.

There's a choice we all have. It's not so much a question of what Jesus taught as what you're prepared to believe. We make him into what we want him to be. We create the kingdom we want. We get the politicians and the world we deserve. It's not difficult to believe in gods coming to earth, in being born again, in our selves living on after death; most people have believed one form or another of this for tens of thousands of years. Believing that God can be what we make Him; that we can create the kingdom of God on earth; that what we create is worthwhile whether we live on to enjoy it or not – that's the hard part.

Go to now, ye rich men, weep and howl for your miseries that shall come upon you.

Your riches are corrupted, and your garments are motheaten.

Your gold and silver is cankered; and the rust of them shall be a witness against you, and shall eat your flesh as it were fire. Ye have heaped treasure together for the last days.

Behold, the hire of the labourers who have reaped down your fields, which is of you kept back by fraud, crieth: and the cries of them which have reaped are entered into the ears of the Lord of sabaoth.

Ye have lived in pleasure on the earth, and been wanton; ye have nourished your hearts, as in a day of slaughter.

Ye have condemned and killed the just; and he doth not resist you.

James 5:1-6 (first century AD)

27. Turning A Man Into A God

John, there must be one man to hear these things from me; for I need one who is ready to hear. This Cross of Light is sometimes called Logos by me for your sakes, sometimes mind, sometimes Jesus, sometimes Christ, sometimes a door, sometimes a way, sometimes bread, sometimes seed, sometimes resurrection, sometimes Son, sometimes Father, sometimes Spirit, sometimes life, sometimes truth, sometimes faith, sometimes grace; and so it is called for men's sake.
The Acts of John (second century AD)

The Acts of John was circulating a generation or so after the Gospel of John, itself several generations after the death of Jesus, and was accepted by parts of the Church as canonical, till it was "consigned to the fire" at the Second Council of Nicaea in AD 787 – the decision-makers in this instance were as far removed in time from Jesus as we are from the twelfth-century French rulers of England. It's one of many interpretations through which the early Christians understood his life and death. At one extreme, with the later John: God on earth, amongst us all, created by us all, working for the good of all. Doesn't matter what you call him, how you define him. Push at the door, and you understand. For the earlier John: God in the heavens, sending a Son to earth, his successors ruling on his behalf, offering salvation to those who believed, and hell for everyone else. Believe in him or perish. One of the many contradictions at the heart of Bible-believing Protestantism is that it accepts the judgment of a Church it regards as flawed, of individuals who were not "saved," on what the Bible itself is. All reasoning on this subject is circular: "We believe in God in the way the Bible says; that way is right because God inspired the people concerned to make the right choices about which books to be included in it, even if we don't think they were real Christians." Those who submit to the authority of the Catholic Church use the same circular logic.

Unpicking the differences between the two gospels would be another book. But for me, the idea that Jesus came from the heavens (or somehow God's sperm was inserted into Mary's womb) two thousand years ago, to save us, is a hard one; an example of the way we change good religion back into superstition. Okay, it made a kind of sense when it was thought the earth was a couple of thousand miles across, and was all there was, when gods had sons, when they and their messengers regularly commuted to earth, but would we give it a moment's consideration if it was put forward as a new idea today? To look at this more closely for a chapter, if Jesus/God really did appear on earth like that, couldn't he/they have tried a little harder? He doesn't write anything down, he appears when most of history is already over, in a remote province of a particular empire, after dozens have already come and gone. He doesn't even travel farther than you could drive in a car today in a couple of hours, depending on the traffic.

In comparison, a contemporary of his, Apollonius of Tyana, a wandering philosopher, traveled over much of the Empire with his disciples, also visiting Ethiopia, Mesopotamia, and maybe even India. He was also believed to be miraculously born, performed miracles, healed the sick, cast out demons, raised the dead, and was worshipped as divine. Much better known than Jesus for some centuries, his historical existence far more certain, he met with many famous people, including the Emperor Domitian, and lived into his eighties, when he was raised to heaven (reportedly).

Jesus doesn't even try to be an Apollonius. Or, indeed, a Paul, who went everywhere he could, traveling thousands of miles, mostly on foot; talked to whoever he could, preferably the top guy; wrote to everyone he could, set up as many churches as he could. As the Son of God, Jesus could more logically have arrived tens of thousands of years earlier. Or he could have waited another two thousand years till we had television or radio, to spread his message. Or he needn't have come at all – God could just have killed him up in heaven, written it up in lights around the planet, in all languages, sent a piece of paper for everyone to sign saying they believed He'd done it – just think how many more people could have been saved. Christians might say that that's too obvious, that we need to have room for faith. But this is exactly how God *does* behave in the Old Testament, and how people of the time believed all gods behaved. He appears in pillars of fire, sends earthquakes and lightning strikes on demand. He has no difficulty in providing the equivalent of detailed architect's drawings for the Tabernacle, the Ark, the Temple. He issues laws that cover every aspect of behavior, for every moment of the day. Jesus even has a mountaintop meeting with God (the Transfiguration; Matthew 17:1-8 etc.) that parallels Moses' encounter on Mount Sinai. This would have been an ideal occasion for him to come back with a scroll that spelt out the new covenant. But it doesn't happen. His followers had to remember, recreate an image in their heads, and maybe they didn't remember everything right, and over the generations brought their own hopes and expectations to the story.

Verses in the Gospels are quoted to show that this Jesus himself believed in his divine mission, like the classic statement in John 14:6, "I am the way, the truth, and the life; no man cometh unto the Father, but by me," repeated around the world millions of times a day. Maybe he did, but then tens of thousands, hundreds of thousands of people have believed the same, of themselves. It's called a messiah complex; or in medical terms, "narcissistic personality disorder" (NPD). Maybe he was schizophrenic – his own family thought he was mad, at least at one point (Mark 3:21-35). And in any case, the Gospel of John, though incorporating earlier oral tradition, is written in a very different idiom from the other Gospels, and is several generations later (with the first three dating from a generation or two after Jesus lived). In John, the Greek style is better, the chronology and selection of events different, the theology more developed. Jesus talks in monologues rather than parables, with carefully constructed literary images of himself (the true shepherd, the vine, and so on). Most scholars would say it's the least likely Gospel to reflect what Jesus actually said, particularly in this instance. It's a later writer (or more probably writers, in the plural), who never knew him, constructing a theology.

Read as a whole, the Gospels show a Jesus who doesn't seem as interested in this kind of role as later teaching makes him out to be. He never tries to "prove" a particular definition of God, he offers no arguments. The closest he comes to a creed is the Lord's Prayer. It doesn't even seem to bother him whether people believe in his God or not. He engages people on their own terms. He has his demands, but they don't amount to "creeds," or "theology," it's only "do this." Living in Nazareth (it's not clear that it existed, it was probably too insignificant a village to have been recorded, but the indications are that if it did, it was a morning's walk from Herod's cosmopolitan and Greek-speaking summer capital of Tiberias), Jesus must have rubbed shoulders with worshippers of Zeus, Osiris, Mithras, Ra, Mercury, Diana, Isis, Adonis, and a host of others. He doesn't mention any of them. The fact that the Roman centurion and the Syro-Phoenician woman whose daughter he heals believe in a different god to him is not an issue. It's how you act that counts, where your heart is, not whether you believe in one God or another. He talks about loving God and loving your neighbor, and that one doesn't count without the other. They amount to the same.

Maybe if Jesus had lived longer he would have passed on his ideas in more detail, more coherently. By comparison Muhammad had over 20 years between his revelation and his death. The Buddha had 45 years, Confucius maybe 50. They had more time to develop their teaching, pass it on to their disciples, to write it down, to organize the succession. Jesus was a relative youngster. How seriously would anyone take a 30-year-old today who made his kind of demands, his kind of claims? He taught for only one year (if you follow Matthew, Mark, and Luke), or maybe three (if you follow John). He was gone before most of his contemporaries knew he was there, one of many flash-in-the-pan troublemakers from the provinces who regularly disturbed the peace of the capital.

Maybe if he had lived longer he would have passed on his ideas more coherently, and in more detail. "Love your enemy" doesn't amount to practical advice. But he seems uninterested in having his teaching handed down to posterity. In so far as the gospels are biography at all, they are unauthorized. They are written in hindsight, by later generations, at a time when some early Christians were trying to make theological sense of what had happened, adding interpretation to story, creating a myth to support their belief. Perhaps Jesus would have been as surprised by their contents as we are.

In contrast Muhammad gave Islam a blueprint for society as well as a religion. Muslims know that they *must* give to the poor. *Zakat*, the giving of alms, is one of the five pillars of the faith. Similarly Buddhists know they *must* practice nonviolence, Jains *must* be vegetarian, to be otherwise would be like cannibalism, etc. These are defining characteristics. It's one reason why Christians argue over so many issues so intently, there are few clear guidelines. And of course it's not that rules make you better either, but they do make for some consistency. So when you begin to doubt the creeds that the Church laid down in the centuries after Jesus, there is less to hold you. Which is maybe one reason why Islam, for example, has been so much less affected by secularism than Christianity.

Jesus is as good an example as we have of the dynamic master teacher, storming into the towns from the desert, blowing away the cobwebs and structures that self-interest has created, bringing people back to universal themes of truth, justice, freedom, equality, spirit; of "oneness." After his death there's a vacuum. The awed disciples, without the same intensity of vision but with an average mortal's share of self-interest, scurry around stitching up the hole and recreating the world as it was before. With time the bureaucrats parcel out the vision into prescribed chunks called doctrine, adding their flourishes; the leadership types organize groups into communities, sometimes called churches; the salesmen go out with the one and only true original product and knock everyone else's; the accountants start to look for profit. It's true of governments as well: the path from vision to compromise, inspirational leadership to deadly hierarchy, cooperation to tax. Much the same happened in Islam, where Muhammad's followers proclaimed him the last prophet soon after his death; though unlike followers of Jesus they didn't go as far as proclaiming him divine.

We have too many gods, and the Christian Church underestimated Jesus by turning him into another one. The ultimate example in business of kicking a colleague upstairs, to an honorary position, to avoid the awkward questions. He was a Jew, in the tradition of the prophets. He wasn't the son of a sky god. The Jews were the least likely people in the Empire to believe that, one of the few peoples who saw an impassable gulf between God and humankind. They were so upset about identifying anything human with God they were prepared to die in their thousands in protest against Roman soldiers carrying standards bearing human images into Jerusalem.

There's an old joke about a priest and a rabbi talking about job promotion prospects.

"I've got a chance next year of being made bishop," says the priest.

"And what after that?" asks the rabbi.

"Well, I couldn't expect anything more, but who knows,

maybe a cardinal?"

"What's after that?"

"Well, there's only the Pope. I couldn't hope for that."

"There must be something else."

"There's nothing after that. Only God comes above the Pope."

"Well, why not? One of our boys made it."

Conservative Christians though insist that the New Testament describes Jesus as being divine, the Son of God, so that's fundamental to Christian belief; they even try to tie him in to Old Testament prophecies, or phrases, as if what we happen to call the Bible makes any kind of coherent literal sense. So let's look at it more closely. They point out that Jesus is frequently referred to in the New Testament as "Lord" (though this can mean anything from "sir" upwards) and "Christ," maybe not identifiable with God but indicating divinity in some form. In one of the earliest documents, in 1 Corinthians 16:22 ("Our Lord, come!" NRSV), the suggestion is that Jesus is prayed to, and Jews prayed only to God. But there may have been many Jews whose perception of God as holy and separate was not as clear as others, and who believed that the coming Messiah would be divine. At no point in the first millennium BC can you say there was a monolithic certainty amongst Hebrews or Jews as to what they believed.

Jesus is also referred to frequently in the Gospels as Son of Man and occasionally as Son of God. They're slippery terms, no more easily defined than "spirit" or "mind." Son of man is the expression that Jesus uses most and seems most comfortable with. "Son of Man" means pretty much "mankind" (Psalm 8:4). Adam, Israel, and kings of Israel are all referred to in the Old Testament as Son of Man. Jesus frequently distinguishes between God and himself (eg: Luke 18:19; Luke 22:42; Mark 13:32). The synoptic gospels all lean in this direction. John takes a higher view (John 6:69; John 8:59), but here Jesus also raises his disciples to the same level as himself (John 20:17) and suggests a distinction between himself and God (John 14:28). In John 10:34 he says to them, "Ye are gods." The meaning overlaps with son of God. "Son of God" is another vague phrase with multiple meanings (capitalization is a late seventeenth-century addition to the Bible text – talking of which, if Jesus is the Son of God, and co-equal with Him, shouldn't pronouns used in relation to him also be capitalized, as in "Him"? Never understood that). Adam, David, Jacob, Ephraim, angels are all called sons of God, as were other prophets around the time of Jesus. Jesus calls peacemakers sons of God (in the Greek text of Matthew 5:9). He's also described as fulfilling the Jewish tradition of the Messiah (Hebrew for "anointed one," the Greek term being "Christ"). The Messiah would be a great leader and obey the Law perfectly, but he is nowhere described as God, or the Son of God. "Messiah" meant someone through whom God worked in history in a striking way. The Persian emperor Cyrus is called *mashiah* in Isaiah 45:1, because through his actions in returning the Jews to Judah he was fulfilling the will of God, even though he may never have heard of Him.

Moreover, many verses in the Gospels suggest that Jesus defined himself as "man" in the ordinary sense of all people being sons of God. He frequently distinguishes between God and himself (Luke 18:19; 22:42; Mark 13:32). This is particularly so in the first of the Gospels to be written, Mark, where there's only one reference to Jesus as Son of God, and that of doubtful authenticity. The references increase through Matthew and Luke, a generation later. And of course there are the words on the cross: *My God, my God, why hast thou forsaken me?*

In Paul's letters he refers to Jesus as "Lord" more than 200 times, which is ambiguous. "Lord" (Greek "Kyrios") can mean "God" or "Sir," or pretty much anything in-between. Paul never comes straight out and says that Jesus is divine. There are one or two verses that suggest it, like Philippians 2:6 or Romans 9:5 (disputed translation) but the balance is on the other side.

Outside church-related institutions the overwhelming scholarly view is that the first Christians did not believe that Jesus was divine, that was idolatry – they even forbad speaking the name of God. The idea of Jesus' divinity developed because non-Jews who believed in him as the "way" to God (and in the first century AD they were increasingly in the majority) would have assumed he was one himself. They wouldn't have been able to understand him *not* being one. But for the first three centuries the highest status he reached was God's Son. Sons, by definition, are not the same as their fathers. They are "begotten," created later. It wasn't till the fourth century AD that the phrase "Son of God" was promoted to mean "God the Son," as coequal with God. Almost all scholars, even conservative Christian ones, would agree on that. By then, Jesus had taken on all the titles that previously belonged to emperors like Caesar Augustus – Savior of the World, Redeemer, Liberator, Emmanuel, Lord of Lords, God from God, the One who established Peace on Earth, etc.

In the first century AD Jews believed that whatever form the Messiah took he was definitely going to make a difference. At the very least, the Romans would be driven out, the exiles would return, and a reign of peace would begin. At best, the dead would be resurrected, God would rule the world and judge humankind. None of these things happened when Jesus came. Few outside Palestine knew for generations that Jesus had lived at all. For these kind of reasons Jesus' own people do not accept him as Messiah, and still regard "Son of God" as an essentially pagan idea. Today, the idea that God has a "son" is hard to take seriously, unless you've been brought up to think that way. It's a return to the old Hebrew, pre-monotheistic way of thinking, like seeing God as a serpent.

Truth seems to come with the final word; and the final word gives birth to the next.
Rabindranath Tagore (nineteenth century AD)

28. Miracles Everywhere

Lead me from the unreal to the real.
Lead me from darkness to light.
Lead me from death to immortality.
The Upanishads

The Christian Church has got this the wrong way round. It wasn't the early Christians who converted the Roman Empire to believing in Jesus as coming from the Father in heaven, but the Empire that converted them. The first "Christians," Jews, did not believe in Jesus as the Son of God. That was blasphemy. The later generation Christians, Greeks and Romans and others, the non-Jews, did. It would have been surprising if they hadn't. The predominant Mediterranean world-view of the time, described by Hesiod eight to nine centuries earlier, was that life was a ladder with animals, people, heroes, angels, and gods on different steps. But they all interacted. Gods in heaven were too remote, they were always coming to earth. Their offspring returned as heroes to heaven. They metamorphosed into one another (look for instance at Ovid's *Metamorphoses*, one of the most influential works in Western culture, which records the history of the world from creation to the deification of Julius Caesar, which was written in AD 8, contemporary with Jesus). An emperor could be divine almost by definition, indeed usually was. You were liable to be crucified for disputing it. Even a great athlete must have something of divinity about him. These divine or semidivine characters were expected to heal and do miracles, that's why they were followed.

We can see examples of this polytheistic way of thinking in the New Testament itself, as soon as we step outside the world of the Jews. There are two curious episodes in Acts. One is at Lystra (Acts 14:8-13), where Paul heals a cripple and as a result he and Barnabas are hard put to prevent the locals from thinking they are the gods Jupiter and Mercury. Another is in Malta (Acts 28:6) where Paul is declared a god because he has survived both drowning and snakebite. I used to put this down to the ignorance and superstition of the locals, amongst whom Paul was moving with the light of knowledge of reason and faith, like a brave nineteenth-century missionary. Far from it. These (in modern Turkey) were prosperous places, much closer to the center of the Empire than Judea. This was normal, it was the way people thought. Almost everybody (apart from Jews and skeptics) believed that gods had sons and they came to earth and had sex with virgins. That's what gods did. It was expected of them.

To put this in a broader context, sons of god in the first century AD were as common as celebrities today. Every other hilltop had a god, a brooding presence or a hyperactive deity chucking thunderbolts or kidnapping the prettiest girls for sex. Zeus fathered hundreds of children by women, mostly virgins. His son Hercules is the best known today, thanks to Walt Disney. Alexander the Great, Plato, Augustus, were all believed to be born of virgins. In fact they're common all over the world. Greek gods and satyrs, Arabian djinni, Celtic dusii, Hindu bhuts, Samoan hotua poro, various demons good and bad, all had human sons and daughters. The births were usually noteworthy in some way, being in difficult times, in the obscurity of a cave, in hiding from angry tyrants, with innocents being slaughtered, with miraculous signs and stars in the sky, foretold by prophets and wise men, under divine protection. This particularly applies to the more prominent sons, like Buddha, Krishna, Muhammad, Zoroaster, Jesus.

Every town in the Empire had statues and temples to a variety of these god-men, drawing variously on a common stock of imagery, iconography, and tradition. Asclepius for instance was a popular one, born of Apollo and a mortal mother, with hundreds of cult centers in the Empire. He heard prayers and healed people, and even raised a man from the dead, but was killed by Zeus for his impertinence. Later he was restored to life and deity. His symbol, like that of the early Hebrews, was a snake coiled round a pole. In contrast, Jesus could not only raise the dead, but defeat death itself (Hebrews 2:14). In this he out-trumps even Hercules, the deliverer and protector, perhaps the most popular god-man of all.

Today the idea that God has a "son" is hard to take seriously, unless you've been brought up to think that way (why even use sex with a virgin on earth to reproduce? Two thousand years ago it wasn't commonly understood that much reproduction in nature is asexual, which is more efficient). It's a return to the old Hebrew, pre-monotheistic way of thinking, like seeing God as a serpent. But as Christianity developed, the followers increasingly added these themes and stories to their own tradition. Take any competing god and you can see the parallels. Mithraism was one of the most popular cults, originating from the old Iranian God of light (still followed in Hinduism today with the god Mitra). Most scholars accept his followers had rituals similar to those of Christians, but which predated Christianity: for instance, baptism, anointing with oil, a eucharist, and Sundays. Christian bishops in many parts of the world still wear a *mithra* or miter and carry a shepherd's staff in imitation of the bishops of Mithras, much as they adopted the dog collar from the Roman civil service and the purple of the bishop's robes from the imperial dress. We still call priests the Mithraic "Father."

Like Jesus, Mithras seems to have been worshipped as "the way, the truth, and the life," as redeemer and savior. He was born on the traditional date for gods born of virgins (as also happened with Adonis, Attis, Bacchus, Horus, Krishna), our 25 December, a date which the Christians took over in the fourth century AD. The shepherds and the Magi visited him as a baby. He performed miracles, healed, was buried in a stone tomb, and rose on the third day, in March, at the time of the spring equinox. The similarities were such that Augustine later said the priests of Mithras worshipped the same God as he did.

Another was Dionysus, born to a virgin goddess in a cave, eaten by the Titans when he was a baby, later resurrected. The symbolic act of eating meat and drinking wine, the flesh and blood of the god (John 6:54-55), at a special meal brought union with him, and he in return granted eternal life. Turning water into wine was his specialty. Legends about it were related at the annual festival held in his honor at the coastal Palestinian city of Sidon. Maybe the Church adopted this tradition into its texts, which is why at a wedding Jesus turns water into a thousand bottles of wine (John 2:3-11), a truly Dionysian quantity for a small village. Maybe it was a useful text of the time which could be turned to illustrate how the "new wine" of the gospel replaced the inferior "water" of Jewish law. The similarities between these incidents in the life of Jesus and those of Attis, Adonis, Osiris, and others are endless.

This is not to say there is no historical basis for these Gospel stories. Take the water into wine for instance. It may be that this scenario appeared first in oral tradition because it was based on Jesus' own wedding. Virtually all Jewish males were married, it would be surprising if Jesus were not. That explains why his mother was the main guest, why the host turned to her for help when the wine ran out, why Jesus felt it his responsibility to supply it. A later writer or compiler may have edited the identity of the bridegroom out of the text to accommodate the increasing sense of Jesus' divinity.

As another possibility, of course, there's the orthodox view that this was a genuine miracle, whatever that means, and the Son of the God of the universe of hundreds of billions of galaxies and umpteen trillions of stars and planets had nothing better to do with his microscopically short time on earth than help a local wedding party get massively hungover.

Most of the miracle stories can be read today in terms of new knowledge (mental illness rather than demons), misunderstanding (he inspired the 5,000 to feed each other rather than somehow multiplied loaves and fishes), mistranslation (walking "by" the water and "on" the water use the same word; or perhaps the disciples just couldn't see him properly in the dark and rain; or perhaps it's just a "borrowed" story – kings like Xerxes and Alexander walked on water, any god could...), or later elaboration. Read the theologians for the ins and outs of which miracles are more credible than others. The number that are seen as such, even by conservative Christian scholars, diminishes with every decade.

Few for example would accept today that the ascension, more significant than the resurrection in Western art, literally happened as the New Testament describes it. It's clearly meant to be taken literally: the disciples are shown looking intently up into the sky as Jesus disappears from sight. But quite apart from the miraculous aspect there are more mundane problems. For instance in Luke 24 Jesus ascends on Easter day itself, whereas in Acts 1 it's 40 days later. Two of the Gospels don't even mention such an apparently significant event. But the main difficulty today is that the account is so clearly based on the world-view of the time, which situates heaven a few hundred feet up in the air. If it were still there now jumbo jets would be knocking holes in it and people falling out. If it's off the edge of the universe, and Jesus is still ascending, invisibly fast, he would barely have started to cross even just our own galaxy yet, assuming he was traveling at the speed of light.

Still, this kind of belief works for many. Millions believe in the divinity of certain individuals. Hindus believe that God manifests himself in avatars, divine beings taking on human form to aid humankind through its spiritual evolution. They can materialize holy ash, or jewelry and watches, heal illness, even raise people from the dead. Recent examples are Swami

Narayan, who has the largest Hindu temple in the UK dedicated to him; Meher Baba, who kept a voluntary silence for 44 years till his death in 1969; Shiva Mahavatar Babaji, who reportedly disappeared in a ball of light in 1922; Sai Baba, whose miracles are better chronicled than anything in the New Testament, and died in 2011. There's a line of holy Mothers, the best known of whom currently is Mother Meera, still living in Germany. Billions have believed, and many still do, that the soul takes flight to the heavens through the hole at the top of the shaman's lodge, or rises in the smoke of the fire, scatters in the sparks, or descends to the underworld through a tomb or cave. It's not difficult to believe in the supernatural. Most scholars though, even conservative ones, would say that to take the ascension event literally undermines rather than reinforces faith.

In respect of this, there's a simple message we can take from the gospels, and from all good religious teaching down the ages. There is no single Son of God. That's idolatry. We are all sons and daughters of God. Or of the Devil. If we want to be.

Such as men themselves are, such will God Himself seem to them to be.
John Smith, the Platonist (seventeenth century AD)

29. How Real Is The Resurrection?

And the Son of God died, which is immediately credible because it is absurd. And buried he rose again, which is certain because it is impossible.
Tertullian (second century AD)

So Christians tend to apply a sliding scale of credibility and significance to miracles. Most you can question, or ignore, but the Resurrection is different. The majority line goes that if the Resurrection isn't true, then nothing is. Faith is meaningless, Christianity pointless. As Paul says, in the first chronological mention of it, in 1 Corinthians 15 ("And Christ be not risen, then is our preaching vain, and your faith is also vain"). It's like Custer's last stand. If you don't believe in it, you can't be a Christian. It seems an odd stand to take, that you can disbelieve the Ascension and go to heaven, but if you disbelieve the Resurrection you go to hell; but there we go.

But there is not an iota of "evidence" of the Resurrection, direct or circumstantial, that would get into a courtroom.

In looking at the Resurrection as it's described in the New Testament, the trouble is, we're relying on stories written by people we don't know, from sources we don't know, with no record of transmission.

The more incredible a story is, the higher the level of "proof" needed to believe it. The philosopher Hume first laid this out in 1748, in his seminal work *On Miracles* – *The wise man proportions his belief to the evidence.* In other words, the more extraordinary the claim, the greater the quality and quantity of evidence that is needed to support it. We shouldn't necessarily believe everything we're told, or even everything we see – we have to evaluate it – that magician didn't really saw that lady in half, did he? Where's all the blood? Imagine the kind of proof we would want if it were claimed of someone today that they had risen from their grave, several days later; the interviews with the risen person, the medical evidence, the video footage (and how sure are we that it hasn't been faked?).

The resurrection of Jesus as a physical, bodily event doesn't seem to feature in the first Christian documents that we have in the New Testament, the letters. There's no mention of the empty tomb, or Mary Magdalene or the other women, or any details. In so far as Paul does talk about the appearance of Jesus to Peter, then James, and all the disciples, then the 500 (a hearsay report which Paul has "received"; who don't appear in the Gospels, no names or testimonies given, no indication of time or place), and finally himself, he mixes up these supposedly factual sightings with his own visionary experience. Again, the word *ophthe* is used – more associated with inner spiritual vision than physical sighting. In Acts 9 he doesn't see a "real," physical Jesus. He sees a blinding light, and hears a voice. His companions don't see or hear anything. It reads like a mental breakdown. To put it perhaps more crudely than Paul would have wanted, any individual's vision of Jesus is as good as anyone else's. And in 1 Corinthians 15:40-47 he talks of resurrection raising "spiritual" bodies, as opposed to "natural." (He also says in 1 Thessalonians 4:15 that Jesus will come again in the lifetime of those present – 2 Thessalonians 2:1-5 was written later by a disciple of his, as if from him, to explain why that didn't come to pass, contradicting the message and declaring it a forgery.)

If we examine this in terms of evidence, no one even claims 2,000 years ago to have seen Jesus rise from the dead. No one records it at the time. There are various stories that circulated decades later about followers who saw an empty tomb, originating from the Gospel of Mark, on which Matthew and Luke are based, written around AD 70, 40 years after the supposed event took place. But the accounts are all different. Different numbers of women, or men, with different names, in each case. They see different things, angels, or men, or Jesus, or nothing. Compare the accounts for yourself if you want to check it out. Jesus doesn't appear again or he appears in Galilee but not Jerusalem, or Jerusalem but not Galilee. Part of the reason for this is that Matthew and Luke draw on Mark, but the last verses of his Gospel on the Resurrection are not in the most reliable manuscripts and almost all scholars agree they were added in the second or third century AD to provide evidence that Jesus was seen alive; in the original it ended at 16:18, with the young man telling the women that he is risen and they flee in terror, telling no one. So because Matthew and Luke didn't have that source to draw on, they went their separate ways.

Then there are problems about the post-Resurrection appearances. The disciples are shown as believing Jesus appeared to them, but again *ophthe* is used. The appearances are also uncertain in that Jesus is variously seen as physical – ready to be touched, asking Thomas to do so (a story about doubt clearly meant to reassure later generations of Christians that if they have faith in Jesus without having seen him they will be blessed rather than disadvantaged; and also to diminish the status of Thomas, the disciple most likely to have actually written a gospel, the *Gospel of Thomas*), eating fish – at other times not, appearing suddenly in their midst, not wanting to be touched (as with Mary), and more of a ghost than a body, materializing twice through a wall (John 20:19, 26). At other times he appears to be human, but not recognizable. In the walk to Emmaus (Luke 24:13-35) he talks with Cleopas and another disciple or wife, they have supper, and it's only when he breaks bread that "their eyes were opened." Then he vanishes. This is not convincing.

The whole episodic nature of the post-resurrection appearances is as confusing as anything in the gospels. Weeks apparently go by without an appearance. What was he doing the rest of the time? And then there are the further appearances after the ascension; to Stephen and Paul. And what about the later appearances to the saints? To people today? Visions of Jesus are not uncommon, to put it mildly.

Associated with the death and Resurrection there are various supernatural events. In Mark (around AD 70) there's darkness over the land. Matthew (around AD 75) has an earthquake and tombs opening, with the dead rising (presumably with new bodies, or they couldn't have appeared to people and been recognized, as Matthew 27:52-53 suggests). Luke (around AD 80) adds the curtain of the Temple being torn in two. Astronomers know there was no eclipse at the time, no darkness. Zombies coming out of tombs would be in the record. This is all invented. Not as conscious deceit – it's just that if you believe your dying Lord rose from the dead, then this is what would have happened. With both the appearances and the supernatural effects it does seem that the detail increases as time goes on, though the latest canonical gospel, John, doesn't mention them at all. As with the Virgin Birth, John (or the writers who built this gospel up in layers over decades) may simply have considered these divine special effects too crude to be taken seriously. They are in any case rather mouse-sized to accompany the death of the Son of the Ruler of a universe of billions of galaxies. You would at least expect them to be felt around the Roman Empire – even around the planet. If no contemporaries on the spot noticed anything out of the ordinary happening, why bother?

The story is expanded further in other gospels not included in the New Testament. In the *Gospel of Peter* (AD 50-100) the soldiers on guard at the tomb see two gigantic angels who come down to bring Jesus out with his cross. Other non-canonical gospels take a more "spiritual" line. In the *Gospel of Mary*, Mary sees Jesus in a vision, not in reality. Peter is suspicious of the vision but Mary is vindicated and joins the apostles as they go out to preach. Later tradition provides a further variety of interpretations. One says that James was the first witness; another says Peter, rather than Mary, giving him more authority. Maybe the New Testament

Gospels are more reliable than the non-canonical ones, but there's little clear reason for saying so, apart from tradition having declared them to be such.

Of course it's hard to read Matthew's account of the passion – the most detailed of the four – and not feel moved by it. Look at all the detail. Nobody would have bothered to invent it all, or had the nerve. And we know it happened because we experience the presence of Jesus. When Peter denies Jesus and the rooster crows, it crows for all of us. We all know that we're weak, we all betray the good when we're afraid, and it's Christ alone who can save us. If he wasn't a savior, who is there to forgive us? How can God forgive if He doesn't understand what it means to be like us?

But things don't just happen in the Gospels because they "happened." They could only happen because God meant them to happen, because He had already foretold it. The writers couldn't conceive of life outside God. Every act, every moment, had spiritual meaning, as it still does for many today. In spiritual autobiographies and missionary stories of today you see the same process at work. The events in their life are interpreted in terms of their faith, as lessons God is teaching them. The tougher the event, the harder but more beneficial the lesson (try hard enough, and you can make anything positive). The truths are all there in scripture. And the writers of the gospels searched scripture for a word or a phrase that had similarities to the event they wanted to describe. Well, it's not like they even had to search, they probably knew much of it by heart, they lived and breathed scripture every moment. And the words they picked were often taken completely out of context, or mistranslated, or misunderstood, or all three, because, like any politician today, they were interested in getting a message across, not looking for the "truth" of what happened. They're "foundation documents," written for the instruction of a community, much of it only marginally more relevant for us today than scrolls like the *Covenant of Damascus* written for the Essene communities around the Dead Sea.

Matthew is writing an idealized spiritual picture of his Savior. So the ride on a donkey into Jerusalem is there because it parallels Zechariah 9:9. Indeed because Zechariah confusingly mentions an ass and her foal Matthew seems to say that Jesus rode both at the same time (21:7). Overturning the money-changers' tables suggests Malachi 3:1, Hosea 9:15, and others. The Gethsemane experience on the Mount of Olives brings to mind David in tears. The arrest and trial echo dozens of references about being surrounded by enemies: making no answer, Psalm 38:13-14; Pilate washing his hands, Deuteronomy 21:6; the suffering on the cross, Isaiah 53:3-12; the two thieves on either side, the evildoers circling the psalmist in Psalm 22; the wine and the gall, Psalm 69:21; being forsaken on the cross, Psalm 22:18; the words on the cross are quoted from Psalm 22:1; dividing the clothes, Psalm 22:18; thirty pieces of silver, Zechariah 11:12; Judas, Obadiah 7; hanging himself, 2 Samuel 17:23; Jesus not having his legs broken, Exodus 12:46; darkness over the land, Amos 8:9; earthquake, Joel 2:10; rising on the third day, Hosea 6:1-2. Why not rise on the next day? Or immediately? Because "three" is one of the "power numbers," like seven, twelve and forty. If something is said three times it's likely to be true. So Jesus returns three times in Gethsemane to find his disciples sleeping (though who was there to report that?). He is mocked three times as he hangs on the cross, in a group of three crosses. Peter denies three times that he is a follower of Jesus (again, no one of the other disciples were there to confirm that). Perhaps more significantly, rising on the third day is one of the oldest tropes in religion, in terms of dying and being reborn, patterned on the three days that the moon descends into darkness before the new crescent moon appears. And so on.

This is not to say definitively none of this could have happened. And of course maybe Jesus chose to ride a donkey, overturned the tables, because he saw himself as fulfilling scripture. No one would claim that of Pilate or Judas though, that they acted as they did to fulfill Old Testament references. Later Christians continued to invent links between the Old Testament and Jesus, like claiming that the fawning poem about the birth of a prince in Isaiah 9:6-7 applies to him.

(This principle, incidentally, accounts for many other stories in the gospels, where there are parallels with the Old Testament; Jesus continues the tradition of water miracles by calming the waves and walking on the sea. Where Elisha heals one leper (Namaan), Jesus heals ten. Where Elisha multiplies 20 loaves and feeds 100 men, Jesus manages to feed 5,000 from five loaves (and two fish), with the added bonus of twelve baskets of leftovers. Etc.) Indeed, there is little in the Old Testament to support the idea of Resurrection itself – Job 7:9 for instance – "As the cloud is consumed and vanisheth away: so he that goeth down to the grave shall come up no more." So it comes down to a choice. You can believe all the miracles actually happened, and Jesus performed them to pattern himself on the Old Testament, or you accept that generations after his death people talked up stories to present him as a figure in that tradition.

The sources for a physical resurrection are tenuous, unconvincing, contradictory, absent, or even point to the opposite conclusion, and there's no way of questioning them. Apologists say this doesn't necessarily mean it didn't happen. Indeed it may even make it more credible in that if the whole thing was a stitch-up the disciples would have made a better job of it, wouldn't have used women as witnesses, etc. Which is somewhat convoluted reasoning – it's like saying if you're a lawyer, in front of a court, the more terrible a case you can put forward for your client's defense, the more likely it is to be true. Most popular Christian apologetics is of this nature, setting up false dichotomies, like: "Well, if God didn't roll the stone away from the tomb entrance, who did? Ha! Got you there!" Which is why fundamentalists of any religion are difficult to argue with. They have no sense of perspective, of judgment; it's like flat earth believers circling the world in planes to attend a Flat Earth Convention.

Perhaps none of this happened at all – to stress again, there are no contemporary records. There was probably no tomb. Crucified people were left hanging, as warnings, to be scavenged by crows and dogs, rather like the corpses of people in England hanged on gibbets in recent centuries. To be denied a proper burial was part of the horror of the death. This is why of all the tens of thousands of people crucified in Palestine in the century around Jesus' death only one skeleton has ever been found, in a casket.

What we are left with is all hearsay, at several degrees removed. In terms of credibility, it's at the level of conspiracy theory. And who knows – maybe the world really is ruled by a cabal of pedophiles, or the Illuminati, or lizards in human guise, or we're all just simulations in a giant computer. The point is that it's easy to see how the story might have arisen. It's not a question of "hoax" or "true," and of having to choose between the disciples being either liars or honest men. That's too simplistic. If we agree to follow the Gospel accounts, the only thing that the four of them (in this New Testament selection of gospels, there are many others that provide different versions again) agree on was that Mary Magdalene (exactly who she was, an individual, a mix of people, fictional or real, is much disputed) went to the tomb – though they disagree on the details; Mark says she goes after sunrise, John says it was still dark; John says she saw the stone had already been removed while it was dark, but in Mark we see her going to the tomb after the sun came up wondering who would move the stone for her.

Anyway, of all the followers she may have been the most committed, or the bravest. Perhaps it's significant that in John's Gospel the disciples don't see the angels in the tomb but she does, after they've left. Perhaps she hallucinated under the stress of the times – even today 10% to 25% of people say in surveys that at least once in their lives they have experienced a vivid hallucination. Perhaps she was an epileptic, prone to visions and imaginary experiences. After all, Jesus had healed her of seven devils.

Perhaps it was less dramatic than that. Experimental psychologists know that it is relatively easy to create false memories that can be stronger than memories of real events. That our real memories are often confused as to their source. That they are influenced by other people's memories of the same event. That we can change our memories in the light of later experience. Perhaps Mary believed she spoke with Jesus but was simply mistaken. Perhaps the gardener was just a gardener. Perhaps she simply went to the wrong tomb. Perhaps she imagined it all much later, having stories drawn out of her by excited grandchildren. Perhaps she lied (it's not exactly unknown for people to lie). In any case, whatever the motive, she started a hare running.

Then as the story gained ground some (but not all) of Jesus' later followers believed it. Other women wanted to be part of it, and added experiences of seeing Jesus, or an angel, or both. Perhaps they couldn't tell the difference. Some of the disciples started to add their bits. A generation, two generations later, after the traumas of the destruction of Jerusalem and the scattering or death of most of the population, second-, third-, or fourth-hand accounts turned into the collection of different stories we have now.

When Paul was writing his letters the core of his message is still the teaching of Jesus, as in Galatians 5:14: *For all the law is fulfilled in one word, even in this; Thou shalt love they neighbor as thyself.* By the time John is writing his gospel, around the end of the century, we're heading back to a blend of Jewish and pagan religion. God loves people, but realizes they're not perfect, like

He is. So rather than punishing them (though they're behaving in the way He made them) He murders His Son for a sacrifice to Himself. Though it's not actually murder, because then He raises him up again, and it's not really a proper sacrifice because it doesn't work unless you have faith that it happened. Even if there's no evidence provided for it.

If you can believe in the Resurrection, good for you. May it make you a happier and better person. But don't waste time and manners trying to force it down other people's throats. The evidence for it is so close to zero as makes no odds. But believing in it isn't necessary to belief in God or being a Christian, any more than believing in the Ascension, or the Virgin Birth, or that donkeys can talk (Numbers 22:28). It's like saying you're only allowed to enjoy Christmas if you believe Santa Claus brought the presents down the chimney. Forcing the issue creates a problem for anyone who wants to think rationally about it.

What we call the beginning is often the end
And to make an end is to make a beginning.
The end is where we start from.
T. S. Eliot (twentieth century AD)

30. How To Read The Resurrection

We have just enough religion to make us hate, but not enough to make us love one another.
Jonathan Swift (eighteenth century AD)

So whereas a Christian today might say that the bodily resurrection is essential, the litmus of the claims of Christianity, it didn't necessarily seem to be that way for the first disciples. It began with vision, not event. Believing in it literally is rather like believing in an earth that's flat or was created 6,000 years ago.

It's not so difficult to believe in it with a small "r," which is probably how Paul meant it – resurrection in a general, spiritual sense. God representing creation, and the Son renewal, is as old as Adam and Eve, it goes right back to the agricultural corn-gods. And by far the best argument for the Resurrection, which Christians don't seem to advance, is that Jesus rose from the dead because people *do* rise from the dead. The world really *is* one of magic and miracle. Millions, perhaps billions of people, have had experiences of accessing patterns of information, of forms, or people, that are incredible in terms of modern science – the effect of healing hands, or of seeing an angel, or a dead relative, or being watched (by some estimates up to 90%), or other forms of the paranormal.

All over the world, from the zombies of Haiti to the Fang people of Gabon and every inhabited place in between many people still do believe in the dead walking, in Elvis Presley still playing, in ghosts, demons, and the supernatural, as a matter of daily experience. There's a vast amount of literature detailing experiences of leaving the body, returning after brain death, communicating with spirits, better documented than the resurrection of Jesus, and more rigorously checked. For New Agers, Christians, Hindus, animists, along of course with virtually everyone in the Roman Empire in Jesus' time, this is the way the world is; it is interpenetrated with the actions of God/gods/spirits. For some, the "literal" truth of it is irrelevant, it's the intention that counts, the "greater truth." Whether a star literally appeared to mark the birth of Krishna isn't significant to Hindus. The story has a truth of its own, which is that one of the three high gods, Vishnu, was prepared to incarnate himself in human form as a divine child. To investigate whether there was such a star in the sky at the time is irrelevant at best, sacrilegious at worst.

So many have had experiences of this world shading off into a different one, of encountering a different kind of reality, and they believe it. Others haven't, and they don't. Many people in the world could believe in Jesus appearing in some form to his disciples after his death, or at least that the disciples believed they saw him in some form.

The real difficulty is in accepting that the Resurrection was unique, physical, and the saving act of God, which transformed the fortunes of humankind, the world and the universe. Most religious people in the world might say that it's the Christians who are lacking in faith, skeptical of the world of spirit and potential, believing that just this story is true and similar ones are not.

So how should we think of the Resurrection today?

In the scales of experience and knowledge we all balance the weights differently. For some, the experience of encountering the risen Jesus or the many other figures perceived as divinely present after their death is such that the Resurrection must be literally true, whatever scientists and scholars and any rationally-minded person might say. The power of love makes anything possible.

For others there are many truths. They recognize the equal power of the experiences of those of different beliefs. The resurrected Jesus might work for me, the reincarnated Buddha for you. But for most belief and knowledge need to go hand in hand, enriching each other. Faith is not credulity. It's personal, and starts from where you are. It's not holding an impossible belief, it's having the courage to live in the light of a good one, the best you can manage. For some Christians the Resurrection is true in a practical sense. The words and actions of our friends, family and teachers still impact us after they've gone. We honor them by living as they would have wanted us to. In doing so, in acting out of love to others we encourage them to do the same, and the kingdom of God on earth gets built. It's our version of "honoring the ancestors," perhaps the most widespread and ancient of all religious practices. Maybe, even, consciousness in some form does survive death, and there are larger dimensions to the world than space and time, and that everything that has happened is still out there, in a real sense; that memories of yesterday are as powerful as the events of today, and shape what happens tomorrow. The impact of Jesus on his disciples was such that his continuing felt presence was more vivid than most.

Some can believe in miracles, others can't. Some have experienced them, most not. A faith for everyone doesn't depend on miracles. It says that there's a vast range of possibilities, from molecules to spirit, and we choose our point on the line. For most in the West our hearts want to believe in the Resurrection, our minds can't. Not today, anyway, or not as a once-only event rather than a matter of common experience.

An argument for the relevance of the Resurrection and that of similar stories might go something like this: Just as the story of the Garden of Eden matters because paradise on earth *is* possible if we live in love and accept our limits, acting as if creation really is beautiful and meaningful, Resurrection *is* possible in the sense that the meaning and purpose we bring to life lives on after our death. Outside space and time, everything we have done, thought and dreamed is still there. The Book of Life is still open.

We shape our lives and our hopes in terms of these stories

we're given, much as billions of believers in other religious figures do. Humbled, scared, thrilled, reconciled, supported, uplifted – these emotions are the common currency of all religion. We give them labels and denominations that make sense to us, or we can't use them. Underneath the labels the emotions run deep. Break the thin ice and our minds are full of shadows, images, fears, the good and bad. Psychology explains some – life hasn't been the same since Freud described the battle between the id and the ego, the subconscious and reason. Perhaps as Jung said we collectively create archetypes that can be more real to us than our individual selves. We might believe in the Resurrection simply because we want to, because we need to, and why not? It's simply the logical step on from the incarnation. God becomes all things, and all things are renewed in different forms.

Religion can't be defined as fact, but it's more literal than symbol. Neither of these languages expresses the world in our heads where the important things in life happen. It models a relationship between ourselves and the world. It pictures a reality that answers our needs. The idea of the man who becomes God or the God who becomes man is one of the most widespread ideas we've developed to link our consciousness with a possible universal one.

Some models are better than others. They, with their stories, change as our views of truth and reality change. A "displacement" model of God sacrificing Himself for humankind is better than the "literal" model of people sacrificing each other for God. Again, if you've ever seen an evangelical preacher whipping a congregation into a frenzy over the "power of the blood" you can see the ancient practice of blood sacrifice still exerting its pull. Better still is a model that recognizes itself as only a model. The value of each lies in the extent to which they develop us as individuals, growing in awareness and practicing love. Not in the miracles that grow up around the models, obscuring the meaning.

The miracles surrounding the birth and death of Jesus are no more important to Christianity than those around the Buddha are to Buddhism. And they are few and trivial compared with those in Hinduism. Our power of will is not so developed that we can turn water into wine or putrefying corpses into living flesh, nor that we can alter our eternal destiny in the universe in a moment. Believing otherwise may be nice, but it's religion in a hurry. Maybe miracles happen, and some are more able to produce them or see them than others. But resting your faith on one is not necessarily helpful, or good religion. It doesn't help us practice it here and now. If it's miracles you want, go live in India.

We don't know what happened to Jesus. Any of the legendary accounts of what happened to him, such as that he survived the crucifixion and traveled to Kashmir, as many Muslims believe, are vastly more credible than the Resurrection. Nor is he going to appear in clouds and lightning tomorrow to judge who believes in him and who doesn't. That's B movie, Hammer horror religion. But a belief that he expresses more clearly than anyone, the divine dimension in human beings, that in some sense he lives on, that maybe we all do, focuses our desires for a life beyond the material, unconstrained by time.

The story expresses our belief that it's the quality of our lives and deaths that's important rather than quantity – the number of years we live or the money and possessions we accumulate. It's by believing we can do good that we do it. By doing it that we become good. By believing in God that we live as His image, aware and active players in the slow grinding of the universe towards self-realization over billions of years. In some way it's by saying yes to life that makes life happen.

Man is certainly stark mad; he cannot make a flea, and yet he will be making gods by dozens.
Montaigne (sixteenth century AD)

Part V

The Early Christians

31. What Did The First Christians Believe?

If you say you see the True,
This seeing is not the true one.
When the True is left to itself,
There is nothing false in it, for it is Mind itself.
When Mind itself is not liberated from the false,
There is nothing true; nowhere is the True to be found.
Hui Neng (seventh century AD)

About the only thing we can be sure of, is that the first Christians didn't believe that God sent His only son Jesus to die on a cross as a sacrifice for the sins of humanity, so that by accepting that in our hearts we can become reconciled with God. That's a much later development.

So what did the first Christians actually believe? Most scholars agree they were known as "Nazareans," or "Nazarenes" – probably nothing to do with Nazareth but implying strict observance of the Law (they're still called by that name in Hebrew). They were one of many Jewish groups opposed to the Temple establishment and Roman rule, probably a minor one compared with the Essenes (who the contemporary Philo writes a whole book on), and the Mandaeans (who still survive today in some communities of the Marsh Arabs in South Iraq, where they fled after the destruction of Jerusalem, still claiming John the Baptist as the true Mandaean), or many others.

There's little doubt they saw themselves as practicing within the Jewish faith, worshipping in the Temple. Virtually all scholars, Christian or not, would agree with this, both from the internal evidence of the New Testament letters and from later writers like Clement of Rome. Indeed they may have followed the Law more zealously than the Pharisees. To get a flavor of what early Christian worship would have been like you would do better today to go to a Sufi mosque rather than a church, or, if you can, to one of the Christian churches in West Syria. There, just down the road from Galilee, they still worship in Aramaic, the language Jesus spoke, foreheads touching the ground, bottoms in the air, a common animal posture of submission to a superior, a practice later largely dropped in Christianity but continued in Islam. (Incidentally, this is the kind of reason why Islam is likely to last longer than Christianity. Look at the varying degrees of hesitation with Christians when it comes to formal prayer and worship. Bowing or kneeling, closing your eyes or not, crossing yourself or not, reciting the creed or not, taking communion or not, tithing or not, it's all pretty optional. Compared to Islam, there's little underlying, commonly understood, real "seriousness" here, across the community as a whole.)

Where scholars begin to differ is in what the Nazarenes believed about Jesus. Christian scholars tend to read back into the first generation the beliefs of the later New Testament writers. But over the last few decades the majority of scholars, including many Christian ones, have come to the conclusion that the Nazarenes considered Jesus to be an ordinary human being, naturally born, but one who managed to follow the Law perfectly. His actual life was probably not very important to them, his death still less so. The Epistle of James scarcely mentions him, nor does that of Jude. They probably believed in the Resurrection, but not as a unique saving event for humankind. Jesus was taken up into heaven in the same manner as Elijah, a similarly divinely anointed prophet with a special relationship to God. For them Jesus was in the radical, uncomfortable tradition of the prophets, calling Judaism back to true, unadulterated worship.

His death on the cross wasn't a sacrifice. Jewish law is specific on what makes a sacrifice to God acceptable. It has to be made on the altar in the Temple (Leviticus 17:11-12), be female rather than male, uninjured, and killed by the priests (Leviticus 4:32; 22:22; 14:9). And nobody can take on the sins of another, as in

Ezekiel 18:20:

> *The soul that sinneth, it shall die. The son shall not bear the iniquity of the father, neither shall the father bear the iniquity of the son: the righteousness of the righteous shall be upon him, and the wickedness of the wicked shall be upon him.*

There's also some evidence that the Nazarenes saw Jesus as the true Prophet, particularly in the Jewish communities from Syria to Iraq, a tradition that again was later taken up and developed by Muhammad. But first and foremost he was a good Jew. In other words, what virtually every Christian believes today about Jesus developed as later teaching. The first Christians weren't "Christian," as we know the word today.

The majority of scholars, across the board, agree that the first leader of the Nazarene community was James, the brother of Jesus, for whom there's more evidence outside the New Testament than for Jesus himself. He was probably stoned to death by the Jewish religious establishment around AD 62, and by AD 85 the Nazarenes were excluded from synagogues, with the liturgy condemning them. In exile they prayed facing Jerusalem, as the Muslims today face Mecca.

Of course, one of these many interpretations of Jesus, which eventually became the dominant one and fed through into what we think of as Christianity today, was that of Paul in the first century AD. Most Jewish scholars see him as the real founder. Christianity as we know it today is, after all, based on the assumption that Jesus didn't really manage to get his message across, and that Paul had to come along to explain it. None of the 27 books in the New Testament are by Jesus, 13 are attributed to Paul, though 4 to 6 of those (some say more) are probably the work of others.

In contrast to James, Paul saw Jesus as more than a prophet come to renew Israel's faith. A Pharisee, he believed, like all the

Pharisees, in the imminent coming of God's kingdom on earth and the resurrection of all believers, a line of thought going back to Daniel. As an educated, cosmopolitan Jew (probably, but a few say Gentile) he would have been familiar with the various competing descriptions of the channel between a transcendent God and people on earth – an intermediary Son, the Greek Logos, the Jewish Wisdom. For first generation Christians Paul's words would not have carried much weight compared with the disciples or brothers of Jesus. Paul himself had never met Jesus, or heard him speak. He doesn't have any interest in him as a person, rarely quoting him, or referring to events in his life. He doesn't seem to have heard of the miracle stories or the Virgin Birth. But he scaled Jesus up, making him the Lord Christ, a cosmic player in the heavenly drama. "Christ is all, and in all" (Colossians 3:11). He may have developed the idea from a "world ruler" prophecy current in Israel at the time, mentioned in the Dead Sea Scrolls. Other widespread contemporary themes were the Man of Righteousness and the Primal Man, and he may have turned this into the beginning of the doctrine of original sin, linking Adam to Jesus. Paul never comes straight out and says Jesus is divine. There are one or two verses that suggest it, like Philippians 2:6 ("being in the form of God"), as mentioned before, but again the balance is on the other side. Adam was the first man, from the earth. Jesus was the last, the spiritual "man of heaven," who lived such a perfect life of service that God "designates" him to be His Son (Romans 1:4). Jesus is not equal to God, but he shows the way. He certainly wasn't a Trinitarian, the concept hadn't been thought of yet. But it is through surrendering ourselves to God through Jesus and understanding our total dependence on him that we're saved. His bloody sacrifice on the cross opened the way for people to come to God (Hebrews 9:22):

And almost all things are by the law purged with blood; and without shedding of blood there is no remission.

(He was wrong about this being the law – blood sacrifice can be replaced by flour – Leviticus 5:11; intercession by others can work – Numbers 14:20; you can pray yourself for forgiveness – Hosea 14:2-3; and so on...) This adoption of Jesus as God's Son seems to happen for Paul at the Resurrection (for example, Romans 1:3-4). Mark, writing later, seems to move it forward to the baptism, starting his story when the Spirit of God descends on Jesus in the form of a dove. Matthew and Luke, writing later still, bring it further forward to the birth, with their two very different narratives of how that happened. A generation or so further away, and John, the last of the New Testament Gospels, skips the birth and says that there was no time in history when Jesus was not God's Son. In John's gospel Jesus is more of a universal Christ figure than the prophet from Nazareth.

Paul's vision of what Jesus was about was one the Gentiles could understand. He could speak their language, literally and figuratively. He scaled up the breaking of bread by introducing pagan sacraments like the taking of bread and wine (1 Corinthians 11:23-26), the food of Demeter and drink of Dionysus, to flesh out the new faith with appropriate ritual, claiming to have received knowledge of this through dreams and revelation. But he went too far for most Jewish Christians. This quickly threw up questions about what the faith actually was, leading to bitter arguments between Paul and the main Nazarene establishment. In Galatians 2 Paul criticizes James for trying to reconvert Paul's converts back to following the Jewish Law. He was mocked by his fellow Jewish Nazarenes as a "man of dreams," or "liar," or the "enemy of God" (Galatians 4:16). The *Pseudo-Clementine Recognitions* even records a possible physical assault by Paul on James.

This sacrificial approach is completely contrary to the teaching of Jesus. He just says, "forgive... seventy times seven" – not "sacrifice." Sacrifice, to protect from the anger of capricious gods, was the dominant religious culture of the time, sure, right across the world. And probably had been for tens of thousands of years. Following the later prophets, Jesus was saying that we don't need to do this anymore. We can approach God directly, we can realize Him in ourselves, He is in everything. Stop the sacrifice and the killing. Stop punishing the innocent.

One impulse from the vernal wood
Will tell you more of man,
Of moral evil and of good,
Than all the sages can.
Thomas Traherne (seventeenth century AD)

32. Different Early Beliefs

The supernatural is the natural not yet understood.
Elbert Hubbard

So how did the kingdom of God on earth for everyone turn, in the eyes of Christians, into the kingdom of heaven for a few? How did the religion of this poor itinerant preacher, in an obscure province of the Empire, become the state religion of the mighty and godless Empire itself? How did Jesus, who defined closeness to God as powerlessness, crucified as a criminal, turn into the living head of the wealthy and powerful Church, a God himself who through his priests on earth was instrumental in torturing and murdering millions? This is the subject of the next couple of chapters. It's a strange story. Following the twists helps us to understand the way in which religions start, change and decline. It shows us something about how societies work, and the extent of the problem we have with our egos. Along the way we find ideas that can still work for us today. But if you're bored with early Christianity, skip to Part VI.

All mainstream biblical scholars today are virtually unanimous in saying that at the heart of Jesus' message in the gospels is his teaching on the kingdom of God. They're not so much in agreement about what that is, but there's no doubt it's a difficult, self-sacrificing, uncompromising message, that involves changing yourself and society. It deals with the things that matter to us – truth, peace, freedom and justice – the great ideals that we still aspire to model in our imperfect world. It never played well to the establishment though, and the Church soon abandoned it, losing the plot very early on, a fact which every Christian sect since has implicitly recognized. The word "kingdom" for instance is mentioned often in the earlier gospels, over 50 times in Matthew. But John, probably a generation or two later, doesn't mention it at all. It was already being written out of the picture. Rejected by the Jews, kingdom teaching was still less likely to appeal to the ruling Romans. And the Church has rarely discussed it since. Both Catholic and Protestant branches have consistently persecuted people who tried to take it seriously.

Tradition and scripture, like history, are written by the victors. Orthodoxy is just what successive generations have turned it into. After thousands of years the chances of it being close to the original are vanishingly small. None of us think like the first Christians did. At a distance history smooths over the bumps. Imagine back 300 years from now, to AD 1700. The ship's wheel has just been introduced to replace the tiller. The Swedes are defeating an alliance of the Russians, Danes, and Poles, and capture Warsaw. The French gain control of the English forts around Hudson's Bay and settle in Texas. Virtually everyone in the West still believes in a divinely-ordained class structure with kings at the top and slaves at the bottom.

Insert any of those lines into a news headline today and see if it would make any sense. The world looked very different, and anyone living then would be astonished to see it today. The difference between first and fourth-century (when Jesus achieved the status of coequality with God) Christians, let alone between them and us, is of the same order. The religion changed, and carried on evolving. What we think is meant by Christianity today has little in common with what Christians of the first few generations meant by it.

It's hard for us today to understand the degree to which all religions evolve because we're so used to thinking that there's only one God, with one right interpretation, and whether or not He exists is a black and white question. We read the Gospels as if everything happened just down the road, yesterday. Jesus either rose from the dead or he didn't, it's all either true or false. We either believe in "God," or we don't.

The Roman view of religion was more sophisticated. Though

in some ways they were obviously more credulous than we are, in others they were more skeptical. They were aware of many gods, both of their own tradition and of the many peoples they had conquered. They judged them on their merits. They used different gods for different purposes, much as today we've farmed out their functions to doctors and dentists, priests and lawyers. They knew that religion was a two-way street, what you got depended on what you put in. Gods were not gods if they weren't worshipped, offered sacrifices. They were there as long as you gave them house room.

There's a simple reason why Christianity succeeded. It didn't emerge clear-cut, as a new, distinct religion with a worked-out creed, to be accepted or rejected. It evolved into a belief that made sense to a lot of people at the time. They turned it into what they wanted. It was as much a reconfiguration of existing religion as a new one. Beliefs evolve out of consensus. Religions all work with the material to hand. They don't appear out of thin air, they are not that different. All the practices, rituals, and symbols that we think of as Christian (sacraments, icons, Christmas, feast days, Sunday, incense, prayer, the Eucharist, speaking in tongues – the list is endless) have been absorbed from other cultures and beliefs. The cross itself, that ancient symbol of the point where God meets us, is a pre-Christian icon, representing the Sun God in Assyria and Central America, Osiris in Egypt. Actually, of all the Christian symbols it's one of the later ones, not really appearing in art till the fifth century AD, when Christianity had taken on a more violent, bloody edge. It later became the hammer of Thor in Scandinavia, and was twisted to form the crooked cross or swastika of the Nazi party. The rosary managed to travel through several traditions, starting off as an aid to meditation in Buddhism, adopted by Islam, and arriving in Europe through the Crusades. All Christian teachings are ancient, universal beliefs that the Church has adapted in a particular way. Salvation, eternal life, the second coming, Son of

God, heaven and hell – anything you can think of.

Over a period of centuries Christianity absorbed existing traditions, rolling up the specialist providers into one divine package headed by a single almighty God. The followers of Jesus overlaid Him with aspects of other gods and heroes – suffering savior-gods were common – and the Church took over their temples, festivals, symbols, and the Old Testament itself. The more powerful the Church became the more it adopted the trappings and beliefs of competing pagan cults, till it was to all intents and purposes indistinguishable from them.

Christianity started to gain traction in the Roman Empire because it was the right religion at the right time. It had the ingredients of a genuinely populist movement. The Empire had been built on conquest and slavery. Tribal identities had been lost, homes and gods uprooted, people displaced. The new faith was for the 90% who did not have "rights" in the form of citizenship, or the money to buy God's favors. They identified with the story of Genesis, of being expelled from the garden, of life as a miserable vale of tears, but with a heaven on offer. And, more importantly, at least for the first couple of centuries, Christianity gave them a new sense of worth, a new dignity. Initially, it was a religion for underdogs, as symbolized by Jesus himself, who celebrated them in his teaching, and who for the first Christians stood for the Jewish people as a whole. It inherited the Judaic principles of caring for widows and orphans, the poor and oppressed. Christians looked after each other. They cared for those in need. Like the Essenes, they shared food, and, at least to begin with, lived communally. Eating around the table together, developing strong relationships, was key. Women were prominent, as leaders, disciples and patrons. In a world ruled by force of arms, where life was generally short and brutal, they offered love and hope rather than stoicism and suffering, and stood against the predominant culture of cruelty. This didn't last, of course. In a few centuries the Church was the largest slaveowner in the Empire, supporting military oppression, pushing the women back into place. But in the meantime not being noble, or wealthy, or a famous soldier, was a positive virtue. Through Jesus the poor had the chance to save themselves. They might not have the villas but their souls were secure and they would be rewarded in the next life. For some, it seemed the best deal on offer.

They became known as the Ebionites, which means "the poor," probably because they stayed true to Jesus' teaching on wealth. Eusebius, the major church historian of the early centuries, describes them as still being strong in Palestine and Syria 300 years later, still believing in Jesus as an ordinary mortal, like the rest of us, and that his message was for Jews only. But the Nazarenes/Ebionites had by then become an embarrassment to the Gentile church, which had moved away from Judaism. Early on, writers begin to edit them out of the story, they came to be persecuted as heretics, and by the end of the fifth century this original Christian Church had died out, killed off by the new Christians.

Many other strands of Christian teaching developed in the first generation. Because Jesus never wrote anything down anyone could pretty make up the religion as it went along. Even in the really early days, the flavor is captured in 1 Corinthians 1:12 – "Every one of you saith, I am of Paul; and I of Apollos; and I of Cephas; and I of Christ" – and that's just in the one small church Paul was writing to. As they spread out from Galilee and Jerusalem the teaching changed, adapting itself to different traditions and beliefs. That's easy to understand – journeys were carried out largely on foot, in difficult conditions. There was no Bible, no creed, no church. Teachers had to support themselves as they went along, making converts on the way, sometimes being converted in turn. Or, some scholars say, the teaching developed separately in a number of different centers, and elements of it focused on the figure of Jesus as giving it human definition.

In the absence of any documentation of what Jesus said or thought, churches and individuals could interpret him pretty much anyway they wanted. Among the earliest, for example, were the Elchasaites in Syria and southwest Turkey. Compared with the foreign offshoots of Christianity springing up in faraway places like Rome, they were just down the road from Jesus' home patch of Galilee. The Elchasaites retained the Jewish law, circumcised their children, rigidly kept the Sabbath, and didn't accept the heretical innovations of Paul. But they believed that two angels had appeared to their founder, Elchasaios, and told him that Jesus was reincarnated anew every century, and born of a virgin on each occasion. Much as Buddha reincarnates for the salvation of humankind. There were many other churches in the area, each with their own angle. Some held that Jesus was being continually incarnated in many individuals, a belief that eventually fed into the Imam doctrine of Shi'ite Islam, as did the "perfect man" tradition and others.

The apostle Thomas started a further group. His supporters claimed he was the twin brother of Jesus. They didn't believe that Jesus came to die for our sins on the cross – they said he came to enlighten those who would hear his words. We don't know much about them – the *Gospel of Thomas* itself wasn't discovered till 1945. But his group of Jerusalem Christians moved to Antioch after the destruction of Jerusalem and became known eventually as the Nestorians. They believed that Jesus had two natures, one human and one divine, and they took this to the point where he appeared to have a dual personality. They spread through Persia to India, central Asia and China. By the seventh century there were Nestorian churches in most Chinese cities. The Mongol Khans nearly converted to this form of Christianity, which would have made them a more powerful church than the Roman Catholics. A few groups still survive. One convert, called Mani, born around AD 217, grew up a Christian, but combined the teaching of Jesus with elements from Zoroaster and Buddha to create a universal, gentle religion that foreswore violence. In many ways it was an improvement on Christianity, with priests committed to poverty and celibacy (both ideas way in the future for the Christian Church). In this form it spread to India and China, where it survived for a thousand years. In its early days it also spread West back to the Roman Empire. Augustine, the most important figure in developing Christian teaching after Paul, was a Manichean before his conversion to Christianity – he needed something more authoritarian to suit his combative nature.

Being dedicated to nonviolence, like Jesus himself, Manichean teaching got up the noses of the establishment everywhere. Mani was hanged by the Zoroastrian Magi, and his followers were persecuted in the Roman Empire first by pagans and then by Christians when they had the power. Manicheans survived persecution in Europe till the seventh century, when they disappear from the record.

Another group were followers of Simon the Magus, a Samaritan teacher who was a contemporary of Jesus. He had a more god-like idea of the Messiah than the Jews and was perhaps an influence on the early Christians. He's mentioned in Acts 8:13. The Church Fathers later reviled him as the fount of all heresy. Then there were the Docetists, who thought that that the idea of God sacrificing His son for the sake of humanity was barbaric, so Jesus only "seemed" to be human, his physical form was an illusion, and so on...

Christianity didn't begin with a common belief, but was more like a wave of ecstatic experience that in a few centuries rippled around the old world from the Atlantic to the Pacific. It was driven by the Jewish belief in a high, single, universal God who actually loved humankind. This love was manifested in a particular man who had died for their sake. They absorbed this new insight into their own traditions, shaping it in a way that made sense to them.

Of course this is all disputed. The balance of scholarly opinion changes with every decade. Scroll forward from now and the outcome by the end of the twenty-first century could be that Jesus is seen as a more historical, political, essentially Jewish figure, and the movement he represented maybe emphasizing the Law still more strongly than the Pharisees. The reverse is equally possible, that Jesus could be seen as a more mythical figure whose essential teachings are irrecoverable. Or the Church can continue dumbing down, and insist on taking all of Scripture literally. All we can be sure of is that our understanding will be different from the one we have now.

Human beings are perhaps never more frightening than when they are convinced beyond doubt that they are right.
Laurens van der Post (twentieth century AD)

33. Where Original Sin Came From

The vision of Christ that thou dost see
Is my vision's greatest enemy.
Thine has a great hook nose like thine,
Mine has a snub nose like to mine.
William Blake (eighteenth century AD)

That our understanding has changed in crucial respects over the centuries is surely undeniable. For instance, to take one particular doctrine, mainstream Christianity is unique today amongst the major faiths in that it teaches that humankind is basically lost, damned, in original sin, caused by Adam and Eve eating the forbidden fruit. We're condemned from the time we're born, unless we accept God through His Son by faith (for Protestants), or through the sacraments (for Catholics).

But the doctrine of original sin goes against the grain of the Jewish Bible, where it's not mentioned (indeed, it contradicts it – in Exodus 34:7 God describes Himself as "visiting the iniquity of the fathers upon the children, and upon the children's children, unto the third and the fourth generation" – He's still vindictive towards descendants, but only up to a point). The Hebrews saw life as innately good. The Jews, whose story it is, see Genesis as a hymn to the greatness and goodness of God, not as an account of the Fall, which leads to redemption, and the story is not mentioned again in the Old Testament. The idea of the individual rather than the family or tribe having clear responsibility for his or her actions doesn't even seem to appear until around the sixth century BC with Ezekiel (Ezekiel 18:2-4; 17-21).

The first century Christians would not have believed in original sin. It runs contrary to the teaching of Jesus, who goes out of his way to affirm people as good rather than bad. The people he condemns are the religious leaders who say the opposite. He says you have to be like a child to enter the kingdom of God (Luke 18:17).

It runs contrary to our understanding of human development today. There is grounding for the idea of inherited traits, sure. Many psychologists say that around half the variation in personality and behavior is inherited, the outcome of our genetic makeup. But the idea that we are all condemned before we start, through an action that had nothing to do with us, goes against common sense.

I remember arguing with my mother about it, as a youngster. Brought up in a Baptist family (Baptists are a major branch of Protestantism who only baptize professed believers; they also believe in salvation by faith alone, and the Bible as the only rule for faith and practice – but who nowadays is really bothered about the differences between Baptists and Presbyterians, Congregationalist and United Reformed?), I hadn't been christened or confirmed. Baptism was an adult choice (or rather teenage, in my case). I didn't feel convinced enough. In fact, the closest I've come to any kind of religious initiation was being blessed by a tribal witchdoctor in Sudan (I still have the cow bracelets). There have been other attempts – being prayed over by a group from the Full Gospel Business Men's Fellowship for instance – that didn't seem to "take." Speaking in tongues has always escaped me.

Anyway, I pointed out that if I wasn't baptized into the Elect I was going to hell. Did she really believe that? She replied that she'd go to hell with me. Love beats doctrine, or should do. That was probably the point where I started to think for myself.

I understand my mother better now that I've had kids of my own, now grown up, who I love dearly. We didn't "raise" them as Christians, that's up to them. But they're better people than most Christians I come across and hear about. And I simply can't comprehend the thinking of Christians I argue with on forums, that if people (traditionally thought of as 999 out of 1,000) aren't "saved" they'll spend eternity in a lake of hellfire. I'd do anything to save them from a minute in that. But I can't believe in an all-loving God who would condemn the vast majority of people who have ever lived to torture, because they haven't made some kind of decision, however nominal, to accept Jesus as their savior. That just seems to me really sick. (It also makes a nonsense of heaven – how could any loving parent enjoy listening to angels playing harps in heaven – or whatever entertainment there is up there – when they know their child/children are being tortured in hell? It equally makes a nonsense of a loving God – how can He be so much less loving than a parent?)

I've never met a parent who thought their children were born evil. True, they're programed to draw attention to themselves, like any animal or bird, to cry when they're hungry or uncomfortable, they can be exasperating and difficult. But they can't be evil when they haven't done anything yet. The idea is obscene. It's also immoral. No teaching has led to more mental agony, physical suffering, and villainy. If an individual's original sin condemns him or her to eternal hellfire, then torturing their bodies to save their souls makes sense. It would be wrong not to. Most Christians down the ages have agreed with the logic of this, including all mainstream church leaders and saints up till a few centuries ago when humanist values began to spread through society. The hardline church leaders of today, the conservative evangelicals and Catholic fundamentalists, are the inquisitors and witch-burners of yesterday, forced (often resentfully) into more mellow positions by secular society.

It's at the root of exploitation and fascism. Some people (usually most, because by definition a "pure" people define themselves against the majority) are seen as born bad, corrupt, contaminated by their ancestral sin, their bloodline. So it was a public service for white Americans to enslave blacks, for German Christians to lead Jews to the gas chambers, to cleanse the homeland.

At a more prosaic level it simply cuts off believers from everyone else. It's not impossible to love people you believe are intrinsically evil, any more than for poor people to be honest in a community of rich people, but it's a lot harder. Indeed, it's a self-fulfilling belief. If you expect people to behave badly, they're more likely to. It's even been shown to be the case in lab experiments on rats. It's self-evident to good teachers that encouragement works better in the long run than punishment.

The idea of original sin runs counter to everything science tells us, from anthropology through sociology to zoology. It is contrary to the teaching of Jesus, the Bible, common sense, experience and morality. It's a poisonous idea that has caused immeasurable individual and social harm down the centuries. So why do so many Christians cling to it as a cardinal doctrine?

The idea was first sketched out by Paul, seven centuries or so after the Genesis story of the fruit and the Fall was written down. Paul hints at the death of Jesus as a sacrifice made by God on our behalf. It was extended by Augustine (354-430), a theologian of genius, the most important of the Church Fathers a few centuries later. Convinced of his own sexual guilt and shame, he projected this onto humanity as a whole, the "multitude of the damned." Because God is wholly good, evil must come from man, and in particular, from women (he wouldn't allow them into his house, even his sisters, who were nuns). For him Adam and Eve were real people (as they were for Jesus, eg: Matthew 19:4), and their sin of disobedience was passed on down the generations through the act of sex. He doesn't explain why a wholly good, loving and all-powerful Creator allows the existence of the Devil, let alone why He should have created him. In the twelfth century AD Anselm develops the idea further, into the doctrine of substitutionary Atonement, where Christ is sacrificed on the cross as a payment for our sins, so God can forgive us. This is a strange creed, running counter to the Old Testament (at least in the later books), where the sacrifice of children to God is detestable. Sacrificial lambs were supposed to be female, uninjured, and offered on the temple altar, not tortured and nailed to wood. But it becomes the central creed of Protestantism, more than a millennium further on, particularly in Calvinism, which sees depravity as our natural state. Not only were you born evil but God has predestined most of us for damnation, with no chance of salvation.

Others churches rejected it, like the eighteenth-century Quakers. But it could have worked out differently at many points. For instance many of Augustine's contemporaries disagreed with him. Pelagius, for instance, Britain's first significant theologian, who tried to reform the Church when he lived in Rome and challenged Christians to live better lives, quoted the Gospels to support the idea that people are born innocent. Augustine vigorously attacked Pelagius, who was tried three times for heresy, and three times acquitted. A supporter of Pelagius, Julian of Eclanum, initially a friend of Augustine, writes movingly against the horrible doctrine of Original Sin:

Explain to me then, who this person is who sends the innocent to punishment. You answer, God... God, you say, the very one who commends his love to us, who has loved us and not spared his son but handed him over to us, he judges in this way; he persecutes new born children; he hands over babies to eternal flames... It would show a just and reasonable sense of propriety to treat you as beneath argument; you have come so far from religious feeling, from civilized standards, so far indeed from common sense, that you think your Lord capable of committing kinds of crime which are hardly found among barbarian tribes.

He could be speaking to Christians today.

Augustine eventually persuaded the Roman Emperor Honorius to pressurize Pope Zosimus into excommunicating his opponent. Augustine was made a saint, and the writings of Pelagius were condemned. But was Pope Zosimus right? Maybe you prefer Augustine to Pelagius, or Jesus. The idea of original sin has its uses. If your life is desperate and miserable, if you can't control your appetites, can't stop doing wrong, you may feel that you're in a state of "original sin." In that case, you might jump at the chance of entering a state of grace. But it's Christianity that generated that definition of sin and grace in the first place. There is no sin in nature, it just is. The lion doesn't eat lambs because it's sinful, but because it can't chew and digest grass. There is no "perfect" creation to fall from because it's constantly evolving. Sin came with self-awareness, with society, with laws. Before laws there was nothing to sin against. God is not so small that we can offend Him.

More helpfully, perhaps, the idea of original sin reflects a deep understanding that we have a dark side to our nature, which we have to understand and gain agency over. We all have the potential to do better, and screw up. We keep falling into "evil" rather than rising to our better destinies. If we seek perfection we're bound to fail, and that needs an explanation. As a spin on the Genesis story it explains how we're capable of the most horrible acts, much as being made in God's image explains acts of greatness and self-sacrifice. It encourages you to search your heart, see what you're capable of, to understand the evil to which you can sink. And we're all complicit in the world's suffering. Any religious teaching, even some of the worst, can stimulate the individual to improve, to have courage, to complete the self in God. That's why religions take hold and survive. They all have these steps that force you to see yourself anew and transcend it, to find a deeper happiness than momentary pleasure.

Hinduism, for instance, describes our condition as one of impermanence. In reading and meditating on the sacred scriptures we recognize this and come to an understanding of our "real" selves, the state of *thuriya*. We can restore ourselves to harmony with the cosmic order by offering everything up

302

in a spirit of sacrifice, and become one with the inner reality
of all things:

> *He who sees Me everywhere,*
> *and sees everything in Me,*
> *I am not lost to him,*
> *nor is he lost to me.*
> *Bhagavad Gita*

This experience is similar to the new birth that Jesus describes.
But, and here's the main difference from the later approach
developed by followers of Jesus, the Brahmins teach that
basically people are good; a teaching that is not just good for
you psychologically, but makes sense metaphysically. If reality
is truth and goodness, then lies and evil must be the illusion.
Good must triumph. Buddhism takes the theme of self as process
even further. I identify my "self" with my sensations, feelings,
emotions, my character, and beliefs. We understand who we
really are by going beyond these, to the awareness that all living
things have in common, to our "Buddha nature," *anatta*, no-self.
We can realize this suddenly, or, more likely, through a long
process of deepening awareness.

Every religion has a different technique. In Taoist China if
you've been a prodigal son and strayed from the right path, you
can return to the fold by reconciliation with your family and
ancestors (though all great religious traditions tend to see the
key issues in the same kind of way; see for instance the parable
of the prodigal son in Luke 15:11-32). All these beliefs work for
the people who think in those ways.

No one is condemned through Adam's disobedience. No one
starts life with a core of evil. That's Satanism, not Christianity.
Of all the teachings in the world this is one of the furthest from
good religion. Let's start with the idea that creation is good, as
God intended it to be, that life is an incredible gift. Recognizing

it and being thankful for it is the start of the road to happiness and wisdom. We're all in need of forgiveness and grace. We're all deeply flawed (and I write this out of conviction of my own inadequacies). But this is a virtuous circle between ourselves, our family, our neighbors, and God. Not a one-track line between God and us. We're not so blessed with goodness that we can afford to dismiss the little we have. The point of believing in God is to expand its area in your life and the world, not diminish it.

Maybe if it hadn't been for the Jewish rebellion against the Romans of AD 68-70 and the consequent dispersal of the Jews things would have turned out differently. We wouldn't have ended up with this guilt-obsessed, flesh-denying new religion (though this kind of transformation is frequent; think for instance of the difference between the *Kama Sutra* and Hindu attitudes to sex today). The Jewish Christians might have carried on growing in strength. They might have remained a reforming movement within Judaism. But two-thirds of the Jewish population were killed or fled the country in the subsequent suppression. The aftermath was hostile and bitter, with some Jews like Josephus switching sides to save their skins. For the Jewish Christians, there was a choice to be made – if the synagogues weren't going to accept Jesus as lord, then perhaps the way forward was to convert the pagan temples.

Moreover the Lord saith, Because the daughters of Zion are haughty, and walk with stretched forth necks and wanton eyes, walking and mincing as they go, and making a tinkling with their feet: Therefore the Lord will smite with a scab the crown of the head of the daughters of Zion, and the Lord will discover their secret parts.
Isaiah (c. sixth century BC)

34. What The Second Century Christians Believed

When a man follows the way of the world, or the way of the flesh, or the way of tradition (i.e. when he believes in religious rites and the letter of the scriptures, as though they were intrinsically sacred), knowledge of Reality cannot arise in him.

Shankara (eighth century AD)

By the end of the first century, Christianity had come a long way from the days when the first worshippers met in the Temple at Jerusalem. It was moving away from Judaism, but wasn't yet a new faith. Different interpretations coexisted for centuries. The letters of Paul's opponents have not come down to us, but we can tell from other letters, for instance from the first century Clement of Rome, that it took generations for Paul's view to get the upper hand.

Most Christians were now Gentiles, with Pauline Christianity one strand amongst many. The "Jewishness" of Christianity was being edited out. The idea that Jesus had been a messiah for the Jews and had come for them only (Matthew 10:5-6) had gone. So had other ideas: that he would return in their lifetimes (Matthew 16:27-28; Luke 9:27; 21:32), that the disciples had a role in establishing the new kingdom and judging it (Matthew 19:27-29), and that a new Temple was going to be built (John 2:19). The heartland of Christianity had migrated from Jerusalem and Palestine to the high-rise urban slums of the major towns and seaports of the Eastern Mediterranean.

In the first century, Jews account for all the main church leaders and writers (with the possible exception of Luke). After that, for twenty centuries, none are Jews. In the view of the Jews, the Nazarenes/Christians had betrayed both faith and people, selling themselves to the Roman enemy for converts and cash. Christians responded by saying that the Jews had murdered God. This began a state of one-sided war that continued for two millennia until its appalling climax in our grandparents' generation, with the Holocaust, within living memory.

As the movement lost its Jewish identity it increasingly appealed to many known today as "Gnostics" ("those in the know," the same meaning as "shaman"). The Gnostics took religion seriously, the "seekers" of their age. They were the first to view organized religion as the opiate of the masses, a drug that kept people enslaved to kings and emperors. They saw themselves as moving beyond the gods of mountaintops and rivers, beyond laws and doctrine, to the worship of God as Spirit. Which means it's hard to know what they thought, their teaching is often vague and contradictory. The central idea is that God is the mind of the cosmos, thinking or dreaming it into existence. And you can know God directly; He is within you. Self-knowledge is knowledge of God. The cosmos is now becoming conscious of itself through conscious beings. In different traditions Gnostics developed a variety of initiation ceremonies and layers of knowledge that enable us to awaken to our shared consciousness with the divine.

There were Gnostics in many religious traditions in the Empire. Most followed various god-men, and it's hard to say how far they adapted some Christian thinking to their own mold (as conservative Christians claim – they weren't really Christians at all) or how far the early Christians adopted some of their ideas. Many of them worshipped in different mystery religions, particularly Mithraism. Mithras was the old Iranian God of light (still followed in Hinduism today with the god Mitra). They had rituals similar to those of Christians – baptism, anointing with oil, Sundays. Paul speaks of the Eucharist in 1 Corinthians – his home town of Tarsus was a stronghold of Mithraism, where followers offered the meat of a sacrificial bull to the sun god, drinking its blood. Like Jesus, Mithras was worshipped as "the way, the truth and the life," as redeemer and savior, as previously stated in chapter 28. Born to a virgin on 25 December, shepherds and Magi visited him as an infant. He performed miracles, healed, was buried in a stone tomb and rose on the third day, and Augustine said the priests of Mithras worshipped the same God as he did.

Some of their books on similar themes are certainly independent of Christianity, or predate it, like the *Apocrypha of John* (20, 1-8) and the *Apocalypse of Adam* (76, 9-77, 18). Those Gnostics who began converting to Christianity saw that the all-too-human books of the Old Testament couldn't have been written by the single almighty good God. Nor could the world, imperfect as it is, have been created by Him. Yahweh, son of El, brother of Baal and Yam, is surely one of thousands of minor tribal deities, with little theology and no sense of individual salvation, or perhaps a rogue god. On their reading of the Jewish scriptures they saw Yahweh as vengeful and arbitrary, favoring the Jews for no good reason, frequently threatening destruction and doing evil; a demonic being who imprisoned man in his material body. Humankind's real father must have been the true God above him, and Sophia (the Holy Spirit of Wisdom, who appears frequently in the Book of Proverbs and in *Ecclesiasticus* in the *Apocrypha*) its mother. So some worshipped the villains and "anti-heroes" of the Old Testament, like Cain. Others went as far as to say that all gods and demons were figments of our imagination. According to the *Gospel of Philip*, "Human beings made gods, and worship their creation. It would be appropriate for the gods to worship human beings" (71:35-72:4). He had a point.

For Gnostics the idea of Jesus as being literally resurrected from the dead may have seemed a crude simplification, if they had heard of it at all. They did not even believe that Jesus died on the cross. Some thought that Simon of Cyrene changed places with him when he carried Jesus' cross. Others believed that Jesus had a separate spiritual form that descended on him at baptism as a dove, and left him to go back to heaven when he died. But in any case his physical existence was unimportant. What mattered to them was their immediate experience of the still-living Jesus who speaks of enlightenment from illusion rather than salvation from sin, a manifestation of God on earth who showed us how to sweep away all the minor gods and bring us direct to the Highest One.

Up until a few decades ago it was assumed that Gnostic Christians were an unimportant offshoot of the main Christian Church. They've been so effectively buried that most of their writings have only been discovered in the last century. Now they're increasingly seen as playing a more important role, though conservatives continue to say that they're not significant, or if they are that they're plain wrong. A few scholars suggest that Christian Gnosticism predates what later became the orthodox tradition and is closer to the teaching of Jesus. Some scholars say, on the basis of hints from hostile writers like Polycarp and Tertullian, that Gnostics were in the majority. The literalists were a minority whose vision for a more controlled religion captured the imagination of an authoritarian ruler, much as you see happening in different countries around the world today. Christians often support would-be or actual dictators in return for them supporting the Church rather than see the democratic process chipping away their privileges. We'll probably never know how significant the Gnostics were, and it doesn't matter, unless you measure truth in terms of numbers of supporters. In which case we're probably only talking at this point about a townful of people anyway, in terms of the modern equivalent.

Whichever, there was probably never a clear-cut divide between Gnosticism and what was to become orthodox Christianity, any more than there is between conservatives and liberals today. Some of their traditions were assimilated, with the origins gradually forgotten. The sacraments are possibly an example. They early on became the center of Christian worship and identity, as they are today for the huge majority of Christians, but they scarcely figure in the New Testament. Jesus performed no rituals. There are references to the Eucharist in 1 Corinthians, and references to baptism (which soon became a rite for infants rather than adults), but Paul scarcely mentions the sacraments, and neither do the other New Testament writers, with the possible exception of Luke in Acts. There's a vast chunk of early Christian experience and practice that's simply not covered in our New Testament. The importance of the sacraments in the early church may originate with Christian Gnosticism where membership rituals were highly important. They probably owe more to works like the early *Gospel of Philip*, which may have been learned and chanted by early Christian believers, than to the New Testament. One of the reasons this gospel didn't make it into the canon was its stress on the earthy, sexual nature of Jesus, particularly in his relationship with Mary Magdalene, which was hard to reconcile with his increasing divinity (*And the companion of the savior is Mary Magdalene. But Christ loved her more than all the disciples and used to kiss her often on the mouth*).

The basic idea of Gnosticism, that the material world is inherently evil and each person is imprisoned within it, to be freed by the spirit of Jesus, comes in the *Gospel of Thomas*, which is probably earlier than any of the New Testament Gospels, and the gospel most likely to have been written by an actual disciple of Jesus, though most Christian scholars dispute this. Some of the non-canonical material is identical or similar to the canonical. Sometimes they elaborate, using similar language, repeating points or extending them. Sometimes they make them more forcibly, for example:

Jesus said: "Whoever does not hate his father and his mother as I do cannot become a disciple to me. And whoever does not love his father and his mother as I do cannot become a disciple to me. For My mother gave me falsehood, but My true Mother gave me life."
Gospel of Thomas

This is close to a saying of Jesus recorded in the Gospel of Luke, but it introduces the important idea of God as Mother as well as Father. Or perhaps we should say, as it is probably earlier than Luke, that Luke takes that idea out. A less patriarchal God is also commonly seen in other non-canonical gospels. In the *Gospel to the Hebrews* Jesus speaks of, "My mother, the Spirit." In the *Apocryphon of John* he says, "I am the Father. I am the Mother. I am the Son." In the *Gospel of Philip*, "Spirit is both Mother and Virgin." Etc.

But the Gnostics, following their individual pursuit of truth, were fragmented and disorganized. The divine Emperor Diocletian outlawed them in AD 295, and their influence waned. By the fifth century they had almost disappeared under persecution by the now official Church of Empire. Their image of the Divine Mother, "The invisible within the All," was written out and destroyed. Though the movement never entirely died out; it resurfaced in the Cathars in Southern France in the eleventh century, until virtually the whole population there was massacred by the 20-year-long Church Albigensian Crusade. Centuries later, it can be seen in the writings of William Blake; and in some ways it's coming back into the frame today. The "anything goes if it feels right" flavor of New Age thinking is reminiscent of Gnosticism. Many of their best-selling books (which nowadays outsell Christian books by something like a factor of ten) are "kind of Christian." Perhaps in the next millennium Christians will increasingly think of themselves as the Gnostics used to, seeing "orthodox Christianity" as a wrong turn that led into the sands for a couple of millennia.

He is never born, nor does he ever die;
Nor once having been, does he cease to
Be. Unborn, eternal, everlasting, ancient, he is not slain when the
body is slain.
Bhagavad Gita

35. How The Bible Came To Be

God in the depths of us receives God who comes to us; it is God contemplating God.
Jan van Ruysbroeck (fourteenth century AD)

In some ways involvement with Gnosticism probably didn't help the Christian cause. Gnostics – and practitioners of the many mystery cults that were common in the Empire – tended to believe that the heart of knowledge was secret. Initiates who passed the early tests got the opportunity to identify with the divine through rituals that simulated death and resurrection. When Christians compounded their secrecy by refusing to worship the Emperor, or serve in the army, Roman authorities regarded them as X-rated. In the public mind Christianity may have had the connotations that witchcraft and sex orgies have today. Christians were accused of incest (marrying their brothers and sisters in Christ) and cannibalism (eating and drinking divine flesh and blood in secret suppers) as well as atheism (refusing to honor the gods). Elements of this secrecy linger, as in the way Greek Orthodox churches still celebrate the Eucharist behind a screen, where not even the congregation can see what's happening.

But by the fourth century AD most believers were taking it all literally, and many had started going to the Holy Land as tourists. As in any pagan cult, places and objects were given sacred status, turned into holy sites and relics. In the choice between the Gnostic idea of Jesus as a teacher of wisdom and God within you, or Jesus as the almighty Son of God coming to rule and deliver judgment, the Almighty won.

But it could have gone the other way, in which case Christianity might have ended up much closer to the Eastern religions of today, as indeed did happen outside the Roman

Empire in the East. In fact there were Buddhist missionaries in the Empire at the time of Jesus, at the port of Alexandria, and the two religions could have developed a fruitful interchange of ideas. In the *Gospel of Thomas* you can substitute the word "Buddha" for "Jesus" without much altering the sense. Later writings like *The Book of the Blessed* by Justin the Gnostic draw on a range of religious experience including the Hindu Lord Shiva, before pointing to Jesus as fulfilling God's plan. This dialogue between the religions has only really been picked up again in the last few decades.

Gnosticism continued through the centuries in Judaism through the Kabbalists, in Islam through Sufi mystics. In Christianity it remained strong in the Pauline churches of Asia Minor and threads continued through the centuries.

So why didn't their interpretation survive in the mainstream of what became Christianity?

Ask many Christians why you should take the Bible literally and they will quote 2 Timothy 3:16:

All scripture is given by inspiration of God, and is profitable for doctrine, for reproof, for correction, for instruction in righteousness.

What we've got is what is right. But what we've got isn't what Paul had, when he wrote to Timothy. The gospels, for instance, hadn't been written yet. Not even the Old Testament had been established yet, let alone the New. But it was during the second century AD that Christians began to think it would be a good idea to collect their very diverse accounts of the words and life of Jesus.

By the second century there were at least a dozen gospels in existence. Over the first three centuries there may have been 70 or more, many of which have only come to light in the last century, which suggests there may be more to follow. We know virtually nothing about any of the writers, canonical or

313

non-canonical. Nor did the people in the council making the decisions. Sometimes the other gospels have a totally different feel from those in the New Testament:

> But they, the archons, those of the place of Yaldabaoth, reveal the realm of the angels, which humanity was seeking in order that they may not know the Man of Truth. For Adam, whom they had formed, appeared to them. And a fearful motion came about throughout their entire dwelling, lest the angels surrounding them rebel. For without those who were offering praise – I did not really die lest their archangel become empty.
> Second Treatise of the Great Seth

We can make a good guess that Jesus didn't actually say this – the tone is too far removed from the bulk of the gospels, and it's over a century later. But who can really decide? And after all, the idea behind the *Treatise of Seth* – that the God of the Old Testament is one god among many, inferior to some, and that Jesus comes from the true heaven above – is not without merit. Actually, the writer probably understood the Old Testament better than Christians today. Would it have appeared any more fanciful than the idea that Jesus was the Son of the often-barbaric God of the Old Testament? Probably not. We live with the assumptions of two millennia. It's quite possible that in the early days a sizable proportion of gentile Christians saw Jesus as a true God revealing the truth to humankind, and the Jewish God of the Old Testament as a deceiver.

There's also a whole library of other texts – letters of Jesus to foreign kings, letters of Paul to Aristotle, histories of the disciples and of many other characters from the life and times of Jesus – most of which have been lost; the Church did its best to burn all those that didn't fit with its teaching (Luke himself refers to a number, since lost, in his first verse). The churches started to feel the need, a dozen or so generations after Jesus, to produce a more coherent, single account. The delay was understandable. Hadn't he said, after all, that the disciples would not have time to visit all the cities of Israel before the end comes (Matthew 10:22-23)? That it would come in the lifetime of his listeners (Matthew 16:27-28; Luke 9:27; 21:32)? But by around AD 70 there could have been very few people still living who had seen or heard him. By then there would have been "Q," a lost source document that was the basis for Mark, Matthew and Luke, and the *Gospel of Thomas*. But they were starting to proliferate, increasingly diverging, becoming more imaginative and magical (and as late as the end of the second century there was still an oral tradition of the words of Jesus which was regarded as having independent authority, separate from the Gospels). But because the Gospels reflected their different beliefs, the scattered churches found it impossible to agree on one. Some Jews preferred Matthew because of its Jewishness and insistence on adhering to every jot of the Law (Matthew 5:18). Gentiles preferred others that supported nonobservance of the Jewish Law. Gnostics liked John, with its rejection of the world, or the *Gospel of Thomas*.

The lead was taken by the Gnostics, those at the cutting edge of the new religion. The first attempt to draw up a definitive list of Christian scripture was made in the middle of the second century by Marcion, a key figure in the early church. He wasn't what we would today call a Trinitarian Christian. The term and the teaching hadn't been thought of yet. And like many Gentiles, he found the morality in the pagan writings to be better than that in what later became known as the "Old Testament." In fact, for him, the God of the Old Testament was clearly a lesser deity, inferior to the one who sent Jesus to redeem the world.

Marcion thought that there should obviously be only one authoritative Gospel, and he chose that of Luke, but edited it to remove all mention of the Jews and references to the Old Testament – wasn't Christianity, after all, a new religion? The use of simple word counts alone shows the difference. "Faith," for instance, scarcely gets a mention in the Old Testament, but occurs about 250 times in the New. He also edited the letters of Paul to make him show Jesus teaching a God of love, not fear.

Valentinus was a leading contemporary of Marcion. He hated the idea of a definitive list. Each believer had the truth within himself, so why shouldn't everyone write their own gospel? He showed the way, with his own *Gospel of Truth*.

In the mid-second century Tatian wrote a single harmonized account, based on the four Gospels (the *Diatessaron*). This was accepted by the Syrian but not the Greek and Latin churches. It was probably more widely read by Christians than the canonical Gospels up to the eighth century, when it was banned.

Many Christians in the second century identified with the teaching of Valentinus or Marcion, rather than Paul or James, Peter or Thomas. Despite persecution by other Christians, Marcionite communities were still flourishing in Syria 300 years later. But as the Church grew in importance over the next couple of centuries, the pressures to create an established official scripture increased. When Christianity became the state religion the impetus was overwhelming. By now it had responsibility for vast tracts of land, multitudes of slaves, and needed to get its act together to play its role in the management of Empire. The Church needed a single "belief" and a "history."

So what was it to be? Was the Church going to splinter into a number of different sects or religions, or were Christians going to stick together and exercise power? Numbers or truth? Impact or purity? It's the problem that bedevils all religions down the ages.

The orthodox Christian argument goes that the books in our New Testament reflect the early apostolic tradition. But it's not as clear-cut as that. Luke wasn't an apostle but his books are in; Thomas was (or may have been) but his is not. We don't even know whether the names Matthew, Mark and John should be attached to the gospels as there's no record of them before AD

185, a century and a half after Jesus' death. Most scholars would say that it's unlikely that any of the New Testament writers had met Jesus. With the books that we do have, there are more variants in the earliest manuscripts than there are words.

The epistles of Paul had widespread support. He was the guy who got it going, who explained the cosmic significance of the Christ figure to the Gentiles. His letters (though the scholarly consensus nowadays is that only seven of the thirteen letters attributed to him were probably written by him, and some of those were later amended) could be read by the now-orthodox as supporting a literal, historical Christ as Savior, but his theology is also close to Gnosticism and the mystery cults, with their dying and rising savior gods. So the Gnostics can still see his letters as supporting a view of Jesus as a spiritual rather than historical figure. He implies further revelation to come in the Gnostic manner. In 2 Corinthians 12:2-4 for instance he refers to a time when he was physically transported to the third heaven (there were usually seven levels, perhaps paralleling the Eastern idea of seven centers of consciousness in the body, described as *chakras*), and also to paradise, where he "heard unspeakable words, which it is not lawful for a man to utter." They were accepted as canonical (authoritative) by around AD 200. Late in the second century Irenaeus declared that just as the earth has four corners and four winds there should be four gospels – so the letters were paired with the purportedly historical narratives of the gospels, and the bulk of the New Testament as we understand it today had general acceptance by AD 300.

Early in the fourth century, a 300-year gap, a similar period from the founding of the USA to now, Eusebius, one of the most underrated figures in history, who wrote the first full-length historical narrative covering both pagan and Old Testament history in his *Chronicles*, drew up what came to be the list that most agree on today. He leaves out the *Acts of Paul*, the *Shepherd of Hermas*, the *Revelation of Peter*, the *Letter of Barnabas*, which up till then many churches had considered authoritative, and he includes *Revelation* and *Hebrews*, which had previously been excluded. The first "Bibles" now begin to appear, though even then they were referred to in the Greek as "the books" rather than "book."

But it wasn't till the fifth century that Eastern and Western Churches in the Empire finally agreed on the selection, with the former accepting Revelation and the latter accepting Hebrews. Agreement was never universal. Some books jumped in and out over the centuries. The Book of Revelation for instance was "out" at the Council of Laodicea in AD 363, "in" at the Council of Rome in AD 382, "in" at the Synod of Hippo in AD 393, but "out" again at the Eastern Orthodox Council in Trulla in AD 692. The Protestant Reformation brought further changes, dropping 12 of the Old Testament books, the "deuterocanonical" writings or the "Apocrypha." Books like *Sirach*, which emphasized the feminine Wisdom tradition, with their erotic charge, didn't stand a chance. Martin Luther wanted to go further and drop James and Revelation as well.

The definitive "Holy Bible" is an illusion. The Syrian Church still recognizes only 22 of our 27 New Testament books; the Armenian Church includes a *Third Letter of Paul to the Corinthians*; the Ethiopian Church has a different selection again. These may be minor Churches in the twenty-first century but at the time they were important ones. The Syrian Church, amongst the wealthiest of the provinces, covered the heartland of Paul's missionary efforts. For the first few centuries more Christians lived there than anywhere else. Ethiopia was one of the first significant Christian areas (King Ezana of the Ethiopian kingdom converted to Christianity around the same time as Constantine – it was a significant place at the time, controlling much of the trade around the Indian Ocean), and Armenia has the oldest national Church in the world, becoming the first Christian state, reportedly through the efforts of two disciples of Jesus who traveled east – Judas Thaddeus and Bartholomew (martyred by being skinned alive). They certainly can't all be right, maybe they all got it wrong.

So where should we draw the line on what to include? Why shouldn't we write a "new" New Testament today? Why stop in the fourth century AD, or the sixteenth? Christians say that the Holy Spirit, working through the bishops in the different Councils, inspired them to reach the right decisions. But oddly enough Protestants don't apply the logic of that to their other decisions, as if the Holy Spirit only came into the room when the composition of the Bible was on the agenda. So why not follow the vision and the courage of the early Christians, open Pandora's Box, and shape our faith to suit our times, as they did? At least select what we want to keep from the Bible and reject the rest? That's what Jesus did, after all, as in flipping the meaning of Isaiah 61:1-2 by dropping "the day of vengeance of our God," and Paul is always doing it when he quotes from the Old Testament, editing the text to promote the bit he wants to convert the Gentiles (eg: Romans 15:8-10). Perhaps we could then find again the exhilarating sense of liberation they had in the first century, when a bunch of motley peasants believed they could turn the world upside down because they had the vision and the faith for a new one.

Man is a credulous animal, and must believe something; in the absence of good grounds for belief, he will be satisfied with bad ones.
Bertrand Russell (twentieth century AD)

36. The Turning Point

The Savior said to them: "For some of them say about the world that it is directed by itself. Some, that Providence directs it. Some, that it is fate. Now, it is none of those. Again, of those opinions I have just described, none is close to the truth, and they are of man. But I, who came from the boundless light, I am here."
The Sophia of Jesus Christ

So the idea that there was ever a "pure" early Church holding a clearly-defined set of beliefs, a single body believing in a common doctrine, is simply not true.

The diverse range of views in the early church about who Jesus was gradually coalesced in the Empire under the influence of some persuasive philosopher/theologians known today as the Early Church Fathers. Christian history tends to treat them as if they were the outstanding intellectual giants of their time, but they represented only a small range of the talent around the Mediterranean world, and were perhaps outshone by Buddhist philosophers of the same period farther East, thinkers like Nagarjuna (he taught the doctrine of "emptiness," arguing that there is nothing which exists in itself, independently from something else – in a way which seems to foreshadow the findings of Quantum Theory). Even so, the majority of scholars, those outside religious institutions at least, do not see them as judicious saints representing the central teaching of Christianity and bringing the Church into some already-existing orthodoxy. They were radical, sometimes unstable, certainly heretical (by later standards) teachers who had very different ideas about how this still relatively new faith should take shape. The one thing they had in common was, to a degree unique in major religions, an obsession with sex. Women were unclean, irrational and carnal. The body itself was wicked. Far from being sacred, the feminine and the flesh need to be controlled, whipped into submission.

Origen (who may have castrated himself), for instance, was the most prolific. He believed that the Father, Son, and Holy Spirit were of descending importance, that the sun and moon had souls, and in the pre-existence of the soul (which seems logical, if you believe in its after-existence, that the soul lives on after death). He was tortured to death under the Emperor Decius, and then 300 years later was excommunicated by the Synod of Constantinople for believing that hell was finite, and that all could be saved from it; so he was sent there retrospectively. Tertullian, crucial in developing the doctrine of the Trinity, ended his life as a Montanist, believing the "new prophecy" that the kingdom of heaven would shortly descend on what is now Turkey. Clement believed that Jesus was not wholly human but had a semidivine body that didn't need to digest food and drink (kind of makes sense – if he was God's Son, how could he be totally human at the same time?). Justin Martyr, a Samaritan, was perhaps the most important of the early ones. He established Christianity as a credible religion for the intellectuals of the Roman world, and did this by gutting it of its Jewish roots (Jews and Samaritans weren't generally fond of each other – hence Jesus' favorable description in the parable of the Good Samaritan – "if even a Samaritan could behave like this, why can't we?"). He describes God as the supreme transcendent Being, operating through His Word, the Logos. This Logos had scattered itself around the world in the hearts of all people, so that everyone had traces of it. For Justin any lover of truth counted as a Christian – even Greek philosophers were Christian without knowing it.

With the exception of Justin none of the half-dozen major early apologists for Christianity up till the year AD 180 (after that, Irenaeus, Clement of Alexandria, Origen, and Tertullian are largely rooted in the Gospel tradition, though they had different ideas as to what that meant, as the Gospels hadn't been settled on) refer to the Gospels in their presentation of Christianity to the Roman world. They appeal to the logic of a single God and a single intermediary, rather than to a historical figure who was born of a virgin and raised from the dead.

The Church Fathers would have been surprised by the beliefs of many Christians today. Much as the later great theologian Aquinas, for instance – who cemented the foundations of Christian theology and was happy to take on board Greek thinking via Muslim scholars like Averroes – would be astonished to see the Church today denying knowledge rather than working with it to create a better natural theology. For example, as a general rule, the Fathers didn't take scripture "literally." They saw that as self-evidently stupid. The purpose of scripture was to convey spiritual truth, in multiple layers of meaning. The literal, historical sense was secondary, even irrelevant. They began the tradition of seeing the Bible as a closed book, a mystery to be interpreted by the Church. And they were quite prepared to invent stories and forge documents to exploit gullibility, because humanity was fallen and needed rescuing. The end justified any means. As Origen says: "Sometimes it is allowable to use deceit and lying as a medicine for the purpose of bringing salvation. For some character are reformed by certain doctrines which are more false than true, just as physicians use similar words to their patients."

The Early Church Fathers made Christianity a credible possibility for those particular times, turning Jesus into a kind of avatar of God, much as Krishna is an avatar of Vishnu (there's little suggestion so far that he's coequal with God). But not a necessary one. And Christianity would probably have remained one of many cults in the melting pot of the Empire, to be forgotten along with the others, or absorbed in the others (if indeed it could even be described as one cult rather than several), were it not for the Emperor Constantine.

Constantine clawed his way to the top of the greasy pole in

the early fourth century AD. Like a corporate empire builder of today, he wanted a new mission statement. The "Roman Way" of the previous centuries was no longer the driving force that had created the world's most remarkable Empire ever. Its resolution was weakening: too many different peoples and cultures had been assimilated at the bottom; too much wealth and corruption had rotted the top. Institutions were breaking down, conflict was endemic. Energetic tribes on the borders were raiding, poverty increasing. The old Roman gods had lost their sway. There were still the mysteries of Eleusis and Orpheus, and the more intellectual faiths of Platonism, Stoicism, and Epicureanism from Greece. But these were remote and abstract for most. With little sense any longer of the public good, people looked for personal salvation. As in the West today a gap was left in the popular imagination into which numerous intermediaries flooded. These included the cults of Isis from Egypt, Cybele from Asia Minor, Astarte from Syria, Mithraism from Persia, Judaism and Christianity from Palestine.

Christianity had an edge in that it rooted the esoteric salvation philosophies of the time in a single god-man, which the majority could readily understand; it wasn't elitist. Exiled from the Jewish tradition, and uncomfortable with worshipping the emperor, its followers were organized into churches and provinces – it could deliver the mobs. Bishops were stepping into the gaps left by a crumbling system. The Christian faith may have won out because it was the best organized (we still talk about church "dioceses," based on the Roman provinces). Now Constantine wanted unity and obedience in matters of state and religion, a common belief that would combine the two. Mithraism had been the main contender in the previous century. The cult of the Sun God, *Sol Invictus*, was also significant – Constantine may have confused this with Christianity, and often switched from one to the other. After all, Christ is apparently spoken of in the Old Testament as the "sun of righteousness," and Clement of Alexandria describes him as driving his chariot across the sky like the sun god. As indeed did the Church, adopting the Sun God's halo for the divine family and saints, and to cement the break from Judaism changed the Sabbath from Saturday to "Sun"day. Perhaps the most persuasive argument for Constantine was that as emperor he was able to usurp some of the functions attributed to Jesus (so Eusebius tells us – he also encourages the increasing trend to blame the Jews for Jesus' crucifixion, though admits it's possible that individual Jews could be saved).

So Constantine converted to Christianity, the key moment apparently being at the Milvian Bridge in Rome on 28 October AD 312 when legend has it that he saw a flaming cross in the sky and the words "In this sign conquer" during his decisive battle with the Emperor Maxentius. This effectively marks the point where the churches lost any connection they might have previously had with the teaching of Jesus. Whoever God might be, Christians are now worshipping the wrong one.

There were approximately ten million people in the Empire at the time of Constantine's conversion, about 10% of the world's population, and about 10% of them were Christians – one million is the best guess we have. About three centuries after the death of Jesus 1% of the world's population were Christian. It's around now that historians start talking of Christianity as a religion rather than a cult.

Christianity had taken a big step, but it was scarcely a coherent religion. By the fourth century there were Adoptionists, Antidicomarians, Apollinarianists, Arians, Cerinthians, Collyridians, Docetists, Ebionites, Gnostics, Monophysites, Montanists, Nestorians, Phibionites, and many others, reflecting different fusions of local traditions. And that's just the ones in the Roman Empire. They variously described Jesus as an ordinary man, a teacher of wisdom, the Teacher of Righteousness, a prophet, the True Prophet, the Primal Man, the Messiah, an angel, God's Anointed, the Son of God, the True God, and a score of others.

These beliefs were not mutually exclusive. Much as many today believe that the universal life force can be tapped through a variety of different methods – aromatherapy, astrology, reflexology, etc. – there were many ways in the first couple of centuries of experiencing the liberation that Jesus brought for those looking for a channel to the universal God. Certain beliefs became more precise and dogmatic as they were teased out and separated in Greek, the language of philosophy, and then codified in Latin, the language of law and confession. But for the first dozen or so generations, the same kind of period that the USA has existed, you could believe at any one of these points on the spectrum and be a Christian. There was no central belief system to persuade converts. What impressed pagans (in the first century or two, anyway) was the love Christians showed, "Christian is as Christian does," not their theology, which hadn't yet been written.

But Constantine wanted clarity and control. He summoned a general assembly of 318 bishops, mostly from the Western provinces of the Empire, none from beyond the borders where his writ did not run, to meet at his vacation home at Nicaea, in Turkey, to sort out the doctrine. They produced the Nicene Creed, in AD 325, as a summary of the essentials of the Christian faith, still taken as authoritative by most Churches today. But the most interesting thing about it is what it leaves out, which is pretty much everything that you would think should go in. It doesn't, for example, quote Jesus at all. It doesn't give any indication of how we should live. It only refers indirectly to the big questions of sin and eternal life. No mention of forgiveness, happiness, justice, love. The core of Jesus' message – "Love the Lord your God... love your neighbor as yourself," and the kingdom itself has disappeared. Most of its ritual chant revolves around Jesus' relationship with the Father, how he was begotten by God and no one else, of the same substance, not a similar one. The creed is a party platform reflecting the intensity of the spiritual power-

politics of the time, every phrase countering what had come to
be regarded as heresy by those wanting an authoritarian state
religion that glorified the emperor.

For those who don't know it, here it is, the distilled wisdom
of orthodox Christianity:

*We believe in one God, the Father Almighty, maker of all things
visible and invisible;*

*And in one Lord Jesus Christ, the Son of God, begotten of the
Father, only-begotten, that is, from the substance of the Father; God
from God, Light from Light, very God from Very God, begotten
not made, of one substance with the Father, through whom all
things were made, both in heaven and on earth; who for us men and
for our salvation came down and was incarnate, was made man,
suffered, and rose again on the third day, ascended into heaven, and
is coming to judge the living and the dead;*

And in the Holy Spirit.

*And those who say: "There was a time when he was not," and:
"Before he was begotten he was not," and: "He came into being
from nothing," or those who pretend that the Son of God is "of
another substance, or essence" (than the Father) or "created" or
"alterable" or "mutable," the catholic and apostolic church places
under a curse.*

(The last paragraph is usually missed out.)

The (probably) historical Jesus has been displaced by the
Lord Christ, raising more questions than answers as to who this
strangely begotten creature exactly was. The Church by now has
completely lost the plot.

*I don't know that atheists should be considered citizens, nor should
they be considered patriots. This is one nation under God.*
George Bush (twentieth century AD)

37. How To Ruin A Good Religion

This doctrine was revealed by God and therefore is to be firmly and steadfastly believed by all the faithful.
Pope Pius IX, Bull *Ineffabilis Deus* 1854 (*Immaculate Conception* – of Mary the mother of Jesus)

So for the last 1,500 years or so the nature of Jesus and his relationship to God have been defined in the doctrine of the Trinity (well, that's an over-simplification; Satan is clearly a god of some kind, albeit a less powerful one; then there's the "Word" of John 1:1, the various saints who each have special powers, like the lesser gods of other polytheistic religions, and so on; but we'll stick with the Trinity for the moment). This is worth exploring further because for many you have to believe in the Trinity to be a proper Christian. Which seems bizarre, as it is such a late development. There's no mention of the Trinity as such in the Bible. The clearest reference is in Matthew 28:19, which is probably a later addition. It still doesn't assert that "the three are one," and non-Trinitarian churches use this formula without drawing the conclusion that it implies belief in the Trinity. There's an oblique reference in 1 John 5:7-8, which doesn't appear in the oldest and most reliable manuscripts and was almost certainly added later, and possibly in a couple of Paul's letters. It doesn't feature in Jesus' teaching. He wouldn't have known what was meant by it. It's one of the Capital Letter Doctrines that the Church developed in the first four centuries, and it took a further five centuries or so to become generally accepted in Europe.

But what did the fourth-century Christians think it meant? Short answer, they didn't know, which is why they argued so much. Are there three separate centers of consciousness here or not – they clearly have separate functions? If God could have one son, why not several? How about daughters? Who was the mother? Doesn't it imply that God had a father himself? No one really understands this; successive church councils over the coming centuries, convened by different emperors, couldn't sort it out, and theologians still argue over it, 1,700 years later.

(In hindsight, I had my own little problem with this. Do Christians pray to God, or Jesus? Are they interchangeable? I guess I used to mostly pray to Jesus, personally; though on more formal occasions, like graces at meals, or in groups, it would be to God; in occasional wilder moments, the Holy Spirit. But I never really figured it out.)

Strictly speaking, in orthodox Christian theology, believing in the Father God and identifying Him with God, which perhaps most Christians do today, is a heresy called Monarchianism. The issue goes to the heart of the complication of Christianity, which evolved as a compromise between the Jewish view of a single omniscient God (as it had now developed), and the Roman/ Greek pantheon of many gods and their different families and relations. It left us a muddle.

Do we now really have one God, or two, or three? It's a new kind of problem, one that didn't exist for those who believed in many gods, or only one God with no family. If Jesus was God's Son, there surely must have been a time when God existed and Jesus didn't. So wasn't he then of secondary importance? If he was not secondary, and had always been around, and was God Himself, then did he have sex with his own mother, in order to be born on earth? That must logically be the case, and the *Epistula Apostolorum*, a book considered canonical by parts of the early church, thought so: *And I, the Word, went into her and became flesh; and I myself was servant for myself, and in the form of an angel; so I will do after I have gone to my Father.*

To reconcile those who thought Jesus must be man, and those who thought he must be God, the doctrine of "hypostatic union" (the union of persons) was developed: he was man and God in one. But this only shifted the problem along. If Jesus and God were the same, what was the point of the different entities? If he was God, and so immortal, how could he have died on the cross? If he hadn't really died on the cross, then his sacrifice wasn't actually a genuine one? An attempt to explain this conundrum was given the name "modalism." This solution, which appeared around AD 200, may have been followed by the majority of Christians. It said that God was one deity with three different phases. God the Father changed into God the Son at the Virgin Birth, and then became God the Spirit at the resurrection.

Modalism kept both the one God and the deity of Jesus intact. But it caused its own difficulties. If God the Father turned into God the Son, leaving heaven empty, then who was Jesus praying to when he was on earth?

There were other solutions, like Patripassianism, which held that it was really God the Father who suffered on the cross. But the main, obvious alternative, called Arianism, was that Jesus was less than the Father but more than human.

It's hard today, after nearly two millennia of taking the Trinity for granted as the definition for correct belief in God, with Jesus as coequal with Him, to get an idea of the intensity with which these positions were debated. Today, when the idea of god-men is so incomprehensible, we've just lost the sense of how central it was to the society of the time. At the Council of Nicaea the followers of Athanasius combined with those of Marcellus to win the day against Arius, fighting it out in the streets, but the controversy continued for 60 and more years afterwards. It was touch and go who would win. Support for one side or the other changed according to fluctuating political and military fortunes, with Athanasius being exiled five times. It was an Arian bishop who baptized Constantine as he lay dying. Success for the Athanasian Trinitarian formula came down to the toss of a political coin, and who could afford the most thugs.

Conservative Christians say that the Spirit of God, who

became known as the Holy Spirit, worked through life on earth to insure that the right decisions were made (which seems a self-evident absurdity; why then so much disagreement over so many centuries?). It's not even as if church councils were peaceful affairs where the mind of God was sought in a spirit of love and tolerance. They were often vitriolic and bloody. The stakes were high. Defeated opponents were exiled, not pensioned off. Athanasius was hesitant about attending the later Council of Tyre (AD 335) as he feared for his safety. One of his supporters, the presbyter Makarios, had been accused of the kidnapping and murder of Bishop Arsenios. Arius himself was ultimately struck down by a mysterious illness – caused, some believed, by poison – and according to Athanasius ended his life "split in pieces in a public lavatory." Others say he was executed for his beliefs.

In an era of common casual cruelty, when seeing people torn apart by animals in the arena was the height of entertainment, Constantine himself stood out as a vicious individual, and being converted did nothing to improve his character. It would be nice to think that the first Christian emperor ushered in a golden period of tolerance, peace, knowledge, artistic achievement, much as did the first Buddhist Emperor, Ashoka, who ruled the Indian subcontinent in the third century BC, and seems to have undergone a genuine conversion. But Constantine murdered his rivals rather than imprisoning or exiling them – the traditional way of doing things. He even executed his eldest son, Crispus, and his brother-in-law. He had his second wife Flavia tortured to death by slow immersion in boiling water.

In later years the Empire itself came apart over these linguistic subtleties. The German tribes of central Europe were largely baptized as Arians, and their war cry as they conquered the later Roman capital of Ravenna was, "The Father is greater than the Son." Arian churches survived throughout Europe till the seventh century, when the last were wiped out. It's reminiscent of Jonathan Swift's Lilliputians in *Gulliver's Travels*, who go to war over whether to cut a boiled egg at the fat or thin end. It was all unnecessary, as Jesus is no more closely related to God than the rest of us.

The Trinity just marks the point where Christianity stopped having much to do with the teaching of Jesus and modeled itself on contemporary pagan religion, hence the priests, bishops and church buildings.

From a personal point of view, of course, believing in the Trinity can be valuable. It's tough to just believe in one abstract, omniscient God out there somewhere, without someone to talk to more directly, someone a bit more human, and a spirit to help you do it. God has many aspects. But there's nothing unique about the Christian Trinity. As soon as gods drop their guard they're likely to be split into threesomes, a magic number of completeness, often representing unity (God), particularity or diversity (Jesus), and a feminine principle (Spirit). There are hundreds of them. The Hebrews would have been familiar with many, some of which feature in the Old Testament. The Egyptians have Osiris, Isis, and Horus; the Babylonians Anu, Ea, Enlil, or the later Apsu, Tiamat, Mummu. Then there's the Sumerian Inanna, Erishkegal, Dumuzi; the Ugaritic El, Ashtoret and Baal; the Alexandrian Serapis, Isis, and Anubis, etc. Many trinities are more comprehensible than the Christian one. For example, the Hindu trinity of the three forms of God – Brahma the Creator, Vishnu the Preserver, and Shiva the Destroyer – at least reflects more of the rhythm of creation, the reality of life as we know it. Still farther east, Chinese religion has the triad of Heaven, Earth, and Man.

The point of taking the Trinity seriously is not that it's uniquely Christian, but common religious currency. Mystics might say the world is one and we can know it as such. Rationalists that we know it through the particular. Most say you leave out the feminine at your peril. By definition the mystics have difficulty in saying what they're talking about. The rationalists must agree that particulars add up to something else. The feminists mostly agree they need a male to define themselves against.

So some Christians explain the Trinity by saying it represents God outside the world, God acting in the world (Jesus), and through the world (Holy Spirit). Much as Hindus talk of the knower (*Rishi*), the act of knowing (*Devata*), and the object known (*Chhandas*), all aspects of a single reality. The twelfth century Joachim, one of the more enlightened Christian thinkers of that period, phrased it progressively: the Hebrew religion centered on God as Father, based on law; Christianity centered on the Son, based on the gospel; today we focus on the Spirit, an age of freedom based on direct spiritual revelation. And there are plenty of other interpretations. Perhaps we can characterize them by different functions. There's the creator Father who gave us life; the Son who came and showed us what matters in life; the Spirit who enables us to do something about it. There's scope here for endless rewriting. It's like having mind, body, and spirit. Ego, superego, and id. But as a precise idea the Trinity is meaningless today to most. Those who believe in it have difficulty saying exactly what it is, or why anyone else should hope to understand it.

The fourth century was the most remarkable ever for Christianity, the turning-point. At the beginning of the century it was a minor cult in the Empire. At the end it was the only permissible religion, and pretty well everyone in the Empire was Christian, around ten million people. Unsurprisingly – you and your family were likely to die horribly if you refused to convert. This meteoric rise in status drove the writing of the creeds, the establishment of the papacy in Rome (rather than the popes in Antioch and other places) as the supreme power in the Church, and the creation of the Bible. The kingdom Jesus talked about for the here and now was pushed into a remote heavenly future, he himself became divine, sacrifice was established as an endless cycle in the Mass. Aristocrats took over the church hierarchy, and in one of history's greatest asset transfers (the biggest of all is going on right now, with the concentration of wealth in the hands of a few) the Church took over much of the Empire's wealth, particularly in the form of lands and slaves. Through history as a whole, around three quarters of the people who have ever lived have been slaves, or serfs with minimum rights – it didn't take the Church that long to become an integral part of the power structures that have always bedeviled us, rather than challenging them in the name of humanity and God, like Jesus did.

The Emperor Julian (reigned AD 361-363) tried to turn the clock back and restore paganism, but failed. Theodosius (379-395) made Christianity the only religion, banning the worship of pagan gods in AD 392. In the *Codex Theodosianus* he declares other religions to be "demented and insane," and states that their followers can be punished and executed, their temples destroyed. The pragmatic Roman approach of accepting any religion as long as the emperor got his dues was abandoned. Their talent for living comfortably with a number of different perspectives on life began to disappear. Ignorance even came to be seen as a positive spiritual virtue, and intelligent criticism and questioning a vice, much as it increasingly does today.

It was Augustine made this possible. He pulled together various strands of early church teaching into a new definition of the relationships between the individual and God, society and the Church. He gave the Church a sacred status of its own. Salvation could now only be obtained through it. Sacraments were even valid if administered by unholy priests who had no idea what they were doing. The laws of God, as interpreted by the Church, were superior to the individual conscience and it was okay to force people into belief. Only God knows and chooses who will be saved. Faith, along the lines started by Paul, was only faith if you could accept what you were told, and by him rather than someone else. He laid the foundations for the Papal Inquisition –

Error has no rights. His successors drove the nails into the coffin of the kingdom, granting the Church a monopoly on permissible belief that lasted for the next millennium.

As Christians gained control of the levers of power in the fourth century it turned from a religion of the persecuted to a religion of persecutors. The Donatists for instance were the most numerous of the various subgroups, who believed in a pure, non-worldly version of the Church, for which they were prepared to suffer and die. Augustine made his name by confronting them, and was the first person we know of in history to advocate war and persecution on theological grounds. Donatists became the first Christians to be murdered in significant numbers by other Christians (let's not get too weepy-eyed here though, it was a Donatist mob that lynched Athanasius' successor in Alexandria, Bishop George). In the fourth and fifth centuries, Christians probably killed more of each other than had been killed by the pagans in the previous three centuries (persecution of Christians had been sporadic and largely localized, prompted by people upset that Christians wouldn't honor their gods; in the these centuries there were only ten years when Christians were executed due to orders from a Roman emperor).

War bands from the East – never particularly numerous, initially, but more effective than bickering Christians – started to pick the Empire apart. The German barbarians, who had been left unconquered in their forests, came under pressure from tribes migrating from further east and started to swarm across the frontiers. Rome itself was sacked by Alaric the Hun in AD 410. Many blamed the Christians, with some truth – turning your back on the world to assure your salvation did not help man the defenses, and many Christians would not serve in the army. Augustine wrote his major work, *The City of God*, to counter the accusations of those who blamed Christians for the collapse, and by the end of the fifth century the Western half had come to an end. In the context of these divisions and developments you may begin to get the drift of why, in the seventh and eighth centuries, many turned with relief to Islam, a faith that simply regards Jesus as a very enlightened prophet. Muhammad had his vision in AD 610, and spent his life preaching justice, equality of all before God, and compassion for the weak. The Byzantine Empire (the surviving Eastern half of the old Roman Empire) was now collapsing, and most Christians in places like Syria and Egypt were Monophysites, believing that Jesus had one nature, whereas the official Church position since AD 451 was that he had two, one human and one divine. Many at first saw Islam as a new Christian movement, maybe even a Reformation. Christians converted to it as a Roman Catholic might convert to Protestantism, shedding a cartload of doctrines and practices that to Semitic speakers may have seemed like foreign Greek imports, in their place restoring the power, presence, and unity of God. Muslims saw themselves as bringing back the faith of Abraham, believing in the one true God, shedding the oppressive theology, and the denial of the grace of good works that had developed in the Christian Churches. They tended to view Christians as heretical Jews, or Judaized pagans. They agreed that the Old Testament was not the final word, and God had more to say, but the New Testament was a misunderstanding. It was the *Qur'an*, not the Christian Bible, which was the perfect word of God.

For Muslims the very idea that God needs to go around begetting bits of Himself to get things done is heresy, reducing His divinity and glory. The Greek language itself is insufficient to convey His majesty. Within a century of Muhammad's death the heartland of Christianity, which was in the Middle East and North Africa, was largely Muslim, and has remained that way.

If there is a God, atheism must strike Him as less of an insult than religion.
De Goncourt (nineteenth century AD)

38. The Religion Of Empire

The most scandalous charges were suppressed; the vicar of Christ was only accused of piracy, rape, sodomy and incest.
Edward Gibbon, on the condemnation of one of the rival popes in 1425 (eighteenth century AD)

We've seen how much beliefs and structures can change over three centuries. Christianity has been going for a further 17. Think of how much England has changed over the same period – the length of recorded history is about the same – England first features significantly in written history when Julius Caesar wrote up his invasion in his Gallic Wars just 50 years before the birth of Jesus. But it was another 13 centuries before there was a recognizable English language, and even then the English upper class still thought of themselves as French. England has been a constantly shifting mix of people and boundaries, shaped by victories and defeats, immigration, emigration and chance. The USA even more so – for that country add genocide to the mix.

The story of Christianity is similar. Sometimes it goes through phases of wholesale change. And so do all religions. Like animals, plants, people and everything else, religions survive by adapting themselves to new conditions; if not, they die out. All societies in history that are isolated by circumstance – losing long-range contact with others, the exchange of ideas, rivals to emulate – wither and fossilize. Hinduism has worked for 5,000 years and more by virtue of its flexibility, adding gods faster than the Hebrew kings added wives. Buddhism, originally an offshoot of Hinduism, developed different forms as it spread; first into Theravada (Ceylon) and Mahayana (Tibet), then with further offshoots like Madhyamika, Tantric, Vajrayana and Zen. Christianity has had to change more than most. Like Buddhism, it has lost its original heartland, and has had to put down new roots in foreign soils. And perhaps more than most it was also "lucky."

Christianity in the West managed to survive the fall of the Empire, converting numbers of the new pagans. The Bible became the foundation document of the Holy Roman Empire, a quasi-religious feudal and fairly ramshackle organization that the barbarians created out of the ashes of the old. And eventually the Bible also became the basis of the self-identity of the new nation states that arose out of feudalism. Christianity achieved this by bending to its purposes the beliefs and traditions of the newcomers.

Catholics nevertheless say that we can rely on the Church to have kept the teaching of Jesus intact. They maintain that Jesus authorized a line of leaders to whom he gave the authority to decipher the intentions of God on earth and provide rulings on them. So no matter that there were conflicting beliefs and always have been, whatever the Vatican says to be true at the time is true. This is based on two verses in Matthew 16:18-19. Most scholars say Jesus didn't speak these words, that they're later additions. There's nothing comparable elsewhere in the gospels and the style is different. And it does seem unlikely that Jesus planned for a long succession when he believed the end of the world was imminent. The general tenor of his teaching seems to be against hierarchies and titles (eg: Matthew 23:5-12). But in any case it was not until the late fourth century AD that they were significantly used as a reason for claiming primacy of the church in Rome. The churches with the closest links to the apostles were in Asia rather than Europe. But as the large majority of Christians down the ages have believed that the Popes are the mouthpiece of God, let's have a quick look at this.

The main justification for the idea that the bishops of Rome rather than any other city are the successors of Peter stems from a legend that Peter went to Rome and was crucified there, upside down, during the persecution by the Emperor Nero in AD 64.

This in itself, even if true, doesn't seem to prove the point. Peter visited many places. He spent far more time in Jerusalem. Why should where he was killed be relevant? But it was an attractive story for the Roman bishops. In fact, several other bishops in the main centers of Christianity – like Alexandria and Antioch – began to call themselves pope. For several centuries, though, none of them, including Rome, claimed power over the other bishops. The first pope to say he could overturn the decisions reached by other bishops was Pope Julius in AD 340-341, when he was supporting Athanasius against the Council of Tyre. Again, as with the creeds and the Bible, it's a 300-year gap from the time of Jesus. The first pope to exercise much authority in the West outside Italy was Pope Leo I, AD 440-461.

As well as the lack of evidence for the idea that the popes were authorized by Jesus to interpret God, there's the more significant problem of the popes themselves. Out of the 266 popes there have probably been many good men. Equally, there have been popes you wouldn't trust to babysit your daughter if you were out of the house, however young she was. Who you wouldn't want to live in the same street with. Corrupt, evil men, who poisoned relatives, raped, murdered, committed every conceivable kind of crime. At least one, Pope Stephen VII, was mad. He had the body of his predecessor, Pope Formosus, exhumed from his grave, dressed up, tried in court, his blessing finger cut off and the body thrown into the River Tiber. Stephen himself was strangled by the Roman mob. The papacy finally reached the pits in the fifteenth century AD, when popes were called "Antichrists" with good reason. Alexander VI (1492-1503) for instance was a man of unbridled immorality. He obtained the throne through bribery, openly advanced his bastard children, and eventually died of the poison he had prepared for some of this cardinals. And he's considered one of the more enlightened popes of the period. And who knows – maybe he wasn't exceptionally bad, that kind of conduct was normal in the Vatican, his enemies who wrote the history books might have been worse, and exaggerated his faults, and so on. But in the twenty-first century the idea that popes can pronounce the will of God by virtue of their position is as bizarre a belief as that kings rule by divine right, that slavery is divinely ordained, or blacks are naturally inferior to whites, or Aborigines aren't even human. It's surely just as likely – far more likely – that this series of individuals, hampered as they have been by the trappings of wealth and power that Jesus so strongly condemned, have consistently led the Church in the wrong direction, further away from his teaching. They are more likely than anyone to be wrong.

By this time, the Christian world had already split into two. In the first millennium it had roughly held together, through a series of councils, about one a century, even if it had nothing to do with what the first Christians believed. But in the eleventh century AD there was the "Great Schism," when it split into what we now call Roman Catholicism and Greek Orthodox. Both figured that there was no more need for councils because they separately had the truth. Basically, the Western Church taught that God would accept the death of Jesus as payment for sin, if believers repented and accepted that they couldn't save themselves from God's righteous judgment. The Eastern Church saw Jesus as a model to be imitated rather than a sacrifice, and through contemplating him they know God and take on His qualities. They didn't cancel their mutual excommunication of each other till 1965; in some respects understandable – at their low point, relationship-wise, the Crusaders sacked Constantinople in 1204, plundering the churches, raping the nuns, slaughtering the civilians; and if Churches can't get their forgiveness/reconciliation act together, nurturing hatred for 800 years, how can they lead the way for the rest of us?

The following millennium brought massive social change, starting with the breakup of feudalism, in part under the pressure of plagues, the Black Death, and the gradual diminution of the powers of the monarchy, the rise of merchants, the beginning of free thought, accelerated by the printing presses.

The Roman Catholic Church remained something of an exception in this process, as it frequently does. As the divine right to rule of czars, emperors, and kings crumbled in nineteenth- and twentieth-century Europe, that of popes actually increased. The doctrine of papal infallibility was pronounced in 1870, and all bishops in the Roman Catholic Church were appointed for the first time by Rome from 1917 onwards. It is similarly going backwards in its treatment of women. In 2010 it raised the ordination of women to one of the most serious crimes in Canon Law, on a level with child abuse.

And of course print can also be used to spread evil. Claims like that of the infallible *Declaration Dominus Jesus* some years back, which declares that the Roman Catholic Church is the "only instrument for the salvation of all humankind," are ugly blots, outcrops of insanity in the landscape of theology. They remind us that no organization in history has burnt so many books (the *Index of Forbidden Books* only ceased publication in 1966), persecuted and murdered its opponents so consistently for so many centuries as the Catholic Church, particularly in the second millennium with its office of the Grand Inquisitor and the Congregation of the Index. The Franciscans cared for the poor in the same way as Mother Teresa, but they also led the way in conjuring up hysteria against the Jews and other minorities. The Dominicans produced great learning and works of art and churches, but they were also involved in setting up the Papal Inquisition. The papal document that launched the Inquisition, the *Malleus Maleficarum*, or *Hammer of Witches*, is up there with *Mein Kampf*. Apart from being highly offensive to victims of the "religion of love" this kind of dogma presupposes that 99% of belief down the ages has been a great mistake. If Christians then doubt the truth of their own 1%, they can be inclined to disbelieve everything, turning to ideologies of cruelty and despair, or they take refuge in superstition or fundamentalism. The twin bastard offspring of Christianity that made the twentieth century a nightmare for so many – Communism and Fascism – are a product of this reaction. The 500 years of censorship, torture and terror orchestrated by Church leaders set a model for future totalitarian states.

There are so many thousands of versions of Christianity we could look at. But indulge me in one more snapshot, because I had to study it. We'll travel in time and place to the land we now call England. The Roman Empire has been long forgotten. The locals look wonderingly at the now grassed-over straight roads, the ruined amphitheaters, temples, aqueducts, palaces, and muse on the race of giants that could have built them – even wondering what they were used for. London has reverted from a powerful metropolis and European trading center to a ramshackle village. The buildings are small, smelly constructions of wood, daub and wattle (cow dung and straw), rather than the grandly-engineered works of brick, stone and marble of Roman times, with fountains and mosaics, under-floor heating, baths and murals.

In the smoky, dark chieftain's hall (this is a couple of centuries before churches start being built) the elders and heads of families are listening to a powerful preacher-poet chanting one of the major hymns of the time, one of the earliest poems in English literature, a hymn that expresses their Christian faith:

Therefore for every warrior the best
Memorial is the praise of living men
After his death, that ere he must depart
He shall have done good deeds on earth against
The malice of his foes, and noble works
Against the devil, that the sons of men
May after praise him, and his glory live
For ever with the angels in the splendor
Of lasting life, in bliss among those hosts.
The Seafarer (translated from the Anglo-Saxon)

This is one of the finest hymns of the period. But there's no dealing with sin here, no awareness of divine justice, of good and evil, no idea of holiness or salvation. The imagery that works for these Anglo-Saxons is military. Jesus has been adopted as a Thor-like god who helps warriors conquer their enemies. Heaven is an adaption of the Nordic Valhalla, where the dead warriors drink and toast their victories – those heads we hewed off, limbs hacked, villages plundered, that spear-thrust, that courage we showed in the face of greater odds. It's in warfare and comradeship that we fulfil our destiny and find our meaning.

It's hard to find a great deal in common between this and the teaching of Jesus, but it was a driving force behind Christianity for the first millennium, and continued way beyond that. There are countless other versions of Christianity. The one most Christians follow is an all-loving God who controls the universe and will reward those who worship Him in this life after they're dead, sending those who don't worship Him to hell – sounds like a giant scam. What should our version be today?

If Christ were here now there is one thing he would not be – a Christian.
Mark Twain (nineteenth century AD)

Part VI

The Way Forward

39. The Damage We Do

Those who can make you believe absurdities, can make you commit atrocities.
Voltaire (eighteenth century AD)

So, how can we look forwards rather than back? Build on worthwhile foundations and have a vision of salvation and renewal for the future?

To do that, if we're Christian, or want to be, we have to go back to square one. We need to acknowledge the harm we've done, and restore and build relationships, in every aspect of life. Which seems to me at the heart of the teaching of Jesus, which built on the best spiritual insights of the time, of all time. It reinterprets God up in the heavens as God living amongst us. In our lives we make Him real. In our actions we create His kingdom.

Later Christians turned this inside out. They interpreted Jesus himself as God coming to earth. They reversed the religion into the pagan ones of the time, putting God back up in the heavens, giving Him a family, turning Him back into Yahweh, a fearsome judge and monarch who threatened to destroy humankind for not recognizing Him as such.

So how did things turn out? Christianity had emerged as a significant religion in the world by the fifth century AD, but it didn't turn it upside down in the way that some of the first disciples hoped and Christians today imagine. The record of success was mixed. Centralized control in the West didn't encourage creativity. There are few significant theologians or writers from the second half of the first millennium. Islam in large part replaced Christianity across the Old World from the Atlantic to the Pacific, with the Church clinging on in Europe. By the end of the first millennium, when Europe was roughly settling down to the kind of shape it has today, there were probably fewer Christians in the world than there had been 500 years earlier. We can, though, recognize the religion we know today. Churches from that time are still standing – there are a couple of eleventh century churches within a few miles of where I live. By a few centuries later we're speaking the same languages in Europe that we speak today. We can relate more directly to the writers. We can look back and make some judgments about the religion's impact on the world. Has it been a "good thing"?

We tend to assume it must have been, even if we don't call ourselves Christian. We've grown up within the results, and they've been good for us. We live today in relatively peaceful, democratic, stable, and wealthy societies (if you just focus on the last decades, anyway), and up till recently at least they were undeniably "Christian." But all these are new developments and we also tend to turn a blind eye to the cost of getting there. And we can't move forwards without some understanding of that cost. Or we have no idea of the scale of what needs to be done.

We could take any century from the last millennium to explore the implications of this, from the feudal period, or that of the Enlightenment, or the period of empires, but let's pick the halfway point, 500 years ago, in the sixteenth century. The majority of the world's population followed one of seven major religions: Christianity, Islam, Hinduism, Buddhism, the South American sun religions, and in the Far East Confucianism and Taoism. Each of these cultures had impressive achievements in various fields – science, astronomy, architecture, engineering, literature, art, and so on, but knowledge transfers were generally one way. China had been more advanced than Europe by now for a thousand years, and the Christian nations had in the previous couple of centuries imported technology from the East like cast-iron tools, the wheelbarrow, the horses' collar, paper, gunpowder, better steering and rigging, the compass, and many others.

Numerically, Christianity was probably the smallest of the seven faiths. Some monarchies of Christian Europe were developing a technological edge in sailing and gunnery. Blocked from access to the East by the Ottomans, with relatively small populations, the coastal nations like Portugal made the most of their disadvantages, and began exploring trade routes by sea rather than conquering by land. But the cities of Europe were like villages compared with the metropolises to be found in the Far East and Central America. The idea that white Europeans always conquer colored natives was still centuries away. Christian Europe itself was still at risk from the Muslims, who in the fifteenth century had penetrated as far as central France and besieged Vienna in 1529. From a global historical perspective it's just as likely in those days that the East could have ended up ruling the West rather than vice versa.

Nevertheless the sixteenth century was a remarkable one for Christianity, full of creativity and conflict, as well as death and destruction – as in the second and third centuries AD, religion was inseparable from power, money and politics, and trying to play a role in it was a dangerous game. Printing changed the rules. Much as writing made organized religion possible, a few thousand years earlier, printing made it impossible – in the sense of organizing the Church and society around a commonly held belief system interpreted down through the priests to the people. When the Bible was translated from Latin to the different vernaculars (at the risk of death), people could read the scriptures for themselves, and spot the difference between façade and reality.

Printing led to numerous splits and divisions, but the religion itself didn't fundamentally change, as it did in the first centuries AD. If anything, Protestantism doubled down on the doctrine of Original Sin and the need of redemption by Christ's blood sacrifice on the cross because of it, becoming even more deeply sadomasochistic. But it shed a cartload of accretions that the

Roman Catholic Church had built up over the previous 1,500 years and, as had happened five centuries earlier with the Catholic/Orthodox split, this again shattered the Church. So in contrast to the paucity of Christian leaders and thinkers in the twentieth century, it gave rise in Europe to a number of men (the idea that women could be church leaders was unthinkable) who went into battle with each other. And in some respects they were needed – by now for instance the focus of worship on relics, forged or stolen, which exchanged hands for vast sums of money. Touching a relic could heal any illness – after all, in 2 Kings 13:21 a dead man is brought to life by being placed in Elisha's tomb. The other large trade was in "indulgences," paying the Church in cash for your sins to be forgiven. Martin Luther led the way, kicking off the Reformation with his *95 Theses,* and translating the Bible from incomprehensible (to most people) Latin into German. A distemperate, scatological writer and personality, in *On the Jews and Their Lies,* which influenced the Nazis (the 38 divisions of the Waffen-SS, the military branch of the Nazi party, who were at the forefront of rounding up Jews for slaughter and massacring civilians, had "God Is With Us" emblazoned on their belt buckles), he calls for their persecution, as in:

> *First, set fire to their synagogues or schools... This is to be done in honor of our Lord and of Christendom, so that God might see that we are Christians...*

(Hitler writes in the same style, in *Mein Kampf – I am convinced that I am acting as the agent of the creator – by fighting off the Jews I am doing the Lord's work.*) More significantly, in supporting princes against peasants and bypassing the Church so the individual could access God directly, he opened up a new front for social Darwinism, nationalism and imperialism to flourish.

Luther was followed by John Calvin, who established a form of theocracy in Geneva, creating the rigid theology of predestination which is still enormously influential in Protestant churches today. His main opponent was another Protestant reformer, Michael Servetus, a brilliant polymath important in many fields, and the first European to describe the function of pulmonary circulation. Calvin had him burned alive at the stake for believing that God was one but manifested Himself in three different ways through Father, Son and Holy Spirit (rather than each of them being coequal). In the prisons of Geneva heretics were handcuffed together to prevent them from committing suicide rather than be forced to look at the torturing of their wives and children. Ulrich Zwingli led the Reformation in Switzerland, and died in battle fighting Catholics. John Knox led it in Scotland, forming the Presbyterian movement. William Tyndale translated most of the Bible into English, and was strangled to death for his pains. Archbishop Cranmer established the liturgy and structures of the Church of England with the *Book of Common Prayer* and the *39 Articles*, and was executed. On the other side, Ignatius Loyola founded the Jesuits, along with Francis Xavier. Thomas More opposed the Reformation in England, and was executed. There were occasional voices of sanity, like that of John Colet and his friend Desiderius Erasmus, the greatest scholar of the time, who promoted humanist principles like human dignity, freedom and the significance of happiness as principal elements of the teaching of Jesus, and refused to take political sides on religious issues. But they were generally drowned out in the vitriol flowing back and forth, magnified through the explosion of pamphlets and books across Europe (in contrast, the Ottomans didn't allow printing into their empire till the eighteenth century), much as happens today with social media. Still, at least they died in their beds.

After Luther, Protestants continued to disagree and to split off from one another over the significance and nature of the sacraments and other issues. Many individuals and groups tried to take the Reformation still further, returning to the Gnostic idea of every individual worshipping God directly, without the need for any organized Church at all. Broadly known as the Anabaptists, these sects were persecuted by Protestants and Catholics alike. Their teaching still survives today in communities like the Mennonites, the Brethren and the Quakers.

Sadly, along with the bad went the good. Almost all the artistic heritage of England, for instance, from the Middle Ages, was destroyed, in one of the biggest acts of cultural vandalism in history.

But none of these larger-than-life characters had quite the same global impact as the mercenary, Fernando Cortez. Columbus had accidentally "discovered" the Americas in 1492, whilst meaning to get to the rich spice islands of the Far East. In 1519 Cortez and 314 fellow-soldiers and adventurers beached their ships at Veracruz (the Rich City of the True Cross) in Central America and set out to conquer the fabled Aztec Empire. The odds against success were incredible; a few hundred against millions. The Spaniards were driven by a powerful combination of extreme greed for gold and glory – for themselves and God. They knew their lives were on the line, it was conquer or die. They took their chance with extraordinary courage and ruthlessness.

They needed these qualities, in abundance. The Aztecs were not peace-loving softies. Their Empire was built on tribute, much of it in the form of human sacrifices. To keep the sun turning in the sky, human beings – usually children, as symbols of innocence and purity – had to die on their altars, with priests ripping out their still-beating hearts; 20,000 were sacrificed at the dedication of the great pyramid of Tenochtitlan, a city four or five times the size of the largest in Europe. They were a society geared to constant warfare, conquering territory to maintain the supply of sacrificial victims. At the time of the invasion, their emperor, Montezuma, was an aggressive leader and campaigner.

Nor were they primitive. In some ways they were more advanced than the Europeans. From the Mayan civilization in the Yucatan Peninsula they had inherited a calendar more accurate in some respects than the one we use today (based on a solar calendar of 365 days and 6 hours, a ceremonial year of 260 days, and a Venus year of 584 days). The Mayans had made astronomical calculations extending over millions of years. A thousand years ago, they forecast the 1991 eclipse of the sun. We have a more accurate knowledge of the dates of their emperors than of the kings who were their contemporaries in the Dark Ages of Christian Europe. And in some respects, morally, they were ahead – women, for instance, could divorce their husbands. Wealth distribution was less inequitable than in Europe.

Yet within a couple of years Cortez was in power and the emperor was in prison, shortly to be strangled. How did it happen? There were many factors, notably the defection to Spain of tribute tribes, but some say the main reason may have been the confusion of the Aztecs as to who these strange godlike people were, with their horses, ocean-going ships, and guns, which they had never seen before. The Aztecs had a god called Quetzalcoatl or "Feathered Snake" (inherited from the Mayan Kukulcan), who was the re-creator of the world. Born of a virgin, with a cross as a symbol, he was resurrected, and dived to the underworld to regain the bones of the dead, who he reanimated. He had promised to return one day from the east to restore his rule and bring prosperity.

The Aztecs mistook the Spaniards, also coming from the east in their feathered ships, riding extraordinary animals, killing at a distance with flashes of noise and light, for the gods in the story. Montezuma is reported as saying, "This is the same lord for whom we are waiting." The Aztecs thought their gods had actually stepped out of the myth and arrived. The year 1519 was their "Year of the One Reed" when the bearded Quetzalcoatl was to return, when the different calendars synchronized.

Maybe this is just a story, maybe the conquest was simply down to guns and armor. But even in the Aztec Empire, 5,000 miles away from the "Old World" of Europe, with no prior contact, we find the same themes of sacrifice and resurrection, virgin birth and second coming. In the Aztec sacrificial system, the victims represented the gods, the priests consecrated the body and blood, and onlookers shared the flesh to identify themselves with the gods. Spanish priests noted the similarity to the Eucharist and saw the Aztec religion as the Devil perverting the truth. And in many ways it was a truly nasty religion, though it has to be said that many victims probably went voluntarily, seeing their death as a passage to paradise.

But it should seem impossible today to think like the Spanish priests, celebrating the expansion of the Church through conquest, particularly when we know the outcome (though Google it, and you'll find Christians who do). It shows the dark side of religions like Christianity, the first major world religion of this kind to have survived to the present, that rely on central authority, claiming to be exclusively true for everyone (rather than just for your own people, like Judaism) and demanding to be believed. Much as Yahweh in the Old Testament uses armies, plagues, flood, fire – whatever came to hand – to smite people who didn't believe in him, European Christian nations used guns to conquer the inhabitants of entire continents. It was driven as much by religion as plunder, and sanction for it was given to Spain and Portugal by papal bulls of the fifteenth century, granting everything on the planet to Christian ownership. Pope Nicholas determined in 1452 that planting a flag on foreign soil made it yours. Natives couldn't own land because they were animals. Pope Alexander VI oversaw the division of South America between the two countries, reflected in the language today, with, broadly, the western half of South America speaking Spanish and the eastern half Portuguese.

By the time Cortez arrived at Veracruz the three million strong native Taino population of Haiti, where Columbus had landed, had already been almost wiped out, with many committing suicide rather than continuing to endure the savage torture and sexual abuse that the Christians routinely inflicted on them (girls aged nine or ten were prized as the best sex slaves). By the middle of the sixteenth century there was not a single Taina left alive.

By the mid-seventeenth century the original population of what is now Mexico had been reduced from 25 million to 1 million. By the mid-eighteenth around 90% of the indigenous population of the whole of South America had been wiped out. In total there are around 1 million pure-blood descendants of the Native American population today, north and south, compared with 100 million in the 1600s.

A few, a very few, churchmen questioned whether European nations had the right to conquer and kill; and the intention was not necessarily genocide, but that was the result. Pope Paul III officially endorsed the practice of enslaving the natives. And the large majority of the churchmen were in the forefront, leading the charge. We have the contemporary reports from the Spanish Dominican priest, Fray Bartolome de Las Casa, in *A Short Account of the Destruction of the Indies* (he argued, against most of his contemporaries, that the natives were actually human, like Europeans, and should have rights). They delighted in torture. Hanging natives wasn't enough, they let their toes touch the ground while they burned them in fire from below, cutting off noses, hands and ears, dashed their babies' brains out on rocks. Wounded warriors who had resisted them were eaten alive by dogs. Aztecs were piled into pits and fed their own flesh. Native lives were held so cheap that in transferring slaves from one Spanish territory to another the ship captains didn't need charts, they could just follow the trail of dead bodies in the water.

The guns began it all; European flu and smallpox counted for most of the deaths. Churchmen and missionaries did their best to stamp out what was left of the original culture. Native scribes were singled out for persecution, to the extent that within a century of Cortez the art of writing itself had almost disappeared amongst the Mayan people, though they had previously equaled the Europeans in literacy and epic works. Their libraries were destroyed, to the extent that we're still trying to figure out their writing system. Their civilization along with that of the Incas and dozens of other nations was obliterated. Indeed, South and Central America have never fully recovered from the exploitative power structures that the conquistadores established there. In some countries like Guatemala the same small group of a few hundred elite families are still in charge.

It was the sixteenth century when Christianity really started to motor. The Atlantic trade winds carried Cortez's successors from Spain and other European nations around the world like a new Black Death (a fourteenth-century plague that wiped out one-third to a half of the population of Europe), reshaping most of it as a series of warring Christian empires, plundering and destroying the local economies. Evangelical Christians might say (they do say), "But they were Catholics, not Christians at all." And Catholics did get to South America first, but much the same happened in North America and Australia with the Protestants, though the numbers involved were fewer, those areas being less densely populated. Africa escaped relatively lightly because the Arabs controlled the north and the mosquitoes the middle. Even so, around 24 million were carried off by Europeans (mostly in English ships) to work as slaves in the newly-emptied lands of the Americas, with another 12 million dying en-route. And we're talking here about a period when the population of England itself was around 5 million. Over 70% of the migrants who were shipped into North America between 1580 and 1820 were black. The reason it remained predominantly white is because their treatment was so inhumane. They died young. It was cheaper to replace slaves than feed them. Especially when they got too old to work.

Historical population figures involve a lot of guesswork. But best estimates suggest that the worldwide population in the sixteenth century was around 500 million. Christians amounted to about 10%, or 50 million. Over the next century or two, by means of conquest and colonization, Christians killed off another 10%. By the twentieth century Christianity had increased its "market share" to around 30% of the world's population, where it remains today, with most, 60% or so, living in the Americas and Africa, compared with around 1% of them in the sixteenth century. It's now the number one religion, with the largest following in the world, though on last-century trends Islam is going to overtake it in this new century.

Of the other six religions mentioned at the beginning of this chapter, the sun religions have been wiped out by Christian conquest. Communism, an offspring of Christian Europe, has made large inroads on Buddhism, Confucianism, and Taoism.

So how did Christianity increase its "market share" of the global population from 10% to 30% over the last half millennium? Quite simply, through the greatest episodes of inhumanity and genocide that the earth has ever seen. Genuine Christian missionary effort, motivated by concern for souls rather than conquest, has had little appreciable effect on the other six religions. Today, after extraordinary efforts by tens, hundreds of thousands of dedicated missionaries, over centuries, there are proportionately fewer Christians in the vast stretch of the globe from Morocco to Indonesia, including all the most populous countries and most of the ancient civilizations, than there were 500 years ago. The areas where Christianity has taken over are those where the local populations were largely eliminated, and replaced, or they were tribal and fragmented, and not strong enough to resist.

So holocaust is not too strong a word to describe aspects of the Christian impact on the world. A comparable genocide today to the sixteenth-century one in Central and South America would involve hundreds of millions, even billions – nuclear war proportions.

Christians see their God as a good God of light and love. But taking a global historical perspective, many more have seen Him as a God of death and destruction, the most monstrous and malign of the many demons that have stalked the earth. Satan's wiliest trick of all was to walk the earth disguised as God the Good. Most Christians have danced to his tune rather than that of Jesus, with his priests pulling the strings. The Gnostics weren't so easily fooled. Humankind has paid the price. The Aztecs thought of hell as a period of time rather than a place, a belief they adopted from the Mayans. Their survivors dated it from 1519 when the Christians arrived.

Every time in history that man has tried to turn crucified truth into coercive truth he has betrayed the fundamental principle of Christianity.

Dostoevsky (nineteenth century AD)

40. Why Aren't Christians Better People?

I want you to just let a wave of intolerance wash over you. I want you to let a wave of hatred wash over you. Yes, hate is good... Our goal is a Christian nation. We have a biblical duty; we are called by God, to conquer this country.
Randall Terry, USA evangelist (twentieth century AD)

Christians prefer to see it differently. But to look at the broader picture, by the beginning of the twentieth century the Western Christian nations, Catholic, Protestant, and Greek Orthodox, controlled up to 90% of the world's surface and its manufacturing output. With the exception of Japan (still a relatively small and mostly agrarian economy) the industrialized nations were all Christian. Here was an opportunity for the Church to help create a new order for the world, to bring peace and justice and prosperity. It was the first and hopefully the last time that any one religion has had so much power.

The moment was ripe for a new Augustine to articulate a vision for a new *City of God*, one that would embrace the whole planet, including the knowledge of the new sciences, to see us through the next millennium. But few in the Church could see beyond the self-interest of national power-politics. Power attracts conflict, the two are inseparable. The most established Christian nations on earth combusted in the first two World Wars. The largest Christian nation in Europe, the home of Martin Luther and Protestantism, Beethoven and Bach, Holbein and Goethe, gave the world the Holocaust itself, humankind's worst crime.

So has Christianity been a "good thing"? Does it make a difference for the better?

The most Christian nations on earth today, those with the highest proportion of churchgoers, have had some of the worst records, being amongst the most racist (South Africa and apartheid), the most genocidal (Rwanda – the home of the great East African Revival in the early decades of the twentieth century), the most tribal (Northern Ireland), the most nationalistic (Serbia), etc. And the evildoers are often part of their communities, sincere Christians, certain of their salvation.

Alternatively you can argue that these are tribal aberrations, nothing to do with the central message; that no sincerely Christian leaders have created suffering and death on the scale of people like Stalin, Hitler and Mao. You can argue that Christians have been at the forefront of abolishing slavery, encouraging human rights, developing one of the most tolerant, life-enhancing, and progressive societies the world has seen. In return you could argue that if the czars and the Church had run Russia more equitably the revolution that devoured itself would never have led to Stalin; that Hitler was voted into power by an overwhelmingly Christian electorate – indeed, as Jung said, he was akin to a mouthpiece for their collective unconscious. Very few ministers and priests spoke out against him; opposition was almost entirely from socialists and communists. You could argue that if the British hadn't effectively brought down the Chinese emperor so they could continue their highly profitable sale of opium to the people there, then the Communist revolution might never have happened; that human rights, etc. are the benefits of a secular society with humanist values that the Church has done more to oppose than encourage. The arguments can run both ways.

But Christianity *should* have made a difference that is *beyond* argument. It makes more explicit claims than any other religion to be both one of love and of equal relevance for everyone. For most of the last 1,000 years Christians have been the overwhelming majority of the indigenous population in the countries where they've lived, with every opportunity to put into practice the teachings of their founder and to be "the light of the world, a city that is set on a hill." Logically history should show a steadily increasing gap between the morality of Christian countries and their pagan neighbors. It hasn't happened.

At the more individual level of course it's different, the record more variable. It's not the point here to sell short the experience of God that Christians have. For hundreds of millions it's the very foundation of their lives. God is as real to them as anything else. Their faith is part of the way they think and act through the day. It's who they are. Many believe life wouldn't be possible without it. Of course, believing in God in the traditional Christian way can work for the individual. Many people have been changed for the better through a commitment to Christ, often dramatically so. As with addiction, if you've hit rock bottom and your life is turned around it's transformational. They're happier, more stable and responsible members of society as a result. There may be few Christians of the stature and worldwide impact of Gandhi or the Dalai Lama in the past century (the exception being Nelson Mandela, who seems to have been a man of deep faith, but kept quiet about it, unlike his more evangelical successors who then unraveled his good work). But there are plenty of outstanding individuals who have worked selflessly and sacrificially for the good of others, as there are in all religions, all societies. The fact that Christian sinners outnumber saints is not necessarily a reason to discredit the ideal. That's just human nature.

But any honest individual who's worked in a Christian organization (or any other religious one) will tell you that strife, abuse, crime are no less rife there than anywhere else. Indeed you can argue that being a Christian can make you worse. It's difficult to believe you are "chosen" by the almighty God of the universe and not feel a little special, that you are right and others wrong. You can see them as "hostile," part of the outside "world." There must be something wrong with them, if they don't accept what you believe as so obviously true. It can be toxic for relationships. Some Christians do not find that their faith makes their lives better. Selfishness can turn to self-righteousness. Problems may be magnified rather than cured. Driven personalities before conversion often remain so afterwards. With membership in overall decline some react by becoming more authoritarian. Many succumb to revivalist or millennial tendencies – they raise the stakes. Double down on the emotion. Revival or the second coming are around the corner. All the little difficulties and messy compromises of life get caught up in a dynamic vision of complete renewal or change, in turn creating a further multitude of little problems when the world disobligingly carries on much as before. Structures like the celibate priestly hierarchy of the Roman Catholic Church (which didn't develop until a millennia after Jesus, and didn't actually become part of canonical law till 1917) actually encourage problems and perversion.

Is there any evidence across the overall numbers that being a Christian makes a scrap of difference? At the personal level it's anecdotal. Some Christians seem very impressive. You can want what they have, and be persuaded into faith. Others are not, they can persuade you out of it. It depends on whom you meet (as Genesis says, we're all made of clay – so be careful who you trust, however persuasive; the snake was the ultimate persuader). Any individual sample is too small to draw conclusions from. But the very few surveys that have attempted to analyze changes in behavior after people have become Christians suggest there's no overall improvement. In a 1991 Roper poll in the USA 4% of born-again Christians said they had driven whilst drunk before conversion and 12% had done so after conversion. Across a range of questions behavior had deteriorated rather than improved. There have been several attempts at analyzing comparable divorce rates in the USA, which all tend to suggest that Christians divorce more frequently than non-Christians – 27% for the born-again, 21% for others, 24% for atheists. You can't put much weight on these figures (maybe, for instance, more Christians get divorced because more of them get married?) but there seems no evidence to point the other way.

In my own very limited experience – I've worked in Christian and non-Christian organizations – the more overtly Christian, the worse the behavior. I no longer have much contact in the flesh with the committed, proselytizing kind of Christians, who believe every word of the Bible is literally true. I don't use social media, but I've looked at and posted on a number of Christian forums – at least those I'm allowed on, as most Christians don't think I qualify as a Christian – and come across them every day. It's depressing. Mentally, I classify them into three groups. There's one dumb and sad group of aggressive shouters where you wonder how they ever got through school. They're often "Bible students" who can debate, for instance, whether the Nephilim (Genesis 6:4) should be classed as sons of God, or fallen angels or giants. Their comments to my posts are generally along the lines of, "You obviously haven't read the Bible." There's another group of decent people for whom loving others and following the teaching of Jesus is more important than thinking through the implications of where the Bible seems to say the contrary. There's another of otherwise sane, intelligent, good people who can say things that make your jaw drop. A recent one for instance was the case of a retired director of a missionary organization who replied to me along the lines of, "people who don't know Jesus as their personal savior and have the fullness of life that he offers don't really 'live,' they only 'exist.'" Which implies that their lives don't really "count." Well, in a sense they do, because through their failure to accept Jesus they're going to spend all eternity burning in hell. The vast majority of the 100 billion or so people who have lived on earth written off with a stroke of the pen. Does it matter that people believe this kind of thing? I used to just ignore it, but I'm afraid it does matter, because, as we've seen throughout this book, delusional beliefs lead to dangerous policies.

The thing is, people aren't stupid where their self-interest is concerned. If there were any clear evidence that being a Christian really made people noticeably better, happier, healthier, or more fulfilled, or that God answered the prayers of Christians rather than those of other faiths or of no faith at all, the churches would be full to the rafters. After 2,000 years everyone in the world would by now be a Christian.

So why aren't Christians better than other people? Partly because the effects of good religion on practice are also true for Buddhists and Muslims, for all believers in all religions. It's the kind of God you believe in that matters rather than the doctrines that churches shape around Him. Sadly, simply believing in God doesn't make you a better or happier person than your neighbor. At most it can make you a better or happier person than you would otherwise have been. Or it can make you a worse person – if you believe that the death of Jesus has washed away your sins it can take away the responsibility for acting virtuously in everyday life.

The blunt truth is that no religion or experience of faith, in itself, necessarily makes you a better person. Individuals can better themselves, develop maturity, improve relationships, come close to God through becoming Christian, or Muslim, or Buddhist, or by leaving formal belief behind. It's down to you. The "God-spot" in your brain is like a spot for music, or sport, or logic. It doesn't improve your character any more than being a concert pianist or a scientific genius does. If you imagine there's a more perfect religious experience, a better group of people, waiting for you around the corner, forget it. Stay where you are. Those who expect much from anything can deliver the least, and the most seemingly unpromising can be the greatest pleasure to deal with.

So how does religion help? Knowledge doesn't bring happiness. Science can't produce it, nor measure it. Nor can wealth. Experience over thousands of generations says that religion can, though which one is immaterial. It adds an extra dimension to the equation, harder to analyze, that happiness is goodness. In transcending the self we can live in unity with the larger world defined by God, live in its goodness. Religion can sort out your life, bring new friendships, self-worth, and give hope – humor less certain. It can give you strength and courage to spread happiness around. Or it can turn you into an intolerable bigot.

People make different choices as to who they want to be, and what kind of religion they want to follow. But there's no necessary connection between the "Church" and "God." Nor is there any necessary connection between Christians and God. If heaven exists, Christians are in a minority there. Judging them by their lives rather than their beliefs, and as a percentage of the population through history, maybe they number one in a hundred.

Religion is as effectively destroyed by bigotry as by indifference.
Ralph Waldo Emerson (nineteenth century AD)

41. The Confusion We're In

The Ninth way is this – to wander from religion to religion seeking enlightenment, but ending up in confusion.
The Sutra of Returning to Your Original Nature, 4.26
(Chinese Christian, eighth century AD)

Religion never stops reinventing itself. The story of the Virgin Birth, for instance, didn't finish with the first two gospel writers, it turned into Christmas. Christmas hasn't always been important to the Church, perhaps because until the advent of hospitals and medicine, the idea of birth was associated as much with death as with life. In the Middle Ages the story developed in art, adding elements we now tend to take as part of the original scene. On the principle that every passage of the Bible illuminates every other, new elements were taken from other verses. So the ox and the ass were added on the basis of Isaiah 1:3. The wise men of Matthew become kings because of Isaiah 60:1-6. The story continued to grow to the modern period, with imported pagan trees, decorations, Christmas cards and presents added in Victorian England.

There are no firm, incontrovertible "truths" in religion. So everything, always, is up for grabs. If Jesus came back today he'd see that the Church is like the Judaism of his own day; nothing much has changed, except that Christian tribes/nations, rather than being oppressed, now dominate the world, economically and militarily. The Church created a new religion of blood sacrifice out of the ashes of his efforts to say that no sacrifice is needed; a religion of fear and obedience out of his attempts to say that fear and laws are what we need to put away. He was turned into what he rejected.

We've covered why we believe, whether it's credible, the differences between good and bad religion, the good teaching of

Jesus, the way that got turned into bad religion by the politicians and bureaucrats. It's easy enough to say that Christianity and religion in general have caused as much harm as good, that Jesus wasn't really God. But what next? What are the good things we can learn and keep from our story, and how can we create a new, better one?

In some ways we're back to the first century AD. There's one superpower, or at least just one global military power, occasionally directing overwhelming technological muscle against unruly tribesmen in far-off regions (bizarrely, even seen recently as self-defense, the "war on terror" – who's been invading who over the last few centuries? When did you last see Muslim troops in New York or London, arresting people?), with many of its citizens believing they have some kind of divinely-ordained right, a manifest destiny, to throw their weight around (like all the European empires before them, and all empires since recorded history began). We spend over a trillion dollars (over 700 billion of those by the USA, more than the next ten countries combined, around five times more than on health, housing and education) around the world every year, fighting or preparing to fight. There's a massive underclass hidden away in the developing world, equivalent to the slave labor of the Empire. The ratio of the net wealth of the few, the less than 1%, to the average is about the same, at 1.5 million times greater. With around half of all income in the US coming from capital income (the real point of "capitalism") – i.e. dividends, interest, rents, etc. – the "labor share" is no better as a percent than it was in the European Middle Ages. Religion and irreligion can be equally toxic. Capitalism reverses the gains of modernity and reinstates the economic inequality of the ancient divinely-ordained monarchies. And capitalism, a corrupted trivialization of Christianity, has effectively become the predominant religion of the USA.

But the "American Century" is unravelling. The push to

establish a more equitable society after the shock of the Second World War has been lost. Since the 1980s, a revolution has taken place – not from the left, but the right. Influenced by media and think tanks owned by the wealthy, a more brutalist social compact has emerged, encouraged by a trend of thought that goes back through Ayn Rand to Nietzsche, who in his later years wrote about subjugation to the "master race." On an accelerating scale, Americans have tended to vote against the idea that people should take care of each other; that they should invest in education, healthcare, care for children and the elderly, for retirement, for "the public good." Maximizing profit for shareholder value is the legal obligation. Milton Friedman's doctrine has triumphed in the US, and to a lesser degree in the UK: "There is only one social responsibility of business… to increase profits." Greed is good. Trying to regulate it, to moderate it, is unnatural, unprincipled, unchristian, communist. Egotism rules. "Not satisfied with a hundred million dollar boat, or house? Get a two hundred million dollar one. Or several."

Modern capitalism encourages people to be their worst selves – if we're each as selfish as possible in business and as consumers everything will work out magically for everyone. It wasn't necessarily meant to be this way – according to the eighteenth-century philosopher of capitalism, Adam Smith, businesses should exist to serve the common good. Profit is the means rather than the end. Today, it's colonialism by other means. It's at odds with our social evolution, our biology, our neurobiology, and all good religious teaching. And as with the Roman Empire, the reasons for its coming decline are already apparent – over-exploitation of resources and labor, increasing inequality, a hollowing out of the middle. American incomes have been static for five decades, with 80% living and dying in debt, whilst millionaires have become billionaires and mega-billionaires, with trillionaires on the horizon. Over the decades since the 1970s the imbalance of wealth between the top 1% in the

USA and the bottom 90% has grown by 50 trillion dollars. If that had trickled down rather than up, half of all Americans would have seen their net worth rise by a factor of eight. Which would have transformed lives, and the overall economy for the better. It could have gone into better education, health care, infrastructure, rather than more possessions than anyone could enjoy, or sitting in tax havens growing more bloated every day, but useless. 15% of the USA economy is spent on public investment, compared to 50% in Canada and Europe. Politics is being poisoned by money and self-interest. Over a trillion dollars every year of revenues stolen from poor countries through tax evasion and the transfer of money within corporations are laundered through tax havens (mostly British dependencies – which is why the UK has been called the most corrupt nation on earth). As with the later Roman Empire, social capital and civic virtue are in decline. Currencies are being debased – in the past governments used to clip coins, or add zeroes to the banknotes, nowadays they just create more out of thin air, called "quantitative easing." It reduces the value of what savings people have, and borrows from the future.

Maybe the capitalist model is the best we have, if you follow a more democratic-socialist kind of version that leads to the generally high standards of living found in the Nordic countries, and maybe it's "moral," but it's not "Christian." Maybe it's going to turn out that following the bizarre financial principles of the Old Testament and the Kingdom of God that Jesus described, and which we've followed for 95% of our history, working together for the common good, might not have been such a crazy idea after all.

As far as public morality goes, truth is as rare a commodity as it was two thousand years ago. A major backwards step was when the Reagan administration ended the fairness doctrine of the US Federal Communications Commission, which required the holders of broadcast licenses to present controversial issues of public importance and do so in a fair, honest and balanced way. It opened the door for more partisan, aggressive politics, and the spiral down to political polarization. The craziest conspiracy theories are now mainstream. Attempts to approach the truth are attacked as "fake news." At the time of writing this, both the USA and the UK are led by the most blatant liars ever to hold the office. Many don't even bother with print any more, they get their prejudices from social media bubbles, where they can be sure they'll only be told want they want to hear, in more extreme form, from sites like Fox News, because that generates the advertising revenue. Most make do with bread and circuses, pop stars and celebrities. Religion is once again more of a supermarket than a corner shop, with a mass of competing beliefs pressing their wares in the marketplace. The mysteries of the East are coming back into the frame, gurus gaining their followers in the Western Empire. Maybe we still believe in the Son of God, but perform our sacrificial rituals without much conviction, salve our consciences with the bread and wine, with the occasional nod of a prayer.

When faced with the big questions, like "What happens when we die?", we're no better off. Worse, really. The traditional Christian picture of heaven and hell doesn't work any longer, and we haven't found anything else to replace it. We don't even ask the question anymore. We're afraid to ask it; we'll hopefully be remembered, sure, by family and friends, but we know there is not going to be a shrine, or a tomb, where we're spoken to, prayed for, as still happens in many parts of the world. The dead, for us, are in the past, not the present. Our roots are shallow. And it's tough to find a meaning and purpose in life, to deepen your roots, if you see death as the end of everything. We've lost our connection with the natural world, with our ancestors, with the sense of life as a rolling stream which continues to include us all, past, present and future. Ironically, as science starts to suggest that reality is there in so far as it's observed, we've lost the sense that life is there in so far as it's witnessed; that our life is real in so far as it's real to others, in the relationships we had and can continue to experience.

As for Christianity – it's unravelling. We can see how it was stitched together. The intentions were often good, inspired. The Book of Job and the searching of the Greek philosophers for instance came from the same kind of enquiring minds that around that time began to rethink our relationship with the world. The one explored suffering and purpose, the other matter and physics. But our idea of God today is an uneasy mix of the two – the metaphysical almighty God of "thought" or "being," beyond space and time, and the friendly wonder-working local tribal God who intervenes on earth and will help us with our exams tomorrow. He is also the Persian God of Zoroaster who is coming again in judgment and will send the wicked to hell. His image has been formed over three millennia, with each generation adding something and interpreting Him in their own way.

So what kind of future does Christianity have? At times in the Dark Ages it threatened to disappear. Then just a century ago it promised to dominate. Now it's going backwards. Today it's hard to imagine it having the same legs as say Hinduism, which has been around nearly three times as long. It's too closely tied to a world-view that's disappeared, a particular version of the God-man/man-God hypothesis, of which there are thousands to choose from. It lacks the inclusive pluralism that characterizes Hinduism on the one hand or the focus and clarity of Islam on the other. Perhaps most of all, in its theology and structures it lacks an intelligent and respectful relationship with the natural world, which, along with cooperation, is one of our most basic human instincts, and one which we've largely lost, other than in the love of many for gardens, flowers and the outdoors. Paganism will still be around in a thousand years' time, assuming there are still humans on the planet; Christianity – less certain.

It's still growing in parts of the world, particularly the

less developed and the rapidly developing, and will carry on doing so. They're taking on board Western technology, and sometimes its political and economic systems, like parliaments and shopping malls. A culture of individual salvation follows a culture of individual success. They may be throwing out cultural traditions that would suit them better. But in any case, as the influence of the West diminishes in relation to that of Islam and China, in the century or two to come these gains are likely to be reversed.

In Western Europe at least Christianity is in dire straits, and on current trends will virtually disappear in the next couple of generations. Of course religion never "disappears" as such. Some followers always remain. The Zoroastrian religion, which predates it by several millennia, still has a few million followers (now called Parsees) in India, having fled there from Persia after the Muslim conquest. Even ancient Egyptian religion is followed by hundreds of thousands. Shamans still summon spirits and foretell the future in Siberia, like they've been doing for tens of thousands of years.

But the problem is that the vision of individual salvation, mediated through the Church, achieved through reconciliation with a probably-historical figure who lived 2,000 years ago but of whom we know little, doesn't persuade many today, if they want to think about it rationally. Of course certainties are attractive. The offer of salvation, a place near God's throne, the warmth of a group bound by strong belief, friendship, hardened even more by small numbers, holds out huge appeal. As cults prove time and time again. Those with the shortest and clearest soundbites, appealing most directly to self-interest, get the most votes, as politicians increasingly prove. Liberals will continue to be edged out of the Church by increasingly conservative and small congregations because they aren't radical enough to attract new ones.

But, short of a catastrophic decline in educational standards, the number of people, in Western Europe at least, who can accept that the Bible is the unique revelation of God to humankind will continue to diminish. And the papacy, particularly the Roman one (there are still others, the Coptic Christian Church for instance, the largest denomination in North Africa and the Middle East, and one of the oldest and most influential Churches, has its own pope), looks increasingly like the ancient Egyptian priesthood, stuck on a riverbank while the world around it moves on and eventually overwhelms it.

To put it another way, it's not so much that the Church's vision doesn't persuade, as that it's hard today to tell the difference between this vision and a thousand others. Substituting literalism in scripture or tradition for moral vision, caught between the rock of age-old creeds and the hard places of modern knowledge, its certainties are crumbling back into the spiritual soup from which they emerged. Many of God's followers, particularly in the growing charismatic and Pentecostal movements, have turned back to the shamanistic practices that have served us well for hundreds of millennia – speaking in tongues, making animal noises, ecstatic dancing, healing, exorcism, and words of knowledge. Here God takes back the characteristics of the ancient weather gods, bringing rain or stopping it, writing the Book of Life for the personal benefit of His followers.

Many more still have turned to New Age practices. When I started in religious publishing over forty years ago traditional Christian books outsold New Age, or mind/body/spirit, in the UK by about four or five to one. Now it's the other way around. It's no longer a passing fashion. Practitioners of alternative medicine, who make a living out of it, outnumber general doctors. More people regularly use them than go to church. The percentage of people who answer "yes" in the UK to the question "Have you ever been aware of or influenced by a power, whether you call it God or not, which is different from your everyday self?" actually seems as if it might have been edging up each decade for the last 70 years. So perhaps people leave the Church to find better ways of believing, not because they can't believe anything any longer. If you think of the Church as the elitist theater, New Age is increasingly the popular religious culture.

It's hard today to see the difference between the Christian obsession with the end times, and the New Age with Aquarius; between angels in the Bible Belt, and Beings of Light in Arizona; the routes to easy money and salvation offered by Western evangelists, or by Eastern gurus. Risen Christ, or core crystals; prayer warriors, or light-workers – there's no difference. Eat this wafer, say these words, and you'll touch God. Follow these paths, or rituals, or horoscopes, tap into this force or that, find your inner self, your previous self, or other self, and you'll realize your true potential. Change your way of thinking, your partner, your company, your colors, the position of your furniture, what you eat, how you eat, when you eat, when you pray, who to, and you'll be happier, wealthier, more fulfilled. It can work. Any of it can work. Of course it can. We can believe anything. As with any religion it's a question of distinguishing the worthwhile from the trivial.

Mainstream Christians dismiss New Age teaching as fantasy, where anything is believed. New Age followers might say with some justification that it's Christianity that's the new upstart, a mere two millennia old, a priestly empire whose time has come and gone. They could argue that Jesus and his disciples would have felt more at home in a New Age community than in today's Church. Their lifestyle had more in common with that of travelers today than with Christians in suburban churches. They could justifiably argue that they're closer to the bedrock of Christianity than the Church is. The New Testament is chockablock with practices many would now think of as New Age if they were given the names used today: clairvoyance, etheric projection, channeling, dream visions, numerous forms of healing (by touch, by saliva, and at a distance), summoning spirits, astrological-type signs in the heavens, apparitions, astral planes. The first disciples practiced divination in recruiting to their number. What are the ascension of Jesus and his walking on water other than masterful examples of levitation, high-ranking miracles in the Buddhist grades of achievement and, so it's claimed, still practiced today?

The Old Testament is richer still, full of practices that are now called shamanistic, astrological, etc. on every other page. Sometimes these practices are condemned, at others not, they're always taken for granted as "real." Communicating through dreams, talking with animals – 2 Kings 2:23-25 for instance describes how Elisha, a relatively peaceful character compared to Elijah, orders two bears to tear up 42 boys because they teased him about his baldness – a level of gratuitous violence which should shock us today. Reading Christian commentators on these kind of episodes, who try to reconcile them with a modern understanding of the world, even with a loving God, is an interesting way of killing some time, if you need some light relief.

But how could it be otherwise? The Hebrews and Jews believed in a world shot through with magic and miracle, in spiritual forces and cosmic struggles, in planetary levels of ascending importance (2 Corinthians 12:2-4), in much the same way as many New Agers do today. The practices and beliefs found in the Bible, also developed before the age of science, are common to societies everywhere. It's the Christians who restrict the spectacular workings of God to the pages of the Bible who are out of step with its spirit. The "rationalists" are in the wrong religion. It might be those who think that Jesus thought about God like they do who understand the least about him.

"New Age" is a misnomer. It's a portmanteau term for pre-scientific beliefs from cultures around the world (often the more exotic and ancient or mythical the better). "Old Age" would be more accurate. Much of its teaching draws on traditions that have been known to work for millennia, probably for millions of years, like the healing powers of particular plants, or the therapeutic benefits of grooming and massaging (you can still see that with the chimps). It's recovering the wisdom of older societies, wisdom that we have lost, insulating ourselves as we do from the world around us with concrete, metal and plastic.

In this sense the Bible is the most significant "New Age" document we have. Christianity the most significant New Age religion. In trying to hang on to its particular version of Hebrew religion and Greek philosophy the Church has simply pushed its congregations out of its doors. With more imagination it could have held on to them. New Age teaching and practice, having had to make its way in the commercial marketplace, without centuries of legacies to support it, is more prepared to meet people where they are. It focuses on the perennials of "well-being" – health and healing, food and diet, sex and love, respect and concern for the planet and other life. It's closer to the Jewish shalom of holistic health in mind, body, and spirit than Christianity is.

Some believers go a long way down this line. They travel beyond any particular idea of God to a mystical blend of different strands of Buddhism, Christianity, Hinduism, speculative science, much as many of the first Christians did. We get into the area of egoic time, species mind, transpersonal experience, and the new humankind. For those living in England rather than California it's harder to take these ideas on board. Maybe we're uniquely disadvantaged, living at the tail end of one major religion and before a new one has taken credible shape (and maybe the new one should be led entirely by women to redress the current patriarchal imbalance).

Intellectually, religious emotions are not creative but conservative. They attach themselves readily to the current view of the world and consecrate it.
John Dewey (twentieth century AD)

42. Moving On

I like your Christ. I do not like your Christians. They are so unlike your Christ.
Mahatma Gandhi (twentieth century AD)

Here's a little example of the growth of New Age belief and decline in Christian support. Around 15 million adults in the UK read their horoscopes regularly. The number roughly matches the number of adults who have stopped going to church in the last century. I'm not suggesting that everyone who stops going to church starts believing in astrology. Many only read their horoscopes out of mild interest in the same way that many go to church for reasons more social than spiritual. But a significant number live by them. Yet there is not a shred of evidence that the movements of the planets have any relation to events on earth – any astronomer would say it's laughable – and Chinese, Indian and Western astrologers use contradictory systems. It's what we've been doing forever – seeing patterns that aren't there, overthinking.

The idea of producing a horoscope was an invention of a journalist on the *Daily Express* newspaper in the 1930s. It struck a chord, and within a couple of years most newspapers around the world had one. Today it's been estimated that professional astrologers outnumber professional astronomers by around 50 to 1. This is despite the fact that if you offer a free horoscope, and the same horoscope is sent to everyone who asks for it, over 90% will say on being questioned that it was relevant to them. So why have people dropped one belief that they feel lacks credibility and personal relevance for one that has no credibility at all?

Reading your horoscope connects you with a feeling that there is a larger plan to life, that it's not just down to you. It advises you; it warns you. It speaks to you on your own level, when you want it. The Church used to provide this kind of assurance in the days when you could believe in the helping hands of innumerable saints, or that any Bible verse could be relevant to your concerns of the moment.

In fact, if you take the Bible literally, shouldn't you embrace astrology? It's riddled with it. Even in the New Testament – the Magi (no number given, Western churches tend to say three, because of the number of gifts, Eastern churches more usually twelve) who visited the baby Jesus in Bethlehem were astrologers, following their star. It worked for them. No messengers had been sent out to call them in.

But today, very few people, maybe one out of a hundred, really believe in the active power of the saints or read the Bible daily. Priests are few (the ratio of clergy to people in the UK is around one to 5,000) and so inevitably remote, often preoccupied with repairing old buildings, church politics and ritual. Not many people, relatively, speak to them honestly and directly, or feel they could ask them for guidance. Authority in the Church is from the top down, and irrelevant to pretty well everyone as the base of the pyramid disappears. Even if we could recover a more meaningful Christian language, there is not the right medium to express it in. You would need to turn the structure upside down.

People don't want to be "saved" today. They don't understand what it means. Saved from what? They want to be happy and healthy. And they'll pay for it, like Christians used to. If the Church doesn't change, the wheel will carry on turning, as it always does, and the New Age teachers will eventually take over and build their new structures over the churches, like the Christians built their churches over the pagan temples. If Christians want to turn this around they need to bring our threads of science and religion, experience and tradition, history and conscience into a better kind of balance. This is what different theologians have always tried to do, but as knowledge has expanded, they've largely lost the plot, continuing to work away in the little diminishing bubbles of their own frame of reference. But then as the great Sufi Ghazali taught, theology is ultimately useless anyway. Just think of it as 200,000 lawyers given 2,000 years to describe love and making a mountainous hash of it. What matters is expressing the awareness of God in the simplicity of a loving life. The more we do this, the more we might understand. The more we understand, the more we realize love is all there is.

Picture religious belief in the shape of a bell, filling the page. You have the few serious, intelligent, committed believers on the left rim, atheists on the right, the bulk of the uncertain in the central body. Those are split between nominal Christians and seekers. The bell's center of gravity is moving across the page, left to right, at a rate of about 1% a year. But it doesn't seem set to carry to the far end. Atheists and humanists, just as much as Christians, struggle with declining memberships in their organizations. When people drop out of believing in Christianity they don't, as a general rule, drop out of belief.

We're looking for answers. New Age ideas seem to run seamlessly from the possible, through the improbable, to the impossible. Maybe our consciousness adds up to more than chimps with extra brain cells, but it's hard to believe that it was passed down to us from higher evolved beings from Atlantis, or space, or angels, or whatever. That's like believing in the Garden of Eden or Noah's Ark. You have to stop somewhere. Christianity has at least spent much of two millennia wrestling with science and philosophy, attempting to reconcile Greek and Hebrew traditions, knowledge and belief. Up till the last few centuries, anyway. New Age ignores them. You can believe anything you want. But astroshamanic space maps are no more credible than God as a King in the sky sending messengers to earth. We need to do better than this, develop some kind of sensible framework of belief, or there's not enough reason for the lazier of us to get out of bed in the morning. So where do you draw the line?

In today's democratic society we start with the principle that everyone has a right to be heard. This after all was true of the first Christians. You couldn't remotely call the early Church a democracy, but every century or so, once they were in power, the bishops voted in councils on what they should believe. Bishops don't do this anymore, the "point" of truth was fixed over a thousand years ago. Perhaps they should start doing it again. Because in the last generation or two we've drifted so far away from this point on the line that most don't even know it's there.

It's not as if the point hasn't moved before. After all, our own Christian tradition tells us that God is not static, but developing. In the second millennium BC, Abraham's God was one for the family. Over the next few centuries the Hebrews enlarged Him to become their tribal God, then the God of the new nation. Over the following few centuries He became the only God. The Christians enlarged Him further. He became not only the God of the Jews, but of all people. In about one and a half millennia God "grew" from a shepherd's tent, through an Ark, then a single temple in Jerusalem to cover the earth. Then nothing changed much for another two millennia. In the face of new knowledge about the earth and the universe our image of God has shrunk and withered. Perhaps it's time for a fresh look.

We need a larger vision, a bigger God. As huge, as extraordinary, as challenging to common practice, as the one Jesus brought to the Jews, or the one expressed in Mahayana Buddhism. One that tells us why we're here and how we should live. Something that lifts us out of who and where we are to where we might get to, what we might become, that ties everything together. That gives enough definition to the uncertainties of life to enable us at least to share the asking of the questions about the journey we're on, even if we can't agree on the answer. We need a vision for that, for what should be at the center of life, for what goodness is and how to be happy. Jesus gave us as good a one as we've got.

The first step is to see where we've gone wrong. For 95% of our history religion has been a collective, tribal matter, a matter of belonging and sharing, of treading lightly on the earth and treating all living things with reverence. With the growth of cities, states, and nations came power, class, and wealth. Within the new religions that grew to accommodate these new structures some continued to find God in solitude, in mysticism, in service, but more used Him as a means of aggrandizement. They defined others as inferior or wrong or even evil rather than just different. The Church, in many aspects, came to represent power, class and wealth. This became embodied in everything from its buildings to its theology.

In the case of Christianity we've developed a religion that gives its opponents reason to describe it, especially in its Western capitalist form, as among the worst of religions, the ultimate expression to date of the sanctification of greed rather than giving; growth and profit rather than holiness and happiness. Maybe the existing Church is past reviving. It's part of the problem rather than the solution. Perhaps the last opportunity to change was earlier in the twentieth century, after the shock of the World Wars and the Holocaust. Most of those prepared to change, to work for a better world, are now outside the Church. The "kingdom shoots" are found more in secular and humanist organizations than Christian ones. Conservatives have been left in charge, and won't let go. And conservatism must be a dead end in the long run. The most secular places in North America and Europe today are those where extremist forms of Christianity had the strongest hold.

The Church today is stuck with the trivia of what used to be a powerful drive to transcendence – with its color and trimmings. Trivial gods concern themselves with what are now trivial issues. They focus on the individual and his/her salvation. They discriminate against those who are different from us, focusing on questions of gender, sexuality, and race, taking primitive tribal laws as universal truth. Serious gods engage with serious issues, and they embrace everyone. Belief today features DNA rather than the Devil, looks for inspiration to the stars rather than saints. It returns to the more immediate problem of how we conduct ourselves to enable survival as a species in this world rather than working for salvation in the next. After all, if we screw this world up why should we be trusted with another one?

Imagine if in the next century aliens make contact with us. They are intrigued by this idea of God, seemingly unique to humankind, an omniscient Being who even sounds superior to them, who they haven't come across before. For them, actually, it's the only interesting idea on the planet (they're not interested in our primitive technology). They want a few-sentences definition – who He/She is, how to approach Him, what the correct procedures are. But there's a proviso, that they'll only take it seriously if representatives of all the peoples in the world who believe in God agree to the wording – they don't want to get bogged down in internal "god politics." If they don't get a coherent answer, they're exploding the planet to re-terraform it into a new galactic space station. Could we e-mail?

I remember a children's Bible I treasured back in the 1950s, which had color plates. One illustration was of the disciples looking up at Jesus rising into the sky: a white, androgynous figure, blue-eyed, about as close to a real historical figure as Captain America. Google images of Jesus today, or sermons, and you can find any amount of the same kind of schmaltz. There are so many ways of picturing God, good and bad. We progress as individuals and as communities, even as a species, by following the good, refusing to make Him just in our image, turning away from the exercise of power, the accumulation of wealth, and seeing others as different. For those who call themselves Christians the way forward is to return to what we can recover of the teaching of the founder, in so far as we can. In his vision of the kingdom Jesus challenged his contemporaries to a new understanding of what it meant to be human. It includes everyone. He said we could give, love, and receive without limit. We just had to "go further." But Christians today are indistinguishable from everyone else. They have the most, give the least. The historical record is probably the bloodiest of any religion. What would Jesus say to us today?

He was born into a people whose self-worth was bound up with their idea of God. The story of how He had succored them as a nation, taken them out of Egypt in the Exodus, out of the Exile in Babylon, enabled them to survive despite the Egyptians, Phoenicians, Assyrians, Babylonians, Persians, Greeks, Romans – this story, whether historical or not, had become the core of their identity. Some of the Jews had backslidden, some had compromised with the oppressors, but some had kept the flame of faith alive. And the most dedicated believers of all were the Pharisees. In the pluralist world of the massive and seemingly impregnable Roman Empire, which had been around for more generations than anyone could remember, they kept the people to the straight and narrow, honoring the commands of God in the Jewish scriptures, refusing to worship the emperor, making Palestine one of the most troublesome provinces for any governor to handle.

And then here's perhaps the most surprising thing in the New Testament. Not the Virgin Birth, or the Resurrection, which was expected of any self-respecting god, but the attitude of Jesus to the Pharisees, the religious lawyers and jurists of their day. Despite the support he got from some of them, and the similarity in some respects of their teaching (for instance Jesus, like them, believed in the afterlife, the Sadducees – the temple priests – did not), the people who Jesus consistently cursed were not the pagans or the backsliders, the Roman oppressors or the cheating Temple priests who cooperated with them – the Sadducees – but the committed believers, the Pharisees. Those who had remained steadfast and faithful in the face of great odds, who had devoted every hour of their waking days to serving God. He cursed them (the "eight woes" in Matthew, or the "six woes" in Luke) not because of what they did, but because of what they did not do. They put law above compassion, God above goodness. He cursed them because they believed they were right, that they were saved in God's eyes. They were proud of what they were doing for God, of the lives they led. They valued the *letter* of their religion, their truth, God's truth, above people, above the *spirit* of unconditional love.

Is the Church much different today? If Jesus really did come back today those he would curse, again, are those most sure of their salvation. The evangelical preachers with their cars and private jets who prate about sin and bless the collection plate when four billion people in the world have no decent sanitation, two billion don't have drinking water, and one billion are hungry; the Catholic bishops who hold up the cross whilst moving pedophile priests from one parish to another; the theologians who surely know that Jesus didn't physically ascend to heaven but teach that if you don't believe he physically rose from the dead then you go to hell. Indeed today we're doubly cursed. We think we're right, and we also have the wealth and power. We're the Pharisees, priests, and Romans together.

Christianity today is as parochial as any of the competing mystery religions of the first century AD. It doesn't preach the kingdom of God. It blesses the status quo rather than challenges it; the few prophets it produces, like Dietrich Bonhoeffer, Martin Luther King and Archbishop Oscar Romero, are murdered – not by fanatics from a different religion, but by people who would call themselves Christian. Christian societies are no more kingdom-like than others, Christians no less selfish or prone to evil than non-Christians. There really is no particular good reason to be a Christian today rather than something else, unless it's the place you're starting from. Given a level playing field and a clear head, who would want to believe in the same kind of God as some supposedly Christian leaders today, any more than that of Muslim terrorists? In any religion where being in the right is more important than admitting your own culpability; spreading your beliefs more urgent than preventing starvation; forbidding condoms more important than the spread of AIDS; demonizing immigrants more significant than protecting the rights of the innocent?

He who steadily observes those moral precepts in which all religions concur, will never be questioned at the gates of Heaven as to the dogmas in which they differ.
Thomas Jefferson (eighteenth century AD)

43. A Glimpse Of The Sacred

Theology is an attempt to explain a subject by men who do not understand it. The intent is not to tell the truth but to satisfy the questioner.
Elbert Hubbard (nineteenth century AD)

Do the big metanarratives of Christianity still make any kind of sense today?

Maybe Christianity simply hasn't yet matured into a good religion. It went off the rails too early. It's still at the cultic stage of making impossible truth claims, venerating the founder as God, commanding blind obedience, creating and worshipping idols rather than loving the life we're part of, following the tortuous logic of "believe in Jesus so that he can save you from what God is going to do to you if you don't believe in him." The orthodox, established Church is a river that meandered into the delta for a couple of millennia, turning back on itself, losing itself in creeds and laws, still searching for the wider sea.

It's missing a huge opportunity. Because contrary to the impression given in the public spheres of life religion today grows rather than diminishes in importance. The more complex the world becomes, and the less self-sufficient we are, and the more we are reliant on others, then the stronger our ideas need to be as the glue that binds us. With better technology, everything from medical to military, we confront increasingly complex problems – anything from what a human being is to where life begins and ends, where the balance lies between freedom and responsibility, force and forgiveness, how we can unite globally to tackle climate change. Defining what our values are and the basis on which we make them have become more important than ever. Bots, data and algorithms cannot replace them.

To shape our questions and answers Christianity needs to

turn itself into something as different from that of today as today's is from the warrior-based, relic-worshipping religion of a thousand years ago. It could happen. Change is as much the lifeblood of religion as of society. Some of the societies in Europe, Christianity's second surviving heartland, have changed in the last couple of generations. They've confronted the demons of racism and nationalism that have been embedded in Christian culture for so long and largely come out the other side. After two catastrophic, self-inflicted wars which went global, they've come to realize that it's not other nations or races who are evil, it's something in all of us. A similar change for the place of Christianity in those societies will mean turning Jesus back from a god into a man, and God back from a personal deity into the Unknown, the ultimate sign of what is beyond our understanding and possession. It will mean taking the kingdom of God seriously on earth, investing our massive economic surplus (relative to the rest of the world) into addressing problems of world poverty rather than fashion and fripperies. Extending rights to all species, respecting the planet as a whole, considering generations down the line rather than the next quarter's profits. Getting involved with politics at every level. Working in local communities to push for fairness. At regional levels creating common infrastructure, meeting the needs for decent housing for everyone, building up jobs. At national levels abandoning the gig economy, giving everyone equal chances in life, taxing wealth and land more than worked-for income. Deepening and widening the safety net. Putting limits on inequality ratios. Yes, even voting for socialist or social democratic parties. At the international level, strengthening the worldwide organizations and agreements rather than playing zero-sum games with other countries. Reducing armament stockpiles, fossil-fuel extraction. Thinking of ourselves as all essentially one people.

It would be hard. Living the kind of life Jesus describes is. He said it would be. The Church should at least try to be there on the line, saying, "This is what it is, what it means. We'll do our best to help you make it." But it's caught up in all this other old stuff. It's turned the teaching of Jesus into another religion of sacrifice. Most religions are based around this idea. God/gods are something "other," fearsome, angry, holy beings who need to be placated. Offerings are made to ensure that the child will be born, our sins forgiven, that the journey will be safe, the crops will grow, the sun will rise again.

Virtually everyone in the Mediterranean area in the first century thought this way. The Greeks, Romans, Jews, all offered sacrifices. Their religions were all temple religions. Sacrifice and law dominated the lives of the Jews. Every hour of the day, in every way, God had to be propitiated. But life itself was still a burden. The Jews were oppressed by the Law, by poverty, by the Romans. They awaited a deliverer, a savior, who would raise their status to what it should be as God's chosen people.

Paul, in a stroke of religious genius, had a new vision of the spiritual world. He turned it upside down. God shows Himself through weakness and shame, not power and strength. He doesn't demand sacrifice, He offers it. In a literal flash of insight Paul saw Jesus as being the sacrifice God Himself had sent as an offering for sin – not just his own, or that of the Jews, but of all humankind. The deliverer had come, and we had crucified him, in line with God's plan. God Himself had freed humankind from the burden of sin and oppression, and all each person had to do in return was realize it.

But Paul was going on hearsay. He was wrong. God is not a remote figure, whether angry or loving, who wants sacrifice, nor does He offer it. His image is in all of us, seen most clearly in those suffering physically and mentally, and children. His love is unconditional, for everyone, not for those who can agree with certain creeds. It's in pouring ourselves out on behalf of others that He is realized. If He exists, it's in so far as we bring Him into being, as Zoroaster first suggested. He is all consciousness, the opposite of building walls of money or power around us.

Today the Trinitarian orthodox God is a glass ceiling on the growth of Christianity, much like the laws of Judaism were for the Nazarenes. True followers of Jesus, as the first of the Early Church Fathers recognized, are those who transcend the self in favor of others, who recognize God everywhere, and are as likely to be found in Kabul as New York. All of life is sacred, it has chosen to be so by coming into being. Smashing this ceiling means being as radical in our approach as Jesus was. And as the previous chapters on the history of belief have suggested the key here is authority, which is the problem in religion much as it is in society, with options ranging from anarchy to tyranny.

Shared systems of belief are helpful in that they encourage individuals to rise above their self-interest. Over the last five millennia we've developed many, much as over the last five centuries we've organized ourselves into many nation states. The trouble is that belief in a system needs commitment. In willingly making the commitment we surrender our power of independent reasoning. Over generations, centuries, a system of collective belief hardens, writes teaching in stone. It even begins to define itself against other systems rather than being open to further sharing. Every now and again it all needs to be pulled down and rebuilt, like Jesus wanted to do with the Temple. Each new religion starts as an act of creative destruction. If Jesus were here today he'd battle with Catholics and Protestants as back then he did with Sadducees and Pharisees.

We can be better Christians with no God at all than with the current Catholic or Protestant God. God is no longer necessary to religion, or to the good life, much as Buddhists have been teaching for longer than Christianity has existed. Perhaps we can just sit lightly to the idea.

This may sound like process theology or Christian atheism of the kind fashionable in the 60s. But perhaps we could think about religion in the same way we think about science. For instance, Newton's law of gravity is of more use to us on a daily basis than Einstein's law of relativity. The first describes the stuff that makes the kettle boil, the tides rise and fall, whereas Einstein's laws operate on a scale beyond our immediate experience, where light bends and time slows. But we can live in the framework of Newton's laws while still accepting those of Einstein as representing a deeper truth. We may know we've moved thousands of miles through space whilst reading this page but it doesn't "matter." We still talk about the sun rising and setting rather than the earth turning even though we know it's not "true."

Similarly Christian atheists are no more "atheistic" than the early Christians, who were themselves called atheists by the Romans. The Romans couldn't understand these people – what were gods if you couldn't represent them in images? Meaningless. How could you worship words?

Churches demonstrate the Roman approach when they insist on Capital Letter Doctrines for truths they've written on paper rather than shaped in marble. The doctrines are no more than the old statues. There comes a point where words are just insufficient, where religious language ceases to matter. Maybe we can still just about talk of God as "He," without assuming He has a penis, or a shape, or any existence we can recognize. But there is in the end no real difference between believing in God and not believing, between Christian and Buddhist. When we transcend the self and escape to distant horizons we might think we see God, but God is infinite and has no handles we can hold on to. He's a dance of possibilities, a void, waiting to be called into being. It's how we respond that determines who God is, and what we in turn are.

It might be difficult to think about Christianity this way. It was shaped by Greek philosophy and Roman paganism, but its driving force was the Hebrew belief that God intervenes. He made the world, made people, changed His mind, chose a particular tribe, and then according to Christian teaching sent a son to earth. We've written this particular story, constructing it around the life of Jesus and overlaying his teaching, and we're good at stories. We've been telling them for hundreds of thousands of years. We shape our response to the real by imagining what our response might be. We turn one into the other. God could be fact or fiction. We change Him at the flick of a switch. And it's not just God. It's ourselves. We can switch ourselves on or off. We can decide to be miserable or happy, to cling to what we have, or let go and travel. You, God, life, it doesn't matter what you call it. One act of friendship to a stranger is worth more than all the God-searching you've done in your life. There's more truth in the patch of grass at your feet than in the theological library.

But if God is not the one the Church describes what is there to hang on to in this religion that it has developed? Maybe it's not so much a question of hanging on as of shedding an old skin when it feels too tight. With the same kind of delight the Romans felt when many of them abandoned their worship of household gods for the invisible, almighty, only God. Think of the new picture of God as a similar step on the journey. As larger than the first-century Christian picture of Him as their picture was larger than the statue of Zeus.

Theology has been moving away from the idea of an objective God for several centuries. Through the major twentieth-century theologians like Rudolph Bultmann, Karl Rahner, and Paul Tillich we move to seeing God as a human projection, with Tillich denying that God exists as other than a symbol. The retreat of theology from the classical idea of God mirrors the decline of orthodox Christian faith. And of course Christians might say it's the fault of the theologians. But it's never wise to shoot the messenger. So why do they still talk about God at all? Because most of us feel there is something ultimately real or worthwhile. And we want to know it's "there." We have language, we need a description, we use our adverbs and adjectives, we seek a noun.

Religions are the different ways in which we emotionally, intellectually, even physically relate to this feeling of reality. They are a kind of language we have spent a million years developing to help us talk in the broadest sense about the important things in life, the ones we can't explain or measure, the ones that aren't rational, but are still "true" – beauty, happiness, wrong, evil, love, transcendence. These are steps on the ladder of self-awareness, ascending from reptiles, through mammals, through human beings, and maybe to God. No one lives as if these intangible qualities don't exist. Our understanding of them is imperfect, our attempts to describe them and pass them on (we call it "religion") worse. But without them we can't love, we can't even think. Each attempt at understanding is worth something, and better than not trying at all. The attempts make a road map of the different journeys we're on. The whole is more than the sum of its parts. It provides a quest to keep us stepping forward. Religion turns this quest into a story, called a myth.

A myth, like the Christian story of God, is our best guess. It condenses truth down to poetic essentials, to appealing metaphors, upon which legends then elaborate. Though it might refer to history it's really outside it, in an eternal "now," using symbols and characters to describe what drives us, which is why it's always relevant. And no religion survives for 2,000 years if it hasn't got a story that helps us along the way. But to say that one story alone is true makes a nonsense of religion, turning it into a lottery. And over time the metaphors are overused, they lose their freshness and value; and when, over successive generations, followers start taking them literally, only the husk is left.

We underestimate the power of religion to do both good and harm. When we lose sight of the best we let the worst run riot. Popes (with the current one being a rare exception), evangelists, and ayatollahs turn the world into a battleground of cosmic forces, the demons of their inherited and collective imaginations played out through the psyches of billions, the Darth Vaders of our time. They create division out of unity, evil out of good, building their castles of limited understanding on the plains with each successive generation fortifying the battlements. Good religion works from the bottom up, not the top down. It grinds away in the tiny daily events, the moments of realization, through which matter evolves into love. Decrees from the top, sweeping away huge swathes of searching and suffering, knowledge and experience, set the universe back. All our certainties are just drops of water in an ocean of probability. What matters is how good our story is, how much it helps us today. Maybe being a Christian today means rejecting the capital C "Church" as it exists now. It has little to do with the teaching of Jesus. Collectively it's responsible for as much human misery as happiness. It acts as a brake on spiritual development as much as a motor. It encourages superstition and ignorance as much as truth, division as much as harmony.

Rejecting it involves working backwards through the last two millennia, undoing the damage the Church has caused, the wrong myths it has created. The first hurdle to be jumped is the crazy modern teaching on the infallibility of scripture, then the doctrine of justification by faith, developed in the Reformation. We work back through the establishment of the Church by Augustine, the sacraments and priesthood, and the cosmic theology of Paul. Along the way go the papacy, Capital Letter Doctrines, original sin, guilt, buildings, and wealth. Indeed the whole religious sphere of life goes. Life is a whole, not to be directed for us by priestly specialists. It will only work if we can live it as a whole. In the Christian tradition the Quakers and Unitarians have come as close to this as anyone.

Being a Christian, for me, means going back to the first couple of centuries, before the religion was corrupted in the process of being taken over by the Empire. I think the Gnostics got Jesus (and God too) more right than Paul, though they lost sight, as

Paul did, of his teaching as a man. If we follow them we can see a nontheistic God everywhere, in everyone, in a similar sense to some Eastern religions.

I think Christianity has to migrate again, this time to take on board the insights of those religions, if it is to survive in the West. But it will remain different from them. The Buddha, for instance, is calm, but remote. He is beyond the suffering of the world, the concerns of the individual. Krishna (the supreme god for many Hindus, who visited the earth around 5,000 years ago) is similarly now immune from suffering, living in constant bliss. Jesus is at the other extreme. On earth he laughed, partied, mixed with prostitutes, wept and suffered. He engages with individuals rather than detaching himself. He died in agony on the cross. In him God has shed His divine remoteness and become human.

A credible Christianity for today starts with the life of Jesus as a vulnerable human being, from the stable to the cross, who believed in putting the divinity into humanity, and taking religion into the real world of doing good, and creating a fair and just society. God is the ideal of the best we can do. He may even exist as the universal mind of which we are fragments. We may be at the beginning of the process that brings Him into conscious being. The closest we get to Him is by embodying love. Jesus saw himself as pointing the way to reconciliation between humankind and God, between one person and another, and within each person, because all are essentially one. In following him, in thought and life, we are Christians. In loving our neighbor we love ourselves. In loving the world we love God. The world *is* God. It's that simple.

Put simply, in a world we now know to be so much bigger, we need to believe in a bigger God. We need to add what we know to what we feel. We need to recognize the breadth of one, the depth of the other, the power of both, and find a new balance. Believing that God will find us a parking place or could bring sunshine on Saturday for our BBQ or cure our cold – okay, all religions have these kinds of beliefs, and in themselves they're mostly fairly harmless. In that sense all religions work, at least as a placebo. Actually healing plays only a small part in Christian tradition compared with most others (at least today, though it was central to the ministry of Jesus), and has very little emphasis on it in its theology and teaching, which is part of the reason for the success today of charismatic and New Age movements. But these beliefs are about as relevant to living a Christian life of the kind Jesus described as an ingrown toenail. Worse, really, because by the time we've filled our heads with this peripheral material there's little space left for the important stuff. We need to join up the dots.

Life is too short and knowledge too vast to do this for yourself. So we'll never know if what we believe is 100% right, or even 50%. If we did it wouldn't be religion, but science. But in every life there comes a point beyond which knowledge doesn't take us, where we set off and say, "I realize that this may not be true, but it works for me. I'm not sure what will happen, but I'll try it." That's what "faith" is. It's believing hopefully. Not a blind trust in formulas, "say these words and you will be saved," but following our conviction that there's something real here, beyond the surface of appearances, something that can challenge and help us. And this is what being human is about – having faith, risking love, making deeper connections, using both reason and intuition to come to a better understanding of who we are and how we should live.

And we need a vision of the sacred to carry us forward. It will balance God "in here" with God "out there." Many scientists now say what people have instinctively felt since self-awareness developed, what monistic religions describe, and mystics of all traditions experience. What we can all feel in a small way. That mind and matter are in some way related. That how we see the world is as important as the world itself. We not only read the map, we draw it.

But "we" is not just you and me. What we can add today is the understanding that consciousness is a line that stretches back millions of years and forward for billions. We shade into chimps on the one hand, into angels on the other: maybe one day we'll all play like Beethoven, draw like Michelangelo, and calculate like a computer. We're moving out into this new world as tentatively as the first human beings moved out of Africa, as tentatively as their ancestors came down from the security of the trees, into a world of riches and diversity they knew nothing about. We'll look back and see the "idiot savants" of today, the victims of autism who are occasionally able to unlock the power of the brain in unbelievable ways, as the equivalent of our "Archaic Humans" from whom we developed. We'll unravel matter down to the fundamental atomic level where it somehow makes a choice, to be or not to be.

All these trillion trillion choices add up to the incredibly complex universe we live in, defying the laws of probability at every point. We'll find ourselves exercising the choice to create this universe. A choice to be loving. We'll live and move in this loving universe like whales in the ocean, rather than amphibians living half in the world of spirit and half in the body. We know this is going to happen in one form or other, because we're here. If there were no mind of God, there would be no matter, no us. The line is a circle; it exists "now."

Religion has called this process "God," and has called God by a thousand names. Any one of them can do.

When all beliefs are challenged together, the just and necessary ones have a chance to step forward and to re-establish themselves alone.
George Santayana (twentieth century AD)

44. The Choices We Face

Either the next century will be a spiritual century or there will be no next century at all.
Robert Muller (former Deputy Secretary-General of the United Nations, twentieth century AD)

We all live in the shadow of the Enlightenment, a movement that dominated the world of ideas in Europe in the seventeenth and eighteenth centuries, which looked to reason and evidence as governing principles of thought and behavior rather than inherited tradition. It promoted individual liberty, freedom of thought and religious tolerance, in opposition to an absolute monarchy or church doctrine. It spawned a scientific revolution, which led to the Industrial Revolution, which triggered the exponential growth in our ability to extract resources from the earth and use them productively, with corresponding rises in standards of living for the majority.

And so it led to the idea of progress. This is a relatively new one. For most of history, until the last couple of centuries, living standards haven't significantly budged from one generation/century/millennium to the next. It was one long, flat line. Previous generations since the year dot have tended to think of their grandparents as more upright, less prone to crime and trivia, wiser than they were. Throughout recorded history most societies have looked back on a past golden age rather than forward to a new one. Things always get worse. The successive ages of gold, silver, bronze, iron, and clay (reflected in Nebuchadnezzar's dream in Daniel 2) represent steps of universal decline from innocence to corruption.

Nowadays though, the prevailing narrative is that things will get better. And in many obvious ways, that's true. In most parts of the world, for instance, we don't enslave, torture, mutilate, rape war victims, buy and sell women, like we used to. We now look on that as barbaric, rather than standard practice, approved by society and God. Murder rates in regions like Europe are one-hundredth of what they were in the Middle Ages. Life expectancy is double that of a hundred years ago. We are ten times more likely to die from obesity than malnutrition, to die by suicide rather than being killed by a soldier. There are ten times more democracies than 60 years ago. And so on. But then maybe we're just rolling our problems up into a bigger and bigger ball to be dealt with by unfortunates further down the road. Nuclear weapons is one. If the Cuban missile crisis hadn't been headed off in the last few minutes that would have given us a quite different perspective on modern life expectancy. Climate change is another. "Ecocide" is another word for it. We're destroying the natural world, on which we depend.

Okay, there are still problems, but we think of them as sortable, generally through better or new technology, whether that applies to crops, manufacturing, medicine, energy sources, whatever. Okay, we've regressed in the US and UK over the last few decades. The shock of the two World Wars and the Great Depression that generated a closer shared identity and an effort at national renewal, leading at least in the UK to more widespread health care, pensions, better education, unemployment insurance, ran into the sands in the 70s and 80s. Average real incomes have been static or falling. CEO pay has risen from 20 times the average pay in their company to 230 times in the US, 500 in the case of banks, with no improvement in performance. Shares in large companies change hands on average 7 times a year in pursuit of short-term gains. The wealthy would no longer accept an 80%+ tax on income. Big internationals often virtually escape tax altogether. The social fabric is unravelling, the viewpoints more divisive and hostile.

We could agree on both the positive and negative. And of course, these things can be remedied. You could say recent decades have been a hiccup, as far as wealth distribution goes. A generation of research has shown the neoliberal economic story to be a false one. The minimum wage does not destroy jobs. Regulation does not restrict entrepreneurialism. Higher marginal tax rates do not stifle growth. Best practices in other parts of the world could be adopted. Trading in shares and currencies could be curbed. Equality of education and opportunity, social mobility, access to health, could all be improved. International institutions could be strengthened to help the closure of tax havens and money laundering. Top tax rates could be raised to the 70% they were before Reagan came to power. Even better, 90%. Inheritance tax could be increased, and a decent wealth tax introduced. The economy would stabilize, inequality would reduce. It's worked before. Ethical standards could be made compulsory in boardrooms. The political center could be restored, the two-party system changed for a more cooperative one.

And even if we couldn't manage it, and if the economies of the US and UK were to go down the tube, sunk by the idolatry of money, so what? That's not exactly a planetary disaster. Just business as usual. No one stays on top forever, whether a corporation, or a dynasty, or a country, or an empire. Electorates will inevitably, sometimes, make a mistake. There's no madness like that of crowds. And the more inequitable the finances, the more easily they can be bought and swayed. But there are plenty of alternatives in the world. When China retakes its previous position as the dominant power perhaps they would undertake the necessary action on climate change that the West won't. So why not keep going as we are, we're on the right path. GNP will continue to grow, almost by definition, worldwide, even if at a slower pace, or with a temporary reverse; so we'll keep having more, and will be happier.

I wish this could be true, that it might happen, even that we could turn rapidly from individual and national competitiveness to social cooperation. And maybe, given how subjective this whole area is, I'm just still too influenced by my Calvinist background, too mired in thoughts of original sin, to take a clear, objective approach. But I struggle to believe the story of inevitable progress. History suggests we're just as likely to spend the next couple of centuries going backwards as forward. It's taken us 2,000 years and more to recover the understanding of the solar system the Greeks had, the flushing toilets of the Cretans, the continent-spanning straight highways of the Romans. The average citizen of New York or London today is probably less educated and cultured than the average citizen of Athens 2,500 years ago. In Athens citizens who didn't regularly engage in lengthy public debate in the Forum were classed as "idiots." Nowadays we don't even have to talk, we can just post garbage and vitriol online.

Worse, is the increasing imbalance between consumption and resources. The world is finite, it's a closed system. Increased productivity with the help of technology won't save us. It takes ten calories of fossil-fuel energy to produce one calorie of food. The energy used per person, on an average worldwide basis, increases exponentially with each passing decade. Going back to the second law of thermodynamics, it's not "free"; it's a cost reflected in climate change. Virtually all commentators agree that our 300 million-year-old stock of fuel is going to run out in the next half century. Renewable energy is more diffuse and still has the costs of harnessing it in the first place (those massive wind turbines aren't cheap to build and maintain). Put these trends together and crunch time is getting closer.

Basically, all civilizations, all hundreds of them, have always failed, with an average lifespan of 250 years. They get too big, too complex; over ten generations or so they all go through the same cycles of adventurism through mercantilism to affluence and then decadence, and collapse. They never factor in the cost of exploiting their natural capital, sucking it dry. They're the planet's ultimate tax dodge. We're no different, we consume at three times the rate we invest, and are on the same kind of time frame, since the start of the Industrial Revolution. The only difference is that with globalization there aren't other, separate regions on earth to pick up the baton and start afresh. Bubbles always burst. And this time, collapse will be global.

And the Enlightenment didn't actually enlighten us. Our "characters" haven't improved; human nature doesn't improve over 100,000 years, let alone over a few hundred. We've just been able to move faster. And in the last century we've had the first two World Wars, Hitler and Stalin, the threat of nuclear destruction, the worst ever famines, the exploration of space, huge advances in knowledge. The best of times, as reflected in the Universal Declaration of Human Rights, and the worst of times, as in the Holocaust. Both generated from Christian societies. But the Church has had little to say that anyone has noticed. We no more listen to the Pope today for the truth about life than we read Hippocrates for the truth about medicine. There are no bestselling books on theology (of a serious nature, not counting the selfish junk) as on cookery, or gardening. No prime-time TV programs, or pages in the color supplements.

But voices are needed. Early in the twentieth century H. G. Wells saw humankind as in a race between education and catastrophe. But education doesn't make us less selfish. It enables us to consume and throw away more, to produce more deadly weapons. There are plenty of educated people in the World Bank, the International Monetary Fund, the World Trade Organization, who are speeding us along on the path to more growth, more pollution and more inequity. The twentieth century was the most "educated," perhaps the least "religious," the world has known. "Self" triumphed over "soul."

We haven't changed over the last 60,000 years since our ancestors left Africa and started to settle around the planet. We now have TVs on our walls instead of ochre drawings, we split atoms instead of logs. But we still have the same kinds of conversations about God as they would have had. The only difference is that our options have narrowed, down to one of John Bunyan's two paths of destruction or righteousness (in *Pilgrim's Progress*, a remarkable book), the alternate visions of Revelation 19 and 20, or 21 and 22. And perhaps the best summary of the world of spirit, the alternative path to catastrophe, is faith in the kingdom of God. The idea that you treat other people with the same respect that you would give to God. The challenge that God is only there in so far as we can imagine Him, and there is no one out there to help us. The idea that we can realize heaven on earth if we can die to ourselves. The idea that's at the heart of all good religion.

To die for an idea; it is unquestionably noble. But how much nobler it would be if men died for an idea that were true!
H. L. Mencken (twentieth century AD)

Part VII

Fanciful Thinking

45. The Dangers Ahead

Religion may have been the original cure. Freud reminds us that it was also the original disease.
P. Rieff (twentieth century AD)

Going back to the first chapter of this book, religion is about how we relate to everything. To our best and worse selves, the people around us, the world around us. So it has to include how we organize society, and our politics. And questions of how to best organize society, questions of justice, run through the Bible. It may be mostly "mythical," but it's also a wholly "political" book. It couldn't be anything else. Its story is that of a people, a nation, being created; how they developed from nomads to agriculturalists, family leaders to kings, pastoralists to warriors, shamans to priests, how family idols propped up each evening in the tent turned into temples. It's about the compulsion to conquer, and the humiliation of being conquered in turn. And all along the way, behind the stories of occasional victory, but more often defeat, there are the whispers of "actually, this is not the right way to go." They're echoed in the myths and stories of all cultures, that attempts to play God end in disaster.

I'm not as confident about the future as most current commentators, because they assume that we're rational people, and, however many wrong turns we take, we'll end up doing the sensible thing. That looks to me like an urban, cosmopolitan myth, of the kind that's discussed in smart dining rooms. I think religions have a more realistic approach. They're more in touch with the darker sides of our nature, as well as the good; they talk about the problems we've always been wrestling with; that we're only partly rational. Our deeper instincts are fight or flight. Create or destroy. Help or kill. And as I see it, throughout history we have always faced a choice. Zoroaster first described it as between Ahura and Ahriman, good and evil. Out of that soil grew Judaism and Christianity, with God and Devil. It doesn't matter how you describe them – empathy or aggression, sacred other or selfishness, whatever. The point is that the arc of the universe *doesn't* bend towards justice, unless we put the work in to make it happen.

And the future is not looking good. One of the basic religious messages, across all traditions, is that there are cataclysmic times ahead, and that seems to be coming true, again. It's expressed dramatically by the Old Testament prophets, among the least-read books in the Bible today. The prophets called on the Israelites to do what was right, to behave differently, to face up to the future they were creating. They saw the connections between injustice, inhumanity, and the ruin of the land. They offered a vision of a better future, a renewed humanity and a renewed earth. A fertile, peaceful one in which we could all share. But it needs a sea change in the way we behave, even the way we think.

Jesus put flesh on this vision, giving us instructions on how to live. He said that the kingdom of God is here. We're actually in the Garden of Eden if only we could see it. The world is wonderful if only we could realize it. There's enough food for everyone if only we could share it. The first Christians lived in the light of this vision. It inspired them to love, to self-sacrifice, and to change themselves and society for the better. Okay, it turned sour; conversion changed to conquest, and now what we're left with is the indifference of materialism, or an obsessive focus on personal salvation. But we still need the vision, or we're living one-dimensional lives.

Which is why the heart of Christianity, the teaching of Jesus, particularly as expressed in the parables, still seems to me relevant and essential. It's why I still think of myself as a Christian. Take, for instance, the parable of the laborers in the vineyard, in Matthew 20:1-16 (the parable of the prodigal son covers something similar, and in richer, more emotional depth). The laborers, poor men working as temporary farmhands in the harvest season, who are hired in the last hour of the evening, get a full day's pay, the same as those who have worked all day. It doesn't seem fair. We couldn't run a business, a society, like that, could we?

But then a full day's pay was what a laborer needed to feed their family. Shouldn't that be the first consideration? The basis of employment? Why should we begrudge anyone the minimum they need? Shouldn't we rejoice that they can get it? And what's fair anyway about a CEO earning hundreds of times more than his coworkers when she's basically stripping the company of its assets for short-term profit, destroying jobs rather than creating them?

This is not "socialist" thinking, just "Christian." And there seems to me to be a deeper underlying message behind the parables. Don't expect life to be "fair." It's not. And you're not going to be able to make it so. Accept it as an incredible gift. Enjoy the moment. It's utterly extraordinary that you're here at all. So give back, rather than take. It's in giving that you are rewarded, not in taking. God is the expression of all life. We are all together in this. Live in the light of this bigger vision, even when it means sacrifice. And the more seriously you take the demands of Jesus/God, the more you are going to have to sacrifice. Skim through the parables in one go. They're urgent – black and white, binary, full of either/or choices. It's wise or foolish maidens, sheep or goats, weeds or wheat. And time is short. The rich man with the well-stocked barns is going to have his life taken that very night. The rich young ruler isn't asked to give up a tenth, or half his wealth, but everything, right there and then, to follow Jesus.

For most Christians around the world today, that probably sounds like heresy. It's God who has provided the sacrifice, in sending his son to the cross, so we don't need to. We just accept the blessing. But however literally or metaphorically you take the Resurrection, and the Atonement, the idea of sacrifice is fundamental to Christianity. It's been fundamental in all religion. "Sacrifice," from *sacer facere*, means to "make sacred." We need to relearn its meaning. At its best, it's about acknowledging the source of everything good. Deciding consciously to give something back, to not take everything. Don't mine the last ounce, don't catch the last fish in the sea. Leave some wilderness. Recognize that we are in a reciprocal relationship. The kind of thinking prevalent today, that we can keep growing GNP indefinitely, preferably at ever better percentages, with everyone enjoying the benefits, with no underlying cost, no sacrifice of our living standards – that seems to me more delusional than believing in God. It's the modern neoliberal idea that exponential growth can continue indefinitely that's the real magical thinking going on in the world today, in comparison to which, believing in the Resurrection seems almost sensible.

The wheel of history always turns again. I don't take karma any more literally than the Resurrection. But I believe there are elements of truth in both. What we sow we reap. In times to come we're going to be on the receiving end of the generosity or brutality of people we currently dismiss as having created their own problems. Global capitalism will go the same way as every other social model, and may be one of the shorter-lived ones. It's sheer hubris to think otherwise. The pursuit of pleasure and wealth at the expense of moral sense and sanity, the lifestyle and economics of Hollywood, will come to be seen as extreme and useless as the Egyptian pursuit of life after death (at over six million tons the Great Pyramid of Giza alone used up more stone than all the churches and cathedrals ever built in England).

And the ascendancy of a particular culture or nation gets shorter as technology develops faster. It took us a few million years to get the hang of language. That led to an increase in brain size of 50% or so, after which nothing much happened for another million years in the Stone Age. Somewhere around 1-200,000 years ago something triggered imagination. We started to produce art, to improve tools, to work skins, to grow crops. And then to write. The rate of change is escalating. 4,000 years in the Bronze/Iron Age. In the period we call BC, it shortens to millennia. In AD, it narrows to centuries; 200 years in the Industrial Age, 100 in the Information Age. Now, we're down to decades. Next, the Genetic Age? Or the Age of AI? Or the Age of Climate Collapse?

And Christianity is becoming so closely identified with capitalism that it may go down with it. Future generations of Homo sapiens or some other species may look at our churches and cathedrals, steeples and spires reaching for the sky, and wonder what on earth the people who built them were trying to achieve, who they were trying to worship. Much as we puzzle over stone circles and pyramids, or the huge stone faces on Easter Island, looking for ever out to the horizon, perhaps for the salvation that never arrived.

Will Homo sapiens even survive? The probability of bringing about our own extinction must be high. The British Astronomer Royal, Martin Rees, an atheist himself but one who has criticized his more militant colleagues for being too hostile to religion, has given humankind only a 50/50 chance of surviving this century. So what are the chances of surviving another 5,000 years? Or 5 million? Will fingers stay off the trigger (nuclear, biological, chemical, or whatever comes next) for that long?

We have the example of past civilizations to show us what happens when the soil, or fuel, has run out, only this time there's no virgin territory to move into. Easter Island itself provides a lesson. It's the only case in history of a society that through circumstance and geography developed in complete isolation. As the trees and soil disappeared the fishhooks got smaller because there were no canoes to get to the fishing grounds, the crops ran out, warfare between the villages increased, till an extraordinary society collapsed and disappeared. In 1992, 110 out of the world's 138 living Nobel Prize winners signed the *World Scientists' Warning to Humanity* that we're at the same point. We're way past that now. The planet is just a larger Easter Island. Our future as a species is in more doubt than at any other time over the last million years, and the best many in the Church can do is bicker over whether women and gays should really have the same status as heterosexual males. And are then surprised that many feel the Church is irrelevant.

Maybe human consciousness, civilization, is just a momentary spark, one that will be extinguished just as it was getting started, unnoticed and unlamented in the history of our galaxy, let alone the universe. Maybe with the wisdom of hindsight future galactic historians of another species will simply say our brains grew too fast. A couple of million years ago the brain spurted to its present size, pushing out the skull to allow room for the skills of communicating and organizing that went with the development of language. But like the insects too heavy to turn themselves the right way up if they fall over, and the arthropods whose brains grew around the food channel and stifled it, we were an evolutionary dead end – suited fine to hunter-gathering, but not for the more complex problems that civilization brings. We won the lottery, and then killed ourselves on the proceeds, competing to accumulate more than others, without a thought for the effects farther down the line, on the generations to come. We were the ultimate virus, consuming everything, till our host, the planet, shrugged us off.

To put it in biological terms the human brain got too big for the body, leading to the pains and dangers of childbirth and midwives. Our jaws retracted, leaving us with too many teeth, so we need dentists. But more significantly, the newer and older parts of the brain haven't integrated well. We've lost many of our natural animal instincts – like regulating our breeding rates according to food supply – without developing an intelligence large enough to compensate. And indeed, there you have the Catholic Church in the forefront waving us, lemming-like, over the cliff edge, discouraging birth control.

Having lost the biological imperative of sharing food along certain genetic lines, we haven't developed enough compassion to avoid absurd inequalities in the distribution of wealth. The result is crime and lawyers, social unrest and police, revolution and armies, obesity and starvation, legacies of suffering and bitterness. We've developed the power of individual choice, but not sufficiently the moral capacity to act out of selflessness rather than greed. We've created monster cities and monster ideologies to match them. We can't even find sufficient self-control to avoid over-fouling our own nest, sawing away the branch on which we're sitting. Homo sapiens is over-congratulatory. Homo idiotus would be more accurate.

Maybe the third millennium will be a time of disaster, human-made, on a scale we haven't seen before. Our imaginary galactic historians will shake their heads and write their epitaph over a desolate planet: "Here are the lords of creation. They weren't doing too badly, till they lost respect for the God who is bigger than they could imagine."

But then it's not the fact that we're perfectly adapted to our environment that makes us human, but that we're such misfits. Otherwise we'd still be up in the trees. It's our sense of separation and inadequacy that drives us forward, creating visions of perfection and salvation in our heads, enabling us to dream of a better, more self-aware, and happier future, a planet that's fit for purpose, a Garden of Eden for humanity. We need a big idea to aim for, something to carry us through the next thousand years, the next million years, or we won't make it. We need to grow to the next level of consciousness.

So hold the idea of God in your head as a possibility. Live it as if it's true. It's in living by faith that we grow. By imagining that we can get to the next step, overriding our genetic programing.

It's in growing that we meet God. Maybe He exists out there, maybe He's all in our heads. Maybe it comes to the same thing. It's worth believing, but it's not worth a moment's argument, a single wrong action.

No one is without Christianity, if we agree on what we mean by the word. It is every individual's individual code of behavior by means of which he makes himself a better human being than his nature wants to be, if he followed his nature only.
William Faulkner (twentieth century AD)

46. Stories For Today

And if we reach, or when we reach, heaven's scenes, we truly will
find it guarded by United States Marines.
Ronald Reagan (twentieth century AD)

I love the old churches in England with the ancient yew trees, relics of the religions practiced on that spot before they were built; surrounded by faded gravestones, with the butterflies amongst the wildflowers (in the more deserted or enlightened ones), the rooks nesting in the trees. You can sense the worship of a hundred generations in the stones, a record of the lives and deaths of a community. There's still a sense of the sacred and of belonging that sum up the meaning of *religio*.

A Little England rural fantasy, I know. But perhaps we can create rituals that bring *religio* back to life for more people. Ones that leaves space for participants to think their own truths, rather than telling them what to think.

Who God is for us today – I think we've lost track of that. We haven't developed the language to describe Him. We're still using words from a minor Bronze Age tribe of a few millennia ago. Jesus made a fresh start, boiling it all down to two commandments, in Matthew 22:37, the whole of life in under 50 words:

Love the Lord your God with all your heart and with all your soul
and with all your mind. This is the first and great commandment.
And a second is like it: Love your neighbor as yourself. All the Law
and the Prophets hang on these two commandments.

I read "your God" as open-ended, he doesn't say "my God." It's whatever "other" you believe in. Perhaps if we started to follow the second commandment, to love our neighbor (which, in reading the gospels, I understand to include everyone, especially the poor, the disabled, immigrants, people of different cultures and faiths, rather than just whoever happens to be living next door), which we can understand, maybe we could learn to see how that applies to the first commandment – rather than define God in our own image, and then apply it to our neighbor.

If you really wanted to go the whole hog; on reading the gospels, canonical and non-canonical, the ones that probably come closest to representing what Jesus might have said, I think it goes something like this:

You are part of everything. I am in you, and you are in me. I and the Father are one. You and the Father are one. We are all in each other, and in every bird, insect and stone. We're all made of stardust. We are all energy, materialized. We are on the way back to the beginning to find our end. So don't worry about the moment. Forget who and what you think you are. Forget hierarchies, armies, wealth. As soon as you have something, give it away. Live happily in your own skin, for the present moment. Live at one with creation. Live at one with God. We are all divine.

Follow me, do as I do, and we can realize the kingdom of God on earth. But it will only happen by taking risks. You have to risk other people, other countries, taking advantage of you, and be happy if they do. You have to risk scorn and poverty, loneliness. Don't protect yourself. You have to be the one to take the first step. If everyone hears this and does it, the kingdom has arrived.

It sounds impossible, and perhaps it is. Perhaps that's why the world hasn't changed since Jesus' time, why the poor are still with us (John 2:8 – a curse on us, incidentally, not a statement of inevitable fact). In reality few practice this, the Church less than anybody. Maybe it should make a start, set a small example.

Patterns of churchgoing are variable around the world. I fully appreciate its strength in the USA, and don't take the UK experience as normal. In my lifetime, Bible Study classes have been replaced by fiction reading groups. The middle class who used to go on church picnics are now on cruises. Prayers before meals have been replaced by background TV and music. When I was a kid, most children went to Sunday School, even if their parents didn't go to church; now they've virtually disappeared. And I don't know much about the different churches around the world. It's often hard to tell where and when a church turns into a different faith altogether. Particularly in the USA, where having largely exterminated the previous inhabitants they're starting off with a relatively clean sheet (culture-wise). Americans invent new religions like they invent businesses. If your church isn't anticipating the coming of the Lord eagerly enough, start your own. Is the Church of Jesus Christ of Latter-day Saints (Mormonism) for instance, with its 16 million members, still a Christian cult or is it shaping up to be the fourth major monotheistic religion, despite its shady and fraudulent origins? Then there's Christian Science, Christadelphians, Seventh-day Adventists, Jehovah's Witnesses, to mention a few.

Or how about the more recent Kimbanguist cult in the Congo, with 25 million members, where the sons and grandson of Simon Kimbangu (who started the movement by reportedly raising a child from the dead, and died himself in 1957, in a Belgian prison) have taken on the functions of God the Father, Jesus the Son and the Holy Spirit? The weekly attendance of that church in the Congo is something like that of all the churches in Western Europe put together.

Europe is less prone to fundamentalism of this kind, though we've had more than our share of its political counterparts. We've had millennia of overlapping and conflicting cultures, several centuries of increasing contact with other religions and beliefs, and a century of reducing influence. Our reliance on the God of Christianity has decreased, as that of North America has increased. We've learned our lessons the hard way. Literal readings of the Bible lead to war. Taking the teachings of Jesus to heart leads to more equality and peace.

As I see it, in a Utopia, there would be no *organized* religion. Its decline in Western Europe is a positive sign. Corruption, violence and murder rates are lower in countries that are less religious. The people are happier (the ten happiest countries in the world are amongst the least religious, and the converse is also true). They are more secure. The principles of justice and fairness that good religion has always promoted, particularly in the later Old Testament prophets and the words of Jesus, have been internalized, absorbed into the mainstream. But will serious Christianity, other than the cultic kind that identifies itself with particular families ("God loves me and my son"), or countries ("God loves America"), ever come back into the frame? What might it look like, what would it take for that to happen?

I'm really not qualified to talk about this, I don't know. I play a small role in our local village life; edit the parish magazine, do some community driving, and so on. I occasionally go to Quaker meetings (but I'm not good at dealing with silence, my "inner light" is pretty dim – not sure it's there at all) or Unitarian ones (it's the place that, spiritually, I feel most at home in – they're open to pretty much anything so long as it comes from a good heart, from good intentions – but there are no groups local to me). I sometimes go to the village church, because it seems a "good thing," and enjoy singing the hymns, and the talks are good, the community aspect is strong, the people are great, and the (female) vicar is brilliant. I keep quiet if the Nicene Creed is spoken, cross my fingers at other points, and don't take communion – technically speaking, in the eyes of the Church, I'm a "pagan," not part of the Body of Christ. And I'm sure there would be no objection if I went up to the rail. But it would offend some stalwarts, somewhere, if they knew what I think, much like some objected to women vicars in the first place (or still do). So why provoke? If anything, I'm envious of the faith many of my family have. I don't mind someone trying to sell the gospel to me, being "proselytized," even if it's by Mormons or Jehovah's Witnesses. They don't know any better. But some people *should* know better. Evangelical theologians and leaders, supporting policies that seem utterly contrary to the teaching of Jesus and the gist of the Bible as a whole, I generally find appalling. So these thoughts are very much from someone on the edge of the Church, or off it altogether.

In the sixteenth century the Church had reached such a pit of corruption that a revolution had to happen. The Protestant Reformation led to the Counter Reformation, on the Catholic side, and though they spent all their time fighting, metaphorically and literally, at least there was a possibility of new shoots. And maybe there's a chance of that again – but I think we've run out of time. It took nearly 2,000 years, for instance, for the majority of Christians to think that slavery was unacceptable. It's *in the Bible*. It's clear that the Bible accepts slavery, even approves of it. In this respect, the founders of modern evangelicalism were right. God gives the Israelites detailed instructions on how long slaves can be kept, how to go about selling your daughter as a slave, what to do with the children of slaves, and how it's okay to beat them to the point of death as long as you don't actually kill them (Exodus 21:1-21). In the New Testament, Paul tells runaway slaves to go back to their masters and behave. There's no hint anywhere that slavery might be wicked, or not part of God's plan for humankind, though you can find this in the pagan literature of the time. We might guess that slavery was not part of Jesus' view of life, but he never mentions it. You can find approval for any kind of evil in the Bible, if you want to.

But we've only got 20 years or so to deal with the issue of climate change. A hundredth of the time it took for the Church to change its mind on slavery.

In the longer run, perhaps a new Christian Church, or the

kind of church I'd like to see, could grow out of the old one, much as Christianity grew out of Judaism, possibly in the same kind of time frame – a century or so. The Bible would play its part in a collection of writings, some more important than others in expressing faith, but a changing one, and different for each community, as in the first centuries. It could edit out much of the Old Testament, leaving it for the Jewish faith, where it belongs. It would add passages from the scriptures of other religions. It would add new writings. This would not be impossible if the will and imagination were there. The compilers of the Jewish Old Testament had more limited and less promising material to work with. The traditions they merged were as different as many of those in different religious traditions today. It's just a question of being faithful to God and the times together, like they tried to be.

The Bible stories are not there to tell us what to think but to drive us under our emotional surface into realizing what we're capable of, into new understandings. They're riveting in the way they picture the extremities of madness, murder, holiness, freedom, sacrifice, redemption. David, Solomon, Jeremiah, Amos, Jesus, Paul – along with many others they've become archetypes of certainty, courage, wisdom, frustration, justice, forgiveness, commitment. Read between the lines, and the whole of life is there. Set against the backdrop of a nation's struggle for identity, for survival and above all for living under the rule of God, taking into account the different agenda and motives of the authors (which is where it gets really interesting) and they can still speak with power if we read them for what they are. They're still relevant to all of us. We still murder Abel, betray like David, scapegoat Jesus. And the greater story of which they're a part can still be our blueprint.

Genesis tells of the creative Spirit breathing life into dust, creating a world that's good in itself. It describes our dawning consciousness, accounting for our sense of separation. God hands over the world to us, and we begin our journey to find our conscious place in it. The prophets warn us against the arrogance of relying on our own resources, the iniquity of oppression, of the disaster to come if we don't keep our faces turned away from ourselves to God and the poor. The birth of Jesus with the shepherds and stable is a celebration of life and love. It tells us that the most insignificant child on earth is as important as any other, indeed more so than our own selves. Love, helplessness, innocence, these are the things we should treasure, not power and position. Maybe somewhere, in each of us, there's a divine child waiting to be born. And, despite the Herods of this world, it will be, because there are no longer gods "out there." The divine Word has become flesh in the world. It will be realized. We want to believe it.

The crucifixion is perhaps the most powerful story we have. The story of the good man who gave himself unstintingly, refusing wealth and power, who saw that the deeper love is the more it hurts. He accepted betrayal and death to remain true to what he believed. He not only spoke of supporting the victims, of identifying with them, of becoming them, he became one in his life, building on the warnings of the prophets, the cries of the oppressed and murdered going back to Abel. It's as far as the kingdom can go. Our destructiveness is not the last word. To be a Christian is to try living without exercising power, to accept without limit. He speaks to us individually because he made it real for himself in his life. If we aren't prepared to follow him as far as he went, it won't happen.

We're close to God today in so far as we are able to relate without dominating, encouraging everyone to be the best they can be. To be the best we can be. It's only through us that He works in the world. He has a hope, a dream, for what we could become. We should not let Him dream alone. In sharing His dream we make it ours, we make our will His will. If we don't, He can't help us off the cross. He won't turn Abraham's knife. We've run out of sacrifices. He's not satisfied with them anymore.

It's in our capacity to forgive and love without limit that we bring the divine into existence. Perhaps the deepest meaning that we can draw from the story of Jesus is that love is sacrifice. It's a sacred, redeeming force. Everything else is compromise. His teaching on the kingdom and his death on the cross were at one on this. It's in the most intense, sacrificial moments of our lives that the ideal becomes real, that love becomes true. The resurrection is the expression of our hope that this is so, that we are eventually part of a greater spirit that we call God, and are not on our own. Christ on the throne in heaven represents the completion of our journey of understanding, where matter is transformed into spirit. Life does come out of death, hope out of fear, love out of indifference. It's been happening for millions of years. Love and hope deeply enough, and the story will triumph. It's not difficult to have faith in God with an army behind you. It's when you're at the bottom of the pit, with no light, when you're wrestling with your own failure or despair, that faith is needed and God becomes real. And we then understand there's no difference between them and us, between the self that despairs and the self that hopes, between the person we could become and the one we are, between the God who is imagined and the one who imagines.

Love and power, God and the Devil, or rather our understanding of God's dual nature, good and evil, struggle throughout the Bible, subverting each other. The best of the New Testament expresses the triumph of the first. But then it stops. We need new texts. And out of a new Bible would come a new religious language for Christians, one that doesn't rely on the old categories of "God out there" and Capital Letter Doctrines. We need a language that works for everyone, in the same kind of way that shamanism worked for everyone before we had revealed religion.

If God were able to slide from the truth I would fain cling to the truth and let God go.

Meister Eckhart (thirteenth century AD)

47. The Church We Need

If your faith is opposed to experience, to human learning and investigation, it is not worth the breath used in giving it expression.
Edgar Howe (nineteenth century AD)

If you've read this far, you'll have an idea where I'm going – all organized religions are basically cults, in one form or other, shaped by the followers for personal or political ends. We're now in a mess – even trying to talk about religion is seen by increasing numbers of rational people as a waste of time, or worse. To get out of it, for religion to be part of the solution rather than part of the problem, healing divisions rather than creating them, there's only one long-term answer – we need to get back to one religion. We're one people, on one planet. Religions that say, "I'm right, and you're wrong," even "if you don't believe like I do, you're going to hell," don't have a place on it. It's a Utopian vision, sure, and will never happen in practice. But there are common principles within which we can respect differences. And underneath those principles – an umbrella of working for the common good – perhaps the religions we have could move in that direction.

Let's draw on the cumulative wisdom and experience of everyone rather than a single tribe or tradition. Flush out the strengths of different religions and bring them together; discard the weaknesses. If it makes sense to be religious it's logical to accept the best practices from the broad range of traditions. Meditation and yoga are as natural parts of a healthy spiritual life as curry and rice are now staples of our diet. It's through embracing diversity that we come closer to truth. It's clear that God didn't want us to be too sure of where it lies. Differences are part of the solution rather than the problem. If we added all the religious insights of the world together we'd get a better picture of a tiny part of who He might be.

I'm not talking about "interfaith dialogue" here. That's a somewhat loaded term, focusing on the Western-orientated emphasis on faith in religion, whereas Eastern religions tend to be more about practice than creeds. It encourages religions to look at points of difference between them. And I totally get the problems of a "buffet" style religion, where people can pick and choose which bit they want. Nobody's going to support a single global football team, it's identifying with your local one that creates the passion. But at least in the game everyone is following the same rules, and aims, rather than demanding that everyone else should play by their rules. The dialogue really needs to be between the religious perspective on life on the one hand, which acknowledges the sacredness of life as a whole, and the materialist consumer-driven perspective on the other. It needs an awakened consciousness, a vision of a world with no poverty, no countries, no wars. Fantasy? Maybe. It's the Kingdom of God on earth that Jesus talked about. Following him is risking something to help make it happen.

As far as Christianity goes, would we still need a Church at all? Faith today may be private, but it's also inevitably collective. We're social animals, needing crowds as well as privacy, constructing our stories out of the collective imagination. In a complex, confusing world, with nations numbering millions, hundreds of millions, rather than the old nomadic units of 150 or so, we need our wider circle, beyond immediate family and friends, our own "tribe." So churches of some form are needed, though perhaps most of what we have is the packaging that can now be left behind, much like the early Christians were thrown out of the synagogues.

A community without a church/temple/synagogue at its heart has lost something. The life-changing, life-affirming, life-questioning rites of passage we used to wrestle with and celebrate communally – birth, commitment, marriage, death –

are now turned into administrative functions – registry offices, hospitals, crematoria. However hard the good people in these places try, it's not the same. They're not designed to be. For this we need churches. But the point is that they should be forces for change as well as celebration. Beacons of light, practicing repentance, forgiveness, openness, love, tolerance, poverty. They should model in a small way the kingdom we would like to see created on earth. They should "go further," be radical. We bridge the difference between where we are and where we want to be by demanding more change of ourselves than we're willing to give.

But churches, like nations, are too big. Nothing in Nature grows big indefinitely. Even whales, reefs and forests have natural limits. Nation states with a population of over 10 million spend disproportionately on armies. They are more prepared to use force than diplomacy. Religions with over 10 million followers are the same. Massive churches, like massive corporations, suck out life from local communities. They become authoritarian. Loose networks of smaller numbers with no hierarchy, no property, will represent the good churches of the future. Something more like the Church in Acts – its first organizational move (Acts 6:1-6) was to ensure the fair distribution of food – it's been estimated that in the first decades 90% plus of Church income was given to the poor, rather than used in supporting leaders and structures/buildings – nowadays it's the other way around. The wealth of the Church worldwide is measured in trillions of dollars. The annual operating budget of many *individual* congregations in the USA is in the tens of millions of dollars. The Roman Catholic Church is still the wealthiest organization in the world. And it's not that the need isn't there... even in the USA, the only significant developed country without universal health insurance (along with by far the most expensive but least effective delivery system).

These smaller churches could draw on different traditions,

as the group agreed. Like the better-functioning societies of today, it would be open to what works best, inclusive in its structures, a pluralist religion. It would embrace "dark green religion," increasingly a major spiritual world-view. Perhaps predominantly Christian in the West, but pagan, humanist, Buddhist, all traditions could play a part. All festivals be honored. Diversity will always be as crucial for religion as it is for species. Let's welcome the coming splits between conservatives and liberals. Let it be clear where they stand, and people be allowed to judge which ideas they want to identify with.

So let's fast with the Muslims, celebrate the festival of Eid, the end of the annual fast (a great idea, wholly suited to today's dietary concerns). Let's celebrate the Hindu festival of Diwali, the triumph of light over darkness, good over evil, knowledge over ignorance. How come there isn't a festival like this in the Christian tradition already? Is it just that we prefer darkness, evil and ignorance? We could continue indefinitely, there's a choice of festivals and celebrations for every day/week/month of the year (and this is how much of the Christian year used to be structured). Let's have a Christian confirmation, marry like the Shinto followers, have a Buddhist funeral, dance with the dervishes, cast spells like the pagans, if that makes sense to us. And out of the mix new practices will emerge. Let the churches be open to anyone to use, focal points for the community. They should be forces for reconciliation, for the awareness of consciousness as "one," underneath the diversity. That's their job. Spirituality is private, churches represent where we come together. Love transcends differences, it never reinforces them.

In this broader kind of religion, would we still have ministers? The standard of ministry is probably higher today than it has ever been. Few go into the Church now for power or money. But they're hampered by the system they're a part of. In themselves religious professionals are no closer to God than you are. They're just more practiced at opening the door. If it's the wrong door that's their problem, not yours. And anybody who talks of religion to people they don't know is risking manipulation. But we need to talk, and listen. That's our history. The trouble is, priests are often poets who have lost the use of their own words, artists who have forgotten how to paint. Ministers of religion should be trained to be just that, ministers of all kinds of religion, those that have a God and those that don't, rather than preachers of a local version of a particular brand. Offering a range of fizzy drinks rather than Diet Pepsi. Or even, perhaps, pointing out that there's always pure water to be had for free.

This already exists in a small way in Eastern religions that are more open to acknowledging truth elsewhere. "The same water is in all the wells," the sage Nisargadatta Maharaj taught in the last century. There is the "Great Church" (*tai chao*), for instance, of the Chinese that blends Taoism, Confucianism, and Buddhism. Cao Dai and Bon Buddhism have the same aim. A nineteenth-century offshoot of Islam, the Bahai faith, preaches world peace and the unity of humankind. Many Hindus also feel comfortable worshipping at shrines devoted to many deities, including Jesus.

In the Christian West, Unitarianism is the strand most open to this, and creates a context for a "do it yourself" religion where individuals can be encouraged to follow their own spiritual journeys. A future "Greater Church," loosely linked, may enable the great religions of the Middle East, India, and the Far East to live peaceably together, at least for those prepared to accept their common humanity and common striving for awareness.

A loosely-connected global "Greater Church" could have an impact on global problems. Already religious institutions worldwide control 8 to 10% of the world's capital markets. Maybe a World Parliament for Religions could match the United Nations and achieve still more. The Parliament would deal with rogue religions like the UN (in theory, if it were given the power and money to do so) deals with rogue states – difficult, when some of its major members are authoritarian, and the USA is in danger of turning into its own version of a rogue state, working against the common interest.

The idea of religions cooperating may seem self-contradictory to many. So at first did the idea of nations doing the same through the League of Nations. But go back a millennium and the idea of nation states would have been incomprehensible. Especially ones where people actually voted for their leaders. Go back ten millennia and there was probably little basic difference between people's beliefs and the way they organized themselves in different parts of the world, despite the fact that it could take many generations for an idea to travel from one end to the other. Go back 60 millennia to when European early modern humans first came out of Africa and there was no difference amongst Homo sapiens physically or culturally. They dressed the same, believed the same, told the same stories. Now go forward a millennia or two and the wheel could have come full circle again. The distinctions that developed between races as they settled around the globe will be blurred through intermarriage. It's started to accelerate in the last few centuries. The differences between religions will have diminished in the same way. Why not start preparing for it? Eventually there may even be one universal faith, just as we have one DNA, one planet, one destiny.

The seeds are already there. Representatives of all the world's religions got together for the first time at the World Congress of Faiths in Chicago in 1893. That might seem a long time ago. But religions move slowly; it's a fraction of the period it took for the creeds and doctrine of the Trinity to be developed. It was influenced by Narenda Nath Datta (Vivekananda, 1863-1902) who emphasized a strain of Hinduism that can accommodate a variety of religious belief. Vivekananda considered that the Divine worked on two levels: the higher level was beyond description, but could be known through meditation. At the lower level God had qualities that were imaged in different ways, through different religions. His teacher, Ramakrishna, had intense spiritual experiences of union with Christ, the Mother Goddess, Kali and Muhammad. All represent different ways to knowledge of the divine. Most of us struggle to realize one. There was another World Parliament in 1993 in Chicago. There are many interfaith organizations, but the establishment Churches support them as a matter of peripheral goodwill (if at all) rather than seeing them as central to their vision. But the principles of Universalism seem to me to be the way forwards, both in politics and religion. Truest to the teaching of Jesus, and the only way we're going to solve the planetary problems we face, with global warming as the major one. It's a faint hope – currently we seem to be going in the other direction. Maybe the opportunity has already passed. The Churches are simply too insular and arrogant to develop into a more mature religion.

And maybe an open-ended religion of this kind isn't distinctive enough to be characterized as "Christian." Or maybe this would turn Christianity into a new religion, the first the West has managed to produce, much as all religions have evolved out of previous ones. A religion that is shaped by the distinctive contribution the West has given to the human inheritance in the form of individual liberty and rights, democracy and common law, much as early Christianity was shaped by the distinctive Hebrew idea of a single God and a chosen people. And why not? Jesus wasn't a Christian anyway, and it's truer to his teaching than a religion that puts dogma before love.

Maybe we can redefine Christianity to be inclusive of truth from wherever it appears, in the same way that Early Church Fathers like Justin the Martyr did, before it got co-opted by the Empire and turned over the centuries into a religion of evangelism, oppression and conquest, and the more enlightened sections of Buddhism and Hinduism still do. Judaism was a "tribal" religion of chosen people, and in the couple of millennia since then we've succeeded in reducing salvation from the tribe to the individual. We've gone in the wrong direction. It's the world that God wants to save. It's all creation that is on the path to consciousness. If we could live in the world as it is, seeing it all as reflecting the love of God, rather than trying to change it into our own image, a reflection of our own greed, then salvation might come.

We're in a time of transition, much as we were back in the fifth century BC, when across the world new understandings of religion developed. The merger of Greek and Hebrew thought in the first few centuries AD may be paralleled by a merger of Christian, Hindu, and Buddhist thought over the next few centuries. Improbable as it may seem today, maybe by then everyone will be believing in God again. But this religion will be as diverse as Christianity was in the first couple of centuries.

And that doesn't matter. The religion you choose to operate in is one that suits the culture you are part of and the temperament you've developed. It's not "truer" than another. God has no interest in your theology. By all means have an orthodox Christian faith, have your personal relationship with God, believe in your personal salvation, or however you want to describe it. But recognize it for what it is, a working model, not a final truth. The path to the sacred, not the sacred itself. It's the psychological equivalent of the "household gods" of Abraham. The personal God of Moses, or Jesus, not the Godhead. It's one of the 99 names of Allah, not the hundredth that is unattainable. The Tao that can be spoken, not the Tao that is beyond words.

The almighty, creator God-beyond-God, whoever or whatever it is that holds every atom in His hand, is beyond our reach, for the moment. But He is the end of all our journeys.

If you know who you are, you can become as I am.
Gospel of Thomas (first century AD)

48. An Image For Now

*The ecstasy of religion, the ecstasy of art, and the ecstasy of love are
the only things worth thinking about or experiencing.*
Don Marquis (twentieth century AD)

The unattainable God, the highest God, the final perfection, the
ultimate silence, the absence of everything, the place outside
time and space, He is pointed to in virtually all religion. All
our traditions are like clumsy rafts we pole out from the shore,
believing that at some point we'll find a current that will take
us to the Promised Land. But there is no Promised Land, and
no map to get us there. The ocean is all there is. How we build
the raft is a question of personal psychology; whether we're left-
brained or right, whether we're optimists or pessimists, focusing
on rules or on freedom, metaphor or fact. Much of the rest is
cultural perspective; whether we see God as "in here" or "out
there," whether we emphasize His workings in the past, present,
or future.

Reaching for the impossible, believing the absurd, this is
the practice religion cultivates. Maybe we kid ourselves that
it's worthwhile. Maybe it never really happens. It's why most
religious founders are relatively indifferent on the description of
God; we don't know who He is. Not particularly bothered about
the belief system; that just defines who He's not. Uninterested in
the organization; that's leading people astray, into thinking they
know where they're going. Their priorities are almost entirely
about how we live. It's how you love that counts.

But most of us need more direction than this provides. The
hard part of loving is not the inadequate beliefs or the structures
they're encoded in. It's coping with suffering and evil that
knocks us back. It's knowing how to reach for the good when
crunch time comes. When the barbarians are at the gates again.

How do we work out what "good" is if it's not the God we've been brought up to believe in? Jesus, however far-sighted he may have been, as a first-century Jew had a conception of God that most of us can't relate to. His God of the Old Testament, of Abraham and Moses, Ezekiel and Daniel, is not ours. His was part of the tradition of the Jewish people, tied into their historical experience and family memories.

One answer to the problems of life is to see them all as illusion. All suffering and illness as self-created. All disasters as a result of collective decisions. If we can raise our awareness high enough we'll no longer suffer. But this seems a long way removed from the daily experience of most. Maybe it's like original sin, with elements of truth but not the whole.

Maybe the Semitic (and Hebrew) view of God as "One" rather than "good" is closer to the truth. We may choose to live a good life. God does not. He is what there is. "Nature" is neutral. Goodness can only be realized through self-awareness and making choices. The Islamic view of "fate" can help us here, *Inshalla*. A large part of suffering is unavoidable. What will be will be. In the process of creation, of matter becoming mind, it is continuously broken and remade. We have to see ourselves as part of the ongoing process of creation, not the end product that gets upset if the process doesn't stop at a time that suits us. We're part of the life of the universe. Like cells in our bodies, the larger spirit continues, grows, remaking us in different forms.

Or maybe there's a deeper truth, maybe nature is not "neutral," but a violent communion. Every living thing fights for survival, and has to. It's in doing this that life has created the planet we're on, right down to the air we breathe. Nature is profligate and inexhaustible, but never gentle. Maybe all religion, from God's sacrifice of Jesus on the cross to Arjuna of the million mouths, is a way of accepting responsibility for what we are. Our guilt at eating other life is transformed into the higher act of eating God, and being consumed in our turn. All our gods reflect different ways of acknowledging our predatory role and our hopes of transcending it. The East emphasizes acceptance of the Source, the West individual effort, conscious surrender to God. In the balance of the two we find our own truth. We are Nature's conscience.

Suffering and self-awareness seem inseparable. Indeed, contentment or happiness can seem at odds with morality. The more compassionate you are, the more you're likely to suffer on behalf of other victims, unless, like the Buddhists, you can rise above it all and see it as illusory. But at a fundamental level, there is surely no appreciation of unity without the experience of separation. Birth and pain, creation and death, they feed on each other. Great artists, musicians, are often suffering individuals, on the edge. They create out of pain. A central religious insight is that perhaps there's no creativity or compassion without suffering. Just as there is no appreciation of "now" without its prior separation into past and future, bittersweet memories and hopeful plans. It's through our developing awareness of it that we grow. Indeed most religions, including Christianity, have traditions that encourage suffering. We articulate the pain, the good, and the evil, that other creatures do not yet feel. In embracing it we transcend it. God is to us as we are to them, a further level of awareness in which suffering and love are reconciled.

The power of the Jesus story is in his suffering. In it we see God, represented in him, become the embodiment of suffering, taking it all on Himself, willingly. We can see Jesus on the cross as the symbol of a God who is brought into being through suffering, of a universe working through death to create new forms of life, recreating the very idea of God every day. We can see Jesus pushing the very idea of God to its limits, asking questions of us to prompt a new answer.

Indeed the point about being a Christian rather than a Buddhist is that suffering can be seen as redemptive rather than illusory. Suffering and love can both break open the ego, open us to others. We can "choose" to offer ourselves, to triumph over disaster, to be better, to grow in love, we can make a difference here on earth, in our lifetimes, now. This doesn't mean it's the better religion, but it can make more sense in the West. We can forgive ourselves for having damaged our "selves" through our own actions. We can ask forgiveness from those we've hurt. This capacity has been hard won over tens of millennia, but we can exercise it. And the point where Christianity and Buddhism merge is that the nature of the quantum world suggests that at some level the choice that Zoroaster asks us to make has already been made. Whatever the universal mind, or God, is, it is the outcome of trillions of choices that have already happened, and are going to happen. We cannot sin against God, because God is self-determining, at every moment. This is the moment. Don't blame God or the Devil, they are us.

This is the paradox of the best of religion. We find that nothing matters, because all is willed. Our will, God's will, random events, there's no difference. Just pictures from different angles. But it's only out of the acceptance that nothing matters that we can act without ego. Acting out of the awareness that nothing you can do makes a blind bit of difference, because it's happening anyway, but that what you do is supremely important, because otherwise it won't – it's the mystery at the heart of the teaching of the Vedic philosophers, of Buddha, of Jesus, perhaps Muhammad most of all. All good religion boils down to one event. It's the moment of understanding, of seeing the universe and our lives as a whole, right now, that enables us to transcend the question, and accept the outcome.

Evil – we don't really know what we mean by the word anymore, it's a theological term – is harder than suffering, but can be seen in the same light. The world is not black and white, people are neither entirely innocent nor guilty, electrons are not either waves or particles – both are true. There's no simple "answer." We're all capable of extremes of selfishness and evil given the right conditions. Evil is simply the harm we're prepared to inflict on others. Experiments have shown that average individuals are easily capable of inflicting suffering on patients if told to do so by a figure in authority. A usually selfish individual can do something heroic, jumping into freezing water and rescuing a child. On the other hand generous and well-meaning people can connive in policies of genocide. Supporting the family can edge into nepotism, sex into rape, self-defense into murder, self-awareness into selfishness. But then you get the occasional stunted serial killer, a businessman or politician who seems to have no conscience, empathy or shame, no sense of any moral standards.

And evil also grows in us collectively; we can become inured to it, as much as any psychopath. It's not the Hitlers that are the problem, but the potential for evil that a Hitler releases in all of us; in the majority of Germans who voted for him, overwhelmingly seeing themselves as Christian, who helped with or turned a blind eye to the rounding up of Jews, gypsies and socialists, who served in the SS. It's not so much the pedophile priests, but the mentality of church leaders that allows them to continue their ministry. It's not so much that we take food from the mouths of starving children, but that it suits us to be part of a system that allows it to happen. It's defining "us" as more important or worthy than "them." Most evil in the world comes in the guise of the good. Good religion points us back to the right path. Conscience is the fruit of tens of thousands of generations working out what that is.

An objective real evil force? Demons, possession, Satan? Obviously there is no "Devil," Christian tradition has just morphed the various different figures in the Bible like Satan, the snake, Lucifer and the Beast, and all the other devils and gods like Moloch and Baal into one simple-minded monster, adding decorative elements from other pagan religions like the horns, red skin, goat hooves etc. The Devil is a bit player in the Bible. He persuades Eve to eat a piece of fruit, runs a bet with God on Job, tempts Jesus in the wilderness – all the savagery, genocide, slavery – that's God's doing. Actually, it's our doing, telling ourselves that we only did it because that pathological God told us to. Sometimes it's individual and collective wickedness. Sometimes it's clearly in the mind of the beholder. There are enough reputable accounts to make it credible in some form. But equally it seems to be more common in the past than today, more common in societies that believe in it than those that don't. The obsession with it creates the conditions in which it flourishes. Like Freudians having a disproportionate share of Freudian dreams, we wish it into existence. It's the same with the paranormal. It happens to those who believe in it. If you try to evaluate it objectively, you're not going to see it. Maybe hell exists for those who want to believe in it badly enough. Maybe Christians who are consumed with preaching damnation for other people find out what it's like.

We need the impulse to goodness that the idea of God provides. We need the channels of inspiration that the Church has historically delivered through God/Jesus/Spirit. We need a reason to believe we can change, and hope to overcome the evil we meet. And to see that it's first of all in ourselves. We're the barbarians. The people in charge often are. The world and everyone in it is what we've made it. The good and evil we see is how we want to describe it. The plank is in my eye, not that of my enemy. Our problem is we don't realize it, any more than the Pharisees did. We need the forgiveness that Jesus talked about, not for some mythical sin that our ancestors committed in eating a piece of fruit, but for what we're doing now; to ourselves, to each other, and to the planet.

Everything we do, even the best, has its shadow side. So humanists and atheists might say their equivalent of God is represented by the finest of our values and achievements. These might be expressed in terms of individual freedom, human rights, democracy, which add up to the highest form of civilization the world has seen. But individualism can lead to the accumulation of exorbitant wealth at the expense of others. Democracy is great, until it's corrupted by gerrymandering, advertising and money, but can elect leaders like Erdogan, Bolsonaro, Duterte, Trump. These are Western ideals, but not universal ones. The more collective ideals of the East, organized around the family, have as strong, and a much older, claim to universality. Human rights are important, but so are those of the creatures on whose backs we tread and whose flesh we eat. All biologists know that animals do suffer, dendrologists know that trees support each other and are interconnected by roots and pheromones. All of life is connected and independent. We're all wired up together.

But we need something more universal than political or social arrangements. Universal values must be something greater than we can understand, more demanding than we can reach, because we don't understand the universe, and probably never will. And if we think we do we create monsters. If we think we've arrived we're just blind to where the shadow falls. We need to learn a better balance between ourselves and our neighbors, ourselves and God, taking God as the totality of everything there is.

How do we keep walking toward the light and away from the darkness we create? Learn what not to do from the Bible. It's a doom-ridden book, starting with the Fall, working through centuries of vicious tribal warfare, exile, the oppression of foreign rule, the warnings of the prophets and the apocalyptic visions of disaster that culminate in Revelation; where, if you take chapter 14 verse 1 literally, 144,000 people will be saved, one person out of each ten million who have lived. It's easy to listen to the crowd, to collectively sleepwalk to disaster. The best wisdom traditions say that the only true wisdom is the one you find within yourself, because we're all different. Recognize your own intrinsic, inalienable worth in the eyes of God. Indeed whatever you believe is only true for you. But embrace the truth of others. Realize that everyone is valued equally, whatever their condition of belief. That's what it means to be fully "human." Make as much of it as you can real for yourself. Look to the different traditions to find the common, best elements that can point you in the right direction. And we need a direction. It's a fearful thing to live in the awareness that everything is down to us. And if we think of "us" as just "me" that's the way to madness. Without a light to aim for and show the way we're struggling in the dark, lost in Plato's cave, squabbling shadows arguing over even more insubstantial words and memories.

If human villainy and human life shall wax in due proportion, if the son shall always grow in wickedness past his father, the gods must add another world to this that all the sinners must have space enough.
Euripides (fifth century BC)

49. A New Trinity

The senses, they say, are subtle;
More subtle than the senses is the mind;
Yet finer than the mind is intellect;
That which is beyond intellect
Is he.
Bhagavad Gita (second century BC)

Our bigger God is the light we live by. The simple belief that our lives have meaning, that there is life beyond our own existence, and that we can find peace through the faith we seek. How to describe Him, without slipping into pantheism? Trinities have proved their worth in dozens of religions. The Christian Trinity – I never really managed to figure it out. So here's a suggestion for a new one; it's along the lines of something I wish I'd been taught more as I grew up; that there are important values in life, supreme ones, that we should try and live by, rather than measure success by exam results, or how many people we've slept with, or how much money we have – or whatever it is that makes you feel good. And, as usual, it boils down to three. We can think of God as truth: the whole, the One, the ultimate reality. The principle of diversity, or particularity, represented in the Christian tradition by Jesus, becomes that of love. The feminine principle, the Spirit, is represented by beauty. What Jesus and other religious teachers have is a moment of insight when they see the underlying patterns in the relationships between people and the world. The pattern is not fixed, it's a discovery, a process. It's the same kind of insight that mathematicians have when uncovering a new formula, or musicians finding the right chord. Scientists talk of the "beauty" of a discovery. The more beautiful and simple the answer, the more likely it is to be true.

What they all suggest is that truth is an aspect of beauty, and vice versa. It's the same with love. All the forces in the universe (gravity, electromagnetism, strong and weak nuclear forces) are creating more and more complex and beautiful forms, turning matter into consciousness. In so far as we play a part in bringing things together, creating rather than destroying, loving rather than hating, we are fulfilled. In rising above our "selves" or losing ourselves in awareness of the patterns at the heart of the universe and the life we lead together we are practicing religion. If it's not beautiful, if it's not loving, it's not true.

"Truth," "love," "beauty"; the experience of the three together is vivid enough for most people to describe them as "real." Let's be hopeful. The divide in the world is not between religions, or between believers and atheists. If there's a divide anywhere it's between those who have faith that the universe is meaningful and act accordingly, looking to something greater than themselves, and those who don't, and act for their own benefit. Between those who will fight to make the world a better place, and those who can't see the point. Between those who are happy helping others along the way of life, and those who see it as a race to win. Between those who will sacrifice their selves in favor of others, and those who want to impose their cultures or creeds. Between those whose first thoughts are: "How can I bring peace to this conflict? How can I resolve the underlying problems?" and those whose first response is aggression or war. Between those who see the potential for unity everywhere and live in its light, and those who see it as reflecting their own interests. Between those who see us as chimps occasionally granted glimpses of the divine mystery, and those who think they're saved and everyone else is going to hell.

We've had to cooperate more and more intensively since we came down from the trees, to face the challenges on the ground. The more complex a society we've created, the more resources we consume to keep it going, the more challenges we face. We're coming up to a turning point, where our future is in doubt.

We have to start to live by a bigger vision, a "religious" one, rather than maximizing "profit," irrespective of costs incurred (trashing the planet, and everyone on it), or we crash and burn.

Faith says we've turned the corner. If enough of us live in its light the world might follow (and current thinking is that it only takes a really active few percent to make a difference to society). It tells us that in our hearts we're more inclined to love than hate, to unity than division, peace than war. Materialism says it's only our own interests, our own beliefs that count, and the rest is nonsense.

Faith says that God is not like we are, interested in saving a few friends or followers in one time and place, careless of the rest. Forgiveness was not offered just once, through one man's life and death. He works through every moment and event, creating beauty and love and truth. The universe is not random, it unfolds from God like a tree from a seed, separating out into the galaxies, stars, plants, and trillions of life forms. There is no other way it could have existed. *God saw the light, that it was good* (Genesis 1:4).

This unfolding is expressed in the beautiful patterns of circles, spirals, and helixes that run through everything. It's seen in the Fibonacci ratios first described in detail in the thirteenth century – though Indian mathematicians were outlining it a thousand years before that – the golden sequences of numbers that dictate the patterns in nature, from the structure of subatomic particles and DNA, to whirlpools and the whorl of galaxies. It's expressed in the most ancient and widespread symbol in religion, that of the spiral, the pathway between this world and its other dimensions, seen in Neolithic temples and graves from Ireland right across Europe through Mesopotamia to India. It's what the universe is made of. Mathematicians might say the secret is in the primes, or the never-ending number pi, or a poet might say:

Beauty is truth, truth beauty, – that is all
Ye know on earth, and all ye need to know.
John Keats

We try, however unconsciously, to imitate these patterns in everything we create. Truth is not what we've been told, it's what we make. The practice of all good religion is the "golden rule." We instinctively believe it's right in relationships. We seek harmony and wholeness. The music most of us enjoy listening to is based on chords that can be divided by whole numbers. We instinctively move toward proportion. The main principle in architecture and art is the golden mean proposed by Pythagoras. We can't prove whether this is true, any more than we can analyze what consciousness means, because we're part of the proof. The thing is, it works. It's a good religion, and we need what religion points to. Its defining characteristics are the search for truth, the appreciation of beauty, and the practice of love. They characterize the experience of "oneness," which is what all the great religious leaders speak of (as opposed to their followers, who turn the teaching upside down). In loving someone, in seeing something as beautiful, in the perception of a truth, we immerse ourselves in the wider reality. We can see what we can become.

Much of what we already appreciate in Christianity is motivated by this. It defines the universe as one of unconditional love. But there's also a lot of "noise" that drowns out the heart of it, a concern to prove things that cannot be proved, to say this picture is better than that one, this definition of God better than that (though when did you ever read any actual definition of God, as opposed to secondary arguments as to why He might be there, or why certain things could only have happened if He was, that made any sense?). There is no such "absolute" truth that we can see or realize, any more than there is absolute beauty or love. To be "real," what is one must be the others as well.

We know aspects of it when we see it, but even then struggle to describe it. We see glancing reflections, "through a glass, darkly," as Paul says in Corinthians. What we take on faith is that we are seeing something "real"; that the universe is the creation of consciousness, the ultimate work of art, and will be seen as a whole when it's complete. Only God knows when that is.

There's nothing scientific in this, nothing that can be proved. And nothing original. It has always played a role in the Christian tradition. In the Middle Ages for instance it was highlighted in a dispute over whether the ultimate vision of God was primarily one of love or of knowledge, with Bonaventura preferring the former and Thomas Aquinas the latter.

In the Renaissance period Marsilio Ficino maintained in his *Theologica Platonica* that the highest Platonic ideals of the Good, the True, and the Beautiful could be found in the human soul. For him these were at the root of all religion. He concentrated on Greek and Persian religions, but another Italian, Giovanni Pico della Mirandola, extended it to embrace Jewish and Muslim wisdom. He suggested that humankind is created to shape itself into whatever form it chooses, and to bear the consequences. Condemned at the time (his *900 Theses* was the first printed book to be banned by the Church), today he seems right, and we extend his vision to everyone.

Art and music are good ways of communicating all three. Fra Angelico will still speak to us when Aquinas is the province of specialist historians. Compare the people wrestling their way on to the divine stage in Renaissance art with the koan-like stillness of Chinese paintings of the same period and you can understand in an instant a lot there is to know about the difference between the Eastern and Western mind, between Confucianism and Christianity. The Europeans pictured God in their image up in the heavens, sending messengers and sons to earth. Simple, glorious, and clear. But impossible to believe today, which is why no one paints like that anymore. The Chinese evoke reality (or nonreality) slipping away behind the mist. It wasn't till the late nineteenth century with Impressionism and then Cubism that Western painting began to picture the process of seeing rather than the object seen. The developments in art paralleled the increasing Western interest in Eastern religion, focusing as it does on the workings of the mind rather than its creations.

Storytelling is also a key. It's why there are so many sacred scriptures around the world. The Bible itself is a baseline on which many further stories have been built, like *The Brothers Karamazov* or *Daniel Deronda*. If you're bored with Obadiah and Nehemiah, read Dostoevsky or George Eliot instead. Don't get stuck on the Bible. Think of religious truth like a great universal novel, the story of consciousness. The main characters are the different religious leaders down the ages. Their sidekicks are the great theologians, mystics and philosophers, the artists and writers. Who's the narrative voice? It's you, all of us. We create our story out of these past lives, much as they have created us. In writing new stories we create the future for our children. We're all characters playing roles in the mind of God. Good religion is good fiction.

Funnily enough the great era of Western fiction coincided with the passing of Christian belief. Broadly speaking, the first atheists and the first novelists were roughly contemporary. The eighteenth-century novel took the idea that characters could explore their own destinies under the controlling pen of the author far further than previous literary forms like drama and poetry. The great flourishing of the novel in the nineteenth and early twentieth centuries seems too remarkable in relation to changing belief patterns to be coincidental. Life came to be seen as a meaningless sequence of ordinary events that we make meaningful, make our own, by giving it shape and form, beginnings and endings. We turn it into our own truth. We make our own novels, our own lives.

The great nineteenth-century novelists knew what they were

doing. George Eliot translated liberal German theologians like Ludwig Feuerbach with tears streaming down her face as she saw the basis of Victorian faith disappearing. Charles Dickens created the sentimental Christmas as a partial substitute for the meaning the Victorians had lost. Thomas Hardy turned the almighty God into a bleak vision of indifference to suffering humankind. In Russia Tolstoy tried to create a new synthesis of rational Christianity and Russian psychology, and Dostoevsky created a Christianity that would survive despite its destruction by reason.

Truth today is a democratic effort, shaped by the consensus of the tribe, as it used to be. A religion that acknowledges its role as fiction and art, a fiction that provides a structure of universal myth and law, will shape our future consciousness. Writers, musicians, and artists are often a generation ahead of their time. Scientists, centuries. Founders of religion, millennia. We need all of them.

Our best protection is that we
In fact live in eternity.
And all our intuitions mock
The formal logic of the clock.
W. H. Auden (twentieth century AD)

50. The Future We Follow

*Life is not spoiled by its ending, and the mere absence of life is not
an object to fear, nor distressing in itself.*
Epicurus (fourth century BC)

Religions exist in the uncertain borderland between our selves
and the world. We're aware today of the extreme difficulty of
saying that a revelation genuinely comes from God, or from "out
there," rather than being shaped or generated in our own heads.
To illustrate this, take a quick look at another religion that *does*
claim this. One of the most curious on earth is that of the Dogon
people in South Mali. They believe that fish-like aliens brought
knowledge to them from a star later identified as Sirius B. In
the 1930s they provided French anthropologists with a detailed
working knowledge of the solar system, down to the rings of
Saturn and the four moons of Jupiter. They described the type
of star it was, and traced its path around the sky. The odd thing
is that Sirius B is not even visible to the naked eye. Its existence
was not confirmed by telescope till the 1860s. The orbits of which
they appeared to have detailed knowledge were not confirmed
till the 1970s. Now *that* looks like confirmation. And the idea
that aliens stopped off in Mali for repairs is a lot more plausible
than the idea of God sending His Son to earth to speak to a few
Palestinians, a couple of thousand years ago.

Of course, there's nothing in the story told by the Dogon
people. We know now that there are 79 moons of Jupiter, with
loads of additional moonlets. Either the aliens couldn't count, or
it was invented. It's like the gospel writers and the Resurrection,
or any aspect of the Bible. A story circulated which writers/
budding journalists wanted to play up, and some individuals
were happy to oblige by confirming it. If Jesus or Christianity
had given us one single fact about the heavens (or anything at

all) which was not known at the time but proved right later, this would be a different book.

As soon as we start to express what we mean by way of spirituality we are shaping our experience in our own terms, not in terms of what might be "real." We project our thoughts across and shape what we see. But this is not just an optional extra, a Sunday occupation for those who have the time to be "religious." It's fundamental to the way we think and act.

So why not believe in a great, loving "God," the thought behind the universe, rather than in the limited ways we describe Him. Original sin, life after death, sacrificial love, these and dozens of other major ideas are there to be tested, adapted, absorbed into a tradition that makes sense to us, that enables us to move forward. Out of these we shape our own definition of God. God is the hook by which we can step into a state of grace. Grace is what happens when truth and love snap together in our heads and we can act unselfconsciously out of that awareness. It's the gift of life, and everything that involves, all the potential it can give; it's not dependent on our beliefs, or on the sacraments. Grace, the natural loving flow of everything, can give us the best kind of happiness; unreserved, undeserved, 15 billion light years' worth of time and space on our side.

Religion describes grace. At its best Christianity is a religion of grace. Grace provides assurance that the universe makes sense, our lives have a purpose, that we are evolving toward a better future than we can imagine. But we'll never know. That's why it's faith, religion rather than science.

And it always will be. There are no clear answers. If this universe is all there is and we could really unravel how it all works there are always further questions: Why is it made this way? Why is there something rather than nothing? What role should we be playing in it? And if we could account for every molecule and event in this universe since time began we would still be left with the idea that there may be vastly more universes than there are molecules in this one. If the universe is infinite God will always be a bigger question than we can find an answer to. Mystery, not certainty, is at the heart of existence, and the acceptance of it at the heart of good religion.

There will always be a "beyond," and there's no reason why it should be within the grasp of our particular animal minds. The sages in the East say even the right questions take the form of unanswerable riddles, and if we can understand them we've probably got it wrong. Most of the great teachers, like Jesus, talk in puzzles, paradoxes, parables, asking questions rather than giving answers. But for the unenlightened, for almost all of us, the questions are worth asking. If we keep questioning we progress. We may get to the point where we don't need the answers, when we simply understand.

Jnana, the path of knowledge, involves exhausting the mind's possibilities, transcending it. Salvation involves the complete surrender to the will of God. The results are the same. It doesn't matter what you believe. It's like your language or your skin color. It's who you become that's important. Better to be a happy and loving Hindu or atheist than a mean and intolerant Christian, and vice versa. Perhaps more significantly it's what you believe that you can become. It's by the collective exercise of faith that we might become what we hope to be.

Imagine a soap bubble. It materializes out of space-time foam and floats free, like a feather on the breath of God. For a fleeting second, threads of biology, history, culture are knitted together by personality. We have this microscopic moment to enjoy, and through a few simple actions hope to leave the world a fraction better than we found it. The actions are hopefully defined by love, which represents the fullest form of self-awareness that we know of.

Developing this is cultivating a state of mind we call prayer. As the sacred scriptures of Zoroastrianism (most of which have been lost) say:

Prayer is the greatest of all spells, the best healing of all remedies.
Zend Advesta

Prayer is neither an offshoot into fantasy, nor a conversation with a God out there in our own image, but is perhaps the most basic way of thinking, an internal dialogue between the two hemispheres of the brain. The right half is artistic/creative, the left more academic/logical. Both are needed to create our picture of reality. We dialogue between the two, between the God we believe has helped bring us into being, and can help us achieve the impossible, and the knowledge that we're just basically chimps who've bootstrapped themselves up out of their comfort zone. We go back and forth between the two halves to find the best course of action, questioning who we are, and where we're going. Seeking guidance from our better self. Changing ourselves, not asking God to change something else. Sitting in silence, paying attention to our thoughts, we can see them generating our feelings, our emotions. These are not physically real, they don't "exist," but they create our reality, they prompt our actions. They put us in touch with the creative life force behind us, behind everything. Hey, I'm hopeless at this, we all struggle with it, but it's what being human is about. We're messed up, confused animals, trying to get to the next step. Sometimes we even prefer our pets to other people. They don't have our kind of problems.

Worship is a state of gratitude. At times this feeling is so overwhelming that it might take on the form of a Higher Power, of God. The flip side of awareness is accountability. We're responsible for what we become and do, for this second of time. The kingdom of God is a measure that we don't live up to. Faith is the belief that the bubble dissolves again back into the mixture we call God; that the awareness we have developed somehow survives in the bubbling ferment of creation. Nothing ever disappears, everything is remembered in the quantum world.

Everything is forgiven, or it could not exist. There is no rubbish bin, no "reset" button in the universe. No hell or heaven. All we do and think and dream is added like yeast to the mixture. The universe for almost all of its existence is likely to be cold and barren, but it doesn't matter, because we can create something worthwhile here and now through what we do. Maybe, even, through faith we can believe it could turn out better, because we're here, because we're having this conversation. Because through 15 billion years the universe has been evolving toward consciousness, and will continue to do so. We're part of this. But you, here, now, is all that matters.

But what of our children, and God in the future?

Think of conscious life on earth as a giant game of snakes and ladders. We've crept past a couple of dozen snakes to get this far. Religious fundamentalism is one of the next big perils. Just ten thousand years ago it didn't exist. A dominant group leader, an overbearing shaman, could only damage his small group of a hundred or so. Now, they could destroy humankind, the planet. If we go down, it's back to cockroaches and rats, if we're lucky. The path to self-awareness that began with the mammals, when the extinction of the dinosaurs gave them their opportunity, would then start anew. The age of reptiles, followed by the age of mammals, will be followed by something different again.

If we get past that snake of global warfare, of climate collapse, that evolutionary test, maybe fueled by different interpretations of God, and manage to work together, reconnect with values like distributed prosperity, justice and love, and keep going, the balance between ourselves and the world might change far more radically than anything we've seen to date. For one thing, we're going to end up looking a lot different. Even in the short span of recorded history the average height of human beings has decreased and risen through changes in lifestyle and diet. As we create our own environment and have the power to genetically manipulate our own bodies the rate of change will increase. It's likely to prove impossible to resist the drive to improve human beings genetically, much as we have already been improving grapes and crops, dogs and cows, for thousands of years. Ironically, in terms of recent history, African genes may be the most highly valued, as they have a greater diversity in the gene pool, from pygmy peoples in the forested Congo to tall, elegant cattle-herders on the savannah – natural selection has had longer to work.

Evolution hasn't had time yet to explore more than a tiny fraction of the potential combinations that exist in DNA, or the possible power of the brain. Artificial evolution can speed this process up by many factors of 10. The replacement of human organs and tissue by that of other species or with man-made materials is already advanced. The ability to clone people may be just a few years away. There's every reason to suppose that the science of genomics will be able to fashion human beings and intelligence in every conceivable form.

But will this be a democratic process, undertaken for the good of everybody, or will it lead to different classes of people more extreme and rigid than anything Hinduism or the Hebrews could have dreamt of? If you successively replace different parts of the human body with organs from other people, or animals, or mechanical devices, how far can you go? Where does a "person" begin and end? How will a thousand-year life expectancy change our view of pleasure, families, salvation (and what would we actually want to do with all that time)? Robots and blockchains can't answer these questions. Traditionally wisdom comes with age, but increased life expectancy over the last couple of centuries doesn't seem to have taken us forward much. Would the sense of adventure, of curiosity, of religion as a series of conversions leading us on to a greater understanding be stronger than the pull of self-righteousness and greed? Is transhumanism, the worship of power over nature, over life and death itself, through technological supremacy, the ultimate port for religion, or its complete perversion?

Maybe this is where our problems will really begin. We struggle at the moment with the "simple" issues of abortion and euthanasia, addiction and mental illness. Even with how to create a reasonably decent, just society. But our very ideas of what a human being is and how to order society accordingly will be up for grabs again. If we can't get our act together now, defining what it means to be human, how we relate to each other fairly, how will we cope with a world of a few million-dollar super-humans who are genetically and physically superior to the rest of us? Will it be like living in the Roman Empire again, with a huge underclass working to keep the privileged few and semi-divine in luxury?

In the beginning there was no death then, nor yet deathlessness.
Of night or day, there not yet any sign.
The One breathed without breath, by its own impulse.
Other than that there was nothing else at all.
Rig Veda

51. If We Survive

Space travel is bilge.
Britain's Astronomer Royal, in the year before Sputnik, 1956

Perhaps we'll go further. The talk at the moment is of nano-robots, cryonics, brain and computer interfaces, and especially AI (Artificial Intelligence), AGI (Artificial General Intelligence), and ASI (Artificial Superintelligence). We're approaching the "singularity" when computers are powerful enough to mimic the human brain, reproducing the thousands of trillions of signals that flash through it every second. But would we then be obsolete? Or would it be a race to enhance ourselves to keep pace with our creation? It's the problem God faced when Adam and Eve ate the fruit, in Genesis 2:22-23 – how are we going to react when our creation becomes as powerful, or even more so, than we are? Will we be as fearful as Him (these ancient myths really can still speak to us – the whole point about them, is that they deal with the fundamental questions that we've always been talking about)?

> *And the Lord God said, Behold, the man is become as one of us, to know good and evil: and now, lest he put forth his hand, and take also of the tree of life, and eat, and live forever: Therefore the Lord God sent him forth from the garden of Eden, to till the ground from whence he was taken.*

We're as yet just a blink of an eyelid in the planet's history. If we can overcome tribal desires to rule and accumulate, rebalance ourselves towards sustainable living, the future will open out, and we'll shape our environment to enable consciousness to continue and develop, rather than be driven to a dead end. But if it's going to be a recognizably human future, loving and alive, rather than an artificial, digital, dead one, it needs to involve everybody. We're all part of the kingdom. We share the same "I."

The world of science fiction could then increasingly become fact. We could start to tap the resources of the planet's core, rather than scratching at the surface. Then we'll tap the energy of the sun, which produces more energy each second than humankind has so far consumed in its history, and be able to work with and create planets. Later the galaxy, working with stars. Perhaps the dialogue between the two halves of our brains will be extended to quarters, to all parts, to all brains. Or perhaps the part that some scientists describe as the fourth level, the prefrontal lobe in the cortex, will grow larger. It's where our empathy and moral sense seem to reside, and doesn't reach its full proportionate size till we're around the age of seven.

Maybe the "mind" will be encased in forms other than the organic – maybe electrical energy, who knows what. The brain by then would be free to grow to an indefinite size, not restricted by the uncomfortably small birth canal, taking it to 10 to the power of 11 neurons, or 12. Maybe we'll develop a more collective kind of consciousness of the kind already possessed by some other species, like the termites, enabling them to build their cathedrals. Jung was fascinated by that; in studying hundreds of his patients' dreams he found similarities across time and cultures, which led him to develop the theory of a "collective unconscious," in which recurrent dream images and situations are related to inherited "archetypes." Maybe we'll go back to our first home, the sea, and talk over family matters with our far-distant cousins, the whales. After all, their proportion of the brain's cortex (the intelligent bit) to body weight, which is the measure of how advanced the brain of a species is, is the same as ours. Okay, they don't wear clothes, because they don't need to, and hands aren't useful in the deep ocean where there are no trees to climb, but maybe they're more intelligent than we are, in ways we don't yet understand – which is why they have four lobes in the brain compared to our three. Maybe they've been seeing God in their image for millions of years before primates and humans were thought of. We could ask forgiveness for the last few centuries of one-sided slaughter. We might learn something from them.

Maybe we'll escape our biology altogether. After all, it's not the case that death is the natural end of everything, that all life is programed to die. Tardigrades, microscopic creatures as complex as cockroaches, are virtually indestructible. They can be boiled, frozen, exist in space vacuums, and come back to life. Bacteria and amoeba do not die. They can be killed, but have no intrinsic lifespan. They're the soup out of which we've emerged, and even the most violent of holocausts are likely to leave the possibility of life reemerging, in forms who might do better than us. Over a couple of billion years we've traded off immortality for complexity, self-awareness, and knowledge. As many of the greatest myths indicate, there's a price to be paid for life, and a still greater one for love. Maybe the next time around, our place at the table will be taken by a different species, who will look back at our fourth level as we look back at our third, and wonder how we ever got to where we are.

With self-consciousness we've come to an awareness of time passing. Is there a further level of consciousness that is aware of time past, present, and future? Of the "one" that includes them all? Where we live with the awareness of dimensions that we can currently only trace in math? Never mind the details of the Christian heaven, or the Nordic Valhalla, or the Celtic Tir na n'Oc, or the Roman Island of the Blessed, or the Greek Elysian Fields, or the Buddhist Pure Land, or whatever. All these ideas have something in common. In all religions time is not actually a straight line, with our lives defined by start and end points. It's more like a little box. In Christianity time is something we've been put into to fulfil God's purpose. He rattles the box occasionally. We're in it for a brief period and then we're taken out to fulfil our real eternal destiny. In Islam the future is already written. In Buddhism we keep getting reborn into this time until we manage to escape the earthly chains and arrive in Nirvana, maybe tens of thousands of generations away. In religion generally it's not the passing moments that matter but how we break free of them. One moment of salvation or enlightenment is worth a lifetime's trudge.

In achieving those moments we step out of the box of time, and our true self escapes from the prison of the body. Time is not seen as an absolute but is shaped by choice. At a deep level, time does not matter, and in moments of profound experience does not exist. This is an idea that all religions try to get a handle on.

Interestingly, in the twentieth century our understanding of time was turned upside down. Time is no longer a straight, unbending line, from past to future, any more than the earth is flat. This idea is as strange to us today as the laws of gravity were to the eighteenth century. But we now live in a world where time slows as you go faster. If we were able to send astronauts to the nearest star and back again at a speed high enough for them to return in a couple of decades, they would come back to find their children older than themselves. If they shot out into space far enough and fast enough they could come back to see themselves being born. Time doesn't even just go in one direction. If you go faster than the speed of light it goes backwards. The math for this hasn't been worked out yet, but it has been for electromagnetic radiation – for waves that instead of diverging from a point converge. The first type are called "retarded" because they arrive after they've been sent, the second "advanced" because they arrive *before* they've been sent.

Time is now a field, like space. The past and future are no less "real" than the present. If we could have surfed a light wave from the beginning of the universe we would see all the past and future simultaneously, and could pick out our lives like an e-mail from the cloud. In the quantum world there's no distance, no time, only "here and now." "Eternity," in this sense, is "real," more so than passing time. Much as "consciousness" could be more "real" than "objective reality" – whatever that means. Can we experience it? Think of a flat horizontal plane transecting a circle. The plane is time and space, across which we move. Maybe our sense of the spiritual is a vertical plane transecting the moment we're in. Occasionally we look up and step outside the moment, and see that everything we are and can be is present now. Now is all that matters. Now is all there is.

> *The disciples said to Jesus: "Tell us how our end will be." Jesus said, "Have you discovered then the beginning, that you look for the end? For where the beginning is, there will the end be. Blessed is he who will take his place in the beginning; he will know the end and not experience death."*
> Gospel of Thomas

So maybe we can change our experience of time? When "we" were single-celled creatures in the sea we had no consciousness of time at all. We moved on to evolve an awareness of passing time, three-dimensional vision, and the ability to interpret objects as images and images as ideas. Maybe we can go further and experience the world in four dimensions? Mathematically, we know that this fourth space-time dimension exists, but we can't experience it directly, we can only see its shadow in algebra, in chalk on the blackboard. We're restricted to mathematical symbols, much as when it comes to "truth" we're restricted to speech, or written words. Could we develop a consciousness that is not subject to the illusions of the ticking clock? The odds seem remote. But any more remote than that descendants of today's rats could, in tens of millions of years' time, be reading and writing books, like we do? If we don't develop this more cosmic kind of consciousness, maybe there's no hope for us. As Einstein said, the problems we face can't be solved from the same level of consciousness that created them.

Perhaps our feeling of impermanence and our yearning for the state of eternity, which are at the heart of religious experience, are the beginning of this consciousness. And maybe dying could be a stage in a progression through experiences of deeper consciousness? Perhaps even if we are stuck in this box, our descendants might not be.

Maybe by then we'll be free of the guilt of flourishing at the expense of other species. Maybe the future for religions of sacrifice is progressively to deny ourselves the "first fruits" of our relatives. We'll encourage life rather than destroy it. Maybe the stardust of which we're made will be converted to starlight. Perhaps the angels some of us think we see are the beings we could become.

Would we still count as "human"? I guess it depends on how inclusive you want to be.

If this took a million years that's only a quarter of the time we've been around for, in one form or other; a fifteenth of the average life of a species; an infinitesimal amount of the time the universe still has to run. If we stay in the game we may be part of the consciousness that in 10 billion or so years' time, when the universe in its current form comes to an end, finds itself at the beginning, ready to play again. Perhaps it's only then that we'll figure out the purpose of creation. Eventual extinction does seem the most likely, with stars disappearing and atoms falling apart, where not even thought can exist, let alone matter. But the "Big Bounce" is a cosmological possibility. Or perhaps by then we could be tunneling into different universes.

That's all so impossibly far ahead... we don't know. But to focus on the shorter term, perhaps we're not going to raise our game, and we'll go the way of Home erectus, Homo neanderthalensis, and our dozens of other cousins. Perhaps the God we've created in our image is more of a destroyer than a savior, a figure of wrath rather than love, and in inventing Him we've simply signed our own death warrants.

For now, though, our story has come full circle. We've found the keys to the Garden of Eden. We can clone species, we're on the edge of creating them, of fashioning ourselves in new forms. We've unpicked the metabolism of life and death, pulling its fruit down from the tree. But we don't have a new story for this. We seem to have lost the facility for writing new chapters. We're still stuck in chapter 2. This story is an interpretation of Genesis that says that to pick the apple, to be self-aware, to gain knowledge, is to transgress against God. Thinking is bad, obedience is good. The Church still promotes this. It has lost the alternative vision of Job, one of the greatest of books in that muddled miscellany we call The Holy Bible, that God is there to be questioned and argued with. That's His role in life, life calling to life, words shaping life. But in the words the writer puts into the mouth of God, the answer will always be beyond us. And the Church has forgotten (or, rather, grew out of the ashes of the teachings that it put on the bonfire) the new story that Jesus offered, where personal growth and sharing take priority over law and self-interest. He called it the kingdom of God.

And the Christian nations who claim to take their morality from Jesus and dominate the world economy have in the last century invented concentration camps and nuclear bombs, colonizing the ocean with submarines, and space with missiles. Roughly half the scientists in the world, mostly Christians, work at least part-time for the military establishment (the world's military/industrial complex is overwhelmingly dominated by the USA, with its allies chipping in some). In the ultimate ironic twist it is as likely to be well-meaning, God-believing Christians, as much as anyone, who will destroy the planet, and the life on it that He's spent four billion years shepherding through to consciousness. That really would give the Devil the last laugh.

This book began out of a question one of my kids once asked me. "Do you believe in God?" I can't answer yes or no. I don't "believe" in those kind of certainties. But I can tell a story. This one's about the grand project of the third millennium AD, which is to produce a quantum computer. It would be made of electrons existing in the "in-between" state, in which they haven't yet "decided" where to appear. In such a system the electrons would calculate probabilities in all the possible universes simultaneously. It would be so powerful that if you enlarged the biggest computer we currently have to the size of the planet it would still take tens of millions of years to calculate what the quantum computer could do in an instant. A microscopic quantum computer with just 300 electrons would have more components in its parallel states than there are atoms in the universe, and the power of larger ones would increase exponentially. In theory it could simulate the universe. It's a difficult thing to build, because organizing electrons that don't exist yet is a hard act. It sounds like science fiction, but scientists around the world are working on it. Anyway, imagine it made. The greatest human achievement ever.

The world leaders gather around it for the opening ceremony.

The Pope is allowed to ask the first question: "There's only one question worthy of this historic moment," he says. "Does God exist?" The machine whirrs, and after a moment comes back with the answer, "She does now."

Believe nothing because a wise man said it.
Believe nothing because it is generally held.
Believe nothing because it is written.
Believe nothing because it is said to be divine.
Believe nothing because someone else believes it.
But believe only what you yourself judge to be true.
The Buddha (fifth century BC)

Afterword

It's tough to acknowledge that for much of your life what you believed and did was wrong. But that's not uncommon. In the 20 years or so since the first edition of this book the number of Americans who identify as "no religion" (not necessarily "no belief") has risen from 8% to 25% – sociologically-speaking, an astonishingly rapid shift, the largest anywhere in the world. Church attendance there is down 20%. In the more secular UK, the "no-religion" figure is now 56%, and at 72% amongst eighteen-to-twenty-four-year-olds. Regular attendance at a church, temple, mosque or synagogue in the UK is down at around 7%.

Funnily enough, that percentage of 7% also applied to the number of people in the USA who used to go to church, back in the 1750s, when it had one of the lowest rates of illiteracy and poverty in the developed world, if you exclude slaves; now it has one of the highest.

We've talked a lot about myths here, how they can convey the essentials of the human story – they can also be highly destructive as well as positive. And one of the most pernicious ones today is that the USA was founded as a Christian nation. Sure, some of the founders were orthodox Christian – Samuel Adams, John Jay, Elias Boudinot and Patrick Henry. But John Adams was a Unitarian, and the majority – Thomas Jefferson, Ethan Allen, Thomas Paine, Benjamin Franklin, George Washington and Alexander Hamilton were deists (deists follow the principle that religious truths should be subject to the authority of human reason rather than divine revelation), either of the non-Christian variety or Christian (upholding the moral value of the teaching of Jesus but doubting his divinity). Constitutional concepts like freedom of expression and the separation of Church and State are Enlightenment values, not biblical ones – more anti-biblical.

But attendance rose through the nineteenth century, with the new flood of immigrants from Europe holding on to the beliefs that were later abandoned by their contemporaries back home. They were then strengthened by the revivalist movements. In the early twentieth century fundamentalism and evangelicalism took off, as a reaction against modern thought and humanist values, and "America" and "Christianity" came to be seen in the USA as synonymous.

It's not difficult to see why many, particularly the young, in the West, find it difficult to believe in the Christian God of the churches today (and it's no coincidence that, with most of their lives in front of them, they are in the forefront of the protest against climate change). After all, incredible though it might seem, a majority of white Christian liberals who voted in 2016 cast their vote for Donald Trump, the antithesis of the behavior and teaching of Jesus (just think "Sermon on the Mount"). Among white evangelicals, the largest religious group in the USA, that number reached four out of five, and they're really committed supporters – though they represent 17% of the population, they account for 26% of the votes.

Wherefore by their fruits ye shall know them (Matthew 17:20) – in this case, by their votes.

I'm writing these last couple of pages shortly after the 2020 election, which Donald Trump is claiming that he won. It looks as if the same proportions of Christians have voted for him again. Trump's supporters include most senior church leaders: ministers, professors and theologians, along with the majority of whites. One of his most distinguished and vocal defenders for instance is the author of the definitive, magisterial, 1,300 page *Christian Ethics: An Introduction to Biblical Moral Reasoning*.

Whoever said God didn't have a sense of humor? You couldn't make this stuff up, unless you're a fantasy or comic writer like Neil Gaiman or Terry Pratchett. In a country like the USA with two parties, one center-right, led by a moderate, highly-experienced, devout Catholic; and the other extreme right, led by the most mendacious and toxic president to hold the office, with no prior experience of politics, now refusing to accept election results, most Christians voted for the latter. Twice. The bulk of the Church today is intellectually and morally bankrupt. It represents religion played out as farce, revealing its underlying pathology. It embraces patriarchy, pseudoscience and white supremacy in its world-view. Pastors peddle illusions of salvation and prosperity to a gullible public like pardoners used to sell indulgences and splinters of the True Cross in the Middle Ages. It's a self-serving religion of exclusion, judgment and fear, a religion devoted to empire rather than love. It's even regressed centuries to supporting the US government policy of allowing suspected enemies of the state to be tortured; to having a religious fanatic from a fundamentalist sect promoted to the Supreme Court. There is no difference *in kind* between believing in the Virgin Birth and Resurrection of a man 2,000 years ago, who we can't be sure even lived, and seeing Donald Trump as an instrument of God's will, or Barack Obama as paving the way for the Antichrist, or COVID vaccination as the Mark of the Beast. The best thing you can say about Donald Trump is that he's given the world a wake-up call on the fragility of democracy and the corruptibility of religion.

The evangelical church in the USA of around a hundred million (along with around five times that many in the rest of the world), and much of the rest of it, has sold its soul (Matthew 4:8-9) for the sake of power and influence. Then around the world there are other churches – Catholic, Protestant, Greek Orthodox, Pentecostals – voting for demagogues and autocrats, from the Philippines (where government death squads roam the streets) through Brazil (wantonly destroying the Amazon rainforest for short-term profit) and Hungary (clamping down on liberty and freedom) to Russia (a murderous, corrupt, secret service state). And the situation is no better in Islam, with elements pushed into extremism after centuries of oppression and exploitation by the West. And elsewhere, Hindu nationalism is on the rise in India; even Buddhist monks (historically one of the more peaceable religions) whip up hatred of minority communities in Burma. Sadly, too often, religions don't look like positive forces in the world. And that's even before you come to the doctrine, the creeds, so much of it unbelievable today.

The glimmer of light is that religions evolve, like life itself. Religions are what we make them. *We* write the books, invent the teaching, change our minds on what to keep or chuck. We create Gods in our image. And good religion sees something of the sacred in *all* people, of whatever belief, or race, or color, or gender, or nationality, or sexual orientation.

Indeed, for the vast bulk of our time on earth, nature, life itself – was sacred. In so far as there was a God, in all that time, she was Mother. With the coming of agriculture, and cities, the ability to reshape the landscape and engineer animals and crops, a mere 12,000 or so years ago, we gained power over nature, with God's blessing – indeed, at His command. With the centralization of wealth, power and kings, the local gods of place, of trees and springs, of hills and rivers, of animals and birds, and the Mother herself, were pushed into the background, replaced by Father Gods up in the sky. We gradually lost that sense of the sacredness and interdependence of life, and started worshipping power instead.

The major world religion at the time of the Hebrews and Israelites was Zoroastrianism. It had developed – centuries, perhaps millennia earlier – the idea of a God of truth and light, Ahura Mazda, who defined himself as "I who am." Out of this came Judaism, which had evolved from its original minor tribal god El – with his companions, the Elohim – to the battle leader Yahweh, and then in the Babylonian Exile developed under Zoroastrian influence into a single, holy God. And out of that came Christianity, which, in the process of making compromises with the pagan world of the Roman Empire, to become established as the official religion and give the emperor control, split God into three (the Trinity). Islam followed, some centuries later, as the third major Abrahamic religion today, restoring the main principle of monotheism – one God.

This story has led us to where we are now. And now we're coming up to payback time. The lead negotiator for the Paris climate agreement said in 2019:

What's at stake over the next decade is nothing less than the future of the planet and of humanity on the planet. That's no exaggeration, that is no hyperbole. That is actually scientific fact.

And it looks as if it might be Christians who could prevent us dealing with it. The USA is the only country to have withdrawn from the Paris Climate Agreement.

There are plenty of lovely, generous, well-meaning people in the churches. But then, within living memory, the electorate in Germany was overwhelmingly Christian and churchgoing when they voted Hitler's NSDAP party (in coalition with his nationalist, anti-Semitic allies, DNVP) into power in 1933, to make Germany great again (MAGA is not new). Hitler returned their support; one of his first acts was to outlaw atheist and free-thinking groups. The Nazis took control of the media, and began rounding up political opponents, Jews and homosexuals the following year. It only takes half a dozen years for reasonable certainties to be overturned, for churchgoing suburban accountants to become war criminals, church wardens to turn into concentration camp guards, for pastors to bless planes as they set off to bomb civilians (and change can happen faster than that; it only took three years for the Soviet Union to disintegrate, between 1988 and 1991). Fascist, authoritarian regimes came close to taking over Europe, and were only prevented from doing so by the military mobilization of the communist USSR on an epic scale, in alliance with the surviving democracies, leaving around 80 million dead.

Europe has recovered through becoming largely post-Christian, whilst incorporating its essentials, like taking care of people, providing safety nets, investing in education and health, restraining inequality. But in the USA, bad religion has been winning the day, with the majority of Christians supporting the president's "Muslim ban," chanting "lock her up," permanently separating immigrant children from parents, encouraging vigilantes – all straight from the Nazi playbook, or that of any dictatorial regime, since the beginning of recorded history. It's always the same; sow division, hatred and chaos. Intimidate. Polarize communities. Weaponize the differences. Then subvert the tools of the state (particularly, nowadays, the judiciary and the voting system) so you can make your power permanent. This is how a democracy slips into dictatorship. Currently, we've even had conspiracy theories like those promoted by QAnon being retweeted by Donald Trump – that he's battling a cabal of Satan-worshipping pedophiles, mostly Democrats, Jews and Hollywood celebrities, who run the world's child sex-trafficking, keeping hundreds of thousands of them in underground tunnels, and are plotting to bring him down. As with Flat Earth fantasists, evolution-deniers, Christian or Muslim fundamentalists (or those from any religion), or people who believe the world is run by the Illuminati, or lizards, or whoever – we do really seem to be dumbing down in countries like the USA and UK.

Christianity today, particularly in the USA, where it's effectively a cult in thrall to a leader who was initially dismissed as a clown, a narcissistic estate sales agent with grandiose ideas of domination, is a destructive force. And in a world where concerted action is desperately needed, it is putting self-interest before the common good, and could bring us all down. Rather than helping to mend and heal society, the Church has become part of the rot. It *is* the rot. Have a look at the Christian online forums, if you need persuading of that; diatribes against gun control, against action to prevent climate change, against action to reduce inequality, to provide safety nets for people, to provide justice – Christian leaders are in the forefront of the charge to take us back to the Middle Ages.

The question "What would Jesus do?" was popularized back in the late 1800s, and has come back into prominence in the last few decades in the USA. It has a particular resonance today, as we face a changing climate and the possible end of civilization. Perhaps Jesus would embrace Christian evangelicals and fundamentalists, try and persuade them through inclusion and love to change their ways. Perhaps he would curse them, as he did the Pharisees. Perhaps, like overturning the market stalls in the Temple, trying to restore its integrity and taking the commerce and money out of it, he would encourage people to take to the streets. I don't know. But I think Zoroaster called the shots right; we're always choosing between good and evil. And that's the religious perspective on life; that we're capable of making moral decisions, acting wisely, out of love rather than greed and ego. There are values we follow, even if it's at our cost. That's the basic ground rule of all good religion. But Christians today generally side with the evil brother, Ahriman.

I don't know what Jesus would do. I don't see how anyone can. And most of the time, anyway, we're all just trying to muddle through; making mistakes, but trying to learn from them. But we have to try and bring Christians back into the rational mainstream, for the sake of the following generations.

The alternative – in the Preface I suggested some might see the Book of Revelation as "mentally unhinged." It reads like it's written by someone on a magic mushroom trip, with its fantastic beasts. It's a popular book with many Christians today, who see in it and others a timeline for Jesus to come again in their lifetimes, bringing the Rapture. But they misread it. Its audience was people suffering under the oppressive rule of the

Roman Empire. Prior to that, the Jews had suffered under the Egyptian, Assyrian, Babylonian and Persian empires. Both Old and New Testaments are one long cry for justice, for freedom from corrupt leaders and foreign rule. Change all the direct or implied references to "Babylon" and "Rome" in Revelation to "America," the equivalent military superpower of today, with its 800 overseas bases and domination of the world economy through the mighty $, and it starts to make sense. The USA could be remembered as the country that, more than any other, killed the planet for us all. So perhaps we should all join with Bible-believing Christians in praying for the Rapture to happen, for them to be taken up into the sky, and to take the fundamentalists from other religions with them. Sadly, the world would be a safer, better place.

Brief timeline of some of the events mentioned

BC

15,000,000,000	Universe created
8,000,000,000	Indian estimate for age of universe
5,000,000,000	Earth formed
4,000,000,000	Life begins
65,000,000	Ancestors of whales return to the sea
24,000,000	Primates
15,000,000	Last time the planet was 4 degrees warmer than today
14,000,000	Homininae (apes) diverge from Orangutan
9,000,000	Hominin (human ancestors and chimps) diverge from gorillas
5,000,000	Human ancestors diverge from chimps
500,000	Persian estimate for age of universe
400,000	Oldest wooden tools
250,000	Oldest cave rituals
100,000	Homo erectus dies off
60,000	Homo sapiens leaves Africa
40,000	Homo floresiensis dies off
34,000	Homo neanderthalis dies off
30,000	Venus figurine
17,000	Lascaux cave paintings
12,000	Agriculture
10,000	Animals domesticated
8,000	First cities
4,000	Christian estimate for age of universe
3,500	Writing invented. First pyramids built. First *Vedas*.
2,000	*Epic of Gilgamesh* written

1,500	Zoroastrianism, first revealed religion
1,400	Abraham leaves Ur
1,360	Amenhotep worshipped as the one God
1,200	Moses and Exodus
1,000	David and the Kingdom of Israel. China the leading economy through to AD 1500. God "hides his face."
Eighth century	First books of the Bible written, including Genesis 2:4-3:24. Parsha and Jainism. King Hezekiah stops Hebrews worshipping the serpent.
Seventh century	Thales, first scientist
722	Fall of the Northern Kingdom of Israel to the Assyrian Empire
621	King Josiah finds the Books of Moses
Sixth century	Buddha, Confucius, Lao Tzu, Mahavira, Pythagoras, Socrates; the Axial Age. *Bhagavad Gita* written. Genesis 1:1-2:3 written. Job written.
586	Fall of the Southern Kingdom of Israel to the Babylonian Empire. Exile.
Fifth century	Histories of Thucydides, Herodotus, the first historians. Compilation of much of the Old Testament.
445	Nehemiah returns to Jerusalem

AD

4BC-AD26	Life of Jesus
50s	First letters of Paul
60s	Last letters of Paul, *Gospel of Thomas*
70s	Gospels of Mark, Matthew

80s	Gospel of Luke. Increasing separation of Jews and Christians.
90s	Acts of the Apostles. Jewish Old Testament agreed.
100	Gospel of John
Second century	Christianity a separate faith. Gnostics. Justin Martyr.
295	Gnostics outlawed
312	Constantine converted
325	Nicene Creed
380	Worship of pagan gods banned in the Roman Empire.
Fourth century	Roman popes begin to claim authority over other popes and bishops. First list of 27 books of the New Testament.
410	Rome sacked
354-430	Augustine
610	Muhammad's vision
Seventh century	Spread of Islam. Text of Jewish Old Testament agreed.
877	The first printed Christian book, a calendar, in China
Ninth to twelfth	Golden Age of Islam
1054	Catholic and Orthodox Churches split
Eleventh to fourteenth	Crusades
Fifteenth century	Renaissance. Papacy in the pits. Printing starts in Europe.
1519	Cortez lands in Mexico.
Sixteenth century	European expansion begins. Reformation; Luther, Calvin, etc.
1633	Galileo faces the Inquisition
Seventeenth century	Enlightenment

Eighteenth century	Industrial Revolution begins
1781	American War of Independence
Early 1800s	Teaching of Biblical inerrancy. Second Great Awakening.
1854	Doctrine of Immaculate Conception
1870	Doctrine of Papal Infallibility
1893	First World Congress of Faiths, in Chicago
1917	All Catholic bishops appointed by Rome
1965	Catholic-Orthodox Joint Communication lifts mutual excommunication
1966	*Index of Forbidden Books* stops publication
1993	Roman Catholic Church admits Galileo was right
1993	*Fatwa* against "round earth" teaching
1998	UK regular Church attendance 3.7 million
2341	Zoroastrian world savior appears
10,000,000	End of humankind if we survive for the average lifetime of a species
5,000,000,000	Sun burns up, life on earth ends
10,000,000,000	Stars disappear

Reading List

A select reading list of a few of the authors I've found helpful. These are some of my favorite nonfiction ones in these subject areas who write for a popular rather than academic audience – I've read pretty much everything they've published. To add all the other individual titles by these and other authors would take up too much space. This is just a microscopically small fraction of the great books that are available.

I was wondering about putting in references to academic literature, but, frankly, in a book of this size, which skims the surface of so many topics, Wikipedia is generally a good bet for checking out the credibility of specific statements. I've just tried to take a consensus of what the majority of the best-qualified people who specialize in a particular subject seem to think – chucking out the net to see what comes in, and making a few connections. If you'd like to discuss any of it, in a constructive fashion, my address is john.hunt@jhpbooks.com.

Science and biology
Cosmosapiens J. Hands
Climbing Mount Improbable R. Dawkins
Wonderful Life S. J. Gould
The Diversity of Life E. O. Wilson
The Demon-haunted World C. Sagan
The Elegant Universe B. Greene
The Road to Reality R. Penrose
Seven Brief Lessons on Physics C. Rovelli
Six Impossible Things J. Gribbin
The Science Delusion R. Sheldrake
The Mind of God P. Davies
A Brief History of Time S. Hawking
The Hidden Life of Trees P. Wohlleben

Our Cosmic Habitat M. Rees
Awakening Earth P. Russell
The Book of Nothing J. Barrow
Life: an Unauthorised Biography R. Fortey
Mapping the Mind R. Carter
The Runaway Brain C. Wills
The Wisdom of Bones A. Walker and P. Shipman

History
Guns, Germs and Steel J. Diamond
The Rise and Fall of the Great Powers P. Kennedy
The Silk Roads P. Frankopan
Prisoners of Geography T. Marshall
Dominion T. Holland
Sapiens Y. N. Harari
A Short History of Nearly Everything B. Bryson
The Pelican History of the World J. M. Roberts
The History of the Ancient World S. W. Bauer
The Story of the Jews S. Schama
The Better Angels of Our Nature S. Pinker
The World's Religions N. Smart
The Penguin History of the Church O. Chadwick
A Little History of Religion R. Holloway
Christianity: A Global History D. Chidester
Civilization F. Fernandez-Armesto
The Outline of History H. G. Wells
The Penguin History of Europe J. M. Roberts
A Distant Mirror B. Tuchman
The Pursuit of the Millennium N. Cohn
The Masks of God J. Campbell
A Study of History A. Toynbee
The Lessons of History W. Durant
Why the West Rules – for Now I. Morris
Why Nations Fail D. Acemoglu and J. A. Robinson

Christianity
An Introduction to the Bible J. W. Rogerson
Religion L. Kolakowski
After God D. Cupitt
Testament J. Romer
The Unauthorized Version R. L. Fox
The Complete Jesus R. Mayotte
The Death of Forever D. Reanney
The Powers That Be W. Wink
The Historical Figure of Jesus E. P. Sanders
The Five Gospels R. Funk
From the Holy Mountain W. Dalrymple
The Phenomenon of Religion M. Momen
Gnosis A. Welburn
Gospel Truth R. Shorto
Images of Eternity K. Ward
Jesus: the Evidence I. Wilson
Honest to God J. Robinson
The Language of God F. Collins
What the Bible Really Teaches K. Ward
The Literary Guide to the Bible R. Alter and F. Kermode
Jesus J. D. Crossan
The First Paul M. J. Borg
How Jesus Became God B. D. Ehrman
Who Wrote the Bible? R. Elliott Friedman
Jesus the Jew G. Vermes
A History of the Bible J. Barton
The Gnostic Gospels E. Pagels
One Jesus, Many Christs G. Riley
Christian Beginnings G. Vermes
A History of Christianity D. MacCulloch
The Rise of Christianity W. H. C. Frend
The Disappearance of God R. Friedman
The Next Christendom P. Jenkins

James the Brother of Jesus R. Eisenman
Myth and Ritual in Christianity A. Watts
Rescuing the Bible From Fundamentalism J. S. Spong
A History of God K. Armstrong
Doubts and Loves R. Holloway
Process and Reality A. N. Whitehead
Pensées Pascal
The Universal Christ R. Rohr

Psychiatry

The Man Who Mistook His Wife for a Hat O. Sacks
The Private Life of the Brain S. Greenfield
Do No Harm H. Marsh
Complications A. Gawande
When Breath Becomes Air P. Kalanithi
The Divided Self R. D. Laing
How the World Thinks J. Baggini

Spirituality

The Way of Zen A. Watts
The Wise Heart J. Kornfield
A New Vision of Reality B. Griffiths
Freedom of Simplicity R. Foster
Amazing Grace K. Norris
The Miracle of Mindfulness T. N. Hanh
Why Buddhism Is True R. Wright
Following Jesus H. Nouwen
Meeting Jesus Again for the First Time M. J. Borg
The Seven Storey Mountain T. Merton
Meditations M. Aurelius
A New Earth E. Tolle
A Grief Observed C. S. Lewis

Related

Letter to a Christian Nation S. Harris
The House of Islam E. Husain
Capital in the Twenty-First Century T. Piketty
The Future We Choose C. Figueres
The Vanishing Face of Gaia J. Lovelock
The Uninhabitable Earth D. Wallace-Wells
The End of Nature B. McKibben
The Ends of the World P. Brannen
The Phenomenon of Man P. Teilhard de Chardin
The Perennial Philosophy A. Huxley
Creative Mythology J. Campbell
The Archetypes and the Collective Unconscious C. G. Jung
The Varieties of Religious Experience W. James
The Tao of Physics F. Capra
The Origins of Virtue M. Ridley
The Origins and History of Consciousness E. Neumann
A History of Western Philosophy B. Russell
The Myth of Sisyphus A. Camus
The White Goddess R. Graves
The Golden Bough J. G. Frazer
The Doors of Perception A. Huxley
Zen and the Art of Motorcycle Maintenance R. Pirsig
Being and Nothingness J. P. Sartre

About the author

Mostly retired, John works in an advisory capacity in his eponymous company (www.johnhuntpublishing.com) providing reader reports and a wealth of industry experience. After getting a Double First in English at Oxford University he worked in a couple of large publishing companies, and set up his own business in 1988, in international co-editions. He has been creating radical ways of working at JHP to enable publishers and authors from around the world to work effectively together, and establishing new paperback lists since 2003.

Thou shalt love the Lord thy God with all thy heart, and with all thy soul, and with all thy mind. This is the first and greatest commandment. And the second is like unto it, Thou shalt love they neighbor as thyself.
Matthew 22:37-39

THE NEW OPEN SPACES

Throughout the two thousand years of Christian tradition there have been, and still are, groups and individuals that exist in the margins and upon the edge of faith. But in Christianity's contrapuntal history it has often been these outcasts and pioneers that have forged contemporary orthodoxy out of former radicalism as belief evolves to engage with and encompass the ever-changing social and scientific realities. Real faith lies not in the comfortable certainties of the Orthodox, but somewhere in a half-glimpsed hinterland on the dirt track to Emmaus, where the Death of God meets the Resurrection, where the supernatural Christ meets the historical Jesus, and where the revolution liberates both the oppressed and the oppressors.

Welcome to Christian Alternative... a space at the edge where the light shines through.
If you have enjoyed this book, why not tell other readers by posting a review on your preferred book site.
Recent bestsellers from Christian Alternative are:

Church Going Gone
Brian Mountford
A priest's memoir covering the 1950s to the COVID-10 crisis –
asking questions about God, sex, faith and the abandonment of
organised religion.
Paperback: 978-1-78904-812-4 ebook: 978-1-78904-813-1

Bread Not Stones
The Autobiography of an Eventful Life
Una Kroll
The spiritual autobiography of a truly remarkable woman
and a history of the struggle for ordination in the Church of
England.
Paperback: 978-1-78279-804-0 ebook: 978-1-78279-805-7

The Quaker Way
A Rediscovery
Rex Ambler
Although fairly well known, Quakerism is not well understood.
The purpose of this book is to explain how Quakerism works as
a spiritual practice.
Paperback: 978-1-78099-657-8 ebook: 978-1-78099-658-5

Blue Sky God
The Evolution of Science and Christianity
Don MacGregor
Quantum consciousness, morphic fields and blue-sky
thinking about God and Jesus the Christ.
Paperback: 978-1-84694-937-1 ebook: 978-1-84694-938-8

Do You Need God?
Exploring Different Paths to Spirituality Even For Atheists
Rory J.Q. Barnes
An unbiased guide to the building blocks of spiritual belief.
Paperback: 978-1-78279-380-9 ebook: 978-1-78279-379-3

Readers of ebooks can buy or view any of these bestsellers by
clicking on the live link in the title. Most titles are published
in paperback and as an ebook. Paperbacks are available in
traditional bookshops. Both print and ebook formats are
available online.

Find more titles and sign up to our readers' newsletter at
http://www.johnhuntpublishing.com/christianity
Follow us on Facebook at
https://www.facebook.com/ChristianAlternative